# CONVEYANCING

# CONVEYANCING

Paul Butt LLB, Solicitor

2002

Published by
Jordan Publishing Limited
21 St Thomas Street
Bristol BS1 6JS

**British Library Cataloguing-in-Publication Data**
A catalogue record for this book is available from the British Library.


ISSN 1352–4534
ISBN 0 85308 786 5

Printed in Great Britain by Hobbs The Printers Ltd of Southampton

# PREFACE

This book is intended as an introduction to conveyancing for those studying on the Legal Practice Course at The College of Law. It is hoped, however, that it will also be of use to others wanting an introduction to conveyancing practice and procedure. Its approach is essentially practical and it does not pretend to contain a detailed analysis of the underlying law. Some background law is included, but it is assumed that readers will have the basic knowledge of land law and contract on which an understanding of conveyancing depends.

In the interests of brevity, both solicitor and client are referred to throughout the book in the male gender. Users of the book are requested to read 'he/she' every time the male pronoun is used, and to accept my apology for omitting specific references to both female solicitors and clients.

I acknowledge with thanks the permission of The Law Society to reproduce the National Protocol, Standard Conditions of Sale, agreed forms of undertaking, formulae for exchange and the Code for Completion by Post. The permission of Solicitors' Law Stationery plc who hold the joint copyright in the Standard Conditions is also gratefully acknowledged.

Although I have been solely responsible for the preparation of this edition, the book still owes an enormous debt to Frances Silverman who was responsible for previous editions. It has been a daunting task taking over from such a renowned conveyancer.

Thanks also to all my colleagues at The College of Law for their assistance, some of it unwitting. Particular mention must, however, be made of Philip Rogers at Chester. I would also like to thank all the staff at Jordans for their help and patience.

My greatest debt, however, is to my wife Anne for her support and encouragement.

The law is generally stated as at 1 April 2002.

PAUL BUTT
*Chester*

# CONTENTS

# TABLE OF CASES

**References in the right-hand column are to paragraph and Appendix numbers.**

xviii *Table of Cases*

# TABLE OF STATUTES

**References are to paragraph and Appendix numbers.**

# TABLE OF STATUTORY INSTRUMENTS, STANDARD CONDITIONS AND GUIDANCE

**References are to paragraph and Appendix numbers.**

# TABLE OF ABBREVIATIONS

| | |
|---|---|
| CGT | capital gains tax |
| CHAPS | Clearing House Automated Payment System |
| END | Electronic Notification of Discharge |
| GPDO | Town and Country Planning (General Permitted Development) Order 1995 |
| LCR | Land Charges Registry |
| LRA 1925 | Land Registration Act 1925 |
| LRA 2002 | Land Registration Act 2002 |
| LRHUDA 1993 | Leasehold Reform, Housing and Urban Development Act 1993 |
| NHBC | National House Building Council |
| NLIS | National Land Information Service |
| nse | no subsisting entries |
| PD | Particulars Delivered |
| PRs | Personal Representative |
| SC | Standard Conditions |
| SEAL | Solicitors' Estate Agency Ltd |
| SPIF | Seller's Property Information Form |
| TT | telegraphic transfer |
| VAT | value added tax |
| VATA 1989 | Value Added Tax Act 1989 |

**Part I**

# INTRODUCTION

**Chapter 1**

# INTRODUCTION TO CONVEYANCING

## 1.1 WHAT IS CONVEYANCING?

A solicitor would probably describe conveyancing as the process by which the safe, speedy and efficient transfer of ownership in land is effected between a seller and a buyer.

Although the public conception of conveyancing is usually closely related to the process of moving house, residential conveyancing is only one aspect of the property lawyer's role. The modern property lawyer will probably be more involved in commercial transactions, ranging from the sale and purchase of a small corner shop to masterminding the development of a vast industrial estate, with all the planning, environmental and construction law implications involved in that type of project. The conveyancing law and procedures involved in acquiring land for an industrial estate are identical to those used to convey a semi-detached house in a suburban street. They are both 'conveyancing'.

This book is intended to provide an introduction to all these various aspects of conveyancing.

## 1.2 THE TWO SYSTEMS OF CONVEYANCING

Two systems of conveyancing exist in England and Wales: the 'registered' and the 'unregistered' systems. The main difference between the two systems lies in the way in which the seller proves his ownership of the property to an intending buyer. The reason for the existence of two parallel systems of conveyancing is historical.

### 1.2.1 The unregistered system

The 'unregistered' system of conveyancing could be described as the traditional way of doing things. It is a method of transferring ownership in land which has existed in England for centuries, although a major overhaul of the law was carried out by the Law of Property Act 1925 and related legislation.

Under the unregistered system, the seller proves his ownership or title by showing the buyer documentary evidence in the form of past conveyances and other documents of the past ownership of the land. Collectively, these are known as the title deeds to the property. The seller is required to show the buyer that he can prove undisputed ownership of the land from a point in time at least 15 years before the present sale/purchase transaction down to the present day. If, for example, A owned the land in question in 1980, it would be necessary for the seller to show to his buyer documents which proved that A, the owner in 1980, had sold to B, who in turn had sold the same land to C, and so on until the land became the property of the present seller. There must be no missing links in the chain, no unexplained jumps from, say, B to E.

This method of conveyancing is safe and logical: if a chain of ownership of at least 15 years in length can be established, it is fair to assume that the seller has sufficient title to the land to ensure that the buyer will acquire a safe and saleable property without fear of its being reclaimed by a third party. However, the process of producing and then checking all the documents needed to establish this chain of ownership is cumbersome, time-consuming and expensive. The system is also not without its flaws, since a competent forger would have little difficulty in producing an authentic and convincing set of fake documents.

### 1.2.2 The registered system

In order to simplify and speed up conveyancing, and to lessen the opportunities for fraud, the 'registered' system of conveyancing was introduced. Placing all the land in England and Wales on the register is a time-consuming process, but it will lead to the gradual elimination of the unregistered system.

The idea of the registered system is that the government maintains a register of land, land transfers take place by notifying the registry of the change of ownership, and the details recorded at the registry are amended accordingly. (This is a similar concept to the DVLA, which keeps a central record of motor vehicles and which must be notified on the change of ownership of a vehicle.)

Each landowner is issued with a certificate which shows the extent of the land which he owns, the benefits enjoyed by the land (eg the right to use a driveway) and the burdens attached to it (eg undischarged mortgages or restrictive covenants which have to be observed by the owner). Proof of ownership rests with the Land Registry itself which, by entering the land on the register, gives a State guarantee of the validity of the title.

When an intending buyer wants to check the state of the title which he is buying, a quick search of the register at HM Land Registry will confirm the information which he needs.

### 1.2.3 The systems exist in parallel

The register is so much quicker, simpler and more reliable for proving ownership than checking through documents supplied by the seller that it is perhaps surprising to find that, after nearly a century-and-a-half, the registered and unregistered systems of conveyancing are still running in parallel with each other. The registered system now dominates conveyancing, but there are still large pockets of land, some in rural areas, others owned by large trusts, which continue to be unregistered.

The progress of the registered system was achieved by gradually making designated areas of the country 'compulsory' areas, so that within these areas, when land was sold, it was obligatory to register it, and, afterwards, to carry out all further dealings with the land using only the registered system. By this approach, much land was entered on the register, but it was only in 1990 that the last compulsory registration order was made, so that it became compulsory to register land on any freehold sale throughout England and Wales. It was only from 1 April 1998 that changes of ownership following death and gifts of land have become compulsorily registerable.

Although all areas of the country are now 'compulsory' as far as registration is concerned, broadly registration will occur only when land changes hands. Thus, although there will, in the future, be a steadily increasing proportion of registered land transactions, some land will be unregistered for the foreseeable future. For this reason, property lawyers need to know and to understand the mechanics of both systems. A brief explanation of the registered land system is set out in Chapter 4.

## 1.3 RELATIONSHIP OF CONVEYANCING AND LAND LAW

Conveyancing is the practical application of land law and the law of contract. It is necessary for the property lawyer to have some knowledge of land law in order to understand, and so to avoid, its pitfalls. A summary of the main points of land law and the law of contract as they affect conveyancing appears in Chapter 3.

## 1.4 APPROACH TAKEN BY THIS BOOK

This book is intended as an introductory work for those who have little or no experience of conveyancing in a practical context. It is set out in a chronological sequence, taking the reader through the steps in a simple transaction in the order in which they would occur in practice. The procedures applicable to the registered and unregistered systems of conveyancing are largely identical and are not specifically referred to except where they differ from one another.

Most land is owned freehold, and the major part of this book concentrates on the procedures relating to freehold tenure. In many cases, the procedure adopted in a leasehold transaction is identical to that used in freehold conveyancing. Where leases differ from freeholds, the differences are highlighted in Part VII of this book.

Similarly, the procedures used in residential and commercial conveyancing are identical to one another. Commercial transactions may involve more money than residential ones, and the large sums of money involved may increase the tension and risk for the solicitor involved, but the object of both types of transaction remains the same – the safe, speedy and efficient transfer of ownership from seller to buyer. If the solicitor does not achieve this, whether in the domestic or the commercial sphere, he will not have done his job properly and risks being sued for negligence. Where the steps to be taken differ in a commercial transaction from a residential transaction, these are indicated at the appropriate stage of the proceedings. A brief overview of commercial conveyancing is also given in Chapter 42. An introduction to the drafting and approving of commercial leases and the security of tenure given to business tenants is also included in Part VII.

This book does not set out to be a definitive academic textbook on conveyancing. It is a beginner's guide to the law and procedures involved in the conveyancing process, and the reader is advised to use practitioner texts to supplement the information given in this book.

### 1.4.1 Practitioner textbooks

#### *General textbooks*

F. Silverman *The Law Society's Conveyancing Handbook* (The Law Society, London, 2001). This contains The Law Society's recommended methods of practice.

### *Specialist works*

Specialist books exist in almost every area of conveyancing from contract drafting to remedies. They are too numerous to mention in this book, but a well-stocked library should contain a selection of appropriate texts.

Of those of more general application, the loose-leaf work *Emmet & Farrand on Title* (Sweet & Maxwell) is known as 'the conveyancer's bible', and is a recognised authority on many aspects of conveyancing law, especially those relating to legal title.

Many precedent books (which are used to trigger ideas for drafting a particular document) also exist. The well-known examples are: *The Encyclopedia of Forms and Precedents*, vols 35–38 (Butterworths), which carry a comprehensive range of model documents and clauses designed to fit most situations, and Parker *Modern Conveyancing Precedents* (Butterworths, 1989), which contains a selection of precedents drafted in simple, modern language.

For a fuller explanation of the land law principles on which conveyancing is based, reference should be made to a standard land law textbook such as *Megarry's Manual of the Law of Real Property* (Sweet & Maxwell, 1995).

## 1.5 E-CONVEYANCING

At the moment, conveyancing is very much a paper-based system. Contracts for the sale of land must be in writing; a deed must be used for the actual transfer of ownership. The various searches and enquiries necessary prior to a purchase must be made by the submission of application forms to the relevant bodies. The Government, however, is very keen that the conveyancing process should be able to be undertaken almost entirely electronically, so that the process can be speeded up. The Land Registry has set up a new 'Land Registry Direct' system which allows direct access to the register via the internet. Another part of this process involves the setting up of the National Land Information Service (NLIS) (see **18.3**) which will enable searches and enquiries to be made almost instantaneously using the internet. Electronic Notification of Discharge (of mortgages) is now also common place.

The Electronic Communications Act 2000 and the Land Registration Act 2002 together provide a framework which will ultimately allow the whole conveyancing transaction to be effected electronically. Contracts will be drafted, approved and exchanged electronically. Searches will be made, and results sent directly to your computer. Contracts and transfers will be 'signed' by a secure electronic signature. On completion, the register will be automatically changed without need for a further application.

It will be some years before a full pilot scheme can be implemented but moves towards this will continue; already applications to remove the name of a deceased proprietor (amongst others) can be made electronically. For the moment, however, this book must concentrate on the paper-based system currently in use, but enormous changes in conveyancing practices are inevitable.

# Chapter 2

# OUTLINE OF A SIMPLE TRANSACTION

## 2.1 HOW A CONVEYANCING TRANSACTION WORKS

A typical conveyancing transaction divides into three stages:

(1)  the pre-contract stage;
(2)  the post-contract (or pre-completion) stage; and
(3)  the post-completion stage.

In terms of time, the pre-contract stage is the longest and much of the legal work involved in the transaction is done at this time. Assuming that matters proceed smoothly, the pre-contract stage of a residential transaction may take 4–6 weeks from the date when instructions are first received. The post-contract stage may then be much shorter, usually no longer than 2 weeks, and the post-completion stage represents the 'tidying up loose ends' process after the buyer has taken possession. It is unrealistic in most circumstances to expect the transaction to be accomplished in less than about 8 weeks from start to finish, and sometimes, due to delays caused by parties over whom the solicitor has no control (eg delays by a local authority in returning a search application or delays by a lender in processing a client's mortgage application), the transaction may take much longer than either the solicitor or the client feels is reasonable. In commercial transactions, different considerations apply, and a much shorter timescale has often to be achieved in order to meet the needs of the clients. However, the procedure to be followed is basically the same.

### 2.1.1 Sellers' packs

There has been much criticism in recent years of the length of time taken to complete a house purchase. The delay between a prospective buyer making an informal offer for a property and the sale becoming legally binding facilitates the practices known as 'gazumping' and 'gazundering'. 'Gazumping' occurs when a buyer, having spent much time and money on surveys and legal work, is told by the seller, just before contracts are to be exchanged, that unless he is prepared to pay a higher price, the property will be sold to another buyer. 'Gazundering' occurs when the buyer, again just before exchange, informs the seller that he will only proceed if the price is reduced.

Towards the end of 1998, the government produced a consultation paper proposing changes in conveyancing procedure aimed at speeding up the process and thus reducing the opportunity for these undesirable practices. The Government introduced its Homes Bill into the House of Commons on 12 December 2000 with the intention of giving effect to its proposals. Although the original Bill was 'lost' when the May 2001 election was called, the Government still intends to reintroduce it when Parliamentary time allows. The Bill will require the seller or the seller's agent, before putting a home on the market, to put together a pack – the contents of which will be prescribed by statutory instrument – of standard and essential information for prospective buyers. This will include a form of structural survey. The Government's proposals have not been universally welcomed. The procedures set out in this book reflect current procedure only, as it may well be some time before any changes are effected. The Government's research, however, showed that, although house purchase in England and Wales was amongst the slowest in the world, it was also amongst the cheapest. If the proposals are implemented, they will inevitably increase the cost considerably.

## 2.1.2  Taking instructions

Whether the solicitor is acting for the seller or the buyer, the first step in the transaction is the same for both of them: instructions must be taken from the client. Those instructions should normally be confirmed to the client in writing, together with written information relating to the costs which the client will have to pay for the work to be done by his solicitor. Following this, the seller's and buyer's solicitors must attend to different aspects of the transaction.

# GENERAL FREEHOLD CONVEYANCING

## OUTLINE OF A SIMPLE CONVEYANCING TRANSACTION

SELLER                           BUYER

| TAKE INSTRUCTIONS | TAKE INSTRUCTIONS |

| PREPARE PRE-CONTRACT PACKAGE |

| PRE-CONTRACT SEARCHES AND ENQUIRIES |

| INVESTIGATE TITLE |

| APPROVE DRAFT CONTRACT |

| EXCHANGE CONTRACTS |

| PREPARE PURCHASE DEED |

| APPROVE PURCHASE DEED |

| PRE-COMPLETION SEARCHES |

| PREPARE FOR COMPLETION | PREPARE FOR COMPLETION |

| COMPLETION |

| POST-COMPLETION MATTERS | POST-COMPLETION MATTERS |

The chart above shows the responsibilities of the parties' solicitors at each stage of the transaction and serves as a reminder of the various procedures which are involved and the stages in the transaction at which they take place.

### 2.1.3  The pre-contract stage

Having taken instructions, the seller's solicitor must prepare the pre-contract package for the buyer. This comprises:

(1)  the draft contract, showing what land the seller is selling and on what terms he is prepared to sell it;
(2)  evidence of the seller's legal title to the property, to prove that he does own and is entitled to sell the land; and
(3)  sometimes, the results of pre-contract searches which the seller has made and other information about the property.

The package may also include such items as copy local authority planning permissions, which the buyer's solicitor will want to see to make sure that the property which his client is buying was permitted to be built on the site.

When the buyer's solicitor receives the pre-contract package from the seller's solicitor, he will check all the documents supplied very carefully to ensure that the terms of the contract accord with his instructions and do not reveal any problems which might make the property an unsuitable purchase for his client. Although the seller has a limited duty to disclose defects in his legal title (but not physical defects), the caveat emptor principle ('let the buyer beware') applies to conveyancing, so that it is the buyer's responsibility to find out all the information which he needs to know about the property before committing himself to the purchase. The Government's proposals for sellers' packs would, to some extent, remove the caveat emptor principle.

### *Title*

The pre-contract package will include documents showing proof of the seller's ownership of the land. The buyer's solicitor must check these documents carefully to ensure that the seller is entitled to sell what he is purporting to sell. Any queries arising out of the title documents are raised with the seller's solicitor by means of 'requisitions'. These are questions or 'requests' addressed to the seller, requiring him to resolve any apparent problems with the seller's ownership, or 'title' as it is usually referred to. The contract usually contains a clause excluding the buyer from questioning the seller's title once contracts for the sale and purchase have been entered into. If the buyer's solicitor discovers problems with the seller's title at this stage, the buyer can withdraw from the transaction without penalty since no formal contract yet exists between the parties.

### *Searches*

It is the application of the caveat emptor principle which makes pre-contract searches necessary. These searches, many of them made with public bodies such as the local authority or HM Land Registry, will reveal a large amount of information about the property, all of which will help the buyer to make up his mind whether or not to proceed with the purchase. In some cases, the seller's solicitor will submit the search applications and pass their results to the buyer's solicitor with the pre-contract package. If this has happened, the buyer's solicitor still needs to check that the correct searches have been made and that their results are satisfactory. In most cases, the buyer's solicitor will make the search applications himself. In this situation the search applications need to be sent to the relevant authorities as soon as firm instructions to proceed have been obtained, otherwise the delay in receiving search replies may cause a delay in the transaction. The Government is setting up a National Land Information Service (NLIS) which will provide an on-line link to the various sources of information to enable searches to be made more easily and much more speedily than at present.

### The buyer's finances

The buyer's solicitor must check that his client is able, in financial terms, to proceed with the transaction. Unless the client has sufficient available cash to purchase the property, he must have received a satisfactory offer of finance and have available sufficient money to pay the balance of the purchase price (it is unusual to obtain a mortgage for the whole of the purchase price). The client must also be able to fund the 10% deposit which is normally payable on entering into a contract to buy land.

### The draft contract

When the buyer's solicitor is satisfied with his search results, with the proof of the seller's ownership (title) and with the terms of the draft contract (he may have negotiated some amendments to the contract with the seller's solicitor), he will be ready to return the draft contract to the seller's solicitor, telling him that the buyer has approved the terms and is now ready to enter the contract. The contract is then prepared for the clients' signatures. Two copies of the contract, incorporating any agreed amendments, are printed off; the seller signs one, the buyer the other. These two parts of the contract are then physically exchanged, so that the buyer receives the part signed by the seller and vice versa. This process is called 'exchange of contracts'.

## 2.1.4 Exchange of contracts

The exchange of contracts marks the stage in the transaction at which a binding contract comes into existence. Until exchange, no contract exists between buyer and seller and either is free to change his mind about the transaction and withdraw from it. It is this aspect of conveyancing procedure that is most frequently criticised; remember, in a residential transaction, there could well be 6 weeks or more between a solicitor being instructed and contracts being exchanged, and, if either party withdraws at the last minute before exchange, this can cause great inconvenience to the other party. It is towards reducing this delay that the Government proposals are aimed. Once exchange has taken place, a binding contract exists and usually neither party can withdraw without incurring liability for breach of contract. On exchange, the buyer will normally pay a deposit. This is customarily 10% of the purchase price and will be held by the seller's solicitor until completion. The money serves as a 'statement of intent' by the buyer that he is serious about the transaction and intends to fulfil his contractual obligations. If he fails to complete, the seller can usually forfeit the deposit and retain the money.

## 2.1.5 Post-contract stage

Since most of the important stages of the transaction have now been accomplished, the pre-completion, or post-contract, stage of the transaction should be less onerous for both sides. At this stage, the first step is normally for the buyer to 'raise requisitions' with the seller. Historically, the purpose of requisitions was to clarify any queries which had arisen out of the seller's proof of ownership of the property, but in modern conveyancing, where proof of title is invariably a pre-contract issue, requisitions are more likely to be directed at the resolution of procedural queries relating to the mechanics of completion itself. For example, the buyer needs to know precisely how much money is required from him to complete the transaction, where completion is to take place and who holds the keys to the property. These queries are usually raised on a standard form which is sent to the seller's solicitor for his replies.

### The draft purchase deed

At the same time as sending the requisitions, the buyer's solicitor sends the draft purchase deed to the seller's solicitor, for his approval. In registered land, this will take the form of a transfer, as prescribed by the Land Registration Rules. In unregistered land, it may take the form of a traditional conveyance, although usually a modified form of Land Registry transfer is used.

Although it was the seller's solicitor's duty to prepare the contract, customarily it is the buyer's solicitor who prepares the purchase deed itself. The contract states what the parties have agreed to do, the purchase deed carries it out. In other words, the purchase deed activates the terms of the contract and brings them alive; this deed must therefore be drafted to reflect the terms of the contract (no new terms can be introduced at this stage) and the seller's solicitor will check the draft deed to ensure that the buyer's solicitor has done the job properly. The seller's solicitor's approval of the draft purchase deed is normally notified to the buyer's solicitor at the stage when the seller's solicitor replies to the buyer's solicitor's requisitions. The purchase deed can then be 'engrossed', ie a copy is prepared containing any agreed amendments; this is the copy which will be signed by the parties.

The seller must always sign the purchase deed, otherwise the legal estate in the land will not pass. Frequently, the buyer also signs but there are circumstances in which it is not in fact necessary for him to do so.

### The buyer's lender

At the same time as the purchase deed is being prepared, it is also necessary for some work to be done on behalf of the buyer's lender. At the time when a mortgage offer was made to the buyer, the lender would have instructed solicitors to act for him in connection with the loan. The lender needs to be certain that the property which he is accepting as security for the loan has a good title (ie he needs to carry out the same investigations as were carried out on behalf of the buyer in this respect) and various documents need to be drawn up to put the mortgage into effect.

### Acting for the buyer and the lender

Frequently, the solicitor who is acting for the buyer will also be instructed to act for the buyer's lender. Acting for more than one party in a transaction is severely restricted by Rule 6 of the Solicitors' Practice Rules 1990, but acting for buyer and lender is usually permitted; see Chapter 6. The solicitor who is acting for the buyer's lender must:

(1) draw up the mortgage deed for signature by the borrower (buyer);
(2) certify to the lender that the legal title to the property is in order (a report on title); and

(3) obtain a clear bankruptcy search against the borrower, since the lender will be reluctant to lend money to a person who is the subject of bankruptcy proceedings.

The buyer's solicitor must also ensure that he is put in funds to complete the transaction. The seller's solicitor will have informed him of the exact amount of money needed to complete the transaction, either in answer to the buyer's requisitions or on a separate document called a 'completion statement'. In residential transactions, the amount needed to complete is often simply the balance of the purchase price, taking into account the deposit which was paid on exchange. In other cases, other sums may be due, for example payment for stock-in-trade in the case of the purchase of a business. The buyer's solicitor will notify his client of the amount due to complete the transaction by sending him a statement of account. The client will also be sent (where appropriate) a copy of the completion statement and, in residential cases, the solicitor's bill showing the fees and disbursements payable in respect of the transaction.

Commonly in house purchases, a large part of the purchase price will be provided by way of loan from the lender and/or by the proceeds of sale of the buyer's present property. This fact will be shown on the statement of account, so that the amount which the client has to find from his own funds is comparatively small.

The money which the client has to pay the solicitor to make up the balance due on completion must be paid to the solicitor in sufficient time before completion to allow that money to be cleared (ie the normal banking process of clearing a cheque) before the solicitor uses that money to complete the transaction. The mortgage loan from the lender must similarly be obtained, so that at the time when the money is required to be sent to the seller's solicitor, all the necessary funds are cleared and are in the buyer's solicitor's client account. Frequently, however, the mortgage advance will not be paid by cheque but will be transmitted directly to the solicitor's bank account.

### Preparation for completion

A few days before completion the buyer's solicitor makes his pre-completion searches to ensure that no last-minute problems have occurred with the title to the property.

At the same time as the buyer's solicitor is preparing for completion, the seller's solicitor is also taking steps to ensure that completion will proceed smoothly and without delay.

### Discharge of seller's mortgage

Very often the seller will have a mortgage on the property which he has agreed with the buyer to remove on completion. The seller's solicitor must now confirm with the seller's lender the exact amount of money which is required to discharge the seller's mortgage, and generally make sure that he has in his possession all the documents required to complete the transaction. This may involve the preparation of a form of discharge of the seller's mortgage if (as is usual) the seller's solicitor is also acting for the seller's lender in connection with the discharge.

### Final checks

Both parties' solicitors check through their respective files and make a 'checklist' of what is to happen at completion. This is to ensure that nothing has been overlooked:

no two transactions are identical, and even the most straightforward of residential transactions can throw up unforeseen last-minute complications. An appointment can then be made for completion to actually take place.

### 2.1.6 Completion

Traditionally, completion took place by the buyer's solicitor attending personally at the seller's solicitor's offices to hand over the money in return for the deeds, but personal attendance at completion is an expensive and time-consuming operation, especially in the context of residential transactions. It is more common today for the parties to agree to complete 'through the post'. In effect, a postal completion means that the seller's solicitor is temporarily appointed to be the agent for the buyer's solicitor, and while acting as such must carry out all the steps which the buyer's solicitor instructs him to do (ie all the things which the buyer's solicitor would be doing if he was physically present at completion).

The method by which completion is to be effected will have been agreed by the respective solicitors at the 'requisitions' stage of the transaction. If a postal completion is to take place, the time at which completion is due to take place will have been agreed in the course of a telephone conversation between the parties' solicitors, and the buyer's solicitor will have given the seller's solicitor precise instructions as to what is required to be done. This is in accordance with the guidelines for postal completions issued by The Law Society (the 'Code for Completion by Post') (see Appendix 5).

On the morning of completion day, the first priority is to transmit to the seller's solicitor the money which is required to complete the transaction. Without tangible evidence that the buyer has paid, the seller will not complete. With a postal completion, the money is usually sent to the seller's solicitor's bank account by what is still called a telegraphic transfer, but is now an electronic transmission of funds from the buyer's solicitor's bank account to the seller's solicitor's account. No physical transfer of the money takes place: the buyer's solicitor's account is debited with the requisite sum, a corresponding credit being entered in the seller's solicitor's account. Computer technology makes this possible even where the two solicitors bank at different banks in different towns.

When the seller's solicitor's bank receives the funds from the buyer's solicitor's bank, the bank should notify the seller's solicitor that the funds have arrived, so that the seller's solicitor can proceed with completion itself. In practice, this is little more than a formality. The deeds may have to be checked on behalf of the buyer's solicitor, the purchase deed dated, the estate agent informed that completion has taken place (so that he can release the keys of the property to the new owner), and the deeds themselves sent by first-class post to the buyer's solicitor. The seller's solicitor will then telephone the buyer's solicitor to inform him of the safe arrival of the money and that completion has taken place in accordance with his instructions.

The clients themselves do not attend completion but should be informed by telephone immediately after completion that it has taken place: the sellers are told that they are now in funds with the proceeds of sale; the buyers are told that they now own, and can take possession of their new property.

## 2.1.7 Post-completion

### *The seller's solicitor*

The seller's solicitor now has some loose ends to tie up. First he must send to the seller's lender the amount required to pay off the seller's mortgage, obtain a receipt for that money and send the receipt to the buyer's solicitor, who will need this receipt to prove to HM Land Registry that the mortgage has been discharged. He must also account to his client for the proceeds of sale and, if not already done, prepare and submit his bill of costs. The proceeds of sale should be dealt with on the day of completion, or as soon as is possible. A solicitor who delays in returning money to a client may have to pay interest on that sum to the client under the Solicitors' Accounts Rules 1998. The seller's solicitor can close his file when he has dealt with these matters.

### *The buyer's solicitor*

The buyer's solicitor must deal with the stamping of documents. Where the purchase price of the property is over £60,000, stamp duty on the amount of the price is usually payable to the Inland Revenue within 30 days of completion. Failure to pay or late payment attracts heavy penalties. Particulars of the transaction (ie who has sold what to whom and at what price) must also be delivered to the Inland Revenue after completion to comply with the Finance Act 1931. This requirement is satisfied by the delivery of a Particulars Delivered (PD) form to the Inland Revenue at the time when stamp duty is paid (or to HM Land Registry as agents of the Inland Revenue in a freehold transaction where no duty is payable).

After these formalities have been completed, the buyer's solicitor must apply to HM Land Registry for his client's title to be registered. HM Land Registry will return to the buyer's solicitor a charge certificate (or land certificate if there is no mortgage over the property) containing details of the buyer's ownership of the land, the mortgages to which it is subject and particulars of any easements or covenants affecting the land. When he has checked that the details contained in the certificate are correct, the buyer's solicitor should forward the certificate, together with any other relevant documents, to the lender, or if the property is not subject to a loan, to the buyer, for safe-keeping. After he has received an acknowledgment from the lender or buyer and all other outstanding matters have been satisfactorily dealt with, the buyer's solicitor may send his file for storage.

## 2.2 LINKED TRANSACTIONS

In many residential transactions, the client will be selling one house and buying another house. His intention is to move from one to the other on the same day, using the money obtained from the sale transaction towards payment of the purchase price of the house he is buying. In such a case, the sale and purchase transactions are inextricably linked: the client cannot afford to buy his new house unless he can also sell the old one, neither does he want to sell his existing house unless he can buy a new one in which to live, since a sale without a related purchase would leave him homeless. This is often described as the 'no home/two homes' syndrome; neither situation is desirable from the client's point of view. The solicitor's objective is to ensure that at any one time the client owns only one house and that at no time is the client without a home. The sale and purchase transactions must therefore be synchronised, and failure to achieve synchronisation where the client has instructed it will prima facie be negligence on the part of the solicitor. It follows that, where the solicitor is acting in linked transactions, he will at the same time be carrying out the steps described above relating to both the seller's and the buyer's solicitor, one set of procedures being relevant to the sale transaction, the other to the simultaneous purchase.

## 2.3 THE NATIONAL PROTOCOL

In 1990, The Law Society issued the first edition of the National Protocol for domestic conveyancing. The Protocol is known by the brand logo 'TransAction' and is intended to standardise, simplify and speed up the procedures relating to domestic conveyancing. Most firms which carry out residential conveyancing are registered with The Law Society as TransAction users.

At the beginning of a residential transaction, the solicitors acting for the parties should ascertain whether the Protocol is to be used in that transaction and, if so, whether there are intended to be any variations to the prescribed procedures. The procedures laid down by the Protocol are intended to regulate the relationship between the seller's and buyer's solicitors and do not affect dealings with third parties such as estate agents or lenders. Broadly speaking, the requirements of the Protocol reflect what is already standard practice within the profession and no special procedures are involved. However, some of the forms used in Protocol transactions are specially prescribed for use in conjunction with the Protocol and some are compulsory (eg a particular form of contract is compulsory). In this book, reference is made to the Protocol in the context of the particular procedural steps being discussed where those procedures differ from accepted practice. If the Protocol is not mentioned specifically, this indicates that the procedure under the Protocol is identical to the procedures described for that particular stage of the transaction. The text of the Protocol is set out for reference in Appendix 1 and provides a further useful checklist of the procedural stages in a simple transaction.

### 2.3.1 Disclosure of related transactions

When a solicitor is instructed to buy or sell a residential property on behalf of his client, he will explain the use of the Protocol to the client and will discuss with him the advantages and disadvantages of disclosing information to the other party about the progress of any related sale or purchase transaction. Disclosure of such information may be helpful to the other party, but might not be helpful to the solicitor's own client if, for example, the client is experiencing difficulties in selling his own property. Disclosure of information about related transactions can be made only with the client's consent, and the client's refusal to give such consent is not deemed to be a departure from the Protocol.

### 2.3.2 Non-solicitors

Where it is in the interests of a client to use the Protocol, a licensed conveyancer acting for the other party should be invited to adopt it. Licensed conveyancers are regarded in the same light as solicitors, so it is possible to rely on a licensed conveyancer's agreement to use the Protocol in a transaction. Since the Protocol procedures are to an extent dependent on undertakings, it is unwise to attempt to use it in a situation where an unqualified person is purporting to represent one of the parties to the transaction, since an undertaking given by an unqualified person is not enforceable in the same way as a solicitor's or licensed conveyancer's undertaking.

**Chapter 3**

# ESSENTIAL BACKGROUND LAW

## 3.1 INTRODUCTION

Conveyancing is about the practical application of land law, and for that reason this chapter contains a brief reminder of some basic principles. It does not pretend to be a comprehensive guide to land law for which the reader is referred to one of the standard texts on the subject.

## 3.2 LEGAL ESTATES, LEGAL INTERESTS AND EQUITABLE INTERESTS

### 3.2.1 Legal estates

Since 1925 there can be only two legal estates:

(1) an estate in fee simple absolute in possession (the freehold estate); and
(2) a term of years absolute (the leasehold estate).

### 3.2.2 Legal interests

The most important legal interests which can subsist today are:

(1) an easement for an interest equivalent to a fee simple absolute in possession or term of years absolute; and
(2) a charge by way of legal mortgage.

### 3.2.3 Equitable interests

Virtually all other estates, interests and charges in or over land other than those mentioned above will take effect as equitable interests (Law of Property Act 1925, s 1).

### 3.2.4 Deeds

As a general rule, a deed is required to convey or create a legal estate or interest, but there are exceptions: certain leases for not more than 3 years and some assents do not need to be by deed. See **27.7** as to the formalities required for a document to become a deed.

## 3.3 THIRD-PARTY RIGHTS

It is often necessary to determine whether or not a buyer of a legal estate in land is to buy free from or subject to a particular existing right or interest in that land belonging to someone else, ie a third party.

For example, assume S owns land which is subject to an easement in favour of E. Will a buyer from S take free from or subject to E's easement?

The way in which third-party rights are protected depends upon whether the title to the land is registered or unregistered.

### 3.3.1  Unregistered land

The protection of third-party rights in land with an unregistered title largely depends on whether or not the particular right concerned is capable of registration under the Land Charges Act 1972.

#### *Land charges*

The following classes of land charge should be noted:

Class C(i)        A puisne mortgage (ie a legal mortgage not protected by the lender's possession of the title deeds).

Class C(iv)       An estate contract (ie a contract to create or convey a legal estate, eg a contract to sell land or grant a lease).

Class D(ii)       A restrictive covenant entered into on or after 1 January 1925.

Class F           A spouse's right of occupation of the matrimonial home under the Family Law Act 1996.

If the third party has registered his right, it will be binding on all persons (such registration being deemed to be actual notice).

If it is registrable, but has not been registered, then the precise effect of failure to register will depend on the nature of the right but, in broad terms, failure to register will render the right void as against a buyer. The fact that the buyer may actually know of the third-party right is irrelevant.

If the right or interest is incapable of registration then whether or not it is binding on a buyer will depend on whether it is legal or equitable.

#### *Legal interests*

Legal easements and legal leases (no matter what the length) and legal mortgages protected by the lender's possession of the title deeds are binding on all persons irrespective of notice.

#### *Equitable interests*

Equitable interests (eg an interest under a resulting trust) bind a buyer unless the buyer falls within the definition of a bona fide purchaser for value of the legal estate without notice.

Notice here includes not only actual notice (ie within the buyer's own knowledge), but also imputed notice (ie within the actual or constructive knowledge of his solicitor), and constructive notice (ie of matters a person would have discovered had he made the enquiries he ought reasonably to have made). However, equitable interests arising under trusts can be overreached (ie transferred to the purchase money) on a sale by two trustees. In such a case, they will not be binding on a buyer, even if he has notice of them.

### 3.3.2 Registered land

How third-party rights are protected in land with a registered title depends upon whether such rights are classified as overriding interests or minor interests. Registered charges, ie mortgages, are for all practical purposes treated as if they were classified as minor interests.

Overriding interests are defined in the Land Registration Act 1925, s 70. If a third-party right is classified as an overriding interest, it will not appear on the register but it will bind a buyer, irrespective of whether that buyer has notice of it (see **4.7.2**).

All other third-party rights are classified as minor interests and must be protected by some entry on the register if they are to bind a buyer. Failure to register (as a notice, caution, inhibition or restriction) will mean that a buyer for valuable consideration in good faith will take free from the minor interest.

## 3.4 EASEMENTS

An easement confers the right to one landowner to use the land of another in some way, or to prevent it being used in a certain way. Examples are: a right of way; and a right of light.

There are certain conditions which must be satisfied before an easement can exist:

(1) there must be a dominant and a servient piece of land;
(2) the right must accommodate (ie benefit) the dominant land;
(3) the dominant and servient pieces of land must not be both owned and occupied by the same person; and
(4) the right must be capable of being granted by deed and therefore must usually be:

   (a) within the general nature of rights capable of being easements; and
   (b) sufficiently definite.

### 3.4.1 Creation of easements

Easements are most frequently created on a sale of part of a piece of land belonging to the seller (see Chapter 40), and it is in these circumstances that the rules relating to their creation are important.

Easements are either legal or equitable. A legal easement must be equivalent to either a fee simple or a term of years, and it is usually created by deed (although it may be acquired by prescription or by statute).

An equitable easement will arise if there has been a failure to observe the formalities necessary to create a legal easement, or if an easement is granted which is not equivalent to either a fee simple or a term of years (eg one granted for life).

In most cases, the easement will be created expressly either by the seller in his own favour over the part of his land being sold (reservation) or in favour of the buyer over the part being retained by the seller (grant).

Where, however, there is no express reservation or grant, certain easements may be created by implication or may be acquired by prescription.

### 3.4.2  Implied reservation

Few easements are implied in favour of a seller and these are generally confined to:

(1)  easements of necessity (eg where the only means of access to the land retained by the seller is over the land being sold); and
(2)  intended easements (eg a right of support on sale of a semi-detached house).

### 3.4.3  Implied grant

Easements similar to those above will be granted impliedly to a buyer. However, the rule in *Wheeldon v Burrows* (1879) 12 Ch D 31 extends the list of easements impliedly granted to cover rights enjoyed by the seller over his own land (quasi-easements) which are continuous, apparent and necessary to the reasonable enjoyment of the land sold.

Also, where the land has previously been occupied by separate individuals (eg where a landlord owns two plots, lets one to a tenant, and then sells one plot), the Law of Property Act 1925, s 62 operates to pass on conveyance rights which have up until then been mere permissions (ie licences), thus elevating them into easements in favour of a buyer.

### 3.4.4  Presumed grant

The grant of an easement will be presumed following the open and unchallenged exercise of a right without permission for a long period of time. This is known as prescription. There are various methods of prescription, but there must be a minimum of 20 years' uninterrupted use before a right can be presumed to have been granted.

### 3.4.5  Public rights of way

A public right of way, often encountered in conveyancing, is not an easement but a right exercisable by anyone, by virtue of the general law, to cross another's land. The surface of the land over which a public right of way exists is known as a highway.

A public right of way can be created at common law by dedication by the owner to the public either expressly or by implication, and by the public accepting that dedication as a highway. It can also be created by statute, for example, under the Highways Act 1980.

Whether or not such a highway is maintainable at the public expense is a separate matter.

## 3.5  COVENANTS

A covenant is a promise made in a deed. In conveyancing, covenants are frequently encountered on a sale of part of land, for example, where B buys part of S's land and covenants in the purchase deed not to build more than one house on the land bought. Here B is the covenantor (ie the person who has accepted the burden of the covenant) and S is the covenantee (ie the person with the benefit of the covenant). As both B and S are parties to the covenant, their rights and obligations are governed by the terms of their contract.

When either S or B later sell their respective interests it has to be decided whether the burden of the covenant will bind a successor of the covenantor, and whether the benefit will pass to a successor of the covenantee. The burden of a positive covenant does not pass to a successor in title. In general, the benefit of a covenant will pass to a successor in title of the covenantee so long as:

(1) the covenant touches and concerns the land of the covenantee; and
(2) the benefit is either expressly assigned or is annexed to the land.

The benefit of a restrictive covenant will also pass where a building scheme has been created.

The burden of a covenant will bind successors in title of the covenantor only where the conditions laid down in *Tulk v Moxhay* (1848) 2 Ph 774 are satisfied. These are:

(1) the covenant must be negative in substance;
(2) it must benefit the land of the covenantee;
(3) the burden must be intended to run with the covenantor's land; and
(4) the successor must have notice of the existence of the covenant.

Where the title to land is unregistered, a restrictive covenant (other than one made between landlord and tenant) must usually be registered as a Class D(ii) land charge.

If the title is registered, such a covenant will be a minor interest.

If the above conditions are not satisfied, a covenant will not ordinarily be directly enforceable against a successor in title, but such a successor may incur liability through a chain of indemnity covenants thus, when B sells to X, he (B) still remains liable to S as the original covenanting party. He therefore requires X to covenant to indemnify him (B) in the event of X breaching the covenant in the S to B conveyance. X, having given an indemnity covenant when he bought, will require a similar one from his buyer when he sells. Both positive and restrictive covenants may be enforced indirectly in this way.

In the case of covenants in leases, the original landlord and original tenant are liable on their respective covenants on ordinary contractual principles. In the case of leases granted before 1 January 1996, they will remain liable on these covenants even after they have disposed of their interests under the lease. However, in the case of leases granted on or after 1 January 1996, the tenant may be released from future liability under the provisions of the Landlord and Tenant (Covenants) Act 1995.

The rule that applies to successors to the landlord's estate and the tenant's estate is that, while the successors hold their respective estates in land linked by the terms of the lease, they are bound by the doctrine of privity of estate. Under that doctrine, it is possible for the landlord for the time being to sue the tenant for the time being, and vice versa, for breach of most covenants in the lease.

## 3.6 SETTLEMENTS

A settlement consists of a disposition of property in a form which creates a succession of interests in the property. Previously they could either exist as strict settlements under the Settled Land Act 1925 or trusts for sale under the Law of Property Act 1925.

The Trusts of Land and Appointment of Trustees Act 1996 now prohibits the creation of new strict settlements, but those which were in existence at the date when the Act came into force remain valid. All settlements created on or after 1 January 1997 will take effect as trusts of land.

## 3.7  TRUSTS OF LAND

A trust of land is defined as 'any trust of property which consists of or includes land'. This includes express, implied, resulting and constructive trusts, trusts for sale, and bare trusts. Trusts of land are governed by the Trusts of Land and Appointment of Trustees Act 1996. Such a trust can be expressly created or will arise under statute, for example where land is held by co-owners or where land passes to personal representatives on the death of the owner.

Under a trust of land the legal estate is vested in the trustees. Trustees have all the powers of an absolute owner, but restrictions may be imposed on such powers by requiring that consent be obtained, for example from a beneficiary, before a power is exercised.

On the death of a trustee, the legal estate automatically vests in the surviving trustee(s) without the need for any document.

On a sale by trustees, a buyer is protected, and need not be concerned with the trusts affecting the proceeds of sale if he pays the purchase money to all the trustees, being at least two in number, or to a trust corporation. In such cases, the trusts which affected the property are detached from it and are overreached.

## 3.8  CO-OWNERSHIP

Co-ownership arises whenever two or more people have simultaneous concurrent interests in land. The most common example is two people buying a house together. Whenever co-ownership occurs, the legal estate can be held only by those to whom it is conveyed as trustees of land, and trustees of land must hold as joint tenants. Thus, the right of survivorship applies to the legal estate (see **3.8.2**).

So far as the beneficial interests in the property are concerned, these may be held by the trustees either as joint tenants (where the right of survivorship applies) or as tenants in common (where it does not).

A conveyance to co-owners should state how the beneficial interests are to be held but, if it does not, they will be held as joint tenants unless either words of severance have been used (eg 'in equal shares') or an equitable presumption of a tenancy in common arises (eg when the purchase money is provided in unequal shares or where property is purchased as partnership property).

If, for example, property is conveyed to a husband and wife, and the husband later dies, on his death the whole legal estate will become vested in the wife. If the beneficial interests were also held as joint tenants, the wife will now be entitled to the whole of the property, both legally and beneficially, but, if they were held as tenants in common, the deceased husband's interest will pass into his estate and fall to be dealt with by his personal representatives, either under the terms of his will or on intestacy.

A buyer from trustees of land only takes free from beneficial interests if he pays the purchase money to all the trustees, being at least two in number or a trust corporation. Thus a sole surviving trustee may need to appoint a second trustee before selling so that the beneficial interests will be overreached.

## 3.8.1 The legal estate

The legal estate will be held by the trustees as joint tenants on trust for themselves (and possibly other persons) in equity. The legal joint tenancy is not severable and there must be a minimum of two trustees (and maximum of four) in order to deal with the legal estate.

## 3.8.2 The beneficial interest

In equity, there is a choice between holding as joint tenants or as tenants in common. The capacity of the buyers, whether as joint tenants or tenants in common, must be stated in the purchase deed or in a separate trust deed.

### (a) *Joint tenants*

The main distinguishing feature of the joint tenancy is the right of survivorship which leads to the interest accruing to the last surviving joint tenant. Because no distinct part of the interest belongs to any individual tenant, no part of it will belong to the estate of a deceased joint tenant.

An interest in a joint tenancy cannot be left by will: the deceased's share passes automatically to the surviving joint tenant(s). A beneficial joint tenancy can be severed inter vivos, for example by serving a written notice on the other joint tenant(s). This has the effect of converting it into a tenancy in common.

### (b) *Tenancy in common*

Where a tenancy in common exists, each co-owner holds a quantified proportion of the equitable interest which is capable of being disposed of inter vivos or by will or passes on the intestacy of the deceased tenant in common. Unless the contrary is stated or evidence to the contrary is proved, a court will usually presume that tenants in common hold the equitable interest in proportion to their original contribution to the purchase price.

In order to avoid subsequent disputes and litigation, it is essential that the shares of each tenant in common are expressly agreed and recorded in a deed of trust (or certified copy transfer) which is signed by the co-owners and kept with the land or charge certificate. This statement or declaration as to the division of the beneficial interest can only be altered by mutual consent of the parties.

An interest under a tenancy in common can be devised by will or pass on intestacy. Where property is held by this method, the parties should be advised as to the desirability of making a will.

### (c)  HM Land Registry practice

Where the co-owners have indicated on the transfer that they will be holding the property as tenants in common, HM Land Registry will place the following restriction on the proprietorship register of the title:

> 'No disposition by a sole proprietor of the land (not being a trust corporation) under which capital money arises is to be registered except under an order of the Registrar or the Court.'

This serves as a warning to any third party dealing with the proprietors that a trust is in existence, and that any disposition of the legal estate must be effected by a minimum of two trustees. This restriction indicates that a tenancy in common exists, but it does not state the proportions in which the co-owners have divided the equitable interest between them. The division of the equitable interest is not a matter with which HM Land Registry is concerned; it is a private matter between the co-owners. No such restriction appears on the proprietorship register if the co-owners have indicated that they wish to hold the beneficial interest as joint tenants. In the absence of a restriction, a third party is entitled to assume that a joint tenancy exists and may therefore safely deal with the survivor of the joint tenants and need not insist on dealing with two trustees.

## 3.8.3  Title in name of sole owner

Instructions will have revealed whether anyone other than the seller is living at the property. If there is, consideration should be given to the question of whether the occupants have any rights in the property which might frustrate the seller's intention of selling with vacant possession.

### The seller is married

If the seller is married, his or her spouse may have statutory rights of occupation under the Family Law Act 1996 and/or an equitable interest in the property through a contribution to the purchase price. Current registration of Family Law Act rights can be checked by inspecting up-to-date office copies of the title (registered land) or by making a Land Charges Department search against the seller (unregistered land) (see Chapter 18). Even if such rights are not presently protected by registration, the spouse may still effect a registration at any time until actual completion. It will be a condition of the contract that any such registration is removed before completion (Family Law Act 1996, Sch 4, para 4). Negotiations must be entered into with the spouse's solicitors for the removal of the charge and a satisfactory solution obtained before exchange of contracts.

It is unsafe to assume that the spouse will not exercise the right to register a charge under the Family Law Act 1996 prior to completion and instructions should be obtained directly from the spouse (through a separate solicitor if there is any possibility of conflict of interests) to confirm the spouse's agreement to the proposed sale. A formal release of rights and agreement not to enforce any such rights against the seller should be prepared for signature by the non-owning spouse before exchange.

A registration under the Family Law Act 1996 can be removed on production of one of the following:

(1)  an application made by the person with the benefit of the rights (ie the spouse);

(2) a divorce decree absolute;

(3) a court order for removal of the charge;

(4) the death certificate of the spouse.

### *Equitable interests*

If it is thought that the spouse may also be entitled to an equitable interest in the property (eg because of financial contributions to the property), it should be assumed that the property is held by the seller on constructive trust for himself and his spouse. The spouse's independent confirmation of agreement to the sale must be obtained (preferably in writing) and the spouse joined as a party to the contract.

### *Sharers and cohabitees*

Sharers and cohabitees may also be able to establish an equitable interest in the property through contribution to the purchase price. Investigation must be made of the exact status of each occupier. If the occupier has an equitable interest, this will be binding on a buyer of registered land as an overriding interest under s 70(1)(g) of the Land Registration Act 1925. In unregistered land it would be binding under the doctrine of notice. The occupier should, therefore, be required to release these rights in the contract. See **19.4.3**.

## 3.8.4 Death of a joint proprietor

### *Registered land*

A restriction registered in the proprietorship register, indicates that the equitable interest is held on a tenancy in common and that two trustees will be needed to transfer the legal estate. The buyer should insist that the seller treats the trust as still subsisting and appoint a second trustee to act with him in the sale. If this is done, the terms of the restriction will be complied with and the buyer is certain of obtaining a good title.

Where no restriction is registered, the equitable interest can be presumed to have been held under a joint tenancy and the sole surviving joint tenant may sell as sole owner on production of the death certificate of the deceased.

### *Unregistered land*

The document under which the joint owners acquired the property must be checked to find out whether it was held on a joint tenancy or a tenancy in common.

TENANCY IN COMMON

A sale of the legal estate by two trustees gives the buyer the assurance that any subsisting beneficial interests will be overreached on completion.

JOINT TENANCY

The deed by which the joint tenants bought the property must be checked to ensure that no memorandum of severance of the joint tenancy is endorsed on it. A bankruptcy search in the Land Charges Department must be made against the names of all the joint tenants (including the deceased) to establish that no bankruptcy proceedings were or are pending against either joint tenant.

Provided there is no memorandum of severance and no bankruptcy proceedings are registered, and that the survivor declares in the conveyance that he is solely and beneficially entitled to the land, it is safe to accept a conveyance from him alone. The death certificate of the deceased joint tenant must, however, be produced. If the joint tenancy has been severed, or if bankruptcy proceedings are pending, the tenancy must be treated as a tenancy in common and dealt with by the appointment of a second trustee (see above).

## 3.9  MORTGAGES

A mortgage is a transaction where the borrower borrows money from the lender and transfers to the lender, as security for the loan, a legal or equitable interest in land.

A legal mortgage must be created by deed and is usually in the form of a charge by way of legal mortgage, but it can also (less commonly) be made by demise (lease) with a proviso for 'cesser on redemption', ie a provision that the term will come to an end if the money is repaid.

An equitable mortgage may arise where the requirements for a legal mortgage are not met, ie it has not been created by deed. An equitable mortgage must, however, be written to comply with the Law of Property (Miscellaneous Provisions) Act 1989, s 2. Equitable mortgages are unimportant in practice.

A lender with a legal mortgage or charge has valuable statutory powers, which may be extended by the mortgage itself. The following are the most important of the legal lender's powers.

(1)  He has power to sue for repayment of the debt.
(2)  He has a power of sale which arises on the legal date for redemption and is exercisable on the terms set out in the mortgage deed. If there are no such terms, the Law of Property Act 1925, s 103 will apply; it provides that the power of sale is to be exercisable if:

    (a)  the borrower has been served with notice requiring repayment of the loan and default has been made for 3 months; or
    (b)  interest is in arrear for 2 months; or
    (c)  there has been a breach of some other provision of the mortgage.

(3)  He has the right to possession of the property. This power, which arises as soon as the mortgage has been entered into, is limited where the mortgaged property is a dwelling house.

## 3.10  THE LAW OF CONTRACT

A working knowledge of the basic law of contract is also essential for an understanding of the underlying framework of a conveyancing transaction.

For a legally binding contract to exist, certain essential elements are required. There must be:

(1)  an offer (as opposed to a mere invitation to treat);
(2)  unconditional acceptance of the offer;
(3)  consideration; and
(4)  an intention to create legal relations.

For a legally binding contract for the sale of land or any interest in land to exist, the requirements of the Law of Property (Miscellaneous Provisions) Act 1989, s 2 must be satisfied.

### 3.10.1 Legal formalities for a contract for the sale of land

In addition to the above, a contract for the sale of an interest in land must comply with the Law of Property (Miscellaneous Provisions) Act 1989, s 2. This requires all contracts for the sale or other disposition of land or an interest in land to be made in writing and signed by the parties. The writing must incorporate all the terms which have been expressly agreed by the parties and the document must then be signed by or on behalf of all the parties.

Where contracts are to be exchanged each part of the contract must contain all the agreed terms and be signed by the appropriate party; it is not necessary for both parties to sign both parts of the contract. It is possible for the signed document to refer to another document which itself contains some or all of the agreed terms. If the document does not contain all the agreed terms, an order for rectification may be sought. The requirement for a written contract does not apply to contracts:

(1) to grant a lease for a term not exceeding 3 years taking effect in possession without a fine (premium);
(2) made at public auction;
(3) regulated under the Financial Services Act 1986.

However, options, equitable mortgages and side letters (variations of contract) issued in connection with sale of land transactions do need to satisfy the requirements of s 2. Failure to satisfy the requirements of s 2 results in there being no contract at all between the parties, and the court has no equitable jurisdiction to allow the enforcement of a contract which does not comply with s 2. The statutory requirements are normally satisfied by the preparation by the seller's solicitor of a formal contract which is usually prepared in two identical parts based on standard conditions of sale amended to fit the particular circumstances of the transaction.

### 3.10.2 Unfair contract terms

The Unfair Terms in Consumer Contracts Regulations 1999, SI 1999/2083, require all contracts to which they apply to be drafted in plain English and also allow a buyer to challenge any term which has not been individually negotiated between the parties on the grounds that the term is unfair. Although the regulations do not expressly state that they apply to land contracts, it is generally accepted, in the absence of an express exclusion, that they do. The Regulations apply only where the seller is a 'supplier', ie acting in the course of a business, and the buyer is a 'consumer', ie a private individual. Therefore, the 'normal' residential conveyancing transaction between a private seller and a private buyer is not affected by the Regulations. Similarly, a commercial lease between a landlord who is in business and a tenant who is in business falls outside the Regulations since in this case the transaction is made between two 'suppliers' as defined in the Regulations. The principal land transactions to which Regulations apply are:

(a) plot sales by a seller/developer (acting in the course of a business) to a private buyer;

(b)   tenancy agreements made between a landlord (in business) and a tenant (private individual);

(c)   mortgages where the lender is acting in the course of business and the borrower is a private individual;

(d)   contracts for financial services made between a broker (in business) and a private individual;

(e)   sales by a mortgagee to a private individual.

Where the Regulations do apply, the burden is on the buyer to prove unfairness. A term will be regarded as unfair if, contrary to the requirement of good faith, it causes a significant imbalance in the parties' rights and obligations arising under the contract to the detriment of the consumer. Various factors, similar to those contained in the Unfair Contract Terms Act 1977 (which does not apply to land contracts), are included in Sch 2 to the Regulations to act as guidelines as to whether 'good faith' exists, for example the strength of the bargaining position of the parties, the circumstances surrounding the contract, whether the consumer has received any special inducement, such as a discount, to agree to the term. An illustrative list of terms which may be regarded as unfair is set out in Sch 3. If a term is held to be unfair, that term is to be treated as void, but the rest of the contract remains binding on the parties, so long as it is capable of continuing without the offending term.

## 3.11 FURTHER READING

Megarry and Wade *Law of Real Property* 6th edn (Sweet & Maxwell, 1995)

# Chapter 4

# REGISTERED LAND

## 4.1 INTRODUCTION

The two systems of conveyancing currently in use in England and Wales, registered and unregistered conveyancing, were introduced in Chapter 1. The substantive law and procedure relating to both systems is broadly similar. Where differences exist it will normally be found that the registered system is less complex than its unregistered counterpart.

Most of the statutes relating to land transactions have equal application to both systems. In particular, the Law of Property Act 1925 applies to both. However, there are some provisions which are exclusive to registered land. The principal statute governing registered land is the Land Registration Act 1925 (as amended). This chapter contains a reminder of the general principles relating to registered land.

To administer the registration of title to land in England and Wales, a system of District Land Registries has been established. Each District Registry deals with the registration of the title to the land in the area of the country allocated to it. This is generally on a regional basis; for example, the registry in Swansea covers the whole of Wales. However, several of the London Boroughs are allocated to District Registries some distance from the capital (eg Birkenhead).

## 4.2 EVENTS WHICH TRIGGER REGISTRATION

The requirement to 'convert' land from the unregistered to the registered system arises when one of the following events occurs:

(1) a qualifying conveyance of the freehold;
(2) the qualifying grant of a lease for a term of more than 21 years;
(3) a qualifying assignment of a lease having more than 21 years still to run;
(4) a first legal mortgage of the freehold or of a lease which on the date of the mortgage has more than 21 years to run.

A conveyance, grant or assignment is 'qualifying' if it is made for valuable or other consideration, by way of gift or in pursuance of a court order. It is therefore necessary to register a transaction following a voluntary conveyance (eg transfer from father to daughter) or an assent (eg when property passes to a beneficiary under a will or intestacy).

There is no requirement to register land except where one of the 'trigger' events listed above occurs, although at any time land can be put on the register voluntarily by the owner.

Both freehold and leasehold land is registrable and it should be noted that it is the *estate* in land which is registrable. So, in the case of a piece of land subject to a lease, there will be one entry on the register dealing with the ownership of the freehold and a separate entry dealing with the ownership of the lease.

### 4.2.1 Estates incapable of registration in their own right

The only two estates in land which are not capable of registration in their own right are:

(1)  a lease which has 21 years or less to run; and
(2)  a mortgagee's term where there is a subsisting right of redemption.

The exception in (1) includes a lease which is for a term of exactly 21 years. Although not capable of existing as a separate title in its own right, the tenant's interest under such a lease will be protected under the registered land system by being either a minor interest or an overriding interest (see **4.7**).

The exception in (2) relates to the protection of a lender during the subsistence of a mortgage. One of the ways of creating a mortgage over land is to grant a long lease in favour of the lender. Also, even if the mortage is created by way of a legal charge, this still gives the lender the same rights as if he had a lease over the land. However, despite having a lease for longer than 21 years, the lender is not entitled to be entered on the register in his own name but must seek to protect his interest by recording it on the borrower's title.

### 4.2.2  Compulsory registration

Although since 1 December 1990 the requirements for compulsory registration of title have applied to the whole of England and Wales, different areas of England and Wales became subject to compulsory registration at different times in the past. This is because the requirement to register was imposed only gradually over a period of more than 50 years. However, it is only with regard to dispositions on and from 1 April 1998 that registration of the freehold has become compulsory on a gift or an assent following death. If land has not been registered after the happening of an event triggering registration in a compulsory area, the legal estate becomes void.

When buying unregistered land, it is therefore always necessary to check the date when the area in which the property is situated became subject to compulsory registration. If it is discovered that the land should have been registered after some earlier disposition, but has not been, the seller must be required to register the title before the transaction to the buyer proceeds. It is not satisfactory to purchase the unregistered title from the seller and then for the buyer to apply for first registration, because the buyer has no guarantee that the unregistered title being offered to him by the seller will be accepted for registration by HM Land Registry. The buyer's lender will also insist that the defect in the seller's title is corrected before completion of the buyer's purchase.

## 4.3  LAND AND CHARGE CERTIFICATES

Once land is registered, title to that land depends on what is entered on the register at HM Land Registry; thereafter the State guarantees the title. Proof of ownership no longer depends on the deeds to the land. A copy of the entries on the register is issued to the landowner (called the 'registered proprietor') in the form of a 'land certificate'. The land certificate is not a document of title as such, but it should be treated in the same way as original documents of title and stored in a safe place since generally no disposition of the land can take place unless the certificate is produced to the Registry. Lost certificates can be replaced, but this is a lengthy and expensive process. Where there is a subsisting mortgage over the land, the land certificate is retained by HM Land Registry who instead issue a 'charge certificate' to the lender. The mortgage to which it relates is attached to the charge certificate. The land certificate is only re-issued to the landowner when the charge is paid off, so that during the subsistence of the mortgage the landowner does not have a land certificate and is therefore not in a position to make a sale of the property to a third party without the consent of the lender. The retention of the land certificate and issue of a charge certificate to the lender help to protect the lender against the borrower's fraud. Up-to-date copies of the register entries ('office copy entries') can be obtained by applying to the district land registry for the area in which the land is situated. A fee is payable for this service, but anyone may make an application as the register is open to public inspection.

Lenders are becoming increasingly concerned about the cost of storage of charge certificates. Under s 63 of the Land Registration Act 1925, a lender may request the Registry to retain the charge certificate in the Registry. Where this has happened, an entry will be made in the charges register stating that the certificate has been retained in the Registry.

## 4.4 DEVOLUTION OF REGISTERED LAND

Once an estate in land becomes registered, all devolutions from that title must also follow the registered system. A separate title number identifies each estate in registered land, so that each separate estate in one physical parcel of land will have its own distinctive title number and corresponding land or charge certificate. If, for example, a landowner registered the freehold estate in a parcel of land, he would be issued with a land certificate identifying the physical area of land which belonged to him. The certificate would also identify the estate as freehold and give him a title number by which to identify the land. If that landowner then grants a 999-year lease of the whole of the land to a tenant, the tenant under that lease has a registrable interest in the land and, on registration of the lease, he will receive a land certificate showing the physical extent of the land (in this example this will be identical to that shown on the freehold certificate), stating that the interest held is leasehold, giving brief details of the lease itself, and giving the tenant an identifying title number which is different from that used by the freehold estate.

On registration of the lease, the freehold certificate will be cross-referenced to show the existence of the lease. Similarly, the leasehold certificate will contain a reference to the freehold title. This cross-referencing system ensures that the tenant of a registered lease is able to trace his landlord should the need to do so arise, and that, because the existence of the lease is noted on the freehold title, a buyer of the freehold cannot do so in ignorance of the existence of the lease.

The 999-year lease used in the above example would probably be a building lease, and the tenant under the lease may then build a block of flats on the land and sell off each flat on a 99-year lease. Each of the tenants under the 99-year leases will also have their own land certificates and title numbers. Each of these will show only part of the land, ie the part which is the subject of the lease – the flat itself – and each will be cross-referenced to the superior titles. It is, therefore, possible for there to be several land or charge certificates in existence at any one time, all of which relate to the same physical plot of land, but each is distinguished from the other because each relates to a separate estate in that land, and each has its own distinctive title number. The title number of an estate in registered land is its sole distinguishing feature and must be referred to in every dealing with that estate.

## 4.5  CLASSES OF TITLE

Once land is entered on the register, the State guarantees the title and compensation is payable in certain circumstances where a defect is found in a registered title. Four classes of title are available and, when an application is made for first registration, the registrar will decide which class of title should be allocated to the interest which is being registered. The class of title which has been given to the interest is shown on the proprietorship register of the title (see **4.6**).

### 4.5.1  Absolute title

The vast majority of registered titles are classed as 'absolute', which in effect means the title is as near perfect as it can be. This class of title can be given to either a freehold or a leasehold interest in the land.

The proprietor of an interest which is registered with an absolute title has vested in him the legal estate, together with all appurtenant rights and subject only to:

(1)  entries on the register (eg covenants);
(2)  overriding interests (these protect some third-party interests in registered land, see **4.7.2**);
(3)  where the proprietor is a trustee, minor interests (third-party rights) of which he has notice, for example, the interests of the beneficiaries under the trust; and
(4)  where the land is leasehold, the express and implied covenants and obligations under the lease.

On an application for first registration, the registrar has a discretion under s 13(c) of the Land Registration Act 1925 to overlook minor defects in the title and to grant an absolute title, so curing the defect.

### 4.5.2  Possessory title

Registration with a possessory title has the same effect as registration with absolute title, except that the proprietor is also subject to all adverse interests existing at the date of first registration. Where, for example, an application for first registration shows that the applicant's title to the land is based on adverse possession, it is likely that the registrar will initially grant only a possessory title to the land, the applicant taking subject to the rights of any person who has a superior interest in the land. This situation can arise where a landowner has acquired an extra piece of garden through adverse possession, perhaps reclaiming wasteland and using it as a vegetable patch for a number of years. Although initially only a possessory title will be granted in these circumstances, it may be possible to upgrade the title to absolute after a period of time. Possessory titles are encountered quite frequently in practice, although statistically they represent less than 1% of all registered titles. This class of title can be given to either a freehold or a leasehold interest in the land.

### 4.5.3 Qualified title

A qualified title, which in practice is very rare, is granted where the title submitted for registration shows a specific identified defect which the registrar deems to be of such a nature that he cannot use his discretion to overlook the defect and grant an absolute title. The registration has the same effect as registration with an absolute title, except that the State's guarantee of the title does not apply to the specified defect. Such a title might be awarded where, for example, the title submitted for first registration showed that a transaction within the title had been carried out in breach of trust. In this situation, the proprietor would take his interest in the land subject to the interests (if any) of the beneficiaries under the trust. This class of title can be given either to a freehold or to a leasehold interest in the land.

### 4.5.4 Good leasehold title

As its name suggests, a good leasehold title applies only to leasehold estates. This class of title will be awarded where the registrar is satisfied that the title to the leasehold interest is sound but, having no access to the title to the superior reversionary interest, he is not prepared to guarantee the lease against defects in the freehold title, or to guarantee that the freeholder had the right to grant the lease. Such a title will, therefore, only be given where the title to the freehold reversion is unregistered or where the freehold is registered with less than an absolute title and where the applicant for registration of the leasehold interest does not submit evidence of title to the freehold reversion when making his application. A good leasehold title is regarded by lenders as being unsatisfactory, and for this reason is sometimes difficult to sell or mortgage.

### 4.5.5 Upgrading title

The registrar may upgrade a title on his own initiative or the proprietor may apply for upgrading.

#### *Possessory title*

A possessory title may be upgraded to an absolute title (or, in the case of leasehold land, to a good leasehold title) if either:

(1) the registrar is satisfied as to the title; or
(2) the land has been registered with possessory title for at least 12 years and the registrar is satisfied that the proprietor is in possession.

#### *Qualified title*

A qualified title may be upgraded to absolute (or, in the case of leasehold land, to a good leasehold title) if the registrar is satisfied as to the title.

#### *Good leasehold title*

A good leasehold title may be converted to an absolute title if the registrar is satisfied as to reversionary freehold title and any intermediate leasehold title. This could occur after the registration of the reversion or of a superior lease.

## 4.6  THE FORM OF THE REGISTER

The register kept at HM Land Registry shows the true state of the title. The land or charge certificate which is issued to the proprietor or his lender is merely a copy of the register entries. District registries now have computerised records and the land or charge certificate issued is a computer-generated printout of the register entries. The register is divided into three sections:

(1)  the property register;
(2)  the proprietorship register; and
(3)  the charges register.

An example showing typical register entries is shown opposite.

### 4.6.1  The property register

The property register describes the estate in land which is registered (ie freehold or leasehold), identifies the property by a short verbal description (eg its postal address) and shows the physical area of the land which is the subject of the registration, usually by reference to a plan. The plan (known as 'the filed plan') is based on the Index Map, which is a large-scale map, based on Ordnance Survey maps, showing the extent of the land which is registered. A copy of the plan is supplied with the land or charge certificate, or can be obtained by an applicant when seeking copies of the register entries. HM Land Registry have a code of colours which they use on plans, thus the land which is the subject of the registration is normally outlined in red, land which used to form part of the title but which has since been sold off is edged in green, and other colours and cross-hatchings are used to show benefits and burdens which affect the land (eg a brown strip of land may indicate the route of a right of way). The property register will also give details of any rights which benefit the land, such as easements or covenants (eg the right to use a pathway over adjacent land). It may also contain reference to easements to which the property is subject. In appropriate cases, the register will contain cross-references to superior and inferior titles (eg to the freehold reversion in the case of a head lease and to any sub-leases granted out of the head lease).

Although the right does exist for a land owner to have his boundaries 'fixed' by HM Land Registry, this right is rarely used and the boundaries shown on the plan supplied by the Registry will give only a general indication of the position of the boundaries. Extraneous evidence (eg from pre-registration deeds) may be required to prove the exact position of boundaries.

Where the land is leasehold, brief details of the lease under which the land is held will be given on the property register. The lease itself is not attached to the land or charge certificate and must be kept safely by the tenant, since it will need to be produced to any prospective assignee as evidence of the terms of the lease.

## OFFICE COPY

This office copy shows the entries subsisting on the register on **4 MAY 1998**.
This date **must be quoted as the 'search from date' in any official search** application based on this copy.
Under s.113 of the Land Registration Act 1925 this copy is admissible in evidence to the same extent as the original.
Issued on 5 May 1998 by HM Land Registry. This title is administered by the
**X X X X X** District Land Registry.

**Edition date : 31 August 1990**          **TITLE NUMBER : LM 12037**

| Entry No. | A. PROPERTY REGISTER<br>containing the description of the registered land and the estate comprised in the Title |
|---|---|
| | **COUNTY**           **DISTRICT**<br><br>**CORNSHIRE**           **MARADON** |
| 1. | (19 December 1989) The Freehold land shown edged with red on the plan of the above Title filed at the Registry and being 47 Queen's Road, Loamster. |
| 2. | (19 December 1989) The land has the benefit of a right of way on foot only over the passageway tinted brown on the filed plan. |
| 3. | (31 August 1990) The land in this title has the benefit of the rights granted by but is subject to the rights reserved by the Transfer dated 29 July 1990 referred to in the Charges Register. |

| Entry No. | B. PROPRIETORSHIP REGISTER<br>stating nature of the Title, name, address and description of the proprietor of the land and any entries affecting the right of disposing thereof<br>**TITLE ABSOLUTE** |
|---|---|
| 1. | (31 August 1990) Proprietor(s) : PAUL JOHN DAWKINS and ANGELA MARY DAWKINS both of 47 Queen's Road, Loamster, Maradon, Cornshire. |

| Entry No. | C. CHARGES REGISTER<br>containing charges, incumbrances etc., adversely affecting the land and registered dealings therewith |
|---|---|
| 1. | (19 December 1989) A Conveyance of the land in this title and other land dated 19 May 1924 made between (1) Allen Ansell (Vendor) and (2) Frances Amelia Moss (Purchaser) contains the following covenants:-<br><br>"And the purchaser for herself her heirs executors administrators and assigns hereby covenants with the Vendor his heirs and assigns that she will perform and observe the stipulations set out in the First Schedule hereto so far as they relate to the hereditaments hereby assured<br><br>THE FIRST SCHEDULE above referred to<br><br>(a) No caravan shall be allowed upon the premises and the Vendor or owners of adjoining premises may remove and dispose of any such caravan and for that purpose may forcibly enter upon any land upon which a breach of this stipulation shall occur and shall not be responsible for the safe keeping of any such caravan or for the loss thereof or any damage thereto or to any fence or wall |

Continued on the next page

## OFFICE COPY

This office copy shows the entries subsisting on the register on **4 MAY 1998**.
This date **must be quoted as the 'search from date' in any official search** application based on this copy.
Under s.113 of the Land Registration Act 1925 this copy is admissible in evidence to the same extent as the original.
Issued on 5 May 1998 by HM Land Registry. This title is administered by the
X X X X X  District Land Registry.

**TITLE NUMBER : LM 12037**

| Entry No. | C. CHARGES REGISTER (continued) |
|---|---|
| | (b) No earth gravel or sand shall at any time be excavated or dug out of the land except for the purpose of excavations in connection with the buildings erected on the land and no bricks or tiles shall at any time be burnt or made nor any clay or lime be burnt on the land." |
| 2. | (19 December 1989) The land is subject to rights of way on foot only over the passageway tinted blue on the filed plan. |

***** END OF REGISTER *****

NOTE : A date at the beginning of an entry is the date on which the entry was made in the Register.

| H.M. LAND REGISTRY | | TITLE NUMBER | |
|---|---|---|---|
| | | **LM 12037** | |
| ORDNANCE SURVEY PLAN REFERENCE | Z Z 8987 | SECTION M | Scale 1/1250 |
| COUNTY CORNSHIRE | MARADON DISTRICT | | © Crown Copyright 1969 |

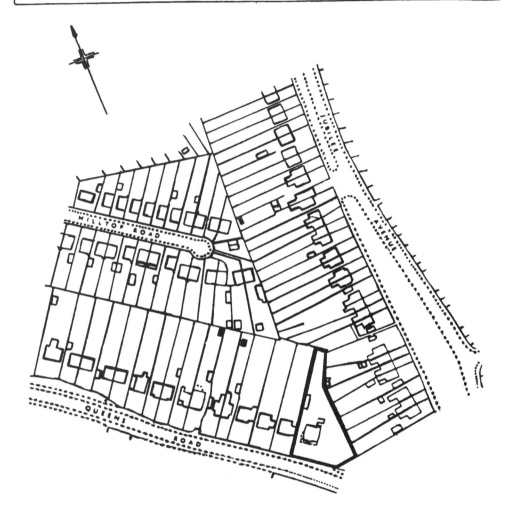

### 4.6.2  The proprietorship register

The proprietorship register states the class of the title which is registered. Although the vast majority of titles are absolute, this part of the register must be carefully checked to ensure that a registration with a title other than absolute is not inadvertently overlooked. This part of the register will also give the name(s) and address(es) of the registered proprietor(s). The address entered on the register is the address which the registrar will use if for any reason he needs to contact the land-owner about the land.

If there are any restrictions on the proprietors' powers to deal with the land (eg if they hold as trustees for another person) a note of the restriction will be entered on this part of the register. The register shows only the position of the legal estate in the land. As with unregistered land, equities are kept 'behind the curtain'. The register may, therefore, reveal the existence of a trust, but will never reveal the details of the trust, such as who the beneficiaries are or their respective interests in the trust.

If, on the transfer to the current proprietors, they entered into personal covenants, for example an indemnity covenant binding only on them and not on future proprietors of the land, this will also be noted on the proprietorship register.

In the case of proprietors registered on or after 1 April 2000, the register will also include details of the price paid for the property by those proprietors.

### 4.6.3  The charges register

The charges register contains details of charges or incumbrances which currently affect the title. Here will be found a note of the burden of easements and covenants which bind the land, often with a reference to a schedule attached to the register. The schedule will contain extracts of the documents which imposed the easements or covenants, with a verbatim copy of the wording of the incumbrance. Only covenants which endure through a change of ownership of the land are noted on the charges register. Covenants which are purely personal in nature, such as an indemnity covenant, are commonly noted on the proprietorship register.

Details of mortgages of the land are also found on the charges register. Two entries are recorded for each mortgage, the first stating the fact that the mortgage exists and the date on which it was created, the second showing the name and address of the lender.

## 4.7  THIRD-PARTY RIGHTS

Third-party rights in registered land fall into one of the following three categories:

(1)  registered charges;
(2)  overriding interests;
(3)  minor interests.

### 4.7.1  Registered charges

The most usual way of protecting a mortgage of registered land is by substantive registration of the charge, which will be noted in the charges register of the mortgaged land. While a mortgage subsists, the land certificate is held at HM Land Registry, a charge certificate being issued to the lender. Second and subsequent lenders are issued with their own charge certificates which will show their own charges on the charges register in addition to those belonging to prior mortgagees.

The priority of mortgages in registered land is governed by the date of registration of the charges.

Other methods of creating a mortgage of registered land do exist but they are beyond the scope of this book.

### 4.7.2 Overriding interests

Overriding interests, as set out in the Land Registration Act 1925, s 70(1), bind a buyer of the land irrespective of whether he has notice of them. They are not entered on the register of the title. The main types of overriding interest are as follows (the lettering corresponds to the appropriate subparagraphs in s 70(1)):

(a)   legal easements and profits (eg a right of way crossing the land);

(f)   rights acquired or in the course of acquisition under the Limitation Act 1980 (eg squatters' rights);

(g)   the rights of every person in actual occupation of the land or in receipt of the rents and profits except where enquiry is made of such person and he fails to disclose those rights (eg the rights of a tenant or of a non-owning spouse);

(h)   rights excepted from the effect of registration where the title is other than absolute (eg the rights of the freehold reversioner in the case of a good leasehold title);

(i)   local land charges (eg planning permissions);

(k)   leases granted for a term not exceeding 21 years.

The above list is not comprehensive, but includes the most commonly encountered overriding interests. At first sight, overriding interests seem to present a major flaw in the registered land system, the basis of the system being that if a matter is not entered on the register it is of no concern to the landowner or to a buyer. Yet overriding interests are not entered on the register, but bind allcomers irrespective of notice. Provided a normal, safe conveyancing routine is followed, overriding interests should not in most cases be a problem in registered conveyancing; almost all will be discovered by the routine searches which are normally undertaken in every transaction; see Chapter 18.

#### *Occupier's rights*

The most problematical of the overriding interests is likely to be in relation to the rights of occupiers under paragraph (g) above. An interest in the property might be claimed under this head by a spouse who had contributed to the mortgage repayments or otherwise made contributions towards the purchase or upkeep of the property. Equally, rights might be claimed by a cohabitee of the legal owner, or by a tenant in possession of the property. A spouse's statutory matrimonial home rights under the Family Law Act 1996 are not overriding, even though the spouse will be in occupation of the land.

To have a right binding on a subsequent buyer under paragraph (g), the claimant must:

(1)  be in actual occupation (or in receipt of rent and profits) at the date of completion of the transaction; and

(2)  have a right recognised under normal land law principles; and

(3)  not have failed to have disclosed that right if an enquiry was made of him.

The House of Lords decision in *Abbey National Building Society v Cann* [1990] 1 All ER 1085 emphasises the need for both occupation and a right in the land before an overriding interest can exist under paragraph (g). It also shows that a lender making an advance to finance a purchase will not be bound by any rights claimed under paragraph (g) by the borrower's spouse, even though she might have been in occupation when the mortgage was created. This is because the spouse's interest cannot arise until the borrower himself becomes legal owner of the land. The House of Lords held that the sequence of events when a person was buying a house with the aid of a mortgage loan, was that the borrower acquired the land and simultaneously mortgaged it. Thus, any equitable interests claimed by an occupier could only arise after the completion of the mortgage, and not before it. Remember that, to claim a right under paragraph (g), both occupation and the right claimed must exist at the date of completion of the transaction in question (ie in this case the mortgage). Contrast this, though, with the situation of a mortgage created some time after purchase of the property, where the danger of the lender being bound is a real one (see *Williams & Glyn's Bank v Boland* [1981] AC 487).

The date at which the existence of other types of overriding interest is to be judged is the date of registration of the proprietor. If, therefore, an overriding interest was created between the date of completion and the later date when the proprietor's title is registered, the proprietor will take subject to that interest.

### *Leases*

Leases granted for a term of not more than 21 years, and so not capable of registration in their own right, may be protected as overriding interests within either or both of paragraphs (g) and (k) above. Paragraph (g) applies only where the tenant is in actual occupation or in receipt of rents and profits but paragraph (k) makes legal leases for not more than 21 years overriding, whether or not the tenant is in occupation.

### *Overreaching*

An overriding interest within paragraph (g) which arises under a trust of land can be overreached on a disposition by two trustees: see *City of London Building Society v Flegg* [1988] AC 54. Note that a trust of land will arise in all cases of co-ownership, and a situation where an occupier has contributed to the purchase of a property will thus give rise to a trust of land. The occupier's rights will therefore be capable of being overreached.

### *Spouses and non-owning occupiers*

A non-owning occupier (of either sex) may be able to claim both a beneficial interest in the property through his or her contribution to it, and rights under the Family Law Act 1996 (these are a minor interest). In appropriate circumstances both possibilities must be considered and dealt with (see **3.8.3**).

### 4.7.3 Minor interests

Minor interests are all third-party interests in registered land which are not registered charges or overriding interests. They include, for example, equitable easements, restrictive covenants and estate contracts. The definition of a minor interest as an interest which is not overriding is not helpful and the easiest way to identify a minor interest is by a process of elimination.

Overriding interests are set out in the Land Registration Act 1925, s 70. If, therefore, the list of overriding interests is consulted and the matter being dealt with does not appear on that list then, by deduction, the interest must be minor and must be protected by some entry on the register. If they are not so protected, they will not bind a buyer, irrespective of whether he has notice of them.

### 4.7.4 Hybrid interests

An interest which would normally be classified as minor, such as an option, can also take effect as an overriding interest if, for example, the person with its benefit is in occupation of the land. See, for example, *Webb v Pollmount Ltd* [1966] Ch 584, where an option, which should have been registered as a minor interest but was not so registered, was allowed to take effect as an overriding interest under s 70(1)(g).

### 4.7.5 Protection of minor interests

To be binding on allcomers, a minor interest must be protected by an entry on the register of the land affected. The four types of entry listed below are those which are used to protect minor interests. The majority of minor interests are protected by the entry of a notice on the charges register of the title. The other three types of entry apply in specific circumstances, and generally appear on the proprietorship register of the title.

#### Notice on the charges register

Most minor interests are protected by entry of a notice on the charges register of the title. This method of protection is suitable for matters such as estate contracts and restrictive covenants. The land certificate must usually be available to the registry before a notice can be entered.

The protection of a spouse's matrimonial home rights under the Family Law Act 1996 is made by notice entered on the charges register. Such a notice does not have to be accompanied by the land certificate.

#### Caution on the proprietorship register

Where it is not possible to protect a minor interest by notice (eg where the proprietor does not consent to the application being made), a caution should be entered on the proprietorship register of the title. This will provide temporary protection for the owner of the minor interest but, on a subsequent application by a third party for registration of his interest or an application by the registered proprietor, the cautioner will be 'warned off' by the registrar and given a limited period in which to establish his rights, failing which the caution will be removed from the register.

A caution could be used to protect, for example, an estate contract where the proprietor of the land had not consented to the entry of a notice on the register.

### *Restriction on the proprietorship register*

Where the registered proprietor's powers of disposition are restricted in some way, this will be signified by the entry of a restriction in the proprietorship register. The restriction must be complied with, otherwise any disposition will not be registered. Typically, such an entry is made where co-owners hold as beneficial tenants in common, where the land is held on trust or strict settlement or where the proprietor is a limited company or charity which is subject to the Charities Act 1993, s 36. Where tenants in common are registered as proprietors the following restriction will be entered:

> 'No disposition by a sole proprietor of the land (not being a trust corporation) under which capital money arises is to be registered except under an Order of the Registrar of the Court.'

### *Inhibition on the proprietorship register*

Where the proprietor is an individual, notice of the proprietor's insolvency is given by entry of an inhibition on the proprietorship register.

### *Personal covenants*

Positive covenants, which do not run with the land, are personal obligations which affect only the proprietor who entered into the covenants. They are commonly noted on the proprietorship register of the title although there is no obligation on HM Land Registry to make reference to them on the title. Such covenants may, however, be enforceable through a chain of indemnity covenants and, in order to give a subsequent buyer of the land notice of the existence and wording of the covenants, a separate copy of the deed imposing the covenants should be kept with the title deeds.

## 4.8 CAUTION AGAINST FIRST REGISTRATION

A caution against first registration (not to be confused with the caution which protects a minor interest) can be lodged by a person who has an interest in land which is currently unregistered. The caution warns any person who attempts to deal with the land that another person purports to have an interest in that land. When a dealing with the affected land is lodged at HM Land Registry, the cautioner is 'warned off' and given a limited period of time in which to establish his rights over the land, failing which the dealing will proceed and the cautioner will lose his interest. This procedure might be used, for example, by a landowner in a rural area where the precise boundaries of the land are uncertain. Registration of a caution against first registration would ensure that the landowner was notified of any purported dealing with the land and would be given an opportunity to defend his rights if a neighbour deliberately or inadvertently attempted to register the land as his own.

## 4.9 MISTAKES ON THE REGISTER

Where there is a mistake on the register, it may be possible to seek rectification of the register under the Land Registration Act 1925, s 82 (as amended). Compensation (indemnity) is payable under s 83 (as amended) where an error in the register is not rectified, where the register is rectified but loss is still suffered, where loss is suffered as a result of rectification or for any other error in the registration system, such as an error in the result of an official search. The conditions for claiming rectification and/or indemnity are stringent and are beyond the scope of this book.

## 4.10 LAND REGISTRATION ACT 2002

The Land Registration Act 2002 (LRA 2002) received the Royal Assent on 26 February 2002. When brought into force it will replace the previous Land Registration Acts and effect major changes to the land registration system; in particular it contains provisions laying down the foundations for the proposed system of e-conveyancing (see **1.5**). It is likely to be mid-2003 before the Act is brought into force, so this book continues to deal exclusively with the pre-existing legislation, however, the main provisions of the LRA 2002 can be summarised as follows.

### 4.10.1 Interests capable of registration and compulsory registration (LRA 2002, ss 3 and 4)

The following interests are capable of registration and compulsory registration under the LRA 2002.

(a) Title to freehold land and rent charges will be registerable as at present.

(b) Franchises (eg a grant from the Crown to hold a market etc) and profits in gross (eg to fish) will be capable of registration with their own title. Also, the Crown will be able to register demesne land (ie land the Crown holds absolutely).

(c) Leases granted for a term of more than 7 years (instead of 21 years as at present) will become compulsorily registrable. This will also apply to leases of any length granted to take effect in possession more than 3 months after the date of grant and leases of any length if the right to possession is discontinuous (eg as in some timeshare schemes).

(d) There is also power for the Lord Chancellor to extend these provisions further; in particular, it is intended that eventually all leases for terms exceeding 3 years will be subject to compulsory registration.

(e) Land belonging to many large landowners still remains unregistered (eg the Crown Estate, Duke of Westminster, etc). Steps will be taken to persuade such landowners to register voluntarily. It is likely that compulsory registration of all land (ie not just on a disposition) will be considered once the LRA 2002 has been in force for a few years.

### 4.10.2 Protection of third party rights (LRA 2002, ss 32–47)

This will only be possible by means of the entry of a notice or a restriction. Inhibitions and cautions (other than cautions against first registration) will be abolished. Notices will either be:

(a) agreed (ie entered with the proprietor's consent); or

(b) unilateral. This type of notice will be entered without the proprietor's consent. The text of the notice will indicate that it is a unilateral notice and state the identity of the person who entered the notice, but will not state the right claimed. Unilateral notices will thus take the place of cautions. The proprietor will be informed of the registration of such a notice and he can then apply to have the notice removed, should he wish to do so – see the current 'warning off' procedure for cautions.

Restrictions will be used in similar circumstances as at present, but will also be used in cases of insolvency and other situations where an Inhibition is presently used.

### 4.10.3 Overriding interests

The LRA 2002 reduces the number of overriding interests and splits them into two categories: those which override a first registration; and those that override a registered disposition.

***Unregistered interests which override first registration (LRA 2002, Sch 1)***
(a)  Leases for terms not exceeding 7 years.
(b)  An interest belonging to a person in actual occupation, except for an interest arising under a Settled Land Act 1925 settlement. The rights of persons in receipt of rents and profits are thus excluded from being overriding. Also, the overriding status of the right claimed only extends to those parts of the land which the person is actually occupying.
(c)  A legal easement or profit; at present certain equitable easements have overriding status, even if not protected by registration under the Land Charges Act 1972, but this situation will not continue.
(d)  A customary right.
(e)  A public right.
(f)  A local land charge.
(g)  Rights to mines and minerals under the Coal Industry Act 1994 and in relation to land first registered prior to 1926.
(h)  A franchise.*
(i)  A manorial right.*
(j)  A right to rent reserved to the Crown.*
(k)  Rights in respect of embankments or sea-walls.*
(l)  A right to payment in lieu of tithes.*

Those marked * will cease to be overriding 10 years after these provisions come into force.

***Unregistered interests which override registered dispositions (LRA 2002, Sch 3)***
(a)  Leases for terms not exceeding 7 years.
(b)  An interest belonging to a person in actual occupation, *except* for:
   (i)  an interest under a Settled Land Act 1925 settlement;
   (ii)  an interest of a person of whom enquiry was made before the disposition and who failed to disclose the right when he could reasonably be expected to have done so;
   (iii)  an interest which belongs to a person whose occupation would not have been obvious on a reasonably careful inspection of the land at the time of the disposition and of which the person to whom the disposition was made did not have actual knowledge at the time of the disposition;
   (iv)  a leasehold interest granted to take effect in possession more than 3 months after the date of the grant and which has not taken effect in possession at the time of the disposition.

(c) A legal easement or profit *except* for an easement or profit which, at the time of the disposition:

   (i) is not within the actual knowledge of the person to whom the disposition was made; and

   (ii) would not have been obvious on a reasonably careful inspection of the land over which the easement or profit is exercisable.

   (This exception will not apply, however, if the person entitled to the easement etc proves that it had been exercised in the 12 months ending with the day of the disposition.)

(d) A customary right.

(e) A public right.

(f) Local land charges.

(g) Rights to mines and minerals under the Coal Industry Act 1994 and in relation to land first registered prior to 1926.

(h) A franchise.*

(i) A manorial right.*

(j) A right to rent reserved to the Crown.*

(k) Rights in respect of embankments and sea-walls.*

(l) A right to payment in lieu of tithes.*

Those marked * will cease to be overriding 10 years after these provisions come into force.

## 4.10.4  Adverse possession (LRA 2002, ss 95–97)

The usual 12-year limitation period will be disapplied to registered land; the law will remain unchanged for unregistered land.

A squatter in adverse possession for 10 years can apply to be registered as proprietor of the land. The application can be made if the squatter is still in possession or has been evicted within the previous 6 months by the registered proprietor.

Notice of the application will be given to the registered proprietor and certain others (eg the proprietor of any registered charge). Any such person so notified has the right to give notice of objection to the registrar within the specified time limit. If such notice is given, then the squatter will not be registered unless certain conditions are complied with.

There are three sets of conditions that must be met. A squatter would only become registered if:

(a) it would be unconscionable because of an equity by estoppel for the registered proprietor to dispossess the applicant and the circumstances are such that the applicant ought to be registered; or

(b) the applicant is for some other reason entitled to be registered as proprietor; or

(c) the land in question is adjacent to land belonging to the applicant and the exact boundary has not been determined under Land Registry rules. Also, for at least the last 10 years of the adverse possession prior to the application, the applicant (or any predecessor in title) reasonably believed that the land belonged to him and the estate in the land in question was registered more than 12 months prior to the date of the application.

Where the squatter is not entitled to be registered under these provisions, the registered proprietor then has 2 years to obtain possession as against the squatter. If he does not do so, and the squatter remains in possession for the further 2 years, the squatter can once again apply for registration as proprietor. He will then be registered unless the registered proprietor is suffering from a mental disability, is an enemy or is detained in enemy territory.

## 4.11  FURTHER READING

Ruoff and Roper *Registered Conveyancing* (Sweet & Maxwell)

# Chapter 5

# TOWN AND COUNTRY PLANNING

## 5.1 INTRODUCTION

The local planning authority (usually the district, unitary or London borough council) is responsible for town and country planning within its own area. The authority's planning policy is contained in 'structure' and 'local' plans (together known as the development plan), which are available for public inspection. The structure plan is a written statement explaining the authority's policy for the whole of its area; more detailed aspects of that policy are shown on the local plans which are large-scale plans, each showing a part only of the local authority's area, supplemented by a written commentary.

### 5.1.1 The Town and Country Planning Act 1990

The principal legislation is the Town and Country Planning Act 1990, as amended. There are also various statutory instruments which affect detailed aspects of this subject. This chapter draws attention to the principles of planning law only insofar as it affects the normal conveyancing transaction and is not a comprehensive guide to the topic.

## 5.2 RELEVANCE OF PLANNING TO THE TRANSACTION

Planning law affects whether a building can be built or extended, and also specifies the particular use to which a property can be put. It is, therefore, important for a buyer to check that the building which he is buying has permission to be on the site where it has been built and also that it is being used for its authorised use. Heavy fines can be imposed for breach of planning legislation and, since planning matters (both permission granted and breaches committed) usually run with the land, an action for any breach which is outstanding at completion could be brought against the buyer after completion, even though the breach was committed by a predecessor in title.

Where the buyer intends to build on the site after completion, or to extend the property or change its use, the buyer's solicitor must consider whether these proposals will require planning permission and advise the client accordingly.

Various planning matters are raised as questions on the local search (LLC1) and the standard form of enquiries of a local authority. An understanding of the principles of planning is required for the correct interpretation of the answers given to these standard questions.

## 5.3 DEVELOPMENT

The word 'development' is the keystone to the understanding of planning law. Basically, any activity which constitutes 'development', as defined, will require planning permission. It is defined in the Town and Country Planning Act 1990, s 55 as:

> 'the carrying out of building, engineering, mining or other operations in, on, over or under land, or the making of any material change in the use of any buildings or other land.'

This definition includes the erection of new buildings, the demolition of, and alterations and additions to, existing buildings and the making of a material change in the use of property. Only a *material* change in use requires permission. 'Material' is not defined and is a question of fact and degree in each particular case.

## 5.4 MATTERS WHICH DO NOT CONSTITUTE DEVELOPMENT

Certain matters which would otherwise fall within the definition of development (and so require planning permission) are specifically excluded from that definition by the Act itself. A summary of the main cases where permission is not required either by the statute or by regulation is given below.

(1)  Works for the maintenance, improvement or other alteration of a building which affect only the interior or do not materially affect the external appearance of a building.

(2)  The use of buildings or land within the curtilage of a dwelling house for any purpose incidental to the use of the dwelling house (eg using an existing garage as a playroom). The 'curtilage' of a dwelling house is the land immediately surrounding the house and, except where the grounds are extensive, will normally encompass the whole of the garden area.

(3)  Change of use within the same use class as specified by the Town and Country Planning (Use Classes) Order 1987, SI 1987/764. There are 15 use classes in all. Class A1 broadly covers use as a retail shop (so a change of use from a newsagent to an ironmonger will not require planning consent). It does not include, however, use for the sale of hot food or for the sale of sandwiches for consumption off the premises. Class A2 covers use of premises for professional and financial services and other services which would be found in a shopping area and A3 use for the sale of food or drink for consumption on the premises or of hot food for consumption off the premises. Class B1 covers offices other than those in A2. Class B2 covers industrial buildings. Changing from one use class to another may be a material change of use and, if so, will require permission. A more detailed consideration of the use classes is beyond the scope of this book.

Note: Changing a single dwelling house into two or more units is a material change of use and is therefore within the definition of development and will require consent.

## 5.5 MATTERS WHICH DO NOT REQUIRE EXPRESS PLANNING PERMISSION

The Town and Country Planning (General Permitted Development) Order 1995, SI 1995/418 (GPDO) automatically grants planning permission to 'development' which falls within its scope without the need for an express application. This covers, for example, erection of fences (subject to a height restriction) or development within the curtilage of a dwelling house. The GPDO will also permit the building of a small extension but is subject to strict conditions on the extent and siting of the extension. Once the size limit for extensions has been used, all further extensions will require express consent. Part 3 of the GPDO also permits certain changes of use between use classes. So, for example, a change from Class A2 to A1 or B2 to B1 or A3 to A1 or A3 to A2 will be permitted development and so not require an application for permission.

The conditions attached to the GPDO must be strictly observed and, if they cannot be complied with, express permission for the development is needed. The local authority has power to restrict the GPDO in whole or in part in relation to its area. This is done by the authority passing an 'Article 4 Direction'. Before the client carries out works which ostensibly fall within the GPDO it should be confirmed that the relevant part of the GPDO has not been restricted in the area concerned. This can be confirmed by making a local search (see Chapter 18).

*ARTICLE 4 = a restriction of the GDPO in the A.*

## 5.6 LISTED BUILDINGS AND CONSERVATION AREAS

Where it is considered that a building is of outstanding historic or architectural interest, the Secretary of State may 'list' it. The effect of the listing depends on which grade of listing is given. Part only of a building may be subject to listing (eg an Adam fireplace). The consequences of listing are, principally, that tighter controls are exercised over development than is the case with an unlisted building and that, in general, the above exemptions from development do not apply. Listed building consent must be obtained for development affecting such a building.

The local planning authority may designate as a conservation area any part of their area which is of special architectural or historic interest, the character or appearance of which it is desirable to preserve or enhance. As a general rule, any non-listed building in a conservation area must not be demolished without conservation area consent. There may also be other restrictions on development.

## 5.7 APPLYING FOR PLANNING PERMISSION

An application for planning permission is made to the local planning authority on a form supplied by them. A fee is payable. It is not necessary for the applicant to be the owner of the freehold of the land over which permission is sought but, if the applicant is not the landowner, he is required to notify the owner of the application. In most cases, the application for permission does not have to be advertised by notice on the building or in a local paper, but many authorities recommend that notice of the application be displayed on the affected building and many local papers publish a weekly list of applications for permission which have been made to the authority.

outline
= PP in principle

Where permission is required for building works, it is possible in the first instance to apply for 'outline' permission only. This will grant permission in principle for the building works, but requires a further application to be made at a later stage for approval of detailed plans. The authority will normally indicate, by way of conditions attached to the outline permission, some of the matters which they require to be incorporated in the final plans for the development. An outline permission is less expensive for the client because it does not involve the preparation of detailed plans for the development.

Detailed plans, including site plans and elevations of the building, will have to be submitted to the authority when approval for detail is sought, at which stage the authority's requirements as specified on the outline permission can be incorporated. Although an authority can restrict a permission to a named individual(s) or company or limit it in time, most planning permissions are not so limited and can therefore be sold with the land. An outline permission granted for development on a site will greatly enhance the value of the site and it is therefore in the seller's interest to obtain such permission before attempting to sell the land.

## 5.8  DURATION OF PLANNING PERMISSION

An ordinary (ie full or detailed) permission is usually subject to a condition that development must be begun within 5 years. An outline permission is subject to conditions that an application for approval of reserved matters must be made within 3 years and that development must be begun within 5 years of the grant of the outline permission or within 2 years of the approval of reserved matters, whichever is the later.

Although there is a time limit within which the development must be commenced, there is no time-limit within which it must be completed. However, if the development has not been completed within a reasonable time, the local planning authority has the power to issue a completion notice under which the development must be completed within a specified further period of time. If it is not so completed then the planning consent is treated as being withdrawn.

## 5.9  ENFORCEMENT

A breach of planning control is enforceable by service of an enforcement notice on the landowner and occupier. An enforcement notice in respect of building works and for changing the use of a building to use as a single dwelling house must be served within 4 years of the alleged breach.

The time-limit for service of an enforcement notice in respect of all other breaches (eg most change of use offences) is 10 years. The notice must state the matters alleged to constitute the breach, the steps required to remedy the breach and the time within which these must be taken. These might be, for example, the removal of buildings or the cessation of any activity on the property. Other remedies which can be employed by the authority include: service of breach of condition notices (for breach of a condition attached to a consent); stop notices which prevent further works or specified activities being carried out on the land; and, in certain cases, an injunction to prevent further breaches from taking place.

Non-compliance with an operative enforcement or other notice may be a criminal offence which is separate and distinct from the civil remedies which are available to the authority.

## 5.10 RESTRICTIVE COVENANTS

When considering a planning matter, the local authority is only concerned with the broad policy of whether they approve of the proposed development on the specified site. They are not concerned with private restrictions on the land. The presence of restrictive covenants on the land will not prevent planning permission from being granted for a development which is ostensibly in breach of the covenants.

A buyer who intends to apply for planning permission for development must also check that his proposals do not contravene any valid restrictive covenants on the land. If the proposals will breach the covenants, consideration must be given to the resolution of this problem, for example, by an application to the Lands Tribunal under the Law of Property Act 1925, s 84 for the release of the covenants, or by taking out an insurance policy which will provide indemnity in the event of breach of any restrictive covenant. It may not be possible to resolve all problems connected with restrictive covenants in this way.

## 5.11 BUILDING REGULATION CONTROL

Building regulation consent from the local authority will be needed whenever building works are to be undertaken, irrespective of whether the works constitute 'development' within the statutory definition, or of whether they require separate planning permission.

Building regulation control is concerned with the health and safety aspects of the building to be erected or altered and regulates the types of materials and construction methods used in carrying out the work. Although the penalties for breach of building regulation control are not as severe as those for breach of the Planning Acts (and prosecutions must be brought within one year of the alleged breach), a buyer who proceeds with his purchase with knowledge of a breach of building regulation control must be advised that, in view of the breach, there is no guarantee of the safety of the structure of the building, which may therefore require expensive repairs or remedial work. On completion of building works for which consent was obtained, a 'final certificate' can be obtained from the local authority. This should be kept with the client's title deeds as evidence of compliance with building regulation control.

The buyer's lender must also be informed of the breach and may be reluctant to lend on a property where such breach exists or may impose conditions on the terms of the loan to ensure that the building work is brought up to standard. A full survey of the property is advisable in these circumstances.

## 5.12 ACTING FOR THE SELLER

Although planning matters do not necessarily fall within the seller's duty of disclosure, the buyer's solicitor will be reluctant to proceed with the transaction unless he is satisfied that the buildings and use of the property comply with current planning regulations. It is, therefore, sensible for the seller's solicitor to satisfy himself as to these matters at an early stage so as to be able to anticipate any problems which might otherwise arise.

The buyer's solicitor will raise pre-contract enquiries to ensure compliance with planning law; the Seller's Property Information Form (SPIF) supplied by the seller to the buyer in protocol transactions also reveals various matters with regard to planning. The following matters should therefore be checked from the documents in the solicitor's possession, from information obtained from the client or from the local planning authority.

(1) The date when the property was first built.
(2) Whether any additions, alterations or extensions have been made to the property or within its grounds since the property was first built and, if so, the date of each addition etc.
(3) If the property has been built or any alteration to it has been made within the last 4 years, either that planning consent was obtained (either expressly or by virtue of the GPDO) or that such consent was not required. Any conditions attached to the planning consent should, if possible, be checked to ensure that they have been complied with.
(4) If the property is leasehold, in addition to (3) above, whether any additions, alterations, etc have been made since the date of the grant of the lease and, if so, whether any restriction on development contained in the lease has been complied with.
(5) What the property is used for, whether any material change of use to the property has occurred during the last 10 years and, if so, whether the appropriate consent has been obtained.
(6) Where alterations or additions to the property have been made, whether building regulation control has been complied with. A 'final certificate' issued by the local authority will show compliance with these provisions.
(7) Whether the property is a listed building or in a conservation area.

## 5.13  ACTING FOR THE BUYER

The matters itemised in **5.12**, if not disclosed by the SPIF (where used), should be raised as pre-contract enquiries with the seller and the answers to the planning questions on the local search and enquiries of local authority should be carefully analysed. Any irregularity revealed by the answers should either be corrected at the seller's expense or, depending on the nature of the breach, an indemnity should be taken from the seller in the contract.

Note that it will be professional negligence for a solicitor to fail to advise a client about the absence of building regulation consent even where the building work in question took place outside the 12-month enforcement period. Lack of consent may mean that the work in question is structurally unsound. If consent was not obtained in relation to any works undertaken within (say) the last 10 years, the client must be advised of the risks involved. A detailed survey of the work may be advisable to ensure its safety. Insurance is also available to cover any works necessary to comply with the regulations.

### 5.13.1  Taking instructions

Instructions should be obtained from the buyer in relation to the following matters.

(1) Does the buyer's intended use of the property correspond with its present authorised use? If not, will planning permission be required for the buyer's intended use and is it likely that the local authority will grant such consent?

(2) Is it apparent on inspection of the property that new buildings or alterations have been made within the last 4 years? If so, check with the seller whether consent for the new buildings was needed/obtained/complied with.

(3) Does the buyer intend to alter the property in any way after completion? If so, will the proposed alterations require planning consent or consent from the person with the benefit of an existing restrictive covenant against development, and is it realistic to expect that such consent(s) will be forthcoming?

## 5.14  ENVIRONMENTAL ISSUES

The responsibility for polluting substances on land rests on the owner or occupier for the time being (including a lender who is in possession of land) under the Environmental Protection Act 1990 and the Environment Act 1995. Civil liability may also exist in tort (see *Scott-Whitehead v National Coal Board* (1987) 53 P & CR 263; cf *Cambridge Water Co v Eastern Counties Leather plc* [1994] 1 All ER 53).

### 5.14.1  Consequences of contamination

The presence of contaminants in land can have very serious consequences on a sale; the site may be 'blighted', making it difficult to sell or mortgage; the use of the land for certain proposed uses may be impossible without extensive (and expensive) clean-up works being undertaken. If the buyer fails to detect contamination, this could potentially lead to liability under the Environmental Protection Act 1990 or at common law. The Law Society has issued a 'warning card' to solicitors reminding them of the need in every transaction (whether a purchase, a mortgage or a lease) to consider whether contamination is an issue and to advise clients of the potential liabilities associated with it.

### 5.14.2  Enforcement

Control of contaminated land falls on the Environment Agency and local authorities. Under new ss 78A–78YC, inserted into the Environmental Protection Act 1990 by the Environment Act 1995, the local authority has the prime responsibility. Each local authority is under a duty to inspect its area for contaminated sites. Once a site has been identified as contaminated, the local authority must then serve a remediation notice on the 'appropriate person'. This will specify the steps necessary to clean up the site so that it is suitable for its intended use.

Liability for remediation falls on the 'appropriate person', as defined by s 78F. This is basically the original polluter, ie the person who caused or knowingly permitted all or some of the contaminating materials to be present in, on or under the land. If such a person cannot be identified, then liability falls on the current owner or occupier; it is this last provision which could result in a buyer becoming liable for remediation costs.

These provisions were brought into force on 1 April 2000.

The local authority also has have powers to serve an abatement notice to remedy a statutory nuisance under ss 79–82 of the Environmental Protection Act 1990 (eg in respect of the emission of smoke, fumes or gases which are prejudicial to health or a nuisance).

### 5.14.3 Searches

Until recently, it was not thought necessary to make enquiries with regard to potential contamination when buying residential property. However, after several cases where land on which new houses had been built was found to be contaminated, the need to make enquiries about environmental matters should be considered in every case. A useful and inexpensive method of doing this, in the case of house purchase, is to make use of Envirosearch Residential. This is available from Jordans Ltd and provides a wide range of environmental information about the property and the surrounding area from information gathered by the Landmark Information Group.

Also, in the case of new houses, the cover given by the NHBC has been extended to include the cost of cleaning up contamination of the site, should this be subsequently discovered. This applies, however, only to houses registered with the NHBC on and after 1 April 1999. There is no protection in the case of other houses.

The standard form of enquiries of the local authority (see **18.6**) now includes questions to ascertain whether the council has served or resolved to serve any notices relating to contamination in respect of the property.

In commercial transactions, and particularly when contemplating the purchase of a green field site or recycled urban land for development ('brown field' sites), it will always be necessary to undertake certain checks and enquiries to ensure that the land which is being acquired is clean or, if not, that the steps needed to clean up the land and related costs are clearly understood by the client. 'SiteCheck', also available from Jordans Ltd, provides an easy method of obtaining information about past land use and other environmental matters.

### 5.14.4 Special enquiries and investigations

Investigations which may need to be undertaken include some or all of the following to discover the uses to which the land has previously been put. The discovery of previous possible contaminatory uses of the land (eg a factory which made gas lamps) may indicate that the land itself is contaminated and will need to be cleaned up before it is developed.

(a) Look at the title deeds back to the stage where the land was a green field site (ie completely undeveloped farmland).
(b) Search old trade directories.
(c) Look at old Ordnance Survey maps.
(d) Make a local search and enquiries and, in particular, raise the specific Part II questions which relate to environmental matters.
(e) Instruct an environmental auditor to do a 'desk-top study' or 'Phase 1 Audit'. This involves obtaining information from a variety of sources to establish current and former land usage. As well as those mentioned in paragraphs

(a) to (d), local newspaper and local historical archives might contain information of past polluting activities.

(f) Purchase environmental data from a commercial search agency.

(g) Raise specific pre-contract enquiries of the seller relating to his use of the land.

If these enquiries indicate previous potentially contaminative uses, it will then be necessary to establish if the site is actually contaminated and, if so, to what extent. This will involve instructing environmental consultants to undertake an actual physical survey of the land. Samples of the soil will be taken on a systematic basis using established techniques and the samples will then be tested in order to discover the extent and nature of the contamination. However, such sampling can always miss isolated pockets of contamination, and so, even if the tests prove negative, the possibility of insuring against contamination and the possible remediation costs should be considered. There is a small, but growing, number of insurance companies offering cover against such risks.

If the land does prove to be contaminated, the costs of remediation to the standard necessary for the proposed use will have to be considered. Remediation can be very expensive, depending upon the nature and extent of the contamination. It might consist of excavating and then safely disposing of the contaminated soil, or encapsulating it so that the contaminants cannot escape. A cost of £1 million per hectare would not be unusual. With such sums at risk, the cost of a desk-top survey – perhaps £500 to £1,000 – seems well worth the expense!

### 5.14.5 Planning permission and contaminated land

Before a proposed development can go ahead, planning permission will be required. In granting such permission, the local authority may impose conditions requiring the site to be cleaned up or requiring investigations to be made to ascertain the full extent of any potential contamination. The Government's Planning Policy Guidance Note 23, issued in 1994, sets out guidance to local authorities in relation to contaminated land. It states that 'where practicable' brown field sites should be recycled into new uses and that 'such recycling can also provide an opportunity to deal with the threats posed by contamination'.

### 5.14.6 Radon

Radon is a naturally occurring gas which is present in the ground and is found at low levels in all buildings. In some high level areas ('Affected Areas' as defined by the National Radiological Protection Board), the Board may recommend that remedial measures are taken to buildings to reduce the radon levels which can cause cancer in human beings.

Radon affects both residential and commercial buildings and, in the Affected Areas, a buyer should raise specific pre-contract enquiries of the seller to ask whether a radon survey has been carried out by the Board and whether remedial measures have been recommended or undertaken. In Affected Areas, the Board will measure radon levels for the owner of property but the Board will not release the results of a survey to a prospective buyer. Optional Enquiry 36 on Part II of the Enquiries of Local Authorities search form should also be raised. Special requirements under the Building Regulations are also in force for new homes built in Affected Areas.

## 5.15 FURTHER READING

Brand and Williams *Planning Law for Conveyancers* 4th edn (Sweet & Maxwell, 1996)

*Butterworths Planning Law Service* (Butterworths)

Hellawell *Environmental Law Handbook* (The Law Society, 2000)

# Chapter 6

# CONDUCT ISSUES RELEVANT TO CONVEYANCING

## 6.1 INTRODUCTION

The principles of professional conduct apply to conveyancing as they do to every other aspect of the solicitor's business.

This chapter contains a summary of the conduct issues which are likely to be encountered during the course of a conveyancing transaction. Those matters which are exclusive to conveyancing are dealt with in detail. Other more general principles are mentioned in outline only and further detail of these can be found in the LPC Resource Book *Pervasive and Core Topics* (Jordans).

## 6.2 ACTING FOR MORE THAN ONE PARTY

### 6.2.1 Conflict of interests

As a general principle of professional conduct, a solicitor or his firm should not accept instructions to act for two or more clients in the same transaction where there is a conflict or a significant risk of a conflict between the interests of those clients. Nor should a solicitor or his firm continue to act for two or more clients where a conflict of interests arises between those clients.

### 6.2.2 The Solicitors' Practice Rules 1990, Rule 6

Rule 6 (as amended) lays down a basic rule that, subject to various exceptions (see **6.2.4**), a solicitor (or a firm of solicitors or associated practices) cannot act for more than one party in connection with conveyancing, property selling or mortgage related services. The prohibition applies to the transfer of land for value at arm's length, the grant or assignment of a lease for value at arm's length and the grant of a mortgage of land.

### 6.2.3 Transactions at arm's length

Whether a transaction is at arm's length will depend on the circumstances of the case and, in particular, the relationship between the parties. A transaction will not usually be at arm's length if the parties are:

(i)   related by blood, adoption or marriage; or
(ii)  associated companies; or
(iii) personal representatives and a beneficiary; or
(iv)  trustees and a beneficiary.

However, even though the rule does not apply in these situations, the general rules of conduct must still be followed. Thus, it would not be possible to act if there was a conflict of interest or a significant risk of a conflict arising.

### 6.2.4 Exceptions to Rule 6

A solicitor may act for seller and buyer only in one of the following circumstances:

(i)   both parties are established clients; or

(ii)  the consideration is £10,000 or less and the transaction is not the grant of a lease; or

(iii) there is no other qualified conveyancer in the area whom either the seller or the buyer could reasonably be expected to consult; or

(iv)  seller and buyer are represented by two separate offices in different localities, and:

    (a)  different solicitors who normally work at each office conduct or supervise the transaction; and

    (b)  no office of the practice (or an associated practice) referred either client to the office acting for that client; or

(v)   the only way in which the solicitor is acting for the buyer is in providing mortgage-related services; or

(vi)  the only way in which the solicitor is acting for the seller is in providing property selling services through a SEAL (see **6.2.6**).

However, even if one of the above circumstances exists, a solicitor still cannot act for buyer and seller:

(i)   without the written consent of both parties; or

(ii)  if a conflict of interest exists or arises; or

(iii) the seller is selling or leasing as a builder or developer.

### 6.2.5 Established clients

The test of whether someone is an established client is an objective one, ie whether a reasonable solicitor would regard that person as an established client. However, a person related by blood adoption or marriage to an established client is deemed to be an established client, as is a person who is selling or buying jointly with an established client.

### 6.2.6 Property selling

A solicitor is permitted to sell property on behalf of his client (see **6.10**). In such a case, special rules apply governing whether a solicitor can also act on behalf of the buyer. This property selling business might be conducted directly by the solicitor himself or through the medium of a Solicitors' Estate Agency Ltd (a SEAL). This is a separate company owned by a least four firms of solicitors which conducts business from separate premises from those of any of the owning solicitors.

When a solicitor (including a SEAL) acts in the property selling for the seller and the same solicitor acts for the buyer, the following conditions must be complied with in addition to those set out in **6.2.4**:

(i)   different persons must conduct or supervise the work for the seller and the buyer; and

(ii)  the solicitor must inform the seller in writing before accepting instructions to deal with the property selling of any services which might be offered to a buyer; and

(iii) the solicitor must explain to the buyer before the buyer gives consent to the solicitor acting for both parties:

  (a)  the implications of a conflict of interest arising; and

  (b)  the solicitor's financial interest in the sale going through; and

  (c)  if the solicitor proposes to offer mortgage-related services to the buyer through a SEAL which is also acting for the seller, that the solicitor cannot advise as to the merits of the purchase.

### 6.2.7  Joint buyers

It is acceptable to act for joint buyers provided that no conflict of interest exists or is likely to arise between them (see Chapter 10).

### 6.2.8  Contract races

The same solicitor must not act for both seller and buyer, nor for more than one buyer, in a transaction where a contract race is in existence (see **6.5**).

## 6.3  ACTING FOR BORROWER AND LENDER

### 6.3.1  General principles

The buyer's lender will frequently instruct the buyer's solicitor also to act for him in connection with the grant of the mortgage. The same situation commonly occurs in relation to the discharge of an existing mortgage when acting for a seller client.

As soon as the solicitor receives instructions to act for the lender, he is effectively acting for both parties in one transaction (ie for both lender and borrower). He has two clients and owes a duty to both (see *Mortgage Express v Bowerman & Partners (A Firm)* [1996] 2 All ER 836). Acting for buyer and lender is governed by Rule 6(3) of the Solicitors' Practice Rules 1990.

A solicitor can act for borrower and lender in the case of an institutional mortgage provided that the following conditions are complied with:

(i)   no conflict of interest arises;

(ii)  the lender's instructions to the solicitor do not extend beyond the limitations contained in Rule 6(3);

(iii) if the property is to be used as a private residence, the certificate of title set out in Rule 6(3) is used.

An institutional mortgage is defined as a mortgage on standard terms provided by an institutional lender in the normal course of its activities (eg a bank or building society).

Rule 6(3) states that the lender's instructions must be limited to certain matters if the solicitor is to be able to act for both parties. These limitations are lengthy and complex. However, most mortgage lenders have adopted the Council of Mortgage

Lenders' *Lenders' Handbook*. This is a standardised set of instructions, subject to variations in certain respects by individual lenders. Adoption of this by the lender guarantees compliance with the Rule 6(3) limitations on the content of the instructions.

Rule 6(3) also sets out a certificate of title to be used when acting for both lender and borrower. This sets out the solicitor's responsibilities and duties towards the lender client and must be used by the solicitor when the mortgaged property is to be used solely for residential purposes.

If the solicitor or a member of his immediate family is the borrower, the lender must first be notified in writing of the circumstances of the transaction. Many lenders will not allow the solicitor to act in such circumstances.

The solicitor may not act for seller, buyer and lender in the same transaction unless the lender has been notified of the circumstances of the transaction.

If a conflict does occur, the solicitor must decline to act for both parties unless he can, with the consent of one party, continue to act for the other.

Conflict may arise if, for example:

(1) the terms of the mortgage offer are unfair to the borrower (eg an extortionate rate of interest is being charged);

(2) instructions reveal that the buyer would be in breach of one of the terms of the offer (eg by allowing tenants into possession of the property);

(3) the buyer or seller is unable to comply with the lender's terms (eg to provide the balance of the purchase price from his own funds).

### 6.3.2 Private mortgages

The solicitor must not act for both lender and borrower in a private mortgage unless the transaction is not at arm's length and no conflict of interest exists or arises. A private mortgage is 'any mortgage other than an institutional mortgage'.

### 6.3.3 Acting for joint borrowers

Provided no conflict of interest exists or is likely to exist, there is no rule of law or conduct which prevents the same solicitor acting for joint borrowers (but see *Barclays Bank v O'Brien* [1993] 4 All ER 417; *Clark Boyce v Mouat* [1993] 3 WLR 1021).

## 6.4 CONFIDENTIALITY

All information received by the solicitor from his client is confidential and remains so even after termination of the retainer. Where, for example, the solicitor is told by his client that the client intends to breach the terms of the mortgage offer by letting the premises to a tenant and will not agree to the lender being told of this, the solicitor, when informing the lender that he can no longer act for him, must tell the lender that the reason for the termination of the retainer is because a conflict of interests has arisen, but he is not at liberty to disclose the nature of the conflict without the buyer client's consent.

## 6.5 CONTRACT RACES

### 6.5.1 Solicitors' Practice Rules 1990, Rule 6A

Where a seller's solicitor is asked by his client to deal simultaneously with more than one prospective buyer, he is required to comply with the Solicitors' Practice Rules 1990, Rule 6A, the text of which is summarised below. Compliance with the rule is mandatory, and breach can lead to disciplinary action being taken against the solicitor. It is the seller's instruction to 'deal' with more than one buyer that triggers the obligation to disclose. This cannot be delayed until a contract is submitted to another purchaser. Any instruction that indicates a decision to deal with more than one party (eg to send out office copy entries to another prospective buyer) requires the disclosure of the decision under Rule 6A. The rule applies to freehold and leasehold transactions, and to commercial transactions as well as residential ones.

### 6.5.2 Withdrawal of papers

Where, having supplied a prospective buyer with a draft contract, the seller later receives a further offer for the property which offer he would prefer to accept, the seller may withdraw his offer and the draft papers from the first prospective buyer before accepting the second prospective buyer's offer and submitting draft papers to him. In this situation, only one buyer is in possession of a draft contract at any one time, thus a contract race does not exist and the rule does not apply.

### 6.5.3 Solicitor acting for seller

Where a solicitor is acting for the seller, he must explain to his client that the solicitor is required to comply with Rule 6A referred to above and, if the seller refuses to allow the solicitor to notify all the prospective buyers of the contract race, the solicitor must decline to act.

Since buyers are themselves wary of entering into contract races, the seller should also be warned of the danger of losing all the prospective buyers if a race is commenced. It is normally preferable to avoid a contract race if at all possible.

### 6.5.4 Disclosure of race to buyers

Having obtained his client's authority, the seller's solicitor must at once disclose the seller's decision to conduct a contract race direct to the solicitor acting for each prospective buyer or, where no solicitor is acting, to the prospective buyer(s) in person. Such disclosure, if made orally, must at once be confirmed in writing or by fax. When the seller's solicitor informs the prospective buyers of the race, he must make clear to each of them the precise terms of the race, ie what has to be done by a buyer in order to secure the property. Commonly, the terms of the race are that the first buyer who presents a signed contract and deposit cheque at the seller's solicitor's office will secure the property.

### 6.5.5 Acting for more than one party

A solicitor must not accept instructions to act for both seller and buyer, even where one of the exceptions contained in Rule 6(2) would otherwise apply. Neither must the solicitor act for more than one prospective buyer where a contract race is involved.

## 6.6 UNDERTAKINGS

There are many situations in conveyancing where a solicitor will be asked to give an undertaking on his client's behalf. For example, an undertaking may be required to enable the buyer client to obtain a bridging loan for the deposit. Similarly, an undertaking may be required from the seller's solicitor that he will discharge his client's mortgage over the property. All the general rules on undertakings apply equally in the context of conveyancing. Failure to honour an undertaking is professional misconduct. Because of the personal liability which attaches to undertakings, it is important that both the giver and recipient of the promise understand precisely what the terms of the promise are. To avoid any misunderstanding, it is recommended that undertakings are always given in writing.

### 6.6.1 Bridging finance for the deposit

Where bridging finance is being extended for the deposit on the client's purchase, the bank or other lender will normally require the solicitor to give an undertaking to repay the loan, usually out of the proceeds of sale of the client's existing property. Such an undertaking should only be given where:

(1)   the solicitor is sure that sufficient funds will be available on completion to repay the loan with interest;

(2)   the solicitor knows the client well enough to feel confident of making a binding commitment on that client's behalf;

(3)   the client has given his irrevocable authority for the undertaking to be given – if in doubt, obtain the authority in writing.

Until contracts have been exchanged on the client's related sale transaction, there is no guarantee that any funds will be available to repay the loan. Ideally, therefore, an undertaking should not be given until contracts have been exchanged on the sale. In practice, it may be necessary to give the undertaking shortly before exchange in order to ensure the availability of funds for a simultaneous exchange on both sale and purchase contracts.

### 6.6.2 Terms of an undertaking on bridging finance

The Law Society has agreed a form of wording for use by solicitors when giving undertakings to banks for bridging finance. The full form of this undertaking is set out in Appendix 7. Even where an undertaking is presented to the solicitor in the standard form or in a familiar and frequently used form of wording, the entire wording should be read carefully in the light of the particular transaction to ensure that the wording is appropriate for those circumstances. If the wording is not wholly appropriate to the circumstances in hand, the undertaking should be amended to reflect the particular requirements of the transaction. The terms of the undertaking should be restricted to repayment:

(1)   of a stated figure, plus interest on that sum if so instructed;

(2)   from a defined source (eg the proceeds of sale of a named property);

(3)   of the net proceeds of sale, having defined what is understood by the word 'net', ie after deduction of specified loans, estate agent's commission, solicitor's fees, disbursements on the sale and purchase and any other known and defined liabilities which will reduce the amount available to repay the loan;

(4)   when the proceeds of sale are actually received by the solicitor, thus protecting the solicitor against having to honour the undertaking in circumstances where the sale of the property is completed but for some reason the funds are never received by him, for example, the client intercepts the money and absconds with it.

### 6.6.3  Change of circumstances

If, having given an undertaking, the circumstances of the client's sale and purchase transactions change, for example the price of the sale property is reduced to take account of a structural defect, the terms of the undertaking must be considered carefully to ensure that they are still capable of performance. The recipient of the undertaking must be informed of the changed circumstances, irrespective of whether they affect the obligations covered by the undertaking.

## 6.7  ESTIMATE FOR COSTS

### 6.7.1  Duty to give estimate

Whenever possible, a solicitor should give a client an estimate of the costs of the transaction. If it is not possible to give an estimate, a general indication of the approximate costs should be given. In residential conveyancing it is normally possible to give the client an estimate of the costs. A precise estimate of costs may not be possible in commercial transactions, but the client should still be given a general forecast of likely costs and the method of calculation of those costs at the outset of the transaction, and informed if that figure is likely to vary substantially.

### 6.7.2  Giving an estimate

In order to avoid misunderstandings an estimate should, if possible, be given in writing. If an oral estimate is unavoidable (eg in response to a telephone enquiry from a client), the estimate should be confirmed in writing either immediately or, at the latest, when the solicitor is instructed to act for the client. In residential conveyancing, it is frequently not possible to avoid giving an estimate over the telephone; many potential clients 'ring round' to obtain the lowest possible price. In such circumstances the prospective client should be advised that the estimate is given on the basis of information supplied by the client and may be subject to variation if unknown factors later emerge which complicate the transaction.

The estimate should be as comprehensive as possible and should be clear as to whether VAT and/or disbursements are included in the given figure. Minor expenses such as postage and telephone must be included in the estimate, not added as a disbursement.

### 6.7.3 Change in circumstances

If events occur which cause the original estimate to become inaccurate, the solicitor must immediately inform the client in writing of the change in circumstances and revise his estimate accordingly. Failure to advise the client of a change in the likely level of fees may render the solicitor liable to prosecution for giving misleading information relating to charges under the Consumer Protection Act 1987, s 20.

### 6.7.4 Quotations for costs

The solicitor should make it clear to the client that an estimate for costs is not a fixed price ('a quotation') for the work unless he intends to charge a fixed price which will not be altered in any circumstances. Where a quotation is given, the solicitor is not permitted to charge the client more than the fixed fee, even if the transaction turns out to be more difficult or complex than had been anticipated. Petty expenses such as postage and telephone must be included in the fixed fee quoted to the client. If a fixed fee is quoted, the client should be informed of that fee in writing and told that the quotation will be valid for a stated period (eg 3 months). If the solicitor has not been instructed by the client within this period, he will then be entitled to issue a revised quotation.

### 6.7.5 Value Added Tax on solicitors' charges

Where a firm is registered for VAT, it will be payable by the client on the solicitor's bill and on some of the disbursements paid by the solicitor on the client's behalf. When giving an estimate or quotation of costs to the client, the solicitor must make it clear whether or not that estimate or quotation includes VAT. If no mention of VAT is made, the client is entitled to assume that the quoted figure is VAT inclusive.

Where an individual or firm is registered for VAT, the firm's VAT registration number must appear on the bills issued by the firm or, if a separate tax invoice is issued, on the tax invoice.

## 6.8 INTRODUCTIONS AND REFERRALS

Many solicitors will have an arrangement with third parties such as estate agents and building societies for the mutual referral of clients. The building society may send the solicitor a client who needs legal advice, and the solicitor may refer to the building society a client who needs to obtain a mortgage. These arrangements must comply with the Solicitors' Introduction and Referral Code 1990 (as amended).

## 6.9 DEALING WITH NON-SOLICITORS

Where the other party to the transaction is not represented by a solicitor, precautions may have to be taken to ensure that the transaction proceeds smoothly and that the interests of the solicitor's client are properly protected. The Law Society has issued notes for guidance for solicitors which are summarised below.

### 6.9.1 Licensed conveyancers

Licensed conveyancers are bound by rules made by the Council for Licensed Conveyancers which relate to conduct, discipline, insurance and accounts. These rules are similar to those which bind solicitors. It is therefore possible to deal with a licensed conveyancer as if the conveyancer was a fellow solicitor.

### 6.9.2 Dealing with unqualified persons

The Solicitors Act 1974, s 22 makes it an offence for an unqualified person to carry out certain acts, including preparing a contract or transfer for the sale of land for gain or reward. At the commencement of a transaction which apparently involves an unqualified person, the solicitor should write to the unqualified person drawing attention to The Law Society's guidelines on this matter and asking for satisfactory evidence that no offence will be committed. The solicitor's client should also be informed of the situation.

Undertakings should not be accepted from unqualified persons because there is no method of enforcing them. Therefore, where a seller who is represented by an unqualified person has a mortgage to be discharged at completion, the buyer's solicitor must require the seller to produce a signed Form DS1 (or receipted mortgage) at completion and must not accept an undertaking for its discharge.

### 6.9.3 Acting for the lender

A solicitor acting for a lender where the borrower is represented by an unqualified person is under no obligation to undertake work which the buyer's solicitor would normally carry out (eg drafting the purchase deed) and should not give the unqualified person additional assistance. However, in such a situation, the solicitor must bear in mind that the interests of his lender client in obtaining a good title to the property are paramount. The advance cheque should be drawn in favour of a solicitor, licensed conveyancer or person properly authorised to receive the money by the borrower. Similar principles apply on redemption of a mortgage.

### 6.9.4 The buyer is not represented at all

Where it appears that the buyer will not be represented or assisted by a solicitor or professional adviser, the seller's solicitor should not prepare a form of contract which he knows will be placed before the buyer for signature without the buyer having had an opportunity to obtain legal advice. This duty in conduct means that the seller's solicitor should advise the buyer in writing to obtain legal advice before signing the contract, but he is under no duty to explain the terms of the contract to the buyer. The solicitor is under a general duty in conduct never to act in a way which is fraudulent or deceitful, nor to act in a way which would gain an unfair advantage either for himself or his client. This provision means that the seller's solicitor must draft a contract which, although properly protecting his own client's interests, does not unfairly disadvantage the unrepresented buyer. Similar considerations apply where it is the seller who is unrepresented.

## 6.10  PROPERTY SELLING

A solicitor is permitted to sell property on behalf of his client, ie he can act as an estate agent for the purpose of selling the property. This activity may be carried out by a solicitor as part of his practice, either through the solicitor's own office or through a separate property display centre. Even when acting in his role as an estate agent, the solicitor is still considered to be a solicitor and therefore remains bound by the Solicitors' Practice Rules 1990, the Solicitors' Accounts Rules 1998 and all other rules, regulations and principles of conduct which affect solicitors in practice. There are special rules relating to advertising and fees which apply where the solicitor is acting as an estate agent. A solicitor can run or be a partner in an estate agency business which is separate from his practice. In this case he must comply with Rule 5 of the Solicitors' Practice Rules 1990, and the Solicitors' Separate Business Code 1994.

### 6.10.1  Surveys and valuations

A solicitor is allowed to carry out a valuation of the property which he has been instructed to sell in order to advise the client on the price at which the property should be advertised for sale. He can also prepare the sale particulars, but may not describe himself as an 'estate agent' nor carry out any other types of surveys or valuations. A qualified surveyor employed by the solicitor may carry out surveys on behalf of a client or prospective client. The solicitor, as the surveyor's employer, would nevertheless remain liable for breach of duty if the surveyor carried out the survey negligently.

### 6.10.2  Application of the Estate Agents Act 1979 and the Property Misdescriptions Act 1991

The Estate Agents Act 1979 does not apply to solicitors who are engaged in property selling as part of the solicitor's business, but the Property Misdescriptions Act 1991 does. The 1991 Act makes it an offence for a person selling property to attach a misleading description to the property which is being sold. The liability is similar to that incurred under the Trades Descriptions Act 1968.

**Chapter 7**

# CAPITAL GAINS TAX AND VALUE ADDED TAX

## 7.1 LIABILITY TO CAPITAL GAINS TAX

A liability to capital gains tax (CGT) may arise on the disposal of an interest in land. A seller's solicitor should be aware of the possibility of potential liability and advise his client accordingly. Similarly, a buyer who is purchasing property other than for use as his principal private dwelling should be made aware of potential tax liability which may be incurred in his subsequent disposal of the property.

### 7.1.1 Chargeable assets

The definition of 'chargeable assets' within the Taxation of Chargeable Gains Act 1992 includes an interest in the proceeds of sale of land held by co-owners. Thus, a disposition by a beneficiary of his equitable interest in land could give rise to a charge to CGT (*Kidson v Macdonald* [1974] Ch 339). Some transactions which are incidental to the sale of land also give rise to a charge to CGT, for example, where a separate payment is made for the release or modification of an easement or covenant. Subject to certain reliefs, gifts fall within the meaning of 'disposal'.

## 7.2 THE PRINCIPAL PRIVATE DWELLING-HOUSE EXEMPTION

The disposal of an individual's principal private dwelling-house (including grounds of up to 0.5 hectares) is exempt from CGT (Taxation of Chargeable Gains Act 1992, s 222).

### 7.2.1 Qualifications

To qualify for the exemption, the seller must have occupied the dwelling-house as his only or main residence throughout his period of ownership. If an individual has more than one residence it is a question of fact which one constitutes his 'only or main' residence. However, the taxpayer can determine the question by making an election within 2 years of acquiring a second property, backdated for up to 2 years.

### 7.2.2 Absences

Under the Taxation of Chargeable Gains Act 1992, s 223, certain periods of absence are disregarded when calculating the amount of relief.

(1) The last 36 months of ownership (in order to facilitate the purchase of another property).
(2) By extra-statutory concession, the first 12 months of ownership (in order to facilitate the sale of another property). If there are good reasons for the period

exceeding one year, which are outside the individual's control, it will be extended up to a maximum of 2 years.

(3)  Any period(s) not exceeding 3 years in total throughout the period of ownership. Absence within this exception may be for any reason (eg an extended holiday) and can be made up of several separate periods of absence, provided that the total under this exception does not exceed 3 years.

(4)  Any period(s) during which the individual was working outside the UK. This exception applies to employees only, not to self-employed persons.

(5)  Any period(s) not exceeding 4 years in total during which the individual was prevented from living in his dwelling-house because he was employed elsewhere. This exception would apply, for example, to a school caretaker who was required to live in accommodation provided by the school, or an employee taking a job in another part of the country.

If the taxpayer is absent for longer periods, the proportion of the gain attributable to periods in excess of those mentioned in cases (3) to (5) above loses the benefit of the exemption, and so becomes chargeable.

*Example*

X spent 4 years wandering through Central Asia in the middle of his 12-year ownership of 'Home'. He makes a gain of £120,000 on its sale.

Three of the 4 years' absence fall within case (3): 'any reason' exemption. So the gain attributable to 1 year out of the 12 years' ownership will be chargeable.

$^1/_{12} \times £120,000 = £10,000$ of the gain will be chargeable.

### 7.2.3  Letting the property

To the extent that the property is let during the period of ownership, it ceases to be the individual's only or main residence (unless such absence can be disregarded under **7.2.2**). The proportion of the gain attributable to the period of letting will be chargeable, but only to the extent (if any) which it exceeds the lesser of £40,000 and the part of the gain which is not a chargeable gain.

*Example*

If X in the example above had let his house during his absence, the £10,000 gain would be exempt as it is under £40,000 (and £40,000 is less than the £110,000 gain attributable to his occupation).

On the other hand, if the gain attributable to the period of letting had been £50,000 and the non-chargeable gain still £110,000, then £10,000 (ie the excess of £50,000 over £40,000) would be chargeable.

### 7.2.4  Houses with large grounds

Where a dwelling-house has grounds of more than 0.5 hectares, the excess is prima facie taxable, but the Inland Revenue has a discretion to allow land in excess of 0.5 hectares to be included within the principal private dwelling-house exemption if the extra land can be shown to be necessary for the reasonable enjoyment of the house.

### 7.2.5  Sale of land alone

The sale of land alone, where the ownership of the house is retained, may enjoy the benefit of the exemption so long as the area of the grounds does not exceed 0.5 hectares. If the house is sold and land retained, a subsequent sale of the land will usually attract CGT.

### 7.2.6  Duality of user

Where part of a principal private dwelling-house is used exclusively for business purposes (eg a doctor who has a consulting room in his home), a proportion of the exemption may be lost, relative to the area of the 'business premises' in relation to the total area of the dwelling house. If a 'duality of user' can be shown, the full exemption may be available. Thus, a person who works from home, but who does not have a separate room for his business from which the other members of the family are excluded, may still take full advantage of the principal private dwelling house exemption.

### 7.2.7  Married couples

Only one exemption is available to married couples. Where a married couple own more than one house they must choose which property is to take the benefit of the exemption.

### 7.2.8  Trustees

The principal private dwelling-house exemption is available where the disposal is made by trustees, provided that the person in occupation of the property was a person who was entitled to be in occupation under the terms of the settlement (eg a tenant for life) (see the Taxation of Chargeable Gains Act 1992, s 225). By virtue of s 12 of the Trusts of Land and Appointment of Trustees Act 1996, a beneficiary under a trust of land now has a statutory right to occupy the trust property.

### 7.2.9  Tenants in common

Tenants in common may be liable for CGT on their respective shares in the equitable interest in the property.

## 7.3  CHARGEABLE GAINS

The gain is calculated by deducting the purchase price of the property (or its base value in 1982 if purchased earlier than this) from its current sale price. Any gain which is chargeable on the disposal is subject to indexation allowances for periods of ownership falling before 6 April 1998. For ownership from that date, the amount of the gain will be 'tapered', ie reduced according to the number of complete years of ownership that have elapsed since 6 April 1998. The taper is greater for business assets than for non-business assets. Any gain is then subject to the individual's annual exemption at the current rate; for details of this and indexation and tapering, see the LPC Resource Book *Pervasive and Core Topics* (Jordans). Over and above this, the gain is chargeable at the highest rate at which the individual pays income tax. Separate taxation is applied to married couples, so each spouse has his or her own annual allowance for CGT purposes. Corporations pay CGT at the corporation tax rate applicable to them, subject to roll-over and other reliefs.

## 7.4 FOUR KEY QUESTIONS

When taking instructions from an individual in relation to the sale of a dwelling-house, the answers to the following four questions will indicate whether there is likely to be a CGT liability on the property. If the client's answers to all the questions set out below match the suggested answers, there is unlikely to be a CGT liability on the transaction. If any of the client's answers differ from those suggested, further enquiries should be raised with the client.

Question 1:       Did you move into the house immediately after you bought it?

Answer:           Yes.

Question 2:       Have you lived anywhere else since moving into this house?

Answer:           No.

Question 3:       Does the garden extend to more than 0.5 hectares?

Answer:           No.

(The answer to this question may be self-evident from the estate agent's particulars of the property.)

Question 4:       Do you (or your spouse) own another house?

Answer:           No.

## 7.5 VALUE ADDED TAX

### 7.5.1 Introduction

A property lawyer will frequently have to consider the impact of Value Added Tax (VAT) on the transaction. VAT is chargeable in respect of a supply of goods or services made in the course of a business. Supplies can be exempt, zero rated or standard rated depending upon the circumstances. Standard-rated supplies are subject to VAT at the then current standard rate (17.5%); zero-rated supplies are taxable, but, as the name suggests, are subject to VAT at a zero rate. Exempt supplies are not subject to tax. Tax paid by a business on supplies made to it ('input tax') can be recovered from HM Customs and Excise provided that it was incurred in making taxable supplies, ie standard or zero-rated, but not exempt, supplies. The tax charged by a business on supplies it makes ('output tax') has to be accounted for to HM Customs and Excise. In practice, the input tax incurred in making those supplies is deducted from the output tax and only the balance is paid over to Customs.

VAT affects property transactions as follows:

(1)   Residential properties:

    (a)   sale of a green field site: exempt, but subject to option to tax (see **7.5.2**);
    (b)   construction and civil engineering works: zero rated;

    (c)   legal and other professional services: standard rated;

    (d)   sale or lease of a new house: zero rated;

(2)  Commercial properties:

    (a)   sale of a green field site: exempt, but subject to option to tax (see **7.5.2**);

    (b)   construction and civil engineering services: standard rated;

    (c)   legal and other professional fees: standard rated;

    (d)   sale of a new freehold building: standard rated;

    (e)   sale of an old freehold building: exempt, but subject to option to tax;

    (f)   grant or assignment of a lease; exempt, but subject to option to tax.

## 7.5.2   The option to tax

When an exempt supply is made, any input tax incurred is not recoverable from Customs. The purpose of the option to tax is to enable the developer to convert an exempt supply into a taxable supply. This will then enable him to recover any input tax incurred in connection with that supply. The details of how to effect this election are outside the scope of this chapter.

## 7.5.3   VAT and residential property

In the case of residential property, the impact of VAT is relatively uncomplicated. The purchase of land by a developer will be an exempt supply, unless the seller has elected to charge tax. The construction work will be zero rated and so no input tax will be incurred on this. Input tax will be paid on the professional fees, however. The sale of the houses will be zero rated. However, this is a taxable supply, albeit at a zero rate, and so any input tax incurred (eg the professional fees or if the seller of the site elected to tax) will be recoverable from Customs and Excise.

## 7.5.4   VAT and new commercial property

The VAT implications here are much more extensive. The sale of the development land is again exempt, but subject to the option to tax. However, the construction and other works will be standard rated. The developer will thus be incurring substantial amounts of input tax. The sale of the new building is, however, standard rated and so the seller will be able to recover the input tax paid on the construction, etc. A 'new' building is one completed within the 3 years prior to the sale and VAT must be charged on the sale.

If a lease is granted of the new building, this is an exempt supply and so no input tax is recoverable. However, it is subject to the option to tax to enable the recovery of input tax.

## 7.5.5   Old commercial buildings

Dispositions of commercial property more than 3 years old are exempt, but subject to the option to tax. The only point in electing to tax is to enable you to recover any input tax incurred; if you incurred none, you will not elect. However, VAT may have been incurred in carrying out repair and refurbishment works on the building. This cannot be recovered on making an exempt supply. Hence again, there is the option to tax, whether on a sale of the freehold or the grant of a lease, to enable the input tax to be recovered by setting it off against the output tax being charged.

### 7.5.6   Conveyancing points

Unfortunately, making a taxable supply or electing to tax does not necessarily mean that the buyer/tenant will have to pay VAT *in addition* to the agreed consideration. The agreed price might be deemed to be *inclusive* of VAT. The terms of the contract between the parties and the operation of s 89 of the Value Added Tax Act 1989 (VATA 1989) have to be considered.

#### *Seller and buyer*

On a sale of a new commercial building there is mandatory VAT on the purchase price. The price agreed is deemed to be *inclusive* of VAT, unless the contrary is agreed. Where the Standard Conditions are used, note that Standard Condition 1.4.2 states that the price is exclusive of VAT. The buyer's solicitor should point this out to the client at the earliest opportunity, as the extra amount payable (17.5%) may affect the buyer's financial arrangements.

On the sale of an old commercial building the position may depend upon when the seller makes the election to tax. If he elects before contract, the position is as above; if he elects after contract, then VATA 1989, s 89 allows the VAT to be added to the purchase price unless the contract expressly states that the price is inclusive of VAT. If the Standard Conditions are used, the position will be the same in both cases. In any event, the buyer should be warned of the danger of the seller electing and should try to negotiate a provision in the contract that the seller will not elect before completion or that the price is deemed to be inclusive of VAT. Otherwise, the buyer should again be advised to make his financial arrangements on the assumption that VAT will be payable in addition to the agreed price.

#### *Landlord and tenant*

The grant of a commercial lease, whether of a new or old building is an exempt supply, subject to the option to tax. If the election is made after the grant of the lease, VATA 1989, s 89 allows the rent to be increased by the amount of VAT, unless there is a clause in the lease making the rent inclusive of VAT. If an election is made before the grant of a lease, s 89 will not apply and so the landlord will only be able to add VAT to the rent if there is a provision in the lease permitting this. In every lease, therefore, there ought to be such a provision.

#### *What if the seller/landlord cannot add on VAT ?*

If an election is made, or a standard rated supply is made and the seller/landlord is unable to add VAT on to the agreed price, the seller is still liable to account for VAT to Customs out of the agreed price. So, for example, a price of £1 million is agreed for a sale of land. If the seller can add VAT, the buyer will hand over £1,175,000, £1 million of which will be kept by the seller, the other £175,000 being handed over to Customs. If the seller is unable to add on the VAT, the buyer need only pay £1 million on completion. Out of this the seller will have to account for £148,936 to Customs and will thus keep only £851,064 himself.

**Part II**

# THE FIRST INTERVIEW

# Chapter 8

# TAKING INSTRUCTIONS

## 8.1 PURPOSE OF TAKING INSTRUCTIONS

The purpose of taking instructions is for the solicitor to obtain from his client sufficient information to enable him to carry out the whole of the client's transaction, not just to enable him to take the first or next step in that transaction. This does not mean that the client is only contacted once during the course of the whole conveyancing transaction; the client must be regularly informed as to the progress of the transaction. From time to time, his further instructions will be needed. However, obtaining as much information as possible in one interview at the commencement of the transaction will save time (both the client's time and that of the solicitor), and will enable the solicitor to obtain a full picture of the transaction and thus to advise the client fully and correctly about his proposals.

Unless full instructions are taken, the solicitor is in danger of overlooking matters which are relevant to the transaction, but which the client had not thought to mention specifically to him (eg a liability to pay capital gains tax on the proceeds of sale).

### 8.1.1 Personal interview

Wherever possible, instructions should be taken from the client in person. The personal interview gives the client the opportunity to ask questions of the solicitor, and the solicitor the benefit of being able to explain matters to the client in an informal and friendly manner.

### 8.1.2 Indirect instructions

Indirect instructions, for example where an estate agent sends the solicitor instructions to act on behalf of one of the estate agent's clients, must be confirmed directly with the client, preferably by personal interview, to ensure that there is no misunderstanding about the instructions and that they comply in all respects with the Solicitors' Practice Rules 1990 (see LPC Resource Book *Pervasive and Core Topics* (Jordans) Part II). This principle applies equally to the situation where instructions are taken from one only of two or more co-sellers or co-buyers (see *Penn v Bristol and West Building Society and Others* [1995] 2 FLR 938). Direct confirmation of instructions must be obtained from all persons who are to be clients of the solicitor.

### 8.1.3 Preparing for the interview

The methods of preparation for the interview and interviewing techniques are dealt with in the LPC Resource Book *Skills for Lawyers* (Jordans) and are not further discussed in this book except for the comments which appear below which are particularly relevant to conveyancing.

Before the interview, the solicitor should find out whether the firm has acted for this client previously in property matters. If it is found that the firm acted on the client's purchase of the property which he is now proposing to sell, the old purchase file should be retrieved from storage and its contents examined before interviewing the client for the purpose of taking instructions on the sale. Much of the information required on the sale transaction may already be contained in the purchase file (eg who owns the boundaries of the property) and it will save time at the interview if this information can be confirmed with the client (to ensure that it has not changed) rather than fresh and full instructions being taken on every point.

### 8.1.4  Acting for both parties

Rule 6 of the Solicitors' Practice Rules 1990 prevents a solicitor from acting for both seller and buyer in the same conveyancing transaction, except in the limited circumstances covered by Rule 6(2) (see Chapter 6). Before interviewing the client, the solicitor should check that the firm has not already accepted instructions to act for the other party in the same transaction or that, if it has, acting for this client is covered by one of the exceptions to Rule 6, complies with the general principles relating to conflict of interests and does not infringe any other practice rule or principle of professional conduct.

### 8.1.5  Protocol cases

Under the terms of the Protocol (see Chapter 2), the seller's solicitor is required to obtain his client's answers to the questions contained in the SPIF (a standard form of pre-contract search, see **18.7**), to obtain from his client any relevant documents relating to such matters as guarantees, building regulation control, etc, and to ask his client to complete the Fixtures Fittings and Contents Form showing which items are to remain at the property after the sale and which are to be removed (see Chapter 11). He must also obtain details of all financial charges over the property (including second and subsequent mortgages), and ascertain the identity of all persons aged over 17 who are resident in the property in order to establish whether or not such persons have an interest in the property.

### 8.1.6  Using checklists

Although checklists cannot be expected to cover every eventuality in every transaction, they are useful in standard transactions to ensure that all necessary information is acquired during the course of the interview. Checklists focus the interviewer's mind on the relevant information, reducing preparation time and, ultimately, saving time in the interview itself, but they do need to be used sympathetically so that the client does not feel he is being processed in an impersonal way. Where checklists are used, it is helpful to have them printed on a distinct colour of paper so that they are easily located in the file, either by the solicitor himself or by another member of his staff who has to work on the file.

### 8.1.7  Mortgage and property fraud

Fraud of all types is on the increase and a solicitor should take steps to minimise the risk of being involved in any way. It is good practice, therefore, in cases where the client is not personally known to you, to ask for some form of proof of identity. Where the solicitor is acting for a borrower and an institutional lender, the *Lenders'*

*Handbook* requires the solicitor to verify the borrower's identity, for example by checking his passport.

## 8.2 MATTERS ON WHICH INSTRUCTIONS MUST BE OBTAINED

A reminder of the matters which will be discussed at a first interview with a client is set out in **8.3** and **8.4**. Although much of the information needed when acting for a seller is the mirror image of, or identical to, the information needed when acting for a buyer, some issues are exclusive to each side of the transaction. For that reason, separate checklists for seller and for buyer are given.

## 8.3 ACTING FOR THE SELLER

### *Full names and addresses of seller(s) and buyer(s), and home and business telephone numbers of seller(s)*

The full names and addresses (including post codes) of all parties involved in the transaction are needed because they have to be inserted in both the contract and purchase deed. 'Full names' includes all middle names (ie names exactly as they appear on the client's birth certificate or passport). The client's home and business telephone numbers are needed in order to be able to contact him during the course of the transaction.

### *Name, address and person to contact at estate agents*

Where an estate agent is involved in the sale, the name, address and telephone number of the person at the agents who is dealing with the sale is needed for contact purposes and in case any queries need to be resolved with the agents.

### *Name and address of other party's solicitors*

The name, address, telephone number, and name of person dealing with the matter as solicitor or representative of the other party to the transaction must be obtained for contact purposes.

### *Full address of the property to be sold*

The full address (including post code) and description of the property to be sold is required for insertion in the draft contract and, later, in the purchase deed.

### *Tenure*

Whether the property is freehold or leasehold will need to be stated in the contract. Where the property is held on a lease, the terms of the lease must also be set out in the contract.

### *Price*

The price at which the property is agreed to be sold must be stated in the contract and the purchase deed.

### Has any preliminary deposit been paid?

There is no requirement for the buyer to pay any money to the seller before the contract is entered into. However, sometimes a small sum of money (a preliminary deposit) is paid by the buyer to the seller's estate agent pending negotiations for the sale. This sum should be noted on the seller's solicitor's file, with a copy of the receipt for its payment and taken into account when calculating the deposit needed later in the transaction (see Chapter 21). The commonest situation in which a preliminary deposit is payable is when the seller is a builder or developer selling a new house (see Chapter 41).

### Fixtures and fittings

It is essential to obtain clear instructions relating to which fixtures and fittings are to remain at the property after completion of the sale, and which are to be removed by the seller (see Chapter 11). Where the Protocol is being used, the client should be asked to complete the Fixtures Fittings and Contents form. Consideration should be given to whether any fittings (eg carpets and curtains) which are included in the sale are included in the purchase price or are to be paid for separately by the buyer.

### Seller's Property Information Form

In cases where the Protocol is being used, the seller should be asked to complete this form. This is a standard form of enquiry dealing with matters such as boundary disputes. It is usual for the client to be given the form to complete in his own time and then return to the solicitor as soon as possible. See **18.7** for details of the form.

### Anticipated completion date

The client should be asked when he anticipates completion taking place. A 'normal' residential transaction takes on average 8–10 weeks from start to finish, although in certain circumstances a shorter time-span can be achieved. Sometimes a longer period of time may be desired by the client owing to particular circumstances (eg where the client finds a buyer for his property in September, but he does not want to move until his children have completed the full academic year at their school the following July).

### The present use of the property

Information relating to the present use of the property should be checked against its authorised use for planning purposes (see Chapter 5) and any restrictive covenants affecting the use of the property to ensure in both cases that no breaches have been committed.

### Does the transaction attract VAT?

Most residential property transactions are not within the scope of the charge to VAT, VAT is, however, an important consideration in a commercial sale. In the case of a 'new' commercial property it is mandatory for VAT to be charged on the sale; in the case of other commercial properties, the seller may elect to charge VAT. He will need to elect if he wishes to reclaim any input tax incurred in connection with the property. If VAT is chargeable on the sale, the seller's solicitor should ensure that the terms of the contract with the buyer enable VAT to be added on to the agreed price (see **7.5**).

## Who is in occupation of the property?

If someone other than the seller(s) is in occupation of the property it will be necessary to ensure that they will vacate on or before completion. Details of any tenancies to which the property is subject must also be obtained as these will have to be disclosed to the buyer.

## Synchronisation

Whether the transaction is dependent on the purchase or sale of another property is one of the most important questions to be raised at the first interview. In residential transactions, the client will often wish to sell his existing house and to use the proceeds of sale to purchase another house in which he will then live. The purchase of the new house cannot be undertaken without the proceeds of sale of the old house. Similarly, if the old house is not sold, the client has no use for the new house – he does not want or need two houses. Where the sale and purchase transactions are interdependent, the solicitor must ensure synchronisation of the two transactions, ie no sale without purchase and vice versa. Failure to do this constitutes professional negligence.

## Whether any terms have been agreed between the parties

It is usually a good idea to ask whether the parties have agreed any other terms between them, ie terms which have not come to light in the interview so far. These terms may have been agreed informally by conversation between the parties or may be recorded in correspondence between them. The solicitor should be aware of all the terms which have been agreed so that they can be incorporated into the contract which is drawn up between the parties.

## Money

The client must be advised as to the costs of the transaction and a financial calculation should be made to ensure that the sale will yield sufficient funds to carry out the client's proposals (eg to pay off the existing mortgage and to purchase a new house).

## Whereabouts of title deeds

The seller's solicitor will need to obtain the title deeds to the property to check that the seller does own and can sell the property and to enable the contract to be drafted. The whereabouts of the deeds should, therefore, be ascertained from the seller. Often they will be in the possession of an existing lender.

## Outstanding mortgages

Where the client has an outstanding mortgage on the property, the solicitor will need to contact the lender to obtain the title deeds (the Charge Certificate in Registered Land), which will usually be in the lender's custody. The client should be asked to supply his mortgage roll number or account number so that the solicitor can obtain the information and documents which he needs from the client's lender. Under s 63 of the Land Registration Act 1925, a lender may request the Registry to retain the charge certificate in the Registry. Where this has happened, an entry will be made in the charges register stating that the certificate has been retained in the Registry. In such a case, there is no need to obtain the charge certificate. Most clients will have a mortgage over their property, some have more than one. All outstanding mortgages will normally need to be discharged before completion of the sale, and therefore the solicitor needs to enquire of the client whether there are any further charges over the property, if so, how many, who the lender is in each case and, in each case, how much money (approximately) is outstanding on the loan. The information yielded by this question affects the financial calculation.

### Amount of deposit

It is customary for a deposit equivalent to 10% of the purchase price to be paid by the buyer to the seller when a contract is entered into. If it is contemplated that a lower deposit will be paid in this case, the client should be fully advised of the consequences of this step (see Chapter 21).

### Proceeds of sale

In many cases, the question of what is to happen to the proceeds of sale of the property will be self-evident – the proceeds are to be used towards the purchase of another property. If the answer to this question is not clear from the information already supplied by the client, the solicitor must find out what the client's wishes are. The proceeds of sale must be dealt with as quickly as possible after completion takes place, otherwise the client may be entitled to interest on his money from the solicitor. If the proceeds are to be sent to the client's bank account, the solicitor needs to know the name and address of the relevant bank and the client's account number.

### Capital gains tax

In certain cases, the sale of the property will be a disposal for capital gains tax purposes (see Chapter 7).

If CGT is payable this should be pointed out to the client at the earliest possible opportunity. The fact that tax is chargeable on the disposition may affect the financial viability of the sale and the seller's decision to sell.

## 8.4  ACTING FOR THE BUYER

Most of the information required when acting for a buyer client is either the same as, or the mirror image of, that required when acting for the seller, with the following modifications.

### Use of the property

In addition to knowing what the present use of the property is, the buyer's solicitor will need to know what the buyer intends to use the property for after completion. In many cases, the answer to this question will be apparent from the circumstances of the transaction (eg the client wants to buy a house to live in it). Any change of use of the property or alteration to its physical structure may require planning permission (see Chapter 5).

### Money

A financial calculation must be undertaken to ensure that the client potentially has sufficient money to purchase the property and pay the related costs of purchase including, in appropriate cases, Land Registry fees and stamp duty. Land Registry fees are payable for registering the land or registering a dealing at HM Land Registry after completion, fees are payable on a scale published by HM Land Registry and the client can therefore be told the exact amount of this cost. Stamp duty is payable at the rate of 1% on the whole of the consideration paid for the property where that price exceeds £60,000, but does not exceed £250,000. Where the price exceeds £250,000, but does not exceed £500,000, duty will be payable at 3% of the price. If the price exceeds £500,000 the duty is 4% of the price. In each case, the stated rate of duty is payable on the whole of the price. Thus a purchase for exactly £60,000 will pay no duty, but a purchase for £61,000 will attract £610 in duty.

Stamp duty is payable only on the consideration for the land, not on that separately attributed to chattels. In marginal cases like this, if the sale includes chattels, it is sometimes possible to reduce the liability to duty by apportioning some of the price to the chattels included in the sale, for example carpets and curtains. The amount apportioned to the chattels must, of course, be a fair reflection of their value, otherwise both solicitor and client could be liable to criminal sanctions. However, in the example given, if £1,000 could be specifically attributed to the purchase of the carpets etc, this would reduce the consideration for the land to £60,000 and thus no stamp duty would be payable, a saving of £610 for the client. Even bigger savings can be made where the purchase price is around the £250,000 or £500,000 thresholds for the higher rates of duty. The rates of duty are changed from time to time by the Finance Act. The rates cited above are those which are current at the time of publication of this book.

In the 2001 Budget, an exemption for stamp duty on all property transactions in specified disadvantaged areas of the country was introduced.

### *Deposit*

The buyer will usually be required to pay a deposit of 10% of the purchase price on exchange of contracts, although sometimes the seller can be persuaded to accept a lower figure. The client may not have ready access to cash to be used for the deposit and the solicitor will have to discuss with his client how the deposit is to be funded. Often it will be possible to use the deposit paid to the client on the sale of his existing property to fund the deposit required on his purchase. Otherwise a bridging loan may be necessary (see **21.4.2**).

### *Mortgage*

Most clients will require some type of mortgage funding to assist with the purchase of the property. Some clients will already have submitted a mortgage application to a lender before coming to see the solicitor, others may require assistance with the sources and types of finance available (see Chapter 9).

### *Survey*

The maxim 'caveat emptor' applies (with limited exceptions) to conveyancing; it is up to the buyer to make sure of his bargain. It is sensible in many cases for the buyer to commission an independent survey of the property to ensure that the property does not have more problems associated with it than the client had bargained for. The solicitor should therefore discuss with his buyer client the need for a survey in appropriate cases (see Chapter 12). The need for an environmental survey should also be discussed (see **5.14**).

### Situation of the property

Enquiries should be made as to the situation of the property, for example, its proximity to railways, rivers, etc, which may indicate the need for special searches to be undertaken (see Chapter 18).

### Insurance

The risk in the property for insurance purposes will often pass to the buyer when a contract is entered into. The client should be warned of this and that you will arrange such insurance on his behalf at his expense. Additionally, there may be a need to discuss with the client arrangements for life assurance (it may be a term of the client's mortgage offer that he takes out a life policy) and buildings contents insurance.

### Who is buying the property?

Where the prospective buyer is married or is intending to live in the property with a cohabitee or friend, the lender who is providing the mortgage finance for the property will insist that the legal title to the property is held in joint names or that they sign a waiver of any rights they may have in favour of the lender. Where the purchase is to be in more than one person's name, the clients must be advised in relation to co-ownership (see Chapter 10). The problems of conflict of interests must be borne in mind when dealing with this issue.

### Custody of deeds

Where there is to be a mortgage of the property, the client's lender will usually take custody of the deeds after completion. In other cases, the client's instructions in relation to custody of the deeds should be obtained. The client may, for example, wish to have the deeds sent to his home, or to his bank, or for the solicitor to keep them in his own strong room.

### The client's present property

It must be ascertained where the client is presently living, and whether it is necessary to sell the client's present house before buying the new one (see *Synchronisation* in **8.3**). If the client is presently living in rented accommodation, he may need to be advised about giving notice to his landlord to terminate that tenancy.

## 8.5  INSTRUCTIONS IN SPECIAL CASES

Information additional to that outlined above will be required where the transaction concerns a newly constructed property (see Chapter 41), a leasehold (see Chapter 35), or a dealing with part only of the seller's property (see Chapter 40).

**Chapter 9**

# FINANCE FOR THE BUYER

## 9.1 INTRODUCTION

The buyer's solicitor should check that the client has sufficient funds available to meet the cost of his purchase and related expenses. This matter should be raised with the client when taking instructions and a further check should be made just before exchange of contracts to ensure that any factors which have altered since instructions were first obtained have been taken into account in calculating the client's financial situation. The client should be advised against entering into a binding contract for purchase unless the financial arrangements are settled and adequate to meet the commitments involved.

The methods used to finance commercial purchases are outside the scope of this book and this chapter concentrates on finance for the purchase of residential property. However, whatever the type of transaction, the buyer's solicitor should always ensure that his client has sufficient funds available.

### 9.1.1 The client has already arranged a mortgage

Many clients will have already considered the financial implications of the transaction before instructing the solicitor to act, in which case all that the solicitor needs to do is to check through the figures with the client to ensure that all necessary items of expenditure have been taken into account. In this situation, the client is likely already to have submitted a mortgage application to a lender and will not require advice on the sources and types of finance available for the purchase of property. The solicitor should not interfere with arrangements which the client has made but, if it appears that the mortgage arrangements are patently unsatisfactory (eg an exorbitant interest rate is to be charged on the loan), there may be a duty on the solicitor to suggest that the client reconsiders his choice of finance on the basis that more advantageous terms could be obtained from another source.

### 9.1.2 Financial services

Generic advice such as 'As you are self-employed, you could consider a pension mortgage' is not within the scope of the Financial Services Act 1986. Advice which suggests that a particular mortgage from a named company should be obtained, or a discussion of the terms attached to a particular mortgage offer, may be within the terms of the Act if the mortgage involved is to be secured with an endowment policy taken out on the borrower's life. Financial services are dealt with in more detail in the LPC Resource Book *Pervasive and Core Topics* (Jordans).

## 9.2 SOURCES AND TYPES OF FINANCE

Where the client has not made any financial arrangements prior to instructing the solicitor, he may require advice on the sources of mortgage finance and types of loan available. In some cases, the client may require assistance with making his mortgage application. The solicitor may have an arrangement with a lender for the introduction of clients; such arrangement must comply with the Solicitors' Introduction and Referral Code 1990.

### 9.2.1 Sources of finance

The main sources of mortgage finance available for the purchase of land in England and Wales are:

(1)  building societies;
(2)  banks;
(3)  insurance companies;
(4)  the client's employer;
(5)  a private mortgage (eg a loan from a relative or from a trust fund); and
(6)  finance houses.

#### *Building societies and banks*

Loans from building societies and banks represent the largest slice of the mortgage market, accounting between them for approximately 85% of all residential loans. There is little to distinguish between the terms offered by these two types of institution: both will offer long-term loans (eg 25 years) at commercially competitive interest rates.

Banks have the reputation of being slightly more flexible in the application of their lending criteria and of being more willing to consider unusual property (eg a derelict barn which is to be converted) and higher value loans. Loans for commercial property and business expansion are also more likely to be funded by banks.

#### *Insurance companies*

Although loans from insurance companies for house purchase represent a small percentage of the loan market, their lending terms are broadly similar to those offered by the banks and building societies. A loan from this source would normally be supported by an endowment policy on the borrower's life. Several insurance companies have now set up their own banking subsidiaries to compete in the mortgage market.

#### *The client's employer*

Some large company employers (eg banks) offer mortgages at concessionary rates to their employees. The terms of these loans may enable the employee to borrow a substantially higher sum at a lower rate of interest than could be obtained on the open market.

Where the rate of interest payable on such a loan is less than the commercial rate being charged by other lenders, the employee may be deemed by the Inland Revenue to be in receipt of a benefit in kind which is taxable in the hands of a higher paid employee. Even with this tax burden, the loan from the employer still usually represents good value for money. The main drawback to such an arrangement is that the employee with this type of loan will find it more difficult to change his job, since ending his employment will result in the withdrawal of the concessionary rates and a consequent increase in mortgage repayments.

### Private mortgage

A client may sometimes be able to arrange mortgage finance through a loan from a relative or from a private trust fund. The terms of such a loan are a matter for agreement between the parties involved, who must always be separately advised. The Solicitors' Practice Rules 1990, Rule 6 prohibits the same solicitor from acting for both lender and borrower in this situation except where the transaction is not at 'arm's length'. It is suggested that, even where the loan is not at arm's length (eg a loan from father to son), the potential conflict of interests between lender and borrower will preclude the same solicitor from acting for both parties.

### Finance houses

Mortgage funding is available from finance houses, but they are not generally considered to be a primary source of finance for a client who is seeking a loan for the purchase of property. The terms offered by a finance house may be less generous than those offered by the banks and building societies (eg a shorter period of loan and higher rate of interest).

However, a client who already owns his house might approach a finance house for a second loan (eg for the purchase of a new car or for improvements to the property). Second mortgages from finance houses for sums not exceeding £15,000 may be affected by the notice provisions contained in the Consumer Credit Act 1974, s 58.

## 9.2.2 Amount of loan

All lenders have slightly different criteria or status qualifications for granting a loan. If the state of the mortgage market means that funds are readily available, the lender may be less stringent in the application of his criteria than at a time when funds are in short supply.

In broad terms, the maximum sum that a borrower can hope to obtain on mortgage is linked to a multiplier of his and his co-owner's salary. For example, a lender may stipulate that it is prepared to lend up to three times the main salary earner's salary plus one times the lesser earner's salary. Thus, if a client earns £40,000 pa, and his co-owner earns £10,000 pa, the maximum loan which the couple could apply for would be £130,000.

This overall limit is usually subject to the further qualification that the amount of the loan does not exceed a fixed percentage of the lender's valuation of the property (not the purchase price). The fixed percentage will vary depending on the lender and the type of property involved but, as a general rule, it is unrealistic to expect to obtain a loan of more than 90% of the valuation (except perhaps for first-time buyers) and the percentage will decrease with the age of the property being purchased. A 90% limit may be placed on a modern property; this figure may drop to 80% or 70% with an older house. It must also be remembered that the lender's valuation of the property is frequently less than the asking price of the property. Where the lender agrees to lend a sum in excess of the normal percentage of the valuation, it may be a term of the loan that the borrower pays for a single premium insurance policy ('a guarantee policy') which is taken out by the lender. If the lender has to exercise his power of sale, he is insured against any loss he may incur due to his having lent more than the normal percentage of the value.

These mortgage guarantee policies have been much criticised as, although they are paid for by the borrower, they protect only the lender. The borrower has no rights under them on a sale at a loss. Indeed, the insurer often has a right of subrogation to reclaim any loss it has had to meet from the borrower. Many lenders now no longer require such policies, or will meet the cost themselves.

### 9.2.3 Types of mortgage

Each lender will apply a different name to the various loan packages which it advertises. These are mainly variations of the three main types of mortgage available, which are:

(1)   a repayment mortgage;
(2)   an endowment mortgage; and
(3)   a pension mortgage.

#### Repayment mortgage

A repayment mortgage is the most straightforward type of loan available. In return for the loan, the borrower grants a mortgage of the property to the lender. Throughout the term of the loan (eg 25 years) the borrower will make monthly repayments to the lender, part of which represents a repayment of the capital sum borrowed. The balance is interest on the loan. At the end of the mortgage term, the loan has been completely repaid and the mortgage is discharged. If the borrower wants to sell the property before the end of the mortgage term, he will pay off the mortgage out of the proceeds of sale of the property, and any sum over and above this amount will belong to him.

The main disadvantage of this type of mortgage is that, if the borrower dies before the mortgage is paid off, the whole of the outstanding balance of the loan becomes immediately repayable from the deceased's estate. This can cause problems if the deceased borrower was the main salary earner for a family, leaving a non-earning spouse and children to cope with the repayment of the mortgage. This difficulty is easily surmounted by the borrower taking out a 'mortgage protection policy' to cover the amount of the loan. Such a policy will guarantee to repay the balance outstanding on the mortgage in the event of the borrower's death. Some policies will also cover permanent disability through accident or illness which prevent the borrower from earning his living. These policies are readily available, inexpensive (a small monthly premium is payable) and, in the case of co-owners, should be taken out over joint lives so that, even if one co-owner is not contributing financially to the mortgage, the repayment of the loan is guaranteed in the event of the death of either of them.

#### Endowment mortgage

An endowment mortgage provides additional security for the loan over the property by means of an insurance policy taken out on the borrower's life. The borrower mortgages the property to the lender and takes out a life policy in the same sum as the amount of the loan. He may also be required to mortgage or to deposit the policy with the lender for safe-keeping. During the mortgage term the borrower makes monthly repayments of interest only to the lender. No capital is repaid during the term of the mortgage. If the borrower dies during the term of the mortgage, the proceeds of the insurance policy will discharge the loan. At the end of the term, the policy 'matures' and should yield sufficient money to discharge the capital sum owing on the mortgage. Most endowment policies do not actually guarantee to repay the amount of the loan on maturity, although they do guarantee to discharge the loan on the death of the borrower. They are 'with profits' policies, which means that the policy holder shares in the profits made by the insurance company over the term of the policy. 'Bonuses', representing this share in the profits, are then added to the amount due on maturity, the expectation being that this will then be sufficient to repay the whole of the loan. Often the profits will be such that there will be an excess over the amount needed to repay the loan and this will then be payable to the borrower.

In the event of the borrower wanting to sell the property before the expiry of the mortgage term, he will have to repay the whole of the mortgage debt out of the proceeds of sale of the property. The insurance policy may then be terminated or transferred as security for another loan. Not all policies can be transferred in this way. The cash value of a policy which is surrendered during the early years of the mortgage will be very small. This type of mortgage may not always therefore be suitable for a borrower who is intending to resell the property within a few years. Since the borrower has to pay monthly premiums on the life policy, in addition to his monthly payments to the lender, this type of loan may be more expensive than a repayment mortgage. This, however, will depend upon the age and state of health of the borrower. Insurance companies will apply normal actuarial principles in assessing the amount of the premium, so that a young, fit and healthy borrower will pay less than an older borrower suffering from a chronic illness.

There has been much controversy in recent years with regard to the mis-selling of endowment mortgages. The danger is that when the endowment policy matures it will not produce enough money to pay off the full amount of the loan, leaving the borrower to find the shortfall from his own funds. It now seems to be accepted that for many people an endowment mortgage is not a good investment.

### *Pension mortgage*

As its name suggests, a pension mortgage links a mortgage of the property which the client is buying with pension arrangements for the client's retirement. This type of mortgage is generally only available to self-employed people and is beneficial (in terms of tax relief on the pension contributions) to high earners.

## 9.2.4 Lender's powers

Almost all mortgage deeds will give the lender power, expressly or impliedly, to repossess and sell the property in the event of default by the borrower. Some borrowers are unaware of this fact and the solicitor, without unnecessarily frightening the client, should point out to the client that these powers do exist and will be exercised by the lender if the need arises. It may therefore be sensible to check that the client is aware of his liability to make monthly repayments of the loan, and insurance premiums where appropriate, and that the amount of these monthly outgoings do not represent an unrealistically high proportion of the client's income. As a very rough guide, the amount of the client's net monthly mortgage repayment should not exceed about 25% of his net monthly income.

## 9.3  TAX RELIEF ON MORTGAGES

Tax relief used to be available on the interest paid in connection with a loan for the purchase of the borrower's home. However, this has been abolished as from April 2000.

## 9.4  FURTHER READING

Myles MacCormack *Mortgage Planning: Guidance for Solicitors Marketing Financial Services* (The Law Society)

# Chapter 10

# ADVISING JOINT BUYERS

## 10.1  ADVISING THE CLIENT

Where it is apparent from instructions that the property is to be occupied and/or financed by two or more adults, the solicitor should discuss with his client(s) the advantages and disadvantages of co-ownership and the various methods by which the client's wishes can be carried out. A note of the client's instructions should be made on the file to ensure that they are implemented at the appropriate stage of the transaction (ie in the purchase deed).

There are three possible alternatives which need to be discussed with the clients:

(a)  sole ownership by one of the clients; or
(b)  ownership by all as joint tenants; or
(c)  ownership by all as tenants in common.

The following points should be borne in mind.

(1)  Instructions should be obtained directly from all proposed co-owners. It is not sufficient to accept the word of one co-owner that his or her cohabitee agrees to the proposals.
(2)  Advising more than one party in the same transaction (ie the two or more co-buyers) may give rise to a conflict of interests between them, for example, where the beneficial interest in the property is to be held in unequal shares. The solicitor must ensure that the co-owners receive separate independent advice in any situation where a conflict arises or is likely to arise (see Chapter 6).

## 10.2  SUITABILITY OF EACH METHOD

### 10.2.1  Sole ownership

This is generally only suitable where the other occupier is not contributing to the purchase price in any way. It will mean, however, that the non-owning occupier will legally have no say in any future disposition of the property. However, a spouse will have rights of occupation under the Family Law Act 1996 and may prevent a sale by registering those rights.

If the occupier is making a financial contribution, it may well be preferable to consider one of the forms of co-ownership. Whatever type of co-ownership is chosen, all co-owners have to join in (and thus agree to) any disposition. However, if there is to be a mortgage on the property, all co-owners will be required to join in this and thus make themselves personally liable to repay the loan. This may well not be what the parties intend.

If an occupier making a contribution were not to become a co-owner, it may well still not be possible for a sale or other disposition to be made without his consent anyway. He will have an overriding interest under s 70(1)(g) of the Land

Registration Act 1925 (see **4.7.2**) and, as such, will be required to release those rights on a disposition; otherwise they will be binding on a purchaser irrespective of notice. In theory, the sole owner of the legal estate can appoint another trustee and thus overreach the overriding interest of the occupier (see *City of London Building Society v Flegg* [1988] AC 54). However, in practice, if a sale is contemplated and the occupier is refusing to leave, it may well still be necessary to obtain a court order to evict the occupier and thus give a buyer vacant possession.

The possibility of a conflict of interest arising should be very carefully borne in mind in advising in this area.

### 10.2.2 Joint tenancy

All cases of co-ownership give rise to a trust of land (see **3.8**). The maximum number of legal owners is four. As with any form of co-ownership, all of the legal co-owners must join in any future disposition of the property. In case of a dispute, an application can be made to the court under s 14 of the Trusts of Land and Appointment of Trustees Act 1996. The court can make whatever order it thinks fit, but will particularly take into account the purpose for which the land was bought.

On the death of a joint tenant, the right of survivorship will apply, and this will make a joint tenancy particularly suitable for married couples and others in a permanent relationship who want their interest in the house to go to the other party on their death. If the parties wish to be able to leave their respective shares by will, eg where they have children from a previous relationship, then a tenancy in common will be necessary.

A joint tenancy can subsequently be 'severed', ie converted into a tenancy in common. This will then destroy the right of survivorship and allow an owner's share to be left by will to whomsoever he pleases.

However, joint tenants always have equal rights in the property, irrespective of their contributions to the purchase price. Thus, if A and B buy as joint tenants, A having contributed 90% of the price and B only 10%, on a subsequent severance, B will acquire a one half share in the land. If the parties want recognition to be given to their respective contributions, then a tenancy in common will be required from the outset.

### 10.2.3 Tenancy in common

This would be usual in the case of business partners and other circumstances where the parties do not wish the right of survivorship to apply, for example where the parties are not co-habiting or not in a long-term relationship, or want to be able to make provision for others out of their interest on death, or want the amount of their contribution to the purchase price to be recognised in the size of their share in the land.

It is essential in a tenancy in common for the respective shares of the co-owners to be expressly recorded. This will be included in the transfer passing the legal estate to them, but this will be retained by the Land Registry for registration purposes. It is sensible, therefore, for a duplicate transfer to be drawn up and executed by the parties; this should then be kept in a safe place as evidence of the parties' rights.

As with a joint tenancy, all of the co-owners of the legal estate must join in a disposition. Disputes can again be resolved by the court under s 14 of the Trusts of Land and Appointment of Trustees Act 1996.

In the case of business partners, it is preferable for the exact shares of the partners not to be recorded in the transfer itself. This is because those shares might change due to a reorganisation of the partnership, for example on the admission of a new partner. It is preferable for the shares of the co-owners to be dealt with exclusively by the partnership agreement and for the transfer to make it clear that they hold as tenants in common in the shares as set out in the partnership agreement.

# Chapter 11

# FIXTURES AND FITTINGS

## 11.1 FIXTURES

Fixtures are generally items which are attached to and form part of the land (eg fitted wardrobes) and will therefore be included as part of the property on sale of the land unless the seller expressly reserves the right to remove them, ie by including a contractual condition to this effect such as 'the seller reserves the right to remove the garden seat and stone ornaments from the property before completion'.

Except where the seller has reserved the right to remove specific items, the buyer can expect to take over the ownership of fixtures on completion; they are part of the property which he has purchased and their value is included in the purchase price.

## 11.2 FITTINGS

Fittings, or chattels (eg carpets and curtains) do not form part of the land and so are not included as part of the property on sale of the land unless the seller expressly agrees to leave them behind. Any fittings which are to be included in the sale should be specifically itemised in the contract or, in residential transactions, a special condition in the contract may refer to the Fixtures Fittings and Contents Form attached to the contract (see **11.6**).

Some fittings may be included in the sale price of the property. These are normally expressly mentioned in the estate agent's particulars of sale; otherwise the seller and buyer will need to reach agreement over an additional price which the buyer is to pay for the purchase of the fittings.

## 11.3 PRACTICAL DISTINCTION

The legal distinction between fixtures and fittings as outlined above is quite clear, but the practical distinction between the two categories is sometimes less obvious. Moveable objects which are not attached to the land, such as carpets, curtains and free-standing furniture clearly fall within the definition of fittings, but items which are attached to the land are not always classified as fixtures. Case-law in this area is unclear and there have been reported cases where items such as greenhouses and garden ornaments have been held to be fixtures, and other cases where the same type of items have been held to be fittings (see *TSB Bank plc v Botham* (1997) 73 P & CR D1).

## 11.4  NEED FOR CERTAINTY IN CONTRACT

Disputes over the unexpected removal of fixtures and fittings are common and frequently cost more to resolve than the value of the disputed items. The estate agent's particulars should be scrutinised to see which items are listed as being included or excluded from the sale, and checked with the client to ensure their accuracy. When taking instructions, it will be necessary to ascertain from the client which items are to be removed, which items he expects to remain at the property, and whether any price in addition to the price of the land is required for the fittings.

In view of the uncertainty of the status of some items in law, it is essential that in appropriate circumstances the contract expressly deals with:

(1)  fixtures which the seller intends to remove on or before completion;
(2)  fittings which are to remain at the property;
(3)  any additional price which the buyer is to pay for the fittings;
(4)  postponement of passing of title to fittings until completion; in the absence of such a condition, the Sale of Goods Act 1979, s 18 will provide that title to the fittings passes to the buyer on exchange (this provision is contained in Standard Condition 9);
(5)  a warranty that fittings are free of incumbrances (eg subsisting hire-purchase agreements). In the absence of an express special condition dealing with this matter, Standard Condition 9, by making the contract one for the sale of goods, implicitly imports s 12 of the Sale of Goods Act 1979 which contains such a warranty.

## 11.5  APPORTIONMENT OF PURCHASE PRICE

The sale of chattels does not attract stamp duty. The value of chattels which have been included in the purchase price of the land can therefore be deducted from the total purchase price, producing a reduction in the value of the land and a possible consequent reduction in the amount of stamp duty payable by the buyer. This apportionment of the purchase price between the land and the chattels is of most value to the buyer when the value of the land and chattels together is marginally above the current stamp duty threshold. Thus a purchase for exactly £60,000 will pay no duty, but a purchase for £61,000 will attract £610 in duty. So if £1,000 can be attributed to the chattels, the purchase price of the land will be reduced to £60,000 and will be exempt from duty, a saving of £610 for the buyer. Similar savings can be made if the purchase price is just above the £250,000 and £500,000 thresholds for the higher rates of duty (see **8.4**).

Only the true value of the chattels may be deducted from the purchase price for this purpose. Any overvaluation of the price of the chattels is a fraud on the Inland Revenue which may render both the solicitor and his client liable to criminal sanctions. Such conduct would also be conduct unbefitting a solicitor which could result in disciplinary proceedings being brought against the solicitor concerned. A further consequence of an overvaluation is that the contract for the sale of the land would be unenforceable by court action, since it could be construed by the courts as being a contract to defraud the Inland Revenue; such contracts are unenforceable on the grounds of public policy (see *Saunders v Edwards* [1987] 2 All ER 651).

## 11.6 FIXTURES FITTINGS AND CONTENTS FORM

The Protocol requires the seller's solicitor to obtain information relating to fixtures and fittings from the seller, using the standard Fixtures Fittings and Contents Form. The completed form should then be sent to the buyer's solicitors with the draft contract. Special Condition 4 on the reverse of the Standard Conditions of Sale form makes reference to the Fixtures Fittings and Contents Form and, in appropriate cases, requires it to be annexed to and form part of the contract.

# Chapter 12

# SURVEYS

## 12.1 WHEN SHOULD A SURVEY BE COMMISSIONED?

In an ideal world, the client should always have a survey carried out before exchange of contracts, but many buyers, particularly first-time buyers for whom the expense of a survey is a major consideration, do not commission an independent survey, preferring to rely instead on the valuation undertaken by their lender. Most lenders disclose their written valuation reports to their customers.

The Government's Homes Bill will require sellers of residential properties to provide prospective buyers with a 'Seller's Pack'. This will contain a simple form of structural survey and may obviate the need for the buyer to commission his own survey. However, at the time of writing it was not intended that the proposed survey would contain a valuation of the property, so mortgage lenders may well still need to commission their own valuation (see **12.3.1**).

## 12.2 REASONS FOR A SURVEY

The caveat emptor rule places on the buyer the onus of discovering any physical faults in the property agreed to be sold. For this reason alone, a survey is always advisable in order to discover physical defects which are not readily apparent on inspection of the property by the lay client.

## 12.3 TYPES OF SURVEY

The client has three main choices open to him:

(1)  to rely on the valuation made by his lender;
(2)  to commission a 'Home Buyer's Valuation and Survey Report';
(3)  to commission a full structural survey.

### 12.3.1 Valuation

A valuation will be undertaken by the buyer's lender in order to establish whether the property being purchased will be adequate security for the amount of the loan. The buyer pays the cost of this valuation and is usually permitted to see the valuer's report, but the report will not necessarily reveal sufficient information about the state of the property to allow the buyer to make a reasoned judgement as to whether or not to proceed with his purchase. As its name suggests, it just assesses the value of the property; it will not contain a detailed commentary on the state of the structure of the property.

### 12.3.2  Home Buyer's Valuation and Survey Report

The Home Buyer's Valuation and Survey Report represents a compromise between the mortgage valuation and the full survey and is an attractive option for a client who is reluctant to commission a full survey. In many cases the buyer's lender will agree (for an additional fee) to instruct the lender's valuer to undertake the survey at the same time as the mortgage valuation is carried out with consequent savings in time and expense for the client. Although of much more value to the client than a mere valuation, this type of survey is still relatively superficial in scope.

### 12.3.3  Full survey

The potential expense of a full survey deters many clients, but the client might be reminded that £500 abortive expense on a survey is preferable to discovering that many thousands of pounds need to be spent on carrying out structural repairs to the property he has just purchased without the benefit of a survey. A full structural survey will provide a detailed commentary on the condition of the structure of the building.

## 12.4  FACTORS INDICATING DESIRABILITY OF A FULL SURVEY

The need for a full structural survey may be indicated by the presence of one or more of the following factors:

(1)  the property is of a high value;
(2)  the amount of the buyer's intended mortgage represents a low proportion of the purchase price (eg 70% or less);
(3)  the property is more than 100 years old;
(4)  the buyer intends to alter or extend the property after completion;
(5)  the property is not of conventional brick and mortar construction;
(6)  the proximity of the property to features which may cause subsidence or other structural problems (eg mines, rivers, clay sub-soils);
(7)  the property is not detached.

## 12.5  SURVEYS IN SPECIAL CASES

A surveyor, even when instructed to carry out a full structural survey, will not normally investigate drainage or electrical systems. A property which does not have the benefit of mains drainage will require a separate drainage survey from an expert in that field, since the cost of repair or replacement of a private drainage system can be prohibitive. Liability for escaping effluent can also involve civil and criminal penalties. An environmental survey may also be required – see **5.14**.

## 12.6  FLATS AND OTHER ATTACHED PROPERTIES

Where the property to be purchased is a flat or is a property which is structurally attached to neighbouring property, a full survey is desirable. The structural soundness of the property being bought is, in these circumstances, dependent on the soundness of the neighbouring property also, and the surveyor must therefore be instructed to inspect the main structure of the building and the adjoining property (if possible) as well as the property actually being purchased.

## 12.7 SURVEYOR'S LIABILITY

The surveyor owes a duty of care to his client to carry out his survey with reasonable skill and care. This common law duty is reinforced by the Supply of Goods and Services Act 1982, s 13, which implies into a contract for services a term that the work will be carried out with reasonable skill and care. Where a client suffers loss as a result of a negligent survey an action can be sustained against his surveyor, subject to the validity of any exemption clause which may have formed part of the surveyor's terms of work. The normal rules relating to remoteness of damage apply, thus the client will not sustain a successful action unless the area of the client's complaint lies within the scope of what the surveyor was instructed to do, hence the importance of giving full and explicit instructions when the survey is commissioned.

Where the client suffers loss after having relied on a lender's valuer's report, an action in tort may lie against the surveyor. No action in contract can be sustained because the survey was commissioned by the lender, and so there is no contractual relationship between the buyer and the surveyor. The success of such an action may again depend on the validity of any exclusion clause contained in the valuation. However, it was held by the House of Lords in *Smith v Eric S Bush (a Firm)* [1990] 1 AC 831 that a valuer instructed by a lender to carry out a mortgage valuation of a modest house, in the knowledge that the buyer would rely on the valuation without obtaining an independent survey, owed a duty of care to the buyer to exercise reasonable care and skill in carrying out the valuation.

# Chapter 13

# ACTION FOLLOWING INSTRUCTIONS

## 13.1 AFTER THE INTERVIEW: BOTH PARTIES

### 13.1.1 Attendance note

An attendance note should be made as soon as possible after the interview, recording exactly what took place at the interview, the instructions received and the advice given. The time spent in the interview should be noted on the attendance note for time-recording purposes.

It is important that a detailed written record of the interview exists on the solicitor's file. The written record provides a reminder to the solicitor of what needs to be done, and evidence of what took place between solicitor and client in case of a later dispute between them.

### 13.1.2 Confirming instructions to the client

In order to ensure that no misunderstanding exists between solicitor and client, instructions should always be confirmed to the client in writing as soon as possible after the interview has taken place. The letter should contain a full record of what happened at the interview, including a repetition of the instructions given by the client and the advice given by the solicitor. The letter should also deal with information as to costs, confirm any action agreed to be taken by the solicitor, and remind the client of anything which he promised to do (eg obtain his building society account number). To comply with the Solicitors' Practice Rules 1990, the letter must also give details of who in the solicitor's firm is dealing with the client's matter and whom the client should contact in the event of a complaint about the solicitor's services.

### 13.1.3 Letters to other parties

If not already done, contact should be established with the representatives of the other parties involved in the transaction, such as the other party's solicitor, the estate agent, and the client's lender. Any such letter is likely to be merely introductory, saying that the solicitor has been instructed to act in the transaction, on what terms the client has agreed to proceed, and that the solicitor will contact the third party further in due course.

#### (1) 'Subject to contract'

For historical reasons, it used to be customary for all correspondence preceding the contract, including this type of introductory letter, to be headed 'Subject to contract'. The purpose of the inclusion of this phrase was to ensure that no contract was inadvertently entered into between the seller and buyer before they fully intended to do so. In view of the provisions of the Law of Property (Miscellaneous Provisions) Act 1989 (see **3.10.1**), it is extremely unlikely that a client could inadvertently form a contract by letter, so the inclusion of the 'subject to contract' phrase is unnecessary on pre-contract correspondence, but it is still frequently encountered in practice.

### *(2) Telephone call*

A telephone call to the third party (provided it is recorded by means of an attendance note on the file) would suffice in place of a letter in these circumstances. The object of the exercise is to establish contact between all the parties who are involved in the transaction, and any method of doing this quickly is therefore acceptable. Sending correspondence by fax is also routinely used to speed up transactions; more and more solicitors are also starting to use e-mail as a method of communication.

### *(3) The estate agent*

Apart from letting the estate agent know the name and address of the solicitor and of his client, it is always useful to have a copy of the estate agent's particulars of sale on file. These particulars can provide useful information relating to the area in which the property is sited, which may indicate to the solicitor that particular searches and enquiries may be required. They will also contain details of the fixtures and fittings at the property and whether or not these are to be included in the sale (see Chapter 11).

## 13.2 FOR THE SELLER

### 13.2.1 Obtain title deeds

The seller's solicitor needs to have access to the title deeds (land or charge certificate in registered land) in order to check that the seller owns and is entitled to sell what he has instructed the solicitor to sell, and to draft the contract of sale.

If the seller does not have a subsisting mortgage on the property, he may have the title deeds himself, or they might be kept, for example, in the solicitor's strong-room or in a bank safe deposit box. The whereabouts of the deeds will have been ascertained from the seller in the initial interview.

Where the seller has a subsisting mortgage on the property, his title deeds (Charge Certificate in Registered Land) will usually be kept in safe custody by his lender who will be reluctant to hand them over to the seller or his representative without a guarantee that the loan is to be repaid.

When writing to the lender to ask for the title deeds, it is customary to pre-empt the lender's request about the repayment of the loan, and to include in the letter an undertaking that the solicitor will either repay the loan to the lender (thus ending the mortgage and entitling the seller to the return of his deeds) or, at the lender's request, return the deeds to him. This type of undertaking is normally acceptable to the lender, who will then release the deeds to the solicitor on the terms of the undertaking. The undertaking is a solicitor's undertaking, subject to the usual rules as to enforceability, and care must therefore be taken in wording it to ensure that what it promises to do is within the solicitor's control to perform (see LPC Resource Book *Pervasive and Core Topics* (Jordans), Part II).

Under s 63 of the Land Registration Act 1925, a lender may request the Registry to retain the charge certificate in the Registry. Where this has happened, an entry will be made in the charges register stating that the certificate has been retained in the Registry. In such a case, there is no need to obtain the charge certificate.

## 13.2.2  Amount outstanding on mortgage

When writing to the lender, it may also be prudent to ascertain the approximate amount outstanding on the seller's mortgage (a redemption figure) to ensure that there will be sufficient funds from the sale to pay off (redeem) the mortgage and the costs associated with the sale and that the surplus (if any) is sufficient for the seller's requirements (eg to put towards the purchase of another property). At this stage, an approximate redemption figure only need be obtained (eg to the nearest £500); nearer completion an exact figure can be confirmed with the lender. Where the seller has several mortgages on the same property, redemption figures should be obtained from each lender.

## 13.2.3  Office copy entries

When the land being sold is an interest in registered land, the seller's solicitor should make an application to the district land registry for the area in which the land is situated for office copies of the register entries. This application is usually made on Form 109, which is an application for copies of the register entries and filed plan only. Where additional documents are known to be filed at HM Land Registry (eg a copy of a conveyance imposing restrictive covenants), it may be necessary to apply for copies of these documents on Form 110.

The application is usually sent to the district land registry by post, although registries will accept applications by telephone and fax. An on-line computer service (Land Registry Direct) is also available, giving direct access to the register and enabling a solicitor to immediately print off copy entries. A fee is payable for obtaining office copies, but this can be paid by credit account, provided the solicitor's 'key number' (account number) is entered on the application form.

The purposes of obtaining office copies are:

(1)  to check that the information supplied by the seller in relation to his title, and that contained in the land or charge certificate, is supported by the information contained in the office copies. The office copies are an official and up-to-date copy of the actual register entries, which therefore represent the true state of the title at the date of their issue. The land or charge certificate in the solicitor's possession may not have been updated by HM Land Registry for several years (eg since the seller bought the land) and it is important for the seller's solicitor to know precisely what entries are now present on the register so that he can take account of these in drafting the contract of sale;

(2)  during the course of the transaction, the seller will need to prove his ownership of the property to the buyer. In registered land this is done by supplying the buyer with (inter alia) office copies of the register entries.

When the office copies are received from HM Land Registry, they should be examined to ensure that they do not contain anything of which the solicitor was previously unaware (if they do, instructions must be obtained immediately), and a photocopy should be taken. The seller's solicitor will need to keep a copy of the register entries in his own file to refer to during the transaction, and he must supply the buyer with the original of the office copies.

### 13.2.4  Preparation of the pre-contract package

The seller's solicitor should then start preparing the pre-contract package which will have to be sent to the buyer. This will contain, as a minimum, two copies of the draft contract (see Chapter 14) and details of the seller's title to the property (see Chapter 16), but if the Protocol is being adopted it will also need to contain the following:

(i)   the Seller's Property Information Form: this was handed to the seller for completion at the initial interview;

(ii)  the Fixtures Fittings and Contents Form: this was also given to the seller for completion at the first interview;

(iii) in unregistered land, an Index Map search at HM Land Registry. This is to ensure that the land is indeed unregistered and that there are no interests registered at the Land Registry adverse to the seller's title. The seller should put this search in hand as soon as possible (see Chapter 18);

(iv)  in unregistered land, a land charges search against the seller and all other previous estate owners revealed by the title deeds against whom there is not already a search with the deeds upon which it is safe to rely (see Chapter 18). This will reveal incumbrances affecting the property and whether any insolvency proceedings have been commenced against the seller;

(v)   copies of planning permissions relating to the property; and

(vi)  copies of any other certificates, consents, etc, relating to the property (eg a guarantee in relation to the insertion of a new damp proof course).

The object of this package is to supply the buyer with all the information he needs to make his mind up whether or not to proceed with the transaction. If the buyer is supplied with a complete package of information at the start of the transaction, it is likely to run more smoothly and speedily, as time will not be wasted in the buyer having to make repeated requests for information and documents from the seller. Although this information is only required in a Protocol transaction, similar packages are also being provided in other transactions. The Government's Homes Bill, currently before Parliament, will require the seller to provide a buyer with a 'Seller's Pack' containing similar information and a form of structural survey.

## 13.3  FOR THE BUYER

### 13.3.1  Search applications

The buyer's solicitor should, as soon as is practicable, put in hand such pre-contract searches as are appropriate to the property in question (see Chapter 18).

### 13.3.2  Mortgage and survey arrangements

The buyer's solicitor should deal with his client's mortgage and survey arrangements if required to do so. In many cases, the client will already have approached a lender and submitted a mortgage application form before seeing the solicitor, and this step will therefore be unnecessary (see Chapter 9). Surveys are dealt with in Chapter 12.

### 13.3.3 The pre-contract package

When the pre-contract package is received from the seller's solicitor, its contents must be studied carefully to ensure that what is being offered for sale by the seller matches the instructions given by, and expectations of, the buyer (see Chapter 19).

**Part III**

# PROCEDURE LEADING TO EXCHANGE

# Chapter 14

# THE DRAFT CONTRACT

## 14.1 PURPOSE OF THE CONTRACT

The purpose of the contract is to define the extent of the land to be sold and to set out the terms on which the seller is prepared to sell. It is the seller's right and duty to draft the contract, since only he will know precisely what he is prepared to sell and on what terms (eg as to price). Drafting the contract is the most important task which the seller's solicitor has to perform. It is arguably the most important task in the whole transaction since, if the terms of the contract are well drafted, the transaction will usually proceed smoothly to completion. Conversely, a badly drafted contract may give rise to problems. It is vital therefore that the utmost care is exercised in drafting the contract.

Although it is the seller's prerogative to dictate the terms on which he is prepared to sell, this does not necessarily mean that he is entitled to draft a contract which is entirely in his own favour and which contains terms prejudicial to the intending buyer. The contract terms are open to negotiation with the buyer and, unless the bargaining strength of the seller is very strong (caused perhaps by the state of the property market generally or, in some cases, by the nature of the property being sold), the seller must be prepared to concede some points in the buyer's favour.

Ultimately, contract drafting is an exercise in the art of compromise. The seller's solicitor must ensure that the terms of the contract adequately protect his own client's interests, but at the same time provide a sufficiently attractive package to persuade the buyer to proceed with the purchase.

Two identical contracts are prepared by the seller's solicitor, both of which are sent to the buyer's solicitor with the pre-contract documentation for his approval. This chapter outlines the legal formalities and contents of a contract for the sale of land, but does not discuss drafting techniques. These are explained in the LPC Resource Book *Skills for Lawyers* (Jordans).

## 14.2 INVESTIGATION OF TITLE

Having obtained office copies of the register of title (registered land) or the seller's title deeds or a copy of them (unregistered land), the seller's solicitor should investigate title before drafting the contract for sale. The method of investigation is dealt with in Chapter 17.

### 14.2.1 Reasons for investigation

Investigation of the title by the seller's solicitor at this stage of the transaction is a precautionary measure to ensure that:

(1) the seller is the owner of, or is otherwise entitled to sell, the whole of the estate which he intends to sell;

(2) any incumbrances on the title can be disclosed in the draft contract in order to satisfy the seller's duty of disclosure (see **14.7**);

(3) any defects in the title are discovered and appropriate steps taken to correct them before exchange of contracts;

(4) any consents which may be necessary from third parties can be obtained;

(5) any queries relating to the title by the buyer can be anticipated.

## 14.2.2 Capacity

While investigating the seller's title, it is necessary to check that the seller is entitled to sell the whole of the estate in the land which he intends to sell. The following circumstances should be considered.

### Sole owner

A sole owner, who owns the whole of the legal and equitable interest for his own benefit (a 'beneficial owner'), will normally have unlimited powers of disposal.

### Trustees (including co-owners)

Where land is held on a trust of land (including a trust arising through co-ownership), any conveyance or transfer of the land must be made by all the trustees, being at least two individuals or a trust corporation, in order to overreach the equitable interests of the beneficiaries. The trustees are normally under a duty to consult with the beneficiaries before selling the land, but a buyer is not bound to enquire whether this has been done (Trusts of Land and Appointment of Trustees Act 1996, s 16).

Trustees of land have the same powers of disposal as a beneficial owner, unless these have been restricted by the terms of the trust. The trust may, for example, require the consent of named persons before a sale takes place, and the sellers must ensure that they obtain all such consents. In registered land, any such limitations on the powers of disposal will be indicated by a restriction on the proprietorship register.

### Personal representatives

Personal representatives have all the powers of trustees of land but are only entitled to exercise those powers during the administration (Administration of Estates Act 1925, s 39). Their powers are joint as to land, whether freehold or leasehold, therefore if a grant of representation has been made in favour of more than one person, they all must be parties to the contract and the purchase deed. However, a grant of representation can be validly made in favour of a single person and in such a case he can act on his own – there is no need for a second personal representative to be appointed. The usual principles of overreaching apply to a sale by personal representatives.

### Mortgagees

In order to sell the property, the lender must have an express or implied power of sale, and that power must have arisen and become exercisable. A power of sale is implied in every mortgage made by deed unless expressly excluded (Law of Property Act 1925, s 101). A legal mortgage must be made by deed (Law of Property Act 1925, s 85). It therefore follows that a legal lender will always have a power of sale unless (exceptionally) that power has been expressly excluded. A lender who is exercising his power of sale must ensure that:

(1) his power of sale exists;
(2) the power has arisen; and
(3) the power has become exercisable.

The power of sale arises on the legal date for redemption. This will be specified in the mortgage and is usually a date early on in the mortgage term (eg one month after the money was advanced). This is so even if the loan is to be repaid over (say) 25 years.

The lender's power becomes exercisable in the circumstances set out in the mortgage deed. If there are no such terms, then it is exercisable if one of the three conditions set out in the Law of Property Act 1925, s 103 is met:

(1) notice requiring payment of the principal money has been served on the borrower and default has been made in payment of the principal money for 3 months; or
(2) some interest under the mortgage is in arrear and unpaid for 2 months after becoming due; or
(3) there has been breach of some other provision contained in the mortgage deed or the Law of Property Act 1925.

### *Charities*

If there is no restriction on the proprietorship register of registered land owned by a charity, a buyer may safely deal with the charity as if it were a sole owner. If there is a restriction on the register or the land is unregistered, consent may be required from the Charity Commissioners under ss 36–40 of the Charities Act 1993. These provisions are outside the scope of this book.

### *Companies*

A company which is regulated by the Companies Acts may deal with land, provided the transaction is within the scope of the objects clause of its memorandum of association (one of its constitutional documents). It would be unusual for a normal trading company to lack the power to hold or dispose of an estate in land, although restrictions on granting mortgages may be encountered. In the case of registered land, if the company's powers are limited, an appropriate restriction will be entered on the proprietorship register.

### *Persons suffering from mental disability*

A contract for the sale or purchase of land entered into by a person who is suffering from mental incapacity sufficient to deprive him of understanding of the nature of the transaction is voidable at the option of the incapacitated party, provided he can prove that, at the time of the transaction, the other contracting party was aware of the disability (*Broughton v Snook* [1938] Ch 505).

Once a receiver is appointed under the Mental Health Act 1983, s 99, the patient loses all contractual capacity and any purported inter vivos disposition by him is void. The receiver has power, subject to the court's approval, to deal with the patient's property (see the Mental Health Act 1983, ss 95 and 96).

*Fiduciary relationships*

Where a fiduciary relationship exists between the parties to the transaction, there is a presumption of constructive fraud which is rebuttable on proof by the dominant party to the relationship:

(1) that the transaction was at a fair price (an independent valuation should be obtained);

(2) that all the circumstances of the transaction were known to the subordinate party; and

(3) that each party received, or was given a proper opportunity to take, independent legal advice.

The transaction is prima facie voidable at the instance of the subordinate party.

A fiduciary relationship is deemed to exist in dealings between the following persons:

(1) solicitor and client;

(2) trustee and beneficiary;

(3) parent and child (where the influence of the parent over the child may be held to have endured beyond the child's majority);

(4) doctor and patient;

(5) religious adviser and disciple;

(6) teacher and pupil;

(7) fiancé(e)s (but not between husband and wife).

A fiduciary relationship may exist in circumstances other than those listed above, but it is not presumed, and the dominance of one party over the other would have to be proved before the court would apply the doctrine of constructive fraud (see, for example, *Lloyds Bank v Bundy* [1975] QB 326 where a fiduciary relationship was proved to have existed between a bank manager and his customer).

If a solicitor is asked to act in dealings between any of the parties listed above or in any other situation where he feels that the relationship between the contracting parties may be classed as fiduciary, he should ensure that:

(1) an independent valuation of the property is obtained;

(2) all the facts pertaining to the transaction are known by and understood by both parties; and

(3) the parties are separately represented.

## 14.2.3 Breach of a restrictive covenant or other defect in title

If investigation of the title reveals a breach of a restrictive covenant which cannot be remedied (eg by obtaining retrospective consent from the person with the benefit of the covenant), consideration should be given to obtaining restrictive covenant indemnity insurance to cover the breach. Insurance is not available for all breaches of covenant.

Other defects or problems with the title which can be corrected (eg by the appointment of a new trustee) should be rectified as soon as possible. Defects which are irremediable will have to be revealed in the draft contract. It must be anticipated that the buyer will require these matters to be remedied before agreeing to purchase the property. Defective title insurance may also be available to cover certain defects.

## 14.2.4  Planning

Although not strictly a matter of title, the seller's solicitor should check at this stage that any necessary planning or building regulation consents have been obtained and complied with (see Chapter 5). Copies of such consents should be obtained from the local authority for the buyer's use. It must be anticipated that the buyer will request sight of these if they are not provided.

## 14.3  THE ANATOMY OF A CONTRACT

A contract for the sale of land usually comprises three distinct parts:

(1)  the particulars of sale;
(2)  the conditions of sale; and
(3)  the memorandum of agreement.

The particulars describe the estate in and physical extent of the land being sold, sometimes by reference to a plan attached to the contract (see **14.5**). The conditions will set out the terms on which the land is agreed to be sold (see **14.6** and **14.7**). The memorandum states that the seller agrees to sell the property and the buyer to buy it at a specified price and contains the signatures of the parties.

## 14.3.1  Terms of the contract

The terms of the contract are dictated by the following.

### *(1)  Open contract rules*

The open contract rules represent the general law on any particular point connected with a contract for sale of land. Some of the rules are based on the common law and some derive from statute (eg Law of Property Act 1925).

The rules imply conditions into a contract where nothing is expressly stated with regard to a particular matter, ie where the contract is 'open' on that point.

Some of the rules operate adequately but others are not satisfactory and are invariably altered by express provision in the contract. Even the rules which do not cause a problem are usually repeated expressly in the contract in the interests of certainty. As most matters are dealt with expressly the open contract rules have little significance in modern conveyancing.

### *(2)  Standard conditions of sale*

As many matters relevant to the sale of land are common to all transactions, standard sets of conditions exist which can be incorporated into a contract of sale. Standard conditions sometimes follow the open contract position but in other cases operate to clarify or amend that position.

### *(3)  Special conditions*

Special conditions are conditions expressly included by the parties because of the circumstances of the transaction or its particular requirements. They are usually used to supplement standard conditions and in some cases will refine or vary the standard condition position.

## 14.4 STANDARD FORMS OF CONTRACT

A solicitor will usually draft a contract either by using a standard form of contract purchased from a law stationers or incorporating a standard set of conditions into a contract generated from his word-processing system. Many of the conditions of sale which are needed in the contract are common to all transactions, so it is advantageous to the solicitor to make use of a standard set of these conditions, which have been drafted by experts and which will be familiar to the buyer's solicitor who will in due course need to look at the terms of the contract very carefully from his own client's point of view.

Many contracts for the sale of land are currently drafted by reference to the Standard Conditions of Sale (The Law Society and Oyez) 3rd edn. These conditions are referred to in context throughout this Resource Book. An example of the front and back pages of the Standard Conditions of Sale form is set out at **14.11**. The centre pages of this document contain the 'small print' of the agreement and are set out in full in Appendix 2.

As an alternative to using the standard form contract purchased from law stationers, the solicitor may produce his own version of the contract on his own word processor, but will then need to include in that document a clause which states that 'the contract is deemed to include the Standard Conditions of Sale, 3rd Edition'. This phrase is necessary to incorporate the text of the Standard Conditions within the typed contract, and to ensure that all the terms of the contract are incorporated in writing as required by the Law of Property (Miscellaneous Provisions) Act 1989, s 2. Use of the Standard Conditions of Sale is encouraged in Protocol cases.

Although the use of the Standard Conditions was widespread in residential transactions, they were not designed for, nor entirely suitable for, commercial transactions. The Law Society and Oyez have now produced the Standard Commercial Property Conditions for use in commercial transactions. These are discussed in Chapter 42 and set out in Appendix 3. Although they are based on the residential Standard Conditions, there are many differences to meet the differing needs of a commercial transaction. The Commercial Conditions use the same numbering scheme as the residential Standard Conditions, so that, for example, Condition 3 in both deals with the seller's duty of disclosure. Most solicitors dealing with sales of commercial property will not use the printed form of contract but will produce their own word processed version incorporating one or other set of Standard Conditions. The word processed version will normally include numerous variations and additions to the Standard Conditions.

## 14.5 THE PARTICULARS OF SALE

The particulars of sale describe the estate in land which is being sold, ie whether it is freehold or leasehold, and the physical extent of that land. They may also contain a reference to easements and covenants which benefit the land (eg the benefit of a right of way). The aim of the particulars is to give a clear and concise description of the property. Where the land being sold can be identified by a regular postal address and has clearly marked boundaries, describing it by reference to its postal address and, in the case of registered land, its title number will suffice. In other cases, for example, the sale of agricultural land or on a sale of part only of the seller's property, a fuller description will be needed and reference must be made to a plan attached to the contract showing the precise delineation of the land to be sold. The existing description of the land as contained in the property register (registered land) or title deeds (unregistered land) can be used as the starting-point for drafting a suitable description in such cases.

## 14.5.1 Plans

A plan must be used on a sale of part of land (which includes the grant of leases of flats) and may be desirable in other cases, for example, where the boundaries of the property are not self-evident, but is generally not necessary for the sale of the whole of a freehold registered title. Whatever type of plan is used, it must be of sufficient size and scale to enable the boundaries and other features of the property to be identified readily (see *Scarfe v Adams* [1981] 1 All ER 843). A plan on a scale of 1:1,250 will be adequate in most cases, but a larger scale will usually be required for sales of flats or the division of buildings into separate units.

### *Boundaries*

Boundaries shown on plans prepared by HM Land Registry are general boundaries only and may not show the precise line of the boundaries of the property (Land Registration Rules 1925, r 278). A Land Registry plan may not therefore be reliable for use as a contract plan.

### *Scale plans*

The use of a scale plan is preferable, but it must be entirely accurate and should show the scale used on the plan itself. A hand-drawn plan which is not to scale may be adequate in simple transactions (eg the sale of part of a garden), but is inappropriate for use in a sale of flats or of a commercial property. Measurements must be shown in metric units.

### *Drawing a plan*

An existing plan in the title deeds may be used as the starting-point for the preparation of the plan but should not be photocopied and reused because photocopying distorts the plan and may make it inaccurate. A filed plan obtained with office copy entries may not be drawn on a sufficiently large scale to enable it to be used. Large-scale Ordnance Survey maps can be obtained from HMSO, but a licence is needed to photocopy these maps. Where the value or complexity of the transaction justifies the expense, an architect or surveyor may be instructed to prepare a plan. If there is any doubt as to the size or extent of the property, an inspection should be carried out and measurements taken. The seller usually bears the cost of the preparation of the plan.

### *Showing features on the plan*

The wording of the contract and of the purchase deed will need to make reference to the plan and its various features and this point should be borne in mind when the plan is drawn (eg a right of way can be more easily described in words in the contract if its beginning and end points are marked 'A' and 'B' on a plan which also shows the demarcation of the route). Markings on the plan should be clear and precise.

The land to be sold should be outlined or coloured in red and any land to be retained by the seller should be outlined or coloured in blue. Other land referred to should be coloured or hatched in distinct colours other than red or blue. The ownership of boundaries should be indicated by 'T' marks. The stem of the 'T' should rest on the relevant boundary, the 'T' being on the side of the boundary which is responsible for the maintenance. Rights of way and routes of services should be marked with broken or dotted lines of a distinct colour, with each end of the route being identified with separate capital letters.

Where the plan is to scale, the scale should be shown. If the plan is not to scale, metric measurements should be shown along each boundary. A compass point indicating the direction of north should be shown. A key should be included to explain the meaning of the various colours and lines used on the plan.

### *Referring to the contract plan*

Care must be taken to ensure that there is no discrepancy between the verbal description of the property and the plan. If there is, it will be a question of construction as to whether the verbal description or the plan will prevail. The contract (and subsequent purchase deed) may refer to the plan as being 'for identification purposes only', or may describe the land as being 'more particularly delineated on the plan'. These two phrases are mutually exclusive and a combination of the two serves no useful purpose (*Neilson v Poole* (1969) 20 P & CR 909).

#### 'IDENTIFICATION PURPOSES ONLY'

Where there is a discrepancy between the land shown on the plan and the contract description, and the plan has been described as being for identification purposes only, the verbal description of the land will normally prevail over the plan. This type of plan is unacceptable for use in connection with registered land and will be returned by HM Land Registry.

#### 'MORE PARTICULARLY DELINEATED'

In the event of a discrepancy between the verbal description of the land and the plan, the plan will prevail over the words where the phrase 'more particularly delineated' has been used. This phrase should not be used unless the plan is to scale.

Note, however, that in many cases there will be no verbal description as such. So, for example, the land being sold may be described as 'All that land edged in red on the plan ... and forming part of property known as ...'. Here the only means of identifying the property is the plan itself and so there can be no question of a discrepancy between the verbal description and the plan.

## 14.5.2 Easements and rights benefiting the property

The seller's investigation of title will have revealed whether or not the property has the benefit of easements or other rights. These may be included in the particulars of sale, although this is not essential as the benefit of them will pass to the buyer in any event under the Law of Property Act 1925, s 62. On a sale of part of land, new rights (eg a right to lay a new water pipe) may be granted to the buyer (see Chapter 40).

### 14.5.3 Errors in the particulars

A mistake in the particulars of sale, for example, describing a freehold property as leasehold, or describing the extent of the land as 5 hectares when in fact it is only 3 hectares, may give the buyer a remedy in misdescription or misrepresentation. These remedies are both explained in Chapter 33.

## 14.6 THE CONDITIONS OF SALE

There are two types of conditions: general conditions and special conditions. General conditions are those which apply in every transaction, such as the Standard Conditions of Sale. Special conditions are those terms which are specially drafted to fit the circumstances of the transaction in hand.

### 14.6.1 Drafting conditions of sale

It is assumed that the seller's solicitor will be using the Standard Conditions of Sale as the foundation of his contract. On this basis, and having considered which matters need to be dealt with by special conditions (see **14.7**), drafting involves the following process.

(1) Look at the relevant Standard Condition of Sale on the point. Does this deal with the matter in a way acceptable to the needs of the client?
(2) If it does not, a special condition will have to be drafted and included in the contract.

The Standard Conditions are in almost universal use in residential transactions. They are not as widely used in commercial transactions, and, where they are so used, they will need amendment to meet the different circumstances of a commercial sale. The more important of the amendments necessary will be mentioned when the relevant part of the contract is discussed. The Standard Commercial Property Conditions are now available for use in commercial transactions.

### 14.6.2 Altering the Standard Conditions of Sale

Where it is necessary to modify one of the Standard Conditions of Sale to meet the requirements of a particular transaction, this can be done by including as a special condition in the contract a clause which contains provisions contrary or different to those contained in the Standard Conditions themselves. It is not necessary to include a special condition which expressly excludes the Standard Condition which is being amended because Special Condition 1(a), printed on the reverse of the contract form, says that where there is a conflict between the general conditions (ie the Standard Conditions printed on the inside pages of the contract form) and the special conditions typed on the reverse of the contract form, the special conditions prevail. However, in practice, the Standard Condition in question will often be expressly stated to be excluded in the interests of certainty. An amendment to the Standard Conditions must be made by special condition on the reverse of the contract form. It is not sufficient merely to strike out or alter the offending condition in the centre pages of the contract form.

## 14.7  MATTERS COMMONLY DEALT WITH BY SPECIAL CONDITIONS

### 14.7.1  The seller's duty of disclosure

The open contract rule provides that the seller is selling a freehold estate free from incumbrances. This is rarely the case since many properties are subject to restrictive covenants which will continue to bind the land after completion of the sale to the buyer. It is therefore necessary to alter this rule in the contract itself, and this is done by Standard Condition 3 which amends the open contract rules.

### *Standard Condition 3*

Under this condition, the seller is deemed to be selling the property free from incumbrances other than those mentioned in Standard Condition 3.1.2. This states that the incumbrances subject to which the property is sold subject are the following.

#### (A) THOSE MENTIONED IN THE AGREEMENT

This is the most important category. Because of the primary implication that the land is being sold free from incumbrances, it is essential that the seller's solicitor investigates his title thoroughly before drafting the contract and includes in the contract details of any and all incumbrances so discovered that will be binding on the buyer after completion. Failure to disclose incumbrances that do not come within one of the remaining paragraphs of Condition 3.1.2 may give the buyer the right to rescind the contract and/or claim damages. The remedies for non-disclosure are discussed in Chapter 33.

#### (B) THOSE DISCOVERABLE BY AN INSPECTION OF THE PROPERTY

Often easements (and some other incumbrances) affecting the land can be discovered by an inspection. If this is the case they are deemed to be patent, ie obvious defects and need not be expressly disclosed. However, to avoid any dispute as to whether a matter is or is not discoverable by an inspection, it is usual to disclose all incumbrances in the contract, whether or not they could be discovered by an inspection.

If the incumbrance is not discoverable by an inspection, it is irrelevant under Standard Condition 3 that the buyer might already know of the existence of an incumbrance, for example because it is on the register in registered land. Such an incumbrance must be included in the contract to comply with the condition.

#### (C) THOSE THE SELLER DOES NOT AND COULD NOT KNOW ABOUT

This is necessary to counteract the strictness of the rule that the property is being sold free from all incumbrances. Apart from this provision, a seller would be in breach of the contractual term that the land was free from incumbrances if it was later discovered to be subject to an incumbrance unknown to the seller. Note that, to come within this provision, it is not enough that the seller did not know about the incumbrance; he must also show that he could not know of it. However, in reality, it is most unlikely that there would be any incumbrances which the seller both did not know about and could not have known about had the seller's solicitor investigated title properly.

(D) ENTRIES MADE BEFORE THE DATE OF THE CONTRACT IN ANY PUBLIC REGISTER
EXCEPT HM LAND REGISTRY OR HM LAND CHARGES REGISTRY OR KEPT AT
COMPANIES HOUSE

This means that any incumbrances registered at Companies House, or entered on the register in registered land or registered as land charges in unregistered land, must be expressly mentioned in the contract (unless they are discoverable by an inspection) in order to satisfy the disclosure requirements of Standard Condition 3. It is not sufficient that they are registered and could be discovered by the appropriate search or are already known to the buyer. On the other hand, matters entered in other public registers, eg the Local Land Charges Register (see Chapter 18), need not be expressly disclosed in the contract.

(E) PUBLIC REQUIREMENTS

This is defined in Standard Condition 1.1.1(j) as being any notice order or proposal given or made by a body acting on statutory authority. This would therefore include matters likely to be revealed by the Enquiries of the Local Authority, for example a public right of way affecting the land (see Chapter 18). These need not be expressly disclosed to the buyer in the contract.

## Defects in title

The open contract implication that the seller is selling the fee-simple, free from incumbrances also implies that there are no other flaws or defects in the title itself. For example, details of some old covenants may be missing, or there may be some other defect in the documents proving ownership (see Chapter 17 on Investigation of Title for details of other possible defects). If these defects are not patent (ie something that is visible to the eye on inspecting the property) then the buyer might again have remedies against the seller for non-disclosure (see Chapter 33). Standard Condition 3 does not change the open contract rules with regard to these defects in title, which, therefore, must be disclosed.

## Matters which will not bind the buyer

These are not defects in title and the seller does not need to disclose them. They would include, for example, the interests of the beneficiaries under a trust of land which will be overreached on a sale by two trustees.

## Physical defects

These need not be disclosed (see Standard Condition 3.2.1) and hence the need for the buyer to commission a survey. However, if the seller deliberately conceals a physical defect (eg 'papering over the cracks'), this may give rise to an action in the tort of deceit.

## Dealing with disclosure in the contract

The seller should make a full disclosure of all incumbrances and defects in title in the contract. He does not want to be faced with an objection that a particular non-disclosed incumbrance or defect was not apparent on an inspection. If an incumbrance is disclosed in the contract, the buyer has agreed to buy subject to it by virtue of Standard Condition 3.1.2(a).

As far as other defects in title are concerned, the disclosure of them will probably give rise to an implication that the buyer has agreed to buy subject to them.

However, if the defect is capable of being remedied, the buyer will be entitled to request ('raise a requisition') that the seller does in fact remedy it. In practice, the seller may not be able or willing to do so. It is, therefore, necessary to include an express provision in the contract preventing the buyer from objecting to it. For example, if the defect in question is an imperfectly executed conveyance, the clause to be inserted in the agreement might be as follows:

**The Buyer shall assume that the conveyance dated ............ is correctly executed and shall raise no requisition or objection in relation to it.**

Note, however, that clauses like this do not become operative until contracts are exchanged. The buyer is free to raise queries about the problem up until that time (although the seller is under no obligation to answer them). It does mean, though, that the buyer is able to consider the risk posed by buying the land subject to this defect and, if he considers it too great, he can withdraw from the transaction without any penalty.

### *The Standard Commercial Property Conditions*

The Standard Commercial Property Conditions also contain provisions dealing with the seller's duty of disclosure. Although these are based on the residential Conditions, there are important differences. There is again the basic premise that the property is sold free from incumbrances other than those set out in Condition 3.1.2, but the provisions of Condition 3.1.2 have been changed from the residential Conditions. Condition 3.1.2(c) has had the word 'reasonably' added so that it makes the sale subject to incumbrances that the seller 'does not and could not *reasonably* know about'. Condition 3.1.2(d) is much wider than the residential Conditions and makes the sale subject to matters 'which would have been disclosed by the searches and enquiries which a prudent buyer would have made before entering into the contract'. This does mean, for example, that the sale would be subject to entries at HM Land Registry even if not specifically mentioned, whereas under the residential Standard Conditions they would need to be.

### 14.7.2 Barring out requisitions

Standard Condition 4.1.1 allows the buyer to raise requisitions at any time within six working days after contracts have been exchanged. In order to save time, however, it is usual to require buyers to raise any queries they have with regard to the title before exchange. In order to do this a special condition will need inserting in the contract along the following lines:

**The Buyer having inspected the Seller's title shall raise no objection to it or requisition on it.**

Note that Special Condition 2 printed on the form of agreement already bars out requisitions on the incumbrances. This will need deleting (and the other special conditions renumbering) as it is no longer required when all requisitions on the title are barred.

Note also, however, that this kind of special condition only prevents the buyer raising objections to the title as presented to him by the seller. If, after exchange, he discovered an undisclosed incumbrance or other defect which ought to have been known to the seller, he would still be able to require the problem to be remedied or assert his remedies for non-disclosure (see Chapter 33).

The Standard Commercial Property Conditions contain the same timetable.

### 14.7.3 Proof of the seller's title

The contract must tell the buyer how the seller intends to prove his legal ownership of the property. This is normally done by showing the buyer documentary evidence of the seller's ownership, the precise nature of which varies depending on whether the property is freehold or leasehold, registered or unregistered. The following sub-paragraphs deal only with freehold land. The relevant leasehold provisions are dealt with in Chapters 35 and 36.

#### *Registered freehold transaction*

The provisions of the Land Registration Act 1925, s 110 form the basis of the requirements for proof of title in a registered freehold transaction. These provisions are regarded as largely satisfactory and a clause which offers less than the s 110 minimum provisions should not be accepted by a buyer. Section 110 requires the seller to supply the buyer with the following:

(1) copies of the register entries; and
(2) a copy of the filed plan; and
(3) evidence as to matters on which the register itself is not conclusive (eg overriding interests).

The items listed in (1) and (2) above cannot be excluded by contractual condition. The only unsatisfactory element of the section is that it requires only ordinary copies of the register entries to be given to the buyer. It is preferable for the buyer to be supplied with office copy entries, because these are official copies with a date stamp, so that the buyer can judge how up to date is the information which they contain.

Both sets of Standard Conditions contain the same provisions which are also identically numbered. Condition 4.2.1 modifies the open contract rule contained in s 110 by requiring office copies of the register to be supplied to the buyer. Condition 4.2.1 is entirely satisfactory and does not need to be altered by special condition. Provided the contract identifies the title number of the land and states the class of title (eg absolute), there is no need for any further condition dealing with title to be added to the contract. The class of title should be stated because the open contract rules assume that an absolute title is being offered unless the contrary is stated. There is space on the front of the Standard Conditions of Sale Form to include these details.

#### *Unregistered freehold title*

Where the sale comprises an unregistered freehold interest, the Law of Property Act 1925, s 44 (as amended) contains the relevant open contract principles. This section provides that the seller must show a good root of title which at the date of the contract is at least 15 years old and all subsequent dealings from that instrument to the present day. This provision is universally regarded as being satisfactory and is rarely departed from. A 'good root of title' is a document which satisfies all three of the following conditions:

(1) it deals with the whole of the legal and equitable interests in the land;
(2) it contains a recognisable description of the land;
(3) it contains nothing to cast doubt on the title.

The documents which are capable of forming a good root of title are:

(i)   a conveyance on sale;
(ii)  a legal mortgage;
(iii) a voluntary conveyance;
(iv)  a post-1925 assent,

provided (in each case) that they satisfy the above requirements.

The forms of agreement incorporating both the Standard Conditions and the Standard Commercial Property Conditions require the seller to insert on the front page what the root of title document will be. It is possible to contract out of the open contract implications, so that, for example, a root could be specified which did not fulfil the open contract definition of a root, or was not at least 15 years old. However, the buyer would almost certainly not accept anything less than the open contract position, and the root document specified should comply with the open contract rules. It is generally accepted that a conveyance on sale or a mortgage are the 'best' roots of title. This is because the buyer under the root conveyance (or the mortgagee) would undoubtedly have fully investigated the title before they bought the land and would not have bought had there then been any problems with the title. On a voluntary conveyance or an assent, title would almost certainly not have been investigated at the time of the gift.

A seller will normally, therefore, look for and insert on the front of the contract a conveyance or mortgage which satisfies the open contract requirements.

Only in extremely unusual circumstances will the seller not be able to comply with the requirements of s 44, and a clause which offers a root which is less than the minimum 15 years in length would be regarded with suspicion by the buyer. He should not accept the short root until he and his lender are satisfied as to the circumstances in which the root is being offered. If the buyer accepts the statutory length of title as prescribed by s 44, he may still be bound by incumbrances which affect the title earlier than the root document but may be entitled to compensation under s 25 of the Law of Property Act 1969. This protection is lost if the buyer accepts a short title and he will be bound by incumbrances on the title behind the root for such length of time as it takes to go back to a good root. In other words, the buyer may be affected by incumbrances which he does not know about, not just over the 15-year period covered by the statutory root, but as far back in time as it would be necessary to go to find such a good root. This potential minefield is not generally acceptable to a buyer. Although the buyer may well have remedies against the seller for non-disclosure in such a situation (see **14.7.1**), he will still own land bound by these incumbrances.

Occasionally it may be found that the seller's reason for offering a short root is because his title is mainly based on adverse possession (squatters' rights). Provided the buyer investigates the situation thoroughly and is satisfied that the title is capable of registration with at least a possessory title at HM Land Registry and that an insurance policy against possible defects can be obtained at reasonable cost, it may be acceptable to proceed on this basis.

Infrequently, it will be found that the reason for the seller offering a short title is because the land is part of a large estate which has not changed hands inter vivos for several centuries and, unless a very recent conveyance is accepted as the root of title, it would be necessary to prove title from some date in the eighteenth century. Again, provided the buyer is satisfied with the seller's explanation and the nature of the risk he is accepting, this may be a reasonable situation in which to accept a short title.

### Proving title by adverse possession

A seller can establish that he has a good right to sell by proving 12 years' adverse possession under the Limitation Act 1980. However, under an open contract, he has to establish not only that he has (together with his predecessors in title, if necessary) been in possession for at least 12 years, but also that the possession has extinguished the title of the true owner. Twelve years' possession on its own might not do this if, for example, the land is subject to a long lease. Twelve years' possession will extinguish the title of the leaseholder, but time will not begin to run against the freeholder until the end of the lease. So it will be necessary to deduce the title of the original owner to the buyer to show that this has been extinguished by the adverse possession. If the original owner's title is registered, this would be possible as the register is open to public inspection, but it is most unlikely to be possible if the land is unregistered. In such a case, therefore, it will be necessary for a special condition to be inserted in the contract setting out how the seller intends to prove his title. This will normally be in the form of statutory declarations by the seller and others, declaring that the seller (and his predecessors if that is the case) have been in sole undisputed possession for the number of years that they claim to have been in possession. The buyer will then be required by the condition to accept this as proof of title and not to raise any objections or requisitions. It is then for the buyer to consider the proof offered and decide, prior to exchange, whether or not to accept the risk. Once contracts have been exchanged, the buyer will then not be able to object to the title offered.

Note also that the Land Registration Act 2002 contains provisions which, when brought into force, will make it unwise in most circumstances for a buyer to accept title to registered land based on adverse possession (see **4.10**).

### 14.7.4 Covenants for title

By including 'key words' in the purchase deed it is possible to give the buyer the benefit of certain implied covenants under the Law of Property (Miscellaneous Provisions) Act 1994. It is usual to specify in the contract which (if any) of the implied covenants the seller is prepared to give. The inclusion of the statement 'the seller sells with full title guarantee' (or its Welsh equivalent) will give the buyer the benefit of the full range of covenants implied by the 1994 Act (see 'full title guarantee' below). A more limited set of covenants is implied if the seller uses the expression 'the seller sells with limited title guarantee' (or the equivalent Welsh expression) (see 'limited title guarantee' below). Where the contract is silent and makes no reference to title guarantee, Condition 4.5.2 in both the Standard Conditions and the Standard Commercial Conditions provides that the seller will sell with full title guarantee. The Standard Conditions of Sale Form of Agreement provides space on the front page to amend this if required. Note that the implied covenants for title are implied into the purchase deed and not the contract. The sole purpose of putting the provision into the contract is to tell the buyer what covenants will be included in the purchase deed when that is executed.

### Details of the covenants

In the following paragraphs:

'disposition'  includes a transfer of land for value, a gift of land, and the grant of a lease;

'seller'  includes a person who sells, gives away, or grants a lease of land;

'buyer'  includes a person who buys for value, a donee, or a person who is granted a lease.

FULL TITLE GUARANTEE

*Disposition of freehold land*

The following covenants are implied into the disposition:

(1) (a) A covenant that the seller has the right to dispose of the land as he purports to. This amounts to a promise that he *can* do what the disposition says he *does* do (eg transfer ownership or grant a leasehold term).

(b) A covenant that he will do all he reasonably can to transfer the title he purports to give. This amounts to a promise that if title is not successfully given to the buyer, the seller will, at his own expense, give reasonable assistance to perfect the buyer's title. This includes assisting the buyer in an application for registration of title under the Land Registration Act 1925.

(2) A covenant that the land is disposed of free from incumbrances, other than those the seller does not know about and could not reasonably know about.

*Disposition of leasehold land*

If the land disposed of is leasehold land, a third covenant is implied:

(3) That the lease is subsisting at the time it is disposed of, and that there is no breach of covenant making the lease liable to forfeiture.

LIMITED TITLE GUARANTEE

*Disposition of freehold land*

If the seller is expressed to dispose of land 'with limited title guarantee', the following covenants are implied.

(1) (a) That the seller has the right to dispose of the land as he purports to (see above).

(b) That the seller will do all that he reasonably can to transfer the title he purports to give (see above).

(2) That the seller has not himself incumbered the land, and also that the seller is not aware that anyone else has done so since the last disposition for value. This means, for example, that if a donee of land later disposes of it with limited title guarantee, the donee covenants that *he* has not incumbered the land, and he also covenants that he is not aware of the donor having incumbered the land.

*Disposition of leasehold land*

(3) A third covenant is added, that the lease is subsisting at the time it is disposed of and that there is no breach of covenant making the lease liable to forfeiture.

*Note:*

(1) The seller is not in breach of the implied covenants in respect of any matters:

(a) to which the disposition is expressly made subject (s 6). This means that if the land is expressly conveyed 'subject to a restrictive covenant contained in a deed dated 1 January 1950 between AB(1) and CD(2)', the seller cannot be sued under the covenants for title in respect of that incumbrance; or

(b) that the buyer knows about at the time of the disposition (s 6). This means that a buyer of registered title could not sue the seller in respect of an overriding interest, if the buyer knew at the time of the transfer that the overriding interest existed.

(2) The seller can modify the effect of any of the covenants by a clause in the disposition (s 8).

### Drafting the agreement for sale

When drafting the agreement on behalf of the seller, it must be decided whether the seller will promise to dispose of the land with 'full title guarantee' or with 'limited title guarantee', or refuse to give any title guarantee at all.

If the seller promises, for example, a 'full title guarantee', that phrase will appear in the subsequent transfer, ie 'the Seller transfers to the Buyer with full title guarantee ...'. The inclusion of the phrase in the transfer will imply the covenants for title into the transfer. Which kind of title guarantee is chosen will depend upon the circumstances of the seller and the state of his title to the land.

### Sale by a sole owner or co-owners

Remember that the seller makes certain promises in the agreement about his title, ie:

* the implied promise that he has a good title to the land; and
* the express promise, by virtue of Standard Condition 3, that he is selling free from incumbrances other than, for example, those mentioned in the agreement and those that the seller does not know about.

He also states what, if any, guarantee of title he will give in the transfer.

The seller's title will be investigated before the agreement is drafted. If the client has, and can prove, a good title, the implied contractual promise that the seller has good title does not need to be amended. Equally, the seller has no reason to refuse to promise a full guarantee, as the covenants implied into the transfer by the 1994 Act will be no wider than the promises about title the seller gives in the agreement.

On the other hand, if the client has no title to the land, or a questionable title (eg title might be based on adverse possession under the Limitation Acts) a special condition will be inserted in the agreement to negative the implied promise that the seller has a good title. Equally, the seller will not want to give any title guarantee in the transfer. So the contract should make it clear on the front page that no title guarantee is to be given.

### Sale by trustees holding on trust for people other than themselves

When drafting the agreement for sale on behalf of the trustees, it must be decided whether or not they should give any title guarantee. If there is satisfactory evidence of title, the trustees should be able to give a guarantee to the buyer. In other words, they should not refuse to give a guarantee simply because they are trustees and not absolute owners. However, they may prefer to give a limited title guarantee. If they give a full title guarantee, they will be promising that there are no incumbrances. If they give a limited title guarantee, they will promise only that they did not create any incumbrances, and that they are not aware of any previous trustees or the settlor having done so.

### Sale by a personal representative

Whether or not a personal representative is prepared to give a guarantee of title will depend on his knowledge, and the evidence that he has, of the title. A personal representative is likely to give a limited guarantee rather than a full title guarantee.

If he gives a limited title guarantee, he will be promising that he has not created any incumbrances, and that he is not aware that the deceased created any.

### Gifts and assents

If a donor makes a deed of gift, or a personal representative assents with a title guarantee, the covenants can be implied. It is not usual, however, for title guarantee to be given in a gift.

### Mortgages

If a borrower mortgages with a title guarantee, the covenants for title will be implied. When acting for the lender, the lender's instructions must be checked to see if the lender requires a full title guarantee in the mortgage, or is willing to accept a limited title guarantee. Usually, full guarantee is required.

### Sales by mortgagees

When a lender sells under his power of sale, there seems no reason why limited guarantee cannot be given; however, in practice, it is common for no title guarantee to be given.

### Assignment of a lease

If the seller assigns the lease with either full or limited title guarantee, he promises that there is no breach of a tenant's covenant, and that there is nothing that would make the lease liable for forfeiture. Standard Condition 3.2.2, however, says that the lease is sold *subject* to any breach of a tenant's covenant relating to the physical state of the property which renders the lease liable to forfeiture.

An express clause should be added to the transfer of the lease to give effect to Condition 3.2.2 in both sets of Standard Conditions; see **36.6.3**.

### Grant of a lease

If a landlord grants a lease with full or limited title guarantee, the covenants for title will be implied into the lease. A tenant who is taking a long-term residential lease and paying a substantial premium is likely to ask for a guarantee to be given. Title guarantee is not usual in a short-term lease.

### Commercial property

On a sale by a large company, where knowledge of matters affecting the property may be scattered amongst many staff in many different departments, it may be wisest for the seller only to give limited title guarantee. In the case of a small company (eg a 'one person' company), there seems no reason why full title guarantee should not be given in the usual way. In practice, however, even large companies will normally give full title guarantee.

## 14.7.5  Vacant possession

Under the open contract rules, vacant possession of the property is to be given on completion. This provision is reflected in the Standard Conditions of Sale, where Special Condition 5 (Special Condition 3 in the Standard Commercial Conditions contract form) on the back page of the contract form provides: 'The property is sold with vacant possession on completion'. An alternative version of this condition is also printed on the form ('The property is sold subject to the following leases or tenancies'). Copies of any leases or tenancy agreements should be supplied to the buyer with the draft contract so that he can see the terms of those agreements.

Schedule 4 to the Family Law Act 1996 implies a term that the seller will secure the cancellation of any rights of occupation enjoyed by a spouse and will give vacant possession on completion. This section needs to be borne in mind in situations where legal title to the property is held by a sole married owner.

## 14.7.6  Date and time for completion

Instructions will have been obtained from the client as to his desired date for completion, but it is not usually possible at this stage of the transaction to insert a definite date for completion in the contract. The actual date for completion agreed between the parties will be inserted in the contract on exchange of contracts, in the space provided for this information on the front page of the contract form. Until that time, this space is left blank. Many factors, including the progress of the client's related purchase transaction, affect the timing of completion and, at the stage when the contract is drafted, it is too early to make a positive decision on the actual date for completion.

If no completion date is inserted in the contract, Condition 6.1.1 in both sets of Standard Conditions sets completion at 20 working days after the date of the contract. This provision is a variation on the unsatisfactory open contract provision which provides that completion shall take place within a reasonable time after exchange of contracts.

Condition 6.1.1 also provides that time is not to be of the essence as regards the completion date except where a notice to complete has been served. Where time is not of the essence, a delay in completion beyond the contractual date will not automatically allow the party not in default to repudiate the contract. Although time can be made of the essence by varying Condition 6.1.1 by Special Condition, this is not usually desirable in a residential transaction and the condition should be left unamended. Problems relating to time being of the essence and to notices to complete are discussed in Chapter 32.

The Standard Conditions do not deal with the precise time on the day of completion by which the transfer must be completed. It is desirable, especially in chain transactions, for this matter to be dealt with by express special conditions in the contract, for example 'completion shall take place by 2 pm'. This is to ensure that there is sufficient time on the day of completion for the seller to use the funds to complete his dependent purchase. Standard Condition 6.1.2, which refers to the time of completion, relates only to the payment of compensation for late completion and does not impose a time-limit on completion itself.

### 14.7.7 Compensation for delayed completion

The contract normally provides for compensation to be paid by one party to the other in the event of completion being delayed beyond the contractual date.

Standard Condition 7.3 contains provisions for the payment of compensation for late completion, and states that the amount of such payment shall be assessed at the 'contract rate' as defined. According to Condition 1.1.1(g) of the Standard Conditions (Condition 1.1.1(d) of the Standard Commercial Conditions), the contract rate, unless altered by special condition, is: 'The Law Society's interest rate from time to time in force'. The Law Society's interest rate is published weekly in the *Law Society's Gazette* and is set at 4% above the base lending rate of Barclays Bank plc.

The object of inserting an interest rate is both to provide an incentive to complete on the due date and to provide monetary compensation to the innocent party for any financial losses caused by the delay in completion. In practice, in residential transactions an interest rate of between 3 and 5% above the base lending rate of a major bank is accepted as being normal. The Form of Agreement for both sets of Standard Conditions contains a space on the front page in which the contract rate can be inserted. If it is wished to rely on Standard Condition 1.1.1(g) (or 1.1.1(d)), this can be left blank. However, it is often used to state expressly that The Law Society's interest rate is to be used. Alternatively, many solicitors will substitute a rate of their own choosing, usually linked to the base rate of their own bankers. Providing for a fixed interest rate (eg 'the contract rate shall be 14% pa') is not normally considered to be desirable in case rates of interest change radically between the time when the contract is drafted and the time when the interest becomes payable. The seller is protected against such fluctuations in interest rates if the contract rate is set to float with a named bank's base rate.

### 14.7.8 Deposit

Although not required by law, it is customary for the buyer to pay a deposit of 10% of the purchase price on exchange of contracts. This acts both as part-payment of the price and as a guarantee of performance by the buyer, since he cannot usually afford to lose this amount of money. If the buyer subsequently defaulted on the contract, the seller would have the right to forfeit that deposit. Condition 2.2 in both sets of Standard Conditions provides for payment of a 10% deposit to be held by the seller's solicitor in the capacity of stakeholder. A special condition relating to the deposit is only needed if it is desired to vary the capacity in which the deposit is to be held. The amount of the deposit is inserted in the space provided for this towards the bottom of the front page of the contract form. There is no need for a special condition to change the amount of the deposit.

Provisions relating to the deposit and the capacity in which it should be held are fully discussed in Chapter 21.

### 14.7.9 Indemnity covenants

If the seller entered into a covenant, whether positive or negative, he will remain liable on that covenant even after he has disposed of the land, unless the wording of the covenant makes it clear that he is not to be bound after he has sold. Where he remains bound, it means that if the buyer breaks the covenant, there is a risk of the seller being sued in respect of that breach. To protect himself, therefore, the seller needs to take an indemnity covenant from the buyer in the purchase deed. However, like other matters, the indemnity can only be included in the purchase deed if this is provided for in the contract. Standard Condition 4.5.4 makes satisfactory provision for such an indemnity. It is, however, considered to be good practice to deal expressly with indemnity by special condition in the contract in order to draw this matter specifically to the attention of the buyer. This can be done by including an express indemnity clause in similar wording to that contained in Standard Condition 4.5.4.

The Standard Commercial Property Conditions contain a similar provision, also numbered 4.5.4.

### 14.7.10  Fixtures and fittings

Fittings (eg carpets and curtains) which are to be included in the sale must be specifically identified in the contract, either by special condition, or by making use of printed Special Condition 4, which refers to the chattels which are itemised on a list attached to the contract. In Protocol cases, the Fixtures Fittings and Contents Form can be used for this purpose. Any separate consideration for the chattels must be expressly stated. Fixtures (items which are attached to the land, eg the central heating system) automatically pass with the land unless a special condition is included giving the seller the right to remove them. Fixtures and fittings are dealt with in detail in Chapter 11.

### 14.8  VOID CONDITIONS

Certain conditions are rendered void by statute if they are included in a contract for the sale of land. Some examples are given below.

#### *Title made with the concurrence of beneficiaries*

It is theoretically possible to conduct a sale of land held on trust by obtaining the consent to the sale of all the beneficiaries. The buyer cannot be required to accept such a situation and can insist that the sale is effected by a minimum of two trustees of the legal estate (Law of Property Act 1925, s 42).

#### *Improperly stamped documents*

If, unusually, in unregistered land, one or more of the documents which form part of the seller's title does not bear the correct amount of stamp duty, the seller is under an obligation to correct this at his own expense and cannot include a contractual condition requiring the buyer to bear the cost of putting this defect right (Stamp Act 1891, s 117). The checking of stamp duties is discussed at **17.6.5**.

#### *Restricting buyer's choice of solicitor*

Any provision which seeks to restrict the buyer's choice of solicitor is rendered void by the Law of Property Act 1925, s 48. Such a provision would also offend Rules 1 and 6 of the Solicitors' Practice Rules 1990.

## 14.9 CONTRACT RACES

From time to time a seller will ask his solicitor to deal with more than one buyer at the same time. This practice, known as a 'contract race', is strictly controlled by Rule 6A of the Solicitors' Practice Rules 1990 and is discussed at **6.5**.

## 14.10 AUCTIONS

Ordinary residential property is not usually sold at auction. Investment property, property which is unique or difficult to value, and agricultural land may, however, be sold by auction rather than privately or through an estate agent. An auction contract is usually prepared by the seller's solicitor in collaboration with the auctioneer. The latter will prepare the particulars of sale, while the solicitor will draft the conditions of sale. The conditions will usually make reference to the incorporation of a standard set of contractual conditions such as the Standard Conditions; Standard Condition 2.3 contains provisions which are needed in order to comply with the Sale of Land by Auction Act 1867.

The Standard Commercial Property Conditions contain the same provisions, with the addition of Condition 2.3.6 which provides that the auctioneer is to hold the deposit as agent for the seller and giving the seller the same rights as in residential Standard Condition 2.2.4 if the deposit cheque is dishonoured.

## 14.11 CONTRACT DRAFTING: A WORKED EXAMPLE

The following instructions have been obtained from Andrew Smith who has instructed Lowe Snow and Co to act for him in connection with the sale of his house.

# AGREEMENT
## (Incorporating the Standard Conditions of Sale (Third Edition))

| | | |
|---|---|---|
| **Agreement date** | : | |
| **Seller** | : | Andrew Smith<br>10 Bolton Park Road, Loamster, Loamshire LM3 5OY |
| **Buyer** | : | Jane Elizabeth Brown<br>17 Milton Drive, Newton, Loamshire LM2 7XZ |
| **Property**<br>(freehold/~~leasehold~~) | : | 10 Bolton Park Road, Loamshire LM3 5OY |
| ~~Root of title~~/Title Number | : | LM 11024 (Absolute Title) |
| **Incumbrances on the Property** | : | The covenants referred to in Entry No 3 of the Charges Register |
| **Title Guarantee**<br>(full/limited) | : | The Seller sells with full title guarantee |
| **Completion date** | : | |
| **Contract rate** | : | The Law Society's interest rate from time to time in force |
| **Purchase price** | : | £55,000.00 |
| **Deposit** | : | £ 2,750.00 |
| **Amount payable for chattels** | : | NIL |
| **Balance** | : | £52,250.00 |

The Seller will sell and the Buyer will buy the Property for the Purchase price.
*The Agreement continues on the back page.*

| WARNING | Signed |
|---|---|
| This is a formal document, designed to create legal rights and legal obligations. Take advice before using it. | <br><br><br>Seller/Buyer |

## SPECIAL CONDITIONS

1.  (a)  This Agreement incorporates the Standard Conditions of Sale (Third Edition). Where there is a conflict between those Conditions and this Agreement, this Agreement prevails.

    (b)  Terms used or defined in this Agreement have the same meaning when used in the Conditions.

    x2.  ~~The Property is sold subject to the Incumbrances on the Property and the Buyer will raise no requisitions on them.~~

2.x3.  Subject to the terms of this Agreement and to the Standard Conditions of Sale, the seller is to transfer the property with the title guarantee specified on the front page.

    x4.  ~~The chattels on the Property and set out on any attached list are included in the sale.~~

3.x5.  The Property is sold with vacant possession on completion.

~~(or) 5.   The Property is sold subject to the following leases or tenancies:~~

4.  The deposit shall be held as agent for the Seller.

5.  The Buyer having inspected the Sellers title shall raise no objection to it or requisition on it.

6.  The Buyer is to covenant in the transfer to indemnify the seller against liability for any future breach of the covenants referred to in Entry No 3 of the Charges Register and to perform them from then on.

**Seller's Solicitors**          :     Lowe Snow & Co.

**Buyer's Solicitors**           :     Bullock Brindley & Ellis

©1995   *OYEZ*   The Solicitors' Law Stationery Society Ltd,
Oyez House, 7 Spa Road, London SE16 3QQ

© 1995 **THE LAW SOCIETY**

4 95  F29334
5065046
* * * * *
*3rd Edition*

**Standard Conditions of Sale**

Andrew Smith is the owner of freehold land known as 10 Bolton Park Road, Loamster, Loamshire. He lives alone in the property. The property is registered with an absolute title at HM Land Registry under title number LM 11024. He has a mortgage on the property which will be paid off when he sells. Entry Number 3 on the Charges Register gives details of various covenants restricting the use of the land. The Proprietorship Register states that when Mr Smith bought the property he entered into an indemnity covenant with the previous owner in relation to these covenants. He has provisionally agreed to sell the house to Jane Elizabeth Brown of 17 Milton Drive, Newton, Loamshire, who has instructed Messrs Bullock Brindley and Ellis to act for her. The price agreed is £55,000, with a reduced deposit of 5% of the purchase price being payable on exchange of contracts because Mrs Brown is obtaining a 95% mortgage. Mr Smith has agreed to the reduced deposit on the basis that he can have that money and use it before completion. There are no chattels to be included in the sale and no fixtures to be removed.

The contract which might be drafted to reflect these instructions is set out in the Agreement above.

The following sub-paragraphs provide a commentary to the contract.

### Date

The contract is left undated at the draft stage. The date is inserted on actual exchange of contracts.

### Parties

The full names and addresses of the parties, as they will later appear on the purchase deed, should be inserted. The seller's solicitor may not at this stage know the full names of the buyer and, if necessary, this information can be supplied later by the buyer's solicitor. Note the inclusion of postcodes in the parties' addresses.

### Property

The property is freehold, so the word 'leasehold' can be deleted. Since the property is registered with an absolute title and is a suburban property with well-defined boundaries, it will suffice to describe it merely by its postal address. This constitutes the 'particulars' of the contract. No plan is needed in this case. Note the inclusion of the postcode in the description of the property; it is now Land Registry practice to include this on the register.

### Title

The property is registered, therefore the reference to 'Root of title' is irrelevant and can be deleted. The title number and confirmation that the class of title is absolute should be inserted here.

### Incumbrances

As the mortgage is to be discharged on completion, this need not be mentioned. The restrictive covenants must be stated to comply with Standard Condition 3. There is no need, however, to set out the covenants verbatim as long as a copy is provided; in this case as it is registered land, office copy entries will be supplied in any event.

*Title guarantee*

The seller is a sole owner and will give full title guarantee. It is customary to insert this on the front page of the contract form, even though in this case the words inserted repeat Standard Condition 4.5.2.

*Completion date*

Completion date is left blank at this stage and inserted on actual exchange.

*Contract rate*

Even though it is not intended to vary Standard Condition 1.1.1(g), confirmation of that fact is included on the front page of the contract form. Unless there are special circumstances, the solicitor would normally decide on the rate of interest to be included in the contract and this is not a matter on which the client's instructions are sought.

*Price*

The price, amount of deposit, amount (if any) payable for chattels (fittings) and balance due on completion are inserted in the appropriate space towards the bottom of the front page of the contract form.

*Agreement for sale*

The words 'The seller will sell and the buyer will buy the property for the purchase price' above the two boxes at the bottom of the front page of the contract form constitute the agreement for sale. A box is provided for the seller/buyer to sign. This is left blank at this stage and will be signed by the client close to exchange.

*Printed Special Condition 1*

Printed Special Condition 1 incorporates the text of the Standard Conditions of Sale (3rd edition) from the centre pages of the contract form. These pages are not reproduced in this example. This condition should not be deleted, since to remove it is to remove the effect of the Standard Conditions. The second sentence of Condition 1(a) confirms that any variation to the Standard Conditions added to the contract by the parties will take precedence over the printed Standard Conditions.

*Printed Special Condition 2*

In this example, printed Special Condition 2 has been deleted and replaced by Special Condition 5. Note that the other conditions have been renumbered to take account of this deletion.

*Printed Special Condition 3 (renumbered as 2)*

Printed Special Condition 3 has been renumbered '2' because the original Printed Special Condition 2 has been deleted from the contract. This condition refers to the implied covenants which are given to the buyer under the Law of Property (Miscellaneous Provisions) Act 1994. In this case, the seller is selling with full title guarantee and this fact is included on the front page of the contract form.

*Printed Special Condition 4*

Printed Special Condition 4 has also been deleted since the sale did not include any chattels (fittings).

*Printed Special Condition 5 (renumbered as 3)*

This Condition provides two alternatives, depending whether the property is to be sold with vacant possession (as here) or is subject to tenancies. In the latter case the details of the tenancies would be given in the condition.

*Typed Special Condition 4*

A new typed Special Condition 4 has been added to the back page of the contract form to deal with the instructions given by the client in relation to the deposit. This clause is necessary in order to vary Standard Condition 2.2 which provides for the deposit to be held as stakeholder. There is no need to insert a provision providing for the deposit to be reduced to 5% (rather than the 10% required under the Standard Conditions) as the insertion of the agreed 5% deposit on the front page will override the Standard Condition. If, however, completion is delayed, Standard Condition 6.8.4 will require the buyer to pay the balance of the 10% deposit if a notice to complete is served (see Chapter 32).

*Typed Special Condition 5*

Another condition has been added to the contract by typed Special Condition 5. Where, as is usual, the seller's title is deduced to the buyer at the pre-contract stage of the transaction, it is customary to include a clause of this type which prevents the buyer from raising queries about the title once contracts have been exchanged.

*Typed Special Condition 6*

The seller gave an indemnity covenant when he bought the property and will remain liable on that after he has sold; see **14.7.9**. To protect himself, therefore, he will need to take a similar indemnity from the buyer. Although one is provided for by Standard Condition 4.5.4, this special condition has been inserted to serve as a reminder that an indemnity needs to be inserted in the purchase deed when it is drafted.

*Solicitors*

The names (and if desired the addresses and references) of the parties' solicitors are inserted at the foot of the back page of the contract form.

## 14.12 ACTION AFTER DRAFTING THE CONTRACT

Two copies of the draft contract should be prepared and both are sent to the buyer's solicitor with the remainder of the pre-contract package. A further copy of the contract should be retained by the seller's solicitor so that he has a copy in his file and can deal with any amendments proposed by the buyer over the telephone.

Consideration of the contract by the buyer is discussed in Chapter 19.

**Chapter 15**

# CONDITIONAL CONTRACTS AND OPTIONS

## 15.1 USE OF CONDITIONAL CONTRACTS

Conditional contracts are generally not desirable since they leave an element of doubt as to the existence and validity of the contractual obligations between the parties.

Most of the situations in which conditional contracts are used benefit the buyer more than the seller (eg 'subject to planning permission'), and the seller should refrain from entering a conditional contract if at all possible.

Conditional contracts carry with them some risks and uncertainties which make them inappropriate for everyday use, but they may be considered for use in the following circumstances:

(1) where the buyer has not had the opportunity before exchange of contracts to make searches and enquiries, or to conduct a survey, or where his mortgage arrangements have not been finalised;

(2) where the contract is dependent on planning permission being obtained for the property;

(3) where the sale is dependent on permission being obtained from a third party (eg landlord's consent).

### 15.1.1 Chain transactions

Conditional contracts should never be used where one or both of the parties has an unconditional sale or purchase contract which is dependent on the conditional contract. In this situation, if the conditional contract was rescinded for non-fulfilment of the condition, this would give rise to great difficulties in the fulfilment of the linked unconditional contract and could result in a breach of that contract.

### 15.1.2 Alternative solutions

Before agreeing to enter a conditional contract, the seller should consider whether there are any alternative solutions which could be used in preference to the conditional contract. For example, it may be preferable to delay exchange until the matter which was the subject of the condition has been resolved. An alternative solution may be to grant the buyer an option to purchase the property to be exercised within a stated period (see **15.5**).

## 15.2 REQUIREMENTS FOR A VALID CONDITIONAL CONTRACT

### 15.2.1 Certainty

The terms of the condition must be clear and certain. In *Lee-Parker v Izzett (No 2)* [1972] 2 All ER 800, an agreement to sell a freehold house 'subject to the buyer obtaining a satisfactory mortgage' was held to be void because the word 'satisfactory' was too vague and there was, therefore, no certainty regarding the circumstances in which the buyer would validly be able to withdraw from the contract. Not all 'subject to mortgage' clauses will suffer the same fate. Provided that the condition is drafted to make it clear that 'satisfactory' mortgage offer means an offer satisfactory to the buyer acting as a reasonable person, then the condition is likely to be valid. There is now an objective standard by which any mortgage offer received can be judged.

The need for certainty must also be borne in mind with regard to other common conditions. So, a contract subject to 'satisfactory searches' will again need a reasonableness provision inserting to avoid being void. See **15.4.1** as to drafting contracts 'subject to planning permission'.

If the condition is void for uncertainty then the whole contract between the parties will also fail.

### 15.2.2 Time for performance

It was held in *Aberfoyle Plantations Ltd v Cheng* [1960] AC 115, that the time for performance of the condition is of the essence and cannot be extended either by agreement between the parties or by the court. The same case also laid down the rules relating to the time for performance of the condition which are summarised as follows.

(1) Where the contract contains a completion date, the condition must be fulfilled by that date, irrespective of whether time was of the essence of the contractual completion date.
(2) If a time is stated for the fulfilment of the condition, that time-limit must be complied with or the contract will fail.
(3) If no time-limit is specified the condition must be fulfilled within a reasonable time. This provision is clearly unsatisfactory, since it leaves room for argument about what is a reasonable time and so a time-limit should always be stated.

## 15.3 WITHDRAWAL FROM THE CONTRACT

Only the party with the benefit of the condition may withdraw from the contract, and only for reasons connected with the condition. No other reason will justify withdrawal, although there is no obligation on the resiling party to prove that he is being reasonable in exercising his rights to withdraw.

It is a question of construction of the condition itself as to whether a party may withdraw before performance of the condition (see eg *Tesco Stores Ltd v William Gibson and Co Ltd* (1970) 214 EG 835).

## 15.4 DRAFTING

The drafting of a condition requires extreme care to ensure that the requirements outlined in **15.2** have been satisfied. No such provision is included in either set of Standard Conditions, although a contract to assign a lease may be conditional on the landlord's consent being obtained under Condition 8.3.4.

The following guidelines should be borne in mind.

(1)  Consider the precise event(s) on which the contract is to be made conditional.
(2)  By what time must the condition be fulfilled? (The specified time-limit cannot be extended.)
(3)  Consider the precise terms on which the party with the benefit of the condition will be able to rescind.
(4)  Make sure that there are no loopholes which would enable one party to escape from the contract other than for the non-fulfilment of the event(s) contemplated in (1) above.
(5)  Use an established precedent, adapting it to fit the exact requirements of the client's circumstances.

### 15.4.1  'Subject to planning permission'

Where a contract is to be made 'subject to the buyer obtaining planning permission', the following matters should be dealt with in the drafting of the condition:

(1)  the form of the application to be agreed by both parties;
(2)  if conditions are attached to the consent, what type of conditions would entitle the buyer to rescind?;
(3)  who should pay the fee for the application;
(4)  whether the buyer can rescind if the local planning authority do not grant permission within a stated period;
(5)  the seller should agree not to oppose the buyer's application;
(6)  whether the application is to be for detailed or outline consent;
(7)  whether the buyer is entitled to rescind if the planning application is never submitted.

## 15.5  OPTIONS

### 15.5.1  What is an option?

An option is a right given to a prospective buyer which allows him to insist on the seller selling the land to him if the buyer wishes to buy within a specified period. There is no obligation on the buyer to buy, but if he does choose to do so, the seller is obliged to sell. Options are common in commercial transactions, but less so in residential transactions.

### 15.5.2  Duration

The option agreement will state the time-limit within which it must be exercised if the seller is to be obliged to sell. The maximum permitted period is 21 years under the Perpetuities and Accumulations Act 1964, but shorter periods (eg 12 months) are much more common.

### 15.5.3 Formalities

An option must comply with the normal requirements for a valid contract – offer, acceptance, consideration, etc. Although the consideration can be a nominal amount (and can be dispensed with altogether if the option is granted by deed), it is common to find that the seller will require a not insubstantial amount to commit himself in this way. The option will also have to provide how the actual sale price of the land is to be arrived at if the buyer exercises the option. If the option is only exercisable for a short period, a fixed price can be specified in the option. In an option exercisable over a period longer than (say) 12 months, the effects of inflation, etc, must be considered and a new price will have to be arrived at. In such a case, the requirements of certainty must be considered, so some formula will need laying down so that the price can be ascertained if the parties are unable to reach agreement. An appointment of a valuer whose decision is final is common. The buyer may wish the consideration for the option itself to be set off against the purchase price; this will need stating expressly.

In addition to the normal contractual rules, as this is a land contract, the provisions of s 2 of the Law of Property (Miscellaneous Provisions) Act 1989 will also need to be taken into account. This requires that the contract is in writing, must incorporate all the agreed terms and be signed by both parties. When the option is exercised, the contract to buy the land comes into existence at that moment. The exercise of the option does not need the signature of both parties.

As the contract for sale comes into existence on the exercise of the option, the terms of that sale contract need considering in the usual way and will need providing for in the option contract. Otherwise, an open contract will be created, which will be unsatisfactory for both buyer and seller. So the option agreement should state that the sale contract will be subject to the Standard Conditions of Sale, how title will be deduced, what incumbrances the land will be sold subject to, what special conditions will apply, etc, in the same way as if the seller were drafting an ordinary sale contract. The buyer will also need to consider these as he would any other contract.

### 15.5.4 Protection of the option

In order to make the option binding on a subsequent buyer of the land, it should be protected by registration. This will be a C(iv) in unregistered land and a notice or caution in registered land. The prospective buyer will probably require a term to be inserted in the option agreement obliging the seller to deposit his land certificate at the Land Registry to facilitate the registration of a notice.

# Chapter 16

# DEDUCTION OF TITLE

## 16.1 DEDUCTION OF TITLE

'Deduction of title' is the expression used to signify the seller's obligation to prove to the buyer his ownership of the interest which he is purporting to sell. Ownership is proved to the buyer by producing documentary evidence of title. The method of doing this varies according to whether the land in question is registered or unregistered.

## 16.2 TIME FOR DEDUCTION

Historically, deduction of title took place only after contracts had been exchanged, so that the buyer had to take the seller's title on trust up until that time and to rely on his right to rescind the contract if the title later turned out to be defective.

The Protocol reflects modern practice and requires the seller to deduce title at the pre-contract stage of the transaction, but both sets of Standard Conditions of Sale maintain the traditional point of view by providing that the seller's evidence of title shall be deduced to the buyer 'immediately after making the contract' (Condition 4.1.1). Where title is deduced to the buyer before exchange of contracts, the contract should contain a condition precluding the buyer from raising queries about the title once contracts have been exchanged. In the absence of such a clause, the buyer would be able to rely on Condition 4.1.1 and could question the validity of the seller's title after exchange, which partly defeats the object of deducing title earlier in the transaction.

## 16.3 SELLER'S OBLIGATIONS

The seller's obligation in relation to the deduction of his title is to supply sufficient documentary evidence to the buyer to prove that he has the right to sell the land.

## 16.4 METHOD OF DEDUCTION FOR REGISTERED LAND

Section 110 of the Land Registration Act 1925 provides that the seller shall supply the buyer with:

(1) a copy of the entries on the register of title; and
(2) a copy of the filed plan; and
(3) an abstract or other evidence of matters as to which the register is not conclusive (eg overriding interests); and
(4) copies or abstracts of any document(s) noted on the register (eg a copy of a conveyance imposing restrictive covenants).

The items listed in (1) and (2) above cannot be excluded by contractual condition.

### 16.4.1 Office copies

Although not required by the statute, both the Protocol and Condition 4.2.1 require the seller to supply office copies of his title to the buyer. Office copies are copies prepared by the Land Registry itself and should always be supplied since they show the up-to-date position of the register. Photocopies of the land or charge certificate may not have been updated by HM Land Registry for several years, and may therefore not reflect the true state of the register. The seller should pay for the office copies.

## 16.5  METHOD OF DEDUCTION FOR UNREGISTERED LAND

The seller will prove his ownership of unregistered land by supplying the buyer with an abstract or epitome of the documents comprising the title. In some cases the evidence supplied will be made up of a combination of these two styles of presentation.

### 16.5.1  Abstract of title

An abstract of title is in essence a précis of all the documents comprised in the title. The preparation of an abstract in traditional form is a skilled and time-consuming task which has largely been superseded by the practice of supplying an epitome of the title supported by photocopies of all the documents referred to.

### 16.5.2  Epitome of title

An epitome of title is a schedule of the documents comprising the title accompanied by photocopies of the documents themselves. On the epitome, the documents should be numbered and listed in chronological order, starting with the earliest in time. Each document should be identified as to its date, type (eg conveyance, assent, etc), the names of the parties to it, whether a copy of the document is supplied with the epitome, and whether or not the original of the document will be handed to the buyer on completion. Photocopies of the documents which accompany the epitome must be of good quality, marked to show the document's corresponding number on the list shown by the epitome, and any plans included in the documents must be coloured or marked so that they are identical to the original document from which the copy has been made.

### 16.5.3 Documents to be included in the epitome

*Root of title*

Under an open contract, the epitome must commence with a good root of title at least 15 years old (Law of Property Act 1925, s 44 as amended). A good root of title is a document which:

(1)  deals with or shows the ownership of the whole legal and equitable interest contracted to be sold;
(2)  contains a recognisable description of the property; and
(3)  contains nothing to cast any doubt on the title.

## Documents capable of being good roots of title

A conveyance on sale or legal mortgage which satisfies the above requirements is generally acknowledged to be the most acceptable root of title, because it effectively offers a double guarantee of the title. The buyer in the present transaction will be investigating the seller's title for a minimum period of 15 years, the buyer or lender under the root conveyance would similarly have investigated title over a period of at least 15 years when he bought the property, thus the present buyer is provided with the certainty of the soundness of the title over a minimum period of at least 30 years.

In the absence of both a conveyance on sale and legal mortgage, title may be commenced with either a voluntary conveyance or an assent dated after 1925. Since voluntary conveyances and assents both effect gifts of the land, no investigation of prior title would have taken place at the time when they were executed, and therefore they do not provide the double check on the title which is given by the conveyance on sale or legal mortgage. For this reason they are less satisfactory to a buyer when offered as roots of title.

## Contractual condition

In the contract, the seller can, in theory, specify any document of any age as the root. However, a buyer will generally not accept a root that does not comply with the open contract requirements.

## Short title

Only in very rare cases will the seller be unable to provide the buyer with a root of title which satisfies the statutory minimum period of 15 years prescribed by the Law of Property Act 1925, s 44 (as amended). A buyer who is offered a short title should not accept the situation until he has received a satisfactory explanation for the reasons for the short root from the seller, and should be advised that, in accepting less than his statutory entitlement under the Law of Property Act 1925, he is also assuming the risk of being bound by incumbrances on the title which he has had no opportunity of discovering or investigating. The risk of being bound by undiscovered incumbrances stretches backwards in time not just to the statutory 15-year period, but to the date of the first document on the title (however old) which would satisfy the requirements for a good root. It follows that a short root should not be accepted by the buyer without a full investigation of the circumstances, the agreement of his lender, and investigation of the possibility of obtaining defective title insurance. The acceptance by the buyer of a short root of title may also affect his ability to obtain registration with an absolute title at HM Land Registry.

## Documents and events to be included in the abstract or epitome

All documents and events affecting the ownership of the land from the root to the present day must be included. There should be an unbroken chain of ownership from the root to the present seller. This includes the following:

(1) conveyances on sale and by gift;
(2) deaths;
(3) grants of representation to deceased owners' estates;
(4) changes of name of estate owners (eg on marriage or by deed poll or statutory declaration);
(5) leases;
(6) mortgages;

(7)  discharge of legal mortgages;

(8)  documents prior to the root which contain details of restrictive covenants which affect the property;

(9)  memoranda endorsed on documents of title (eg recording a sale of part, assent to a beneficiary, or severance of a beneficial joint tenancy);

(10) powers of attorney under which a document within the title has been executed.

### *Documents which need not be included in the abstract or epitome*

Certain documents need not be included in the abstract or epitome, although in some cases their inclusion will be helpful to the buyer. These include:

(1)  documents of record (eg death and marriage certificates) and land charges department search certificates. It is, however, good practice to include search certificates so that the buyer can see which searches have been correctly made in the past, in which case he need not repeat the search during his own investigation of the title. Documents of record should also always be abstracted so that the buyer receives a complete picture of the title;

(2)  leases which have expired by effluxion of time;

(3)  documents which pre-date the root of title, except where a document within the title refers to the earlier document (Law of Property Act 1925, s 45). Where a document within the title has been executed under a power of attorney, the power must be abstracted whatever its date.

### 16.5.4  Production of original documents

Condition 4.2.3 in both sets of Standard Conditions requires the seller to produce to the buyer (at the seller's expense) the original of every relevant document, or an abstract, epitome or copy with an original marking by a solicitor of examination, either against the original or against an examined abstract or against an examined copy. 'Marking' is a certification by a solicitor that the copy has been examined against, and is a true copy of, the original.

### 16.5.5  Documents which will not be handed over on completion

The epitome must specify which documents will be handed to the buyer on completion and which will be retained by the seller. The buyer is entitled on completion to take the originals of all the documents within the title, except those which relate to an interest in the land which is retained by the seller. For example, on a sale of part, the seller will retain the title deeds in order to be able to prove his ownership of the land retained by him. Similarly, a general power of attorney will be retained by the seller, because the donee of the power needs to keep the original document in order to deal with other property owned by the donor, and personal representatives will retain their original grant in order to administer the remainder of the deceased's estate.

## 16.6  LEASEHOLDS

Deduction of title to leaseholds is discussed in Chapter 36.

**Chapter 17**

# INVESTIGATION OF TITLE

## 17.1  SELLER'S INVESTIGATION OF TITLE

The seller's solicitor should investigate his client's title before drafting the contract for the sale of the property. The purpose of this investigation is to ensure that any problems which might exist with the title can be resolved without delay or, if this is not possible, that steps can be taken to disclose the defects to the buyer and to protect the seller by the inclusion in the contract of an appropriate exclusion clause (see Chapter 14). The method used by the seller's solicitor to investigate title is identical to that undertaken by a buyer's solicitor who is carrying out this task on behalf of his client. The paragraphs which follow apply equally to both situations.

## 17.2  BUYER'S INVESTIGATION OF TITLE

When the seller has supplied the buyer with evidence of his title, the buyer's task is to investigate that evidence to ensure that the seller is able to transfer that which he has contracted to sell and that there are no defects in the title which would adversely affect the interests of the buyer or his lender. Any matters which are unclear or unsatisfactory on the face of the documentary evidence supplied by the seller may be raised as queries (requisitions) with the seller within the time-limits specified in the contract for raising requisitions. It is usual to find that the contract will contain a special condition preventing the buyer raising requisitions on some or all aspects of the title. This will only become binding, however, on exchange of contracts and does not prevent the buyer from raising queries at the pre-contract stage.

## 17.3  LENDER'S INVESTIGATION OF TITLE

Where a lender is advancing money secured by a mortgage over the land, he will be concerned to ensure that there are no defects in title which would adversely affect his ability to sell the land should he need to do so to recover his loan. Where the same solicitor is acting for both the buyer and his lender in a simultaneous transaction, investigation is carried out only once, taking account of the particular requirements of each client. Where the lender is separately represented, the solicitor acting for the lender may undertake his own investigation of title. However, in commercial property transactions the borrower's solicitor may be required instead to provide the lender with a 'Certificate of Title'. This is a certificate signed by the borrower's solicitors certifying that the borrower has a 'good and marketable' title to the property. This certificate will be relied on by the lender in lieu of its own investigation of title. Special care should be taken in giving such certificates as the lender will be able to sue the borrower's solicitors should there in fact be any problem with the title. The City of London Law Society has produced a standard form of certificate which is in widespread use.

## 17.4  TIME FOR INVESTIGATION

Traditionally, investigation of title followed deduction of title as a procedure which was undertaken after exchange of contracts and was subject to time-limits imposed by the contract (see Condition 4.1.1 in both sets of Standard Conditions). In practice, the seller will invariably supply his evidence of title at the draft contract stage of the transaction (and in Protocol cases must do so) and may, by inclusion of a contractual provision to such effect, prevent the buyer from raising his requisitions after exchange of contracts, thus compelling the buyer to carry out his investigation at the pre-contract stage of the transaction.

## 17.5  REGISTERED LAND

Investigation of title of registered land comprises:

(1)  an examination of the office copy entries and filed plan supplied by the seller (including a copy of the lease where the title is leasehold and documents which are referred to on the register such as a transfer imposing restrictive covenants on the land);

(2)  checking for evidence of overriding interests since these are not on the register but are binding on the buyer irrespective of notice; and

(3)  pre-completion searches (see Chapter 28).

### 17.5.1  Looking at the office copies

The examination of office copies in registered land is a straightforward procedure. A written note should be kept of any matters on which requisitions need to be raised or further investigation carried out. A buyer should never accept office copies dated more than 12 months previously. Prior to completion the buyer will need to make a search at the registry to make sure no entries have been placed on the register since the date of the office copies, and this date must be no earlier than 12 months prior to the date of the search application.

The points in the following paragraphs should be checked.

***The property register***
(1)  Does the description of the land agree with the contract description?
(2)  Does the title number match the one given in the contract?
(3)  Is the estate freehold or leasehold? Does this accord with expectations from the contract?
(4)  Which easements are enjoyed by the property? Do these match the needs of the client?

***The proprietorship register***
(1)  Is the class of title correct?
(2)  Is the seller the registered proprietor? If not, who has the ability to transfer the land?
(3)  Are there any other entries? What is their effect?

***The charges register***
(1)  Are there any incumbrances?

(2) How do these affect the buyer?

(3) Which of them will be removed or discharged on completion?

(4) Have you agreed in the contract to buy subject to the incumbrances which remain?

### *The filed plan*

(1) Is the land being bought included within the title?

(2) Are there any colourings/hatchings which may indicate rights of way, the extent of covenants or land which has been removed from the title?

### *Miscellaneous points*

(1) Check that the office copies are recent; the date of issue is stated on them. The Land Registry will not accept a search in relation to office copies dated more than 12 months previously.

(2) Check that you have been given a copy of all covenants, etc, referred to on the Register.

## 17.5.2 Adverse entries on the proprietorship register

The most commonly found adverse entry on the proprietorship register will be a restriction. The wording of the restriction will indicate what procedure must be followed in order to conduct a valid disposition of the land. The buyer must therefore either follow that procedure (eg payment of money to two trustees in the case of land held on a trust of land) or require the seller to remove the restriction from the register on or before completion.

In some cases, an inhibition will be found on the proprietorship register (usually only in connection with the bankruptcy of the proprietor) which will prevent any disposition of the land until it is removed.

A third party who asserts rights over the land may place a caution on the proprietorship register which means that no dealing with the land can be registered until the cautioner has been given the opportunity by the Chief Land Registrar to show cause why the dealing to the buyer should not proceed. A buyer should not generally proceed with his purchase until the caution has been removed.

## 17.5.3 Overriding interests

The existence of most overriding interests can be discovered through:

(1) disclosure by the seller in the contract;

(2) pre-contract enquiries of the seller under which the seller will normally be asked to reveal details of adverse interests and occupiers' rights;

(3) a local land charges search (local land charges are overriding interests);

(4) inspection of the property before exchange which may reveal evidence of such matters as non-owning occupiers, easements and adverse possession.

## 17.5.4 Other matters

Other particular points which may arise out of the examination of a registered title are dealt with in **17.7**.

## 17.6 UNREGISTERED LAND

Investigation of title to unregistered land comprises:

(1) an examination of the documents supplied in the abstract or epitome to check that:

    (a) the root document is as provided for by the contract – if the wrong document has been supplied, the buyer is entitled to insist on the correct document being supplied in its place;

    (b) there is an unbroken chain of ownership beginning with the seller in the root document and ending with the present seller, ie the documents show the progression of the title from A to B, from B to C, from C to D and so on with no apparent breaks in the chain;

    (c) there are no defects in the title which will adversely affect the buyer's title or the interests of his lender;

(2) verification, ie inspection of the original deeds (in practice this is frequently postponed until completion and not carried out at this stage of the transaction);

(3) checking for evidence of occupiers (this is normally done by inspection of the property);

(4) pre-completion searches (see Chapter 28);

(5) the date when the area became subject to compulsory registration should also be checked to ensure that no transaction or event requiring registration has occurred since that time (see **4.2.2**).

### 17.6.1 Method of investigation of an unregistered title

Each of the documents within the abstract or epitome must be scrutinised carefully to ensure that it is in order. In order to ensure that nothing is overlooked on investigation, the solicitor should adopt and follow a systematic and thorough method of investigation of an unregistered title. One of the best methods is to read through the documents several times following the procedure set out in **17.6.2**. By following this routine, many of the common defects should be spotted. You should then move on to consider the nature of each document in the title and consider the particular problems which may arise in relation to such a document. These are set out in **17.7**. When investigating title on behalf of the buyer, the seller's solicitor should be required to resolve any problems discovered. If investigating title on behalf of the seller prior to drafting the contract, you must expect the buyer to request that any defects are rectified. If this is not possible, consideration should be given to inserting a special condition in the contract preventing requisitions on the point in issue; see **14.7.1**.

Whichever procedure is adopted, the following three basic rules must be adhered to.

(1) Notes must be made in writing. It is too dangerous to rely on memory, particularly when the title is long or complex.

(2) Investigation must start with the root document and move forwards chronologically from that point. If this is not done, gaps in the title may not be spotted.

(3) Investigation involves looking for omissions in the documentation as well as for errors on the face of the documents. It is therefore sensible to refer to a pre-prepared standard list which contains a reminder of all the items which need to be checked in each type of document.

### 17.6.2 Suggested method of investigating title

Before considering particular problems, the epitome and accompanying documents should be checked for the following, which will be looked at in turn:

(1) root of title;
(2) links in the chain;
(3) stamp duties;
(4) description;
(5) incumbrances;
(6) execution;
(7) searches.

### 17.6.3 Root of title

Check that the epitome begins with the root of title specified in the contract. Does that document satisfy the definition of a good root?

Generally, it is not possible (or necessary) to require evidence of title prior to the root (Law of Property Act 1925, s 145). It is possible, however, in the following circumstances:

(a) when an abstracted document is executed by an attorney, the buyer is always entitled to a certified copy of the power, whenever that might be dated;
(b) when the property is described by reference to a plan in a pre-root document, the buyer is entitled to see that plan;
(c) when the property is sold subject to or together with matters contained in a pre-root document (eg the land is sold subject to pre-root covenants), the buyer is entitled to a copy of those matters.

### 17.6.4 Links in the chain

There should be an unbroken chain of ownership from the root of title up to the present seller. Legal estates can be transferred only by means of some form of document (usually a deed), so there should be documentary evidence of every change of ownership. There should be a chain of ownership which shows the transfer from A to B and then from B to C and so on up to the present seller.

Any changes in the names of owners should also be evidenced, for example a marriage certificate if a name was changed on marriage.

### 17.6.5 Stamp duties

Unstamped or incorrectly stamped documents are neither good roots of title nor good links in the chain. They cannot be produced in evidence in civil proceedings, nor will they be accepted by the Land Registry on an application to register the title. The buyer must, therefore, check that all the title deeds have been correctly stamped. The payment of duty is evidenced by an embossed stamp (or stamps) being placed on the deed, usually in the top margin. If stamping defects are discovered, the buyer is entitled to insist that the seller remedies the deficiency at his own expense. Interest and a penalty are usually charged if stamp duty is not paid at the correct time. Any contractual provision requiring the buyer to meet the cost of putting the defect right will be void (Stamp Act 1891, s 117).

The following points should be considered:

(1)  Ad valorem duty. A conveyance on sale is liable to an ad valorem duty, ie a duty varying according to the amount of the consideration. Rates of duty have changed over the years and in practice a table of stamp duties should be used to check the applicable rates for a particular document. For some lower value properties a reduced rate or total exemption from duty was possible if the consideration was below a certain threshold; again this has changed over the course of time. However, the reduced rates could be claimed only if a certificate of value was included in the conveyance. The wording of the certificate is:

**'It is hereby certified that the transaction hereby effected does not form part of a larger transaction or of a series of transactions in respect of which the amount or value or the aggregate amount or value of the consideration exceeds ................ pounds.'**

Therefore, a conveyance on sale which does not have a certificate of value in it and does not bear an ad valorem stamp has not been correctly stamped.

(2)  Stamp duty does not have to be paid on mortgages executed after 1971.

(3)  A conveyance or transfer by way of gift executed after 30 April 1987 is exempt from stamp duty, provided it contains a certificate that it is an instrument within one of the categories of exempt documents under Stamp Duty (Exempt Instruments) Regulations 1987, SI 1987/516.

This is an example of such a certificate:

**'The Donor certifies that this deed falls within category [insert category] in the Schedule to the Stamp Duty (Exempt Instruments) Regulations 1987.'**

The category differs according to the circumstances of the transaction, which should be checked with the Regulations.

(4)  A power of attorney is not liable for stamp duty (s 85 of the Finance Act 1985).

(5)  Particulars delivered stamp. The Finance Act 1931 provides that certain documents must be produced to the Inland Revenue, together with a form giving particulars of the documents and any consideration received. The form is kept by the Inland Revenue (it provides useful information for the assessment of the value of the land) and the document is stamped with a stamp (generally called the 'PD stamp') as proof of its production. Without the PD stamp the document is not properly stamped and the person who failed in his responsibility to produce it (ie the original buyer) can be fined. The document must be produced irrespective of whether any ad valorem duty is payable.

The documents that need a PD stamp are:

(i)   a conveyance on sale of the freehold;
(ii)  a grant of a lease for 7 years or more;
(iii) the transfer on sale of a lease of 7 years or more.

### 17.6.6  Description

The buyer should check that the description of the property corresponds with the contract and is consistent throughout the epitome, ie that the ownership of the land presently being sold is included in the deeds. Particular care should be taken where the deeds show that part of the land included in the root document has been sold off separately. Copies of any plans referred to should be obtained, even if they are pre-root.

## 17.6.7 Incumbrances

Particular care should be taken with incumbrances. You should check to ensure that there are none disclosed by the deeds other than those disclosed in the contract. Copies of all covenants, easements and other burdens affecting the land should be supplied, even if they are pre-root. Burdens should be checked to ensure that they will not impede the client's proposed use for the property. If they appear to do so, you should consider whether they will in fact bind the client if he buys the land, applying normal land law principles. So, for example, in the case of a restrictive covenant, check if it has been registered as a D(ii) land charge; it will not be binding on a purchaser otherwise.

## 17.6.8 Execution

You should check that all deeds and documents in the title have been properly executed. If a seller did not execute, then the legal estate would not have passed to the buyer and there will be a break in the change of ownership.

The formalities for execution of a deed changed on 31 July 1990.

### (1) Execution of a deed by an individual on or after 31 July 1990

A conveyance of a legal estate must be executed as a deed. A document will only be a deed if:

(a) it is signed by its maker;
(b) that signature is witnessed and attested. This means that the signing of the deed by a party must be witnessed by another person who then also signs the deed to signify that he was present when the deed was so signed. There is no need for the same person to witness all of the signatures;
(c) it is clear that the document is intended to be a deed. That intention can be made clear either by describing the document as a deed (eg 'This Deed of Conveyance is made 1 September 1993 …') or because the document is expressed to be executed or signed as a deed (eg the attestation clause might say 'signed by the seller as his deed in the presence of …');
(d) the document is delivered as a deed.

The delivery of a deed may be a matter of intention only. A deed is delivered by a seller when it is signed by him with the intention that he will be bound by it.

It is possible for an individual to direct another person to sign a deed on his behalf, provided that the signature is made in his presence and there are two attesting witnesses.

### (2) Execution of a deed by a company on or after 31 July 1990

For a document to be executed as a deed by a company, it is necessary for the document to be executed and delivered as a deed.

A document can be executed either:

(a) by the affixing of the company seal; or
(b) by being signed by a director and the secretary, or by two directors of the company, provided that the document is expressed to be executed by the company. In other words, it must be made clear that the signatures amount to execution by the company, rather than execution by the directors personally.

If the executed document makes it clear on its face that it is intended to be a deed, it will be a deed when delivered as a deed. It is presumed, unless the contrary appears, to be delivered at the time it is executed.

A purchaser for value can presume:

(a) that the document has been properly executed as a deed by the company if it bears two signatures purporting to be those of a director and the secretary, or those of two directors; and

(b) that it has been delivered as a deed, providing it is clear on its face that it is intended by the signatories to be a deed.

The purchaser will be content, therefore, if he sees a statement in the document that it is signed as a deed by the company and sees accompanying this statement two signatures purporting to be those of directors or director and secretary.

This is an attestation clause used when a company is executing a deed, but not using its company seal:

Executed as a deed for XYZ Co Ltd

by the signature of

.................................................    Director

.................................................    Secretary

### (3) Formalities for deeds executed before 31 July 1990

(A) BY AN INDIVIDUAL

A deed executed before 31 July 1990 had to be signed and sealed by its maker, and delivered as his deed. If these formalities were not observed, the document was not a deed, and could not create or convey a legal estate.

The seal was usually only a red, self-adhesive circular piece of paper. However, it was still essential that a seal was placed on the conveyance before the maker signed. If a conveyance does not bear a seal, evidence is needed that a seal (or something representing a seal, such as a printed circle) was in position at the time of execution. If a seal was never there, then the document is not a deed, and could not have conveyed the legal estate.

The delivery of the deed is a matter of intention. A deed is delivered when it is signed by the maker with the intention that he is to be bound by it. If a person signs and seals a deed, it is inferred from this that the deed is also delivered, so no evidence that a deed was delivered is required.

(B) BY A COMPANY

If a conveyance was executed by a limited company, before 31 July 1990, the execution was valid if the conveyance was executed in accordance with the company's articles of association.

By s 74 of the Law of Property Act 1925, if the company seal had been affixed in the presence of the secretary and director, the deed was deemed to have been duly executed, even if in fact the articles demanded different formalities. Further, a buyer could assume that the deed had been executed so as to satisfy s 74 if there was on the deed a seal that purported to be the company seal, and signatures that purported to be those of secretary and director.

### 17.6.9 Searches

Although not essential, a seller should supply with the epitome copies of all previous land charges and company searches made against the previous owners of the land. These would have been made prior to previous dispositions of the land. If the Protocol is being used, a search against the seller should also be produced. Before he can safely buy the land, a buyer needs clear, correctly made searches against the names of all the estate owners revealed by the epitome. However, he need not repeat searches that have been previously made (with the exception of the seller, who must be searched against again), if they have been correctly made. The following matters should, therefore, be checked carefully.

(1)  Was the search made against the correct name of the person as set out in the deeds? The full name must be searched against and the spelling must be correct.
(2)  Was the search made for the full period of the person's ownership? The years of ownership searched against is set out on the search result and whether it is the correct period can be checked from the epitome.
(3)  Was the transaction which followed the search completed within the priority period of the search? The priority period is set out on the result of the search and this should be compared with the date on the appropriate deed.
(4)  In the case of changes of name (eg on marriage) is there a search against both old and new versions of the name?

If the above checks reveal any problems, eg a transaction not completed within the priority period, there is a danger that other entries could have been on the register which would not have been revealed by the search, but which would be binding on a buyer. It will, therefore, be necessary to repeat any such searches to ensure that there are no problems.

## 17.7 PARTICULAR PROBLEM AREAS

Having studied the epitome, checking the above general points, the nature of each document and transaction in the epitome should then be considered to see if any of the following particular problems areas are involved. These particular problems will also be relevant to the present transaction with the seller, whether the land is registered or unregistered. The points raised apply to both systems of conveyancing, unless otherwise stated.

### 17.7.1 Conveyance by trustees to themselves

In the case of a conveyance by trustees or personal representatives to one of themselves, enquiry must be made into the circumstances of the transaction because, on the face of it, such a conveyance is in breach of trust and is voidable by the beneficiaries. Such a transaction can be justified if one of the following situations exists:

(1)  there is proof of a pre-existing contract in favour of the trustee or personal representative;
(2)  the personal representative was a beneficiary under the will or intestacy of the deceased;
(3)  the consent of all the legally competent (ie adult and sane) beneficiaries was obtained to the transaction;

(4)  the conveyance was made under an order of the court;

(5)  the transaction was sanctioned by the trust instrument.

## 17.7.2  Trustees of land

### *Registered land*

In registered land, a restriction may be entered on the proprietorship register which will indicate to the buyer what must be done to overreach the beneficiaries' interests. Provided the terms of the restriction are complied with, the buyer will get good title. In all cases, the disposition must be made by all the trustees, being at least two in number, or a trust corporation.

### *Unregistered land*

Since 1 January 1997, trustees of land (including trustees for sale) have the same powers of disposition as a sole beneficial owner, unless the trust deed varies these or imposes a requirement for consents to be obtained. If the trust deed indicates that consents are required to a sale, a buyer is not concerned to see that the consents of more than two persons are obtained and is never concerned with the consent of a person under mental incapacity. Where the person whose consent is required is not of full age, the consent of the minor's parent or guardian must be obtained. A buyer must pay his money to all the trustees, being at least two individuals or a trust corporation, to take the land free from the equitable interests of the beneficiaries (see the Law of Property Act 1925, ss 2 and 27). A sale by trustees for sale prior to 1 January 1997 will be subject to similar rules, but the provisions of the Law of Property Act 1925, ss 26–28 should be checked in transactions other than a sale or where consents are required.

### *Appointing a further trustee*

If there is only one trustee, then the buyer must insist that a second trustee is appointed in order to overreach the interests of the beneficiaries. The appointment will usually be made by the surviving trustee (although the trust deed can confer the power of appointment on someone else). The appointment can be made prior to the contract for sale being entered into. In this case, the new trustee will thus be a party to the contract and bound by its terms. This is particularly useful where the new trustee is also in occupation of the property (see **19.4.3**). Alternatively, the sole trustee can enter into the contract on his own and then appoint a further trustee prior to completion in order to receive the purchase price and thus ensure overreaching takes place. A special condition can be included in the contract requiring the seller to appoint the further trustee, although he would be under an obligation to do so anyway in order to comply with the duty to make good title.

## 17.7.3  Personal representatives

### *Registered land*

On production of the grant, personal representatives may become registered as proprietors of the land, in which case, provided the buyer deals with the registered proprietors and complies with any restriction on the register, he will get good title. Personal representatives would not normally register themselves as proprietors unless they intended to hold on to the land without disposing of it for some period of time, for example, during the minority of a beneficiary. In other cases, the personal representatives will produce their grant of representation to the buyer as proof of their authority to deal with the land. Provided the buyer takes a transfer from all the proving personal representatives and submits an office copy or certified copy of the grant with his application for registration, he will obtain a good title. An assent made by personal representatives to a beneficiary must be in the form prescribed under the Land Registration Rules 1997. Unlike in unregistered land (see below), there is no danger of the same piece being mistakenly disposed of twice.

## *Unregistered land*

### *(1) Powers of personal representatives*

Personal representatives enjoy the same wide powers as trustees of land. If there is only one proving personal representative, he has all the powers of two or more personal representatives and, consequently (unlike a sole individual trustee), can convey the land on his own and give a valid receipt for the proceeds of sale. If, however, the grant is made to two or more personal representatives, they must all join in the assent or conveyance. A buyer must therefore call for the grant to see who has or have been appointed as personal representative(s) and must insist that all the personal representatives named in the grant join in the assent or conveyance, or call for evidence of the death of any personal representative who will not be a party to the purchase deed.

### *(2) Assents*

An assent made by personal representatives must be in writing in order to pass the legal estate in the land to the beneficiary. The beneficiary who is to take the land must be named in the document, which must be signed by the personal representatives. If the document contains covenants given by the beneficiary (eg indemnity in respect of existing restrictive covenants), it must be by deed. Even where the beneficiary is also the sole personal representative (eg where a widow is her deceased husband's sole personal representative and sole beneficiary) a written assent is required (*In re King's Will Trusts; Assheton v Boyne* [1964] Ch 542). Where there is an assent on the title, it is essential to check that a memorandum of that assent was endorsed on the grant of representation. Otherwise there is a danger that a later sale by the personal representatives will deprive the assentee of the legal ownership; see *(3) Section 36 statement*, below.

### *(3) Section 36 statement*

The purpose of s 36 of the Administration of Estates Act 1925 is to provide protection for a buyer who purchases from personal representatives. It is based on the premise that personal representatives, not dealing with their own property, and perhaps dealing with a large complicated estate, may be more likely than other owners of land to attempt (mistakenly) to dispose of the same property twice. A buyer will take good title from personal representatives, even if there has been a prior disposition by them, provided that:

(a) the conveyance to the buyer contains a statement given by the personal representatives that they have not made any previous assent or conveyance of the same land; and

(b) no memorandum of a previous conveyance or assent of the land is endorsed on the grant; and

(c) there has been no earlier conveyance of the land.

This latter provision means that an assentee is at risk of losing title to a later purchaser who relies on the section, whereas a buyer is not. To prevent this happening, the assentee should have insisted that a memorandum of the assent was endorsed on the grant of representation. A subsequent assentee is not able to rely on the provisions of s 36; it only benefits a 'purchaser', ie a person who has given value.

Where, as now, the transaction induces first registration, an endorsement on the grant is not required. The need for registration of any disposition will prevent any land being disposed of twice.

*(4) Acknowledgment for grant*

A disposition by personal representatives should contain an acknowledgment of the right to production of their grant of representation because this is a document of title the inspection of which may be required by subsequent buyers of the land. The grant should be inspected to check for endorsements which have been made on it.

*(5) Naming the beneficiary*

An assent or conveyance by personal representatives of a legal estate is sufficient evidence in favour of a buyer that the person in whose favour it is made is the person entitled to have the legal estate conveyed to him, unless there is a memorandum of a previous assent or conveyance on the grant. In effect, this means that a buyer from an assentee of land, having checked the grant and found no adverse endorsements, does not have to look at the deceased's will to check that the assentee was entitled to the land, but this provision will not protect the buyer if it is apparent from some other source (eg the assent itself) that it was made in favour of the wrong person (see the Administration of Estates Act 1925, s 36).

*(6) Investigation of title points*

The result of all the above is that, when investigating an unregistered title, the following points should be checked:

(a)  On a sale by personal representatives:

– inspect grant to check authority of personal representatives;
– ensure all proving personal representatives joined in conveyance;
– check grant contains no memorandum of a prior disposition of the land;
– check conveyance contains a s 36 statement;
– check conveyance contains an acknowledgement for production of the grant.

(b)  On an assent by personal representatives:

– inspect grant to check authority of personal representatives;
– ensure all proving personal representatives joined in assent;
– check grant contains no memorandum of a prior disposition of the land;
– check grant does contain a memorandum of the assent;
– check assent contains an acknowledgement for production of the grant.

### 17.7.4 Co-owners

Co-owners hold land on a trust of land, and the remarks relating to trustees in **17.7.2** apply.

## Registered land

### *(1) Tenants in common*

If the co-owners are tenants in common in equity, a restriction will be entered on the proprietorship register. In the event of death of one or more of the co-owners, so that at the time of sale there is only one surviving trustee, the restriction ensures that a second trustee is appointed to join with the survivor in the transfer. This is the preferred and safest method of dealing with this situation. Alternatively, the buyer can deal with the survivor alone, provided that the restriction is removed from the register. Proof of death of the deceased must also be provided.

### *(2) Joint tenants*

If the co-owners are joint tenants in equity, no restriction is placed on the register and a buyer may deal with the survivor of them on proof of the death of the deceased co-owner.

## Unregistered land

The conveyance under which the co-owners bought the land should be inspected to see whether they held as joint tenants or tenants in common in equity.

### *(1) Tenants in common*

The sole survivor of tenants in common does not automatically become entitled to the whole legal and equitable estate in the land, because a tenancy in common is capable of passing by will or on intestacy, so the trust still subsists. A buyer from the survivor should, therefore, insist on taking a conveyance only from two trustees in order to overreach any beneficial interests which may subsist under the trust. This is the safest and preferred method of dealing with the survivor of tenants in common. Alternatively, if the survivor has become solely and beneficially entitled to the whole legal and equitable interest in the land, he may convey alone as sole owner on proof to the buyer of this fact. Such proof would consist of the death certificate of the deceased, a certified copy or office copy of the grant of representation and an assent made in favour of the survivor.

### *(2) Joint tenants*

The survivor of beneficial joint tenants becomes entitled to the whole legal and equitable interest in the land, but a buyer from him will accept a conveyance from the survivor alone only if he can be satisfied that he will benefit from the protection of the Law of Property (Joint Tenants) Act 1964. The problem is that the joint tenancy could have been severed, turning it into a tenancy in common.

This Act (which is retrospectively effective to 1925) allows the buyer to assume that no severance of the joint tenancy had occurred before the death of the deceased joint tenant. To gain the protection of the Act, the following three conditions must all be satisfied:

(1)  there must be no memorandum of severance endorsed on the conveyance under which the joint tenants bought the property;
(2)  there must be no bankruptcy proceedings registered against the names of either of the joint tenants at HM Land Charges Registry;
(3)  the conveyance by the survivor must contain a statement that the survivor is solely and beneficially entitled to the land.

If any of the above conditions is not met, the survivor must be treated as a surviving tenant in common and the procedure (above) relating to tenants in common must be followed.

Should it be necessary to appoint a further trustee, the procedure outlined in **17.7.2** should be followed.

### 17.7.5 Disposing lenders

#### *Existence of the power of sale*

The Law of Property Act 1925, s 101 gives a power to sell the legal estate vested in the borrower, subject to prior incumbrances but discharged from subsequent ones, to every lender whose mortgage is made by deed. Thus, unless expressly excluded, the power is available to a lender under a legal mortgage. In relation to registered land, only the proprietor of a registered charge has a power of sale. Where a lender sells in exercise of his power of sale, the mortgage deed will not bear a receipt but the buyer nevertheless will take free from it and from subsequent mortgages.

#### *Power of sale arises*

The power of sale arises when the mortgage money becomes due under the mortgage, ie on the legal date for redemption, which is usually set at an early date in the mortgage term. The power only becomes exercisable by the lender as provided for in the mortgage deed, or when one of the events specified in the Law of Property Act 1925, s 103 has occurred. These events are:

(1) a demand has been made for the principal sum outstanding on the mortgage and this demand is unpaid for 3 months; or
(2) any interest due under the mortgage is in arrears for 2 months; or
(3) there is breach of any other covenant in the mortgage.

A buyer from the lender must check (by looking at the mortgage deed) that the power of sale has arisen, but need not enquire whether the power has become exercisable.

### 17.7.6 Attorneys

#### *Powers of attorney*

A power of attorney is a deed under which the donor appoints someone (the attorney or donee) to carry out certain actions on his behalf. In the context of conveyancing, it might be necessary for a seller to give someone a power of attorney to execute documents on the seller's behalf because the seller was going abroad and would not be available when the documents needed to be signed.

#### *Types of power*

There are four types of power of attorney:

(1) a general power, under the Powers of Attorney Act 1971, s 10, entitles the attorney to deal with all of the donor's assets;
(2) a special power, which permits the attorney only to deal with certain specified assets or categories of assets;
(3) a trustee power, which is used where property is held on trust;

(4) an enduring power, which is made under the Enduring Powers of Attorney Act 1985. This type of power endures through the donor's mental incapacity (subject to registration of the power).

### Revocation

Subject as below, a power of attorney can be revoked expressly by the donor or will be revoked automatically on the donor's death, mental incapacity, or bankruptcy. Once registered, enduring powers are irrevocable except by order of the court.

A person who buys from an attorney (and subsequent buyers) will get good title if the power:

(a) authorises the transaction which is to take place between the attorney and the buyer; and

(b) is valid and subsisting at the date of completion of the transaction.

The buyer is therefore concerned to ensure that the power had not been revoked at the date of completion of his purchase from the attorney. A summary of the protection given to the buyer by the Powers of Attorney Act 1971 is set out below.

### Copy of power

The buyer is entitled to a certified copy of any power of attorney which affects the title (even if the transaction involves land which is unregistered and the power is dated earlier than the root of title).

### Terms of the power

By checking the terms of the power itself the buyer should ensure that the transaction was authorised by the power. A general power of attorney under the Powers of Attorney Act 1971, s 10 entitles the attorney to take any action the donor could have taken with regard to any of the donor's property. Other types of power should be carefully checked to ensure that they authorise the particular transaction in relation to the particular property concerned.

### Registered land

The original or a certified copy of the power must be submitted when an application is made to register a disposition made in exercise of the power. If the transaction between the attorney and the buyer is not made within 12 months of the grant of the power, a statutory declaration made by the buyer to the effect that he had no knowledge of the revocation of the power must accompany the application for registration. For Land Registry purposes, a certified copy of a power of attorney must be certified on every page.

### Unregistered land

NON-ENDURING POWERS

A person who buys directly from an attorney holding any type of non-enduring power of attorney will take good title under the Powers of Attorney Act 1971, s 5(2), provided he buys in good faith without knowledge of the revocation of the power. Death revokes such a power, thus the buyer cannot take good title if he is aware of the death of the donor. A subsequent buyer (a person who buys from the person who bought from the attorney, in this paragraph referred to as 'C') obtains the protection of the Powers of Attorney Act 1971, s 5(4) if either:

(1)  the dealing between the attorney and his immediate purchaser (P) took place within 12 months of the grant of the power; or

(2)  the person who buys directly from the attorney (P) makes a statutory declaration within 3 months of completion of the sale between P and C to the effect that he (P) had no knowledge of the revocation of the power.

Where a person (P) buys from an attorney more than 12 months after the date of the grant of the power, P's solicitor should require P to make the requisite statutory declaration immediately on completion of the transaction, since this document will be required as evidence of non-revocation on a subsequent disposition of the property. If the declaration is not made immediately and P dies before making the declaration, there will be a defect in title, since the subsequent buyer (C) will not be able to take the protection of the Powers of Attorney Act 1971, s 5(4).

ENDURING POWERS

An enduring power of attorney under the Enduring Powers of Attorney Act 1985 must be in the form prescribed by that Act. Until the incapacity of the donor, the power takes effect as an ordinary power and the Act contains provisions to protect buyers which are similar to those outlined above. On the incapacity of the donor, the attorney's authority to act becomes limited to such acts as are necessary for the protection of the donor and his estate until such time as the power is registered with the Court of Protection. Once registered, the power is incapable of revocation and the attorney's full authority to act is restored.

Where a person is buying from an attorney who holds an enduring power, he should make a search at the Court of Protection to ensure that no application for registration of the power is pending. If the power has already been registered, the attorney should produce the registration certificate to the buyer. An office copy of the power can be produced as evidence both of the contents of the power and of its registration.

### Trustees – The Trustee Delegation Act 1999

The law regarding the use of powers of attorney by trustees was changed, non-retrospectively, as from 1 March 2000.

In the case of powers of attorney created prior to that date (even if exercised after it), trustees could not use a general power. They had to use a trustee power under Trustee Act 1925, s 25. However, this only permitted delegation for a maximum of 12 months and could not be used to delegate in favour of a sole human co-trustee. This had profound implications in relation to co-owners, who hold the land under an implied trust. Take the case of a husband and wife who were co-owners. They could not use a general power, and if using a trustee power could not appoint the other as attorney; a stranger would have to be appointed.

However, due to the wording of s 3 of the Enduring Powers of Attorney Act 1985, one co-owner could validly appoint the other as attorney if an enduring power was used.

### Powers created prior to 1 March 2000

The rules set out above continue to apply. However, any enduring powers created prior to 1 March in favour of a sole human co-trustee will cease to be effective in relation to the trust property on registration of the power with the Court of Protection or on 28 February 2001, whichever is the earlier unless the donor has a beneficial interest in the land. In such a case, the power will continue to be effective in relation to the trust property. Thus an enduring power made by one co-owner in favour of the other in (say 1999) can still be used today, as the donor has a beneficial interest under the implied trust under which the co-owners hold the land.

*Powers created on or after 1 March 2000*

Trustees can now use a general power provided the donor of the power has a beneficial interest in the land. In favour of a purchaser, this is to be taken conclusively if the donee of the power, ie the attorney, makes a statement to that effect either at the time of the disposition by him, or within 3 months afterwards.

Section 25 of the Trustee Act 1925 has been rewritten to provide for a new general trustee power of attorney. This still allows delegation only for a maximum period of 12 months. Such a power can be an enduring power.

Co-owners can thus use either an ordinary general power or a general trustee power and can in both cases validly appoint a sole co-owner as attorney. The 1999 Act makes it clear, however, that a person acting both as trustee and as attorney for the other trustee, cannot give a valid receipt for capital money; remember that the receipt of two trustees is required to overreach the beneficial interests under a trust.

So, the end result of these complicated provisions is that if one of two co-owners wishes to appoint an attorney to execute a deed selling the land, the co-trustee cannot be appointed as the co-trustee will not be able to give a valid receipt. In such a case, a stranger will need to be appointed and this rule cannot be evaded by using an enduring power.

## 17.7.7  Discharged mortgages

### *Registered land*

A mortgage over registered land which has been discharged will be deleted from the charges register of the title and is thus of no further concern to the buyer. As far as the seller's existing mortgage is concerned, the buyer should raise a requisition requiring this to be removed on or before completion. Discharge of a mortgage of registered land is effected by filing a completed Form DS1 at HM Land Registry.

### *Unregistered land*

Discharged legal mortgages should be abstracted by the seller and checked by the buyer's solicitor to ensure that the discharge was validly effected.

Where a lender has sold the property in exercise of his power of sale, the mortgage deed will not bear a receipt.

### *(1)  Building society mortgages*

Provided that the receipt (usually endorsed on the mortgage deed) is in the form of wording prescribed by the Building Societies Act 1986 and is signed by a person authorised by the particular society, the receipt may be treated as a proper discharge of the mortgage without further enquiry being made.

*(2) Other mortgages*

By the Law of Property Act 1925, s 115, a receipt endorsed on the mortgage deed operates to discharge the mortgage, provided it is signed by the lender and names the person making repayment. However, where the money appears to have been paid by a person not entitled to the immediate equity of redemption, the receipt will usually operate as a transfer of the mortgage. Thus, if the person making repayment is not the borrower named in the mortgage or a personal representative or trustee acting on his behalf, the receipt should make it expressly clear that the receipt is to operate as such and is not intended to be a transfer of the mortgage to the person making payment.

### 17.7.8  Voluntary dispositions

When a voluntary disposition is presented as a link in the chain of title, or when acting for the donee taking a voluntary conveyance from a donor, care needs to be exercised, since the transaction could be set aside by the donor's trustee in bankruptcy under the Insolvency Act 1986 (as amended by the Insolvency (No 2) Act 1994) at any time until 5 years has elapsed from the date of the voluntary transaction.

The rules relating to voluntary dispositions apply to any transaction at an undervalue, and this includes pure gifts, assents, inter spouse transfers on marriage breakdown (including those made by court order) and any inter vivos transaction where the full market value consideration is not paid for the property.

#### *Disposition by an individual within the past 2 years*

A disposition by an individual within the 2 years immediately preceding the current transaction may be set aside by the trustee in bankruptcy if the donor is made bankrupt. It is therefore unsafe to proceed with the current transaction until at least 2 years have elapsed since the date of the voluntary disposition. However, in the case of registered land, unless a restriction appears on the register, the buyer will be protected.

#### *Disposition by an individual between 2 and 5 years ago*

In the case where a buyer knows of a voluntary disposition from A to B between 2 and 5 years ago, is it safe for a buyer to buy from B, or is there a danger that, if A becomes insolvent, the trustee in bankruptcy could claim against the buyer? The basic principle is that a buyer from B is protected provided that he has acquired in good faith and for value. The buyer is presumed *not* to be in good faith in either of the following cases:

(1)  when the buyer acquired the property, he had notice of the bankruptcy proceedings and that the disposition to B was at an undervalue; or

(2)  the buyer was an associate of either A or B. Associate is widely defined to include a person's spouse or ex-spouse, members of his family and his spouse's family, his partner and his partner's family and his employees.

Registration of bankruptcy proceedings will amount to notice, so a buyer will need to make a bankruptcy search against A, not just for the period of A's ownership, but also up until the date of his own acquisition. This is to ensure that he is not presumed to be lacking in good faith under paragraph 1. If the search reveals bankruptcy entries against A, then the purchase cannot proceed. Similarly, if the buyer is an associate of either A or B, then the sale cannot proceed even if the bankruptcy search is clear; in the case of A becoming bankrupt after the purchase, the buyer will be deemed not to be in good faith because he is an associate, even though he had no notice of the bankruptcy when he bought.

### Disposition by an individual more than 5 years ago

No problems arise with a disposition made by an individual more than 5 years before the date of the present transaction, unless the donor went bankrupt within 5 years of the voluntary disposition. It will therefore be necessary to conduct a Land Charges Department search against the name of the donor from the date when the donor acquired the property until 5 years after the date of the voluntary disposition.

### Disposition by a company within the past 2 years

If a disposition made by a company within the 2 years preceding the date of the current transaction was to a person connected with the company, it may be set aside by the liquidator on the company's subsequent insolvency. The current transaction cannot therefore proceed until at least 2 years have elapsed since the voluntary disposition. A 'person connected' is defined by the Insolvency Act 1986, ss 249 and 435 as a director of the company and any associate (as defined above) of a director and associates of the company.

If the disposition was made within the past 2 years to someone not connected with the company, the liquidator's power to set the transaction aside on the company's subsequent insolvency applies only if the present buyer has notice of the insolvency proceedings and of the undervalue transaction. These rules also apply to a transfer of property between two companies in the same group.

### Disposition by a company more than 2 years earlier

Where a disposition was made by a company more than 2 years earlier, no problems arise unless the company went into liquidation or became subject to an administration order within 2 years of the disposition. A company search should be made against the donor company to ensure that no liquidation or administration proceedings were commenced within the 2 years following the date of the voluntary disposition.

### Summary

A buyer who buys for value and in good faith will generally now be protected under the Insolvency Act 1986 (as amended by the Insolvency (No 2) Act 1994). However, some lenders are reluctant to lend on property where there has been a voluntary disposition within the past 5 years unless an insurance policy is obtained covering the possibility of the donor's insolvency within this period.

### Registered land

Once the donee has become the registered proprietor there is no problem, since a subsequent buyer is subject only to entries on the register and to overriding interests. However, in the case of dispositions registered on or after 1 April 2000, the register includes details of the price paid by the proprietor. If this appears to be nil or something of no monetary value, then the provisions of the Act should be borne in mind. Where first registration is based on a voluntary disposition, a note will be added in the proprietorship register to the effect that the title is subject to the provisions of the Insolvency Act 1986. Where such a note appears, a buyer from that proprietor will need to consider the effect of the Insolvency Act 1986 as outlined above.

## 17.8 VERIFICATION OF TITLE

Verification of title consists of checking the evidence of title supplied by the seller against the original deeds. In registered land, the true state of the register can be confirmed by the buyer when making his pre-completion search at HM Land Registry.

In unregistered land, the abstract or epitome should be checked against the seller's original deeds. In most cases, where the title is not complex, the buyer's solicitor postpones his verification until actual completion. If he then finds an error on the title which had not previously been disclosed by the seller, although Condition 4.1.1 in both sets of Standard Conditions allows a further period of six working days to raise further requisitions, there will inevitably be a delay in completion. However, where photocopies of the original deeds have been supplied with the epitome, verification will normally be a formality.

Condition 4.2.3 in both sets of Standard Conditions requires the seller, at his own expense, to produce to the buyer the original of every document within the title or, if the original is not available, an abstract, epitome or copy with an original marking by a solicitor of examination either against the original or against an examined abstract or against an examined copy.

## 17.9 RAISING REQUISITIONS

If the buyer's solicitor's investigation of title reveals any problem then the buyer should raise a 'requisition on title' of the seller's solicitor. A requisition is a question asked about the problem which requires a remedy from the seller.

If the seller ultimately cannot show good title then the buyer may consider whether defective title indemnity insurance is available (perhaps at the seller's cost) in order to protect him should he decide to proceed and accept the defect. If such insurance is unavailable or the defect is such that it may affect the buyer's enjoyment of the property then the buyer is unlikely to proceed.

The buyer (and the buyer's lender) should be advised of any defects in title as soon as they become apparent.

Traditionally, title was deduced by the seller only following exchange. In such a situation, the seller's inability to make good title would have constituted a breach of contract entitling the buyer to withdraw from the contract and/or claim damages. Where requisitions are raised prior to exchange, a buyer will have no remedy should he choose to withdraw because of defects in title as there is no contract between the parties. Equally, of course, the seller would have no remedy if the buyer chose to withdraw for no good reason.

Condition 4.1.1 in both sets of Standard Conditions requires the buyer to raise requisitions within 6 working days of the later of exchange or the delivery of the epitome. This is so whether or not title is deduced prior to exchange. Remember, however, that it is usual nowadays for the seller to insert a special condition in the contract barring out requisitions (see **14.7.2**). This will not prevent the buyer raising queries prior to exchange (although the seller need not answer them), but it will prevent the buyer raising requisitions after exchange on matters disclosed by the epitome.

## 17.10  WORKED EXAMPLE OF AN UNREGISTERED TITLE

An example of an abstract of title to unregistered land which has been prepared in traditional form is set out below. The following points would need to be noted if the title was being investigated by the buyer's solicitor on behalf of his client.

(1)  The first entry on the abstract is a note of a Land Charges Department search (LCR search) made on 20 June 1967. This reveals a D(ii) entry (ie a restrictive covenant). Provided that the buyer's solicitor checks this entry and it is consistent with restrictive covenants which have been revealed to him in the contract, no further action will be required. The search shows no other entries ('n.s.e.' means 'no subsisting entries').

(2)  This search is followed by a conveyance dated 23 June 1967, just 3 days after the date of the search certificate and well within the priority period of the search. This conveyance is the 'root document': it is a conveyance on sale (note the consideration and receipt clauses), dealing with the whole of the property and is more than 15 years old (see the Law of Property Act 1925, s 44). This conveyance must be checked carefully to ensure that the chain of title which starts with this document follows down the subsequent line of documents without break or interruption. The property conveyed by the deed (commencing with the words 'ALL THAT') is 17 Lakeside Road, Burley. Does the same property carry on through the subsequent dealings, is it added to or detracted from? Is it the property which the present buyers have contracted to purchase? In this document the property is described by reference to a plan ('more particularly delineated on the plan') which is attached to an earlier, pre-root document (the conveyance dated 14 March 1956). Because a document within the title itself refers to an earlier document, the Law of Property Act 1925, s 45 will allow the buyer to call for production of the earlier document. Without sight of the plan attached to the 1956 conveyance, it is not possible to ascertain precisely the land which is being sold in the 1967 conveyance. A requisition must therefore be raised requiring the seller to produce a copy of this plan.

(3)  The property in the 1967 conveyance is also described as having the benefit of rights and easements granted by the conveyance (ie the 1956 conveyance). Unless the 1956 document is produced, the buyer will be unable to find out what these rights and easements are. Similarly, the property is described as being subject to covenants imposed by the 1956 conveyance, so once again production of this document must be called for, relying on the right given by the Law of Property Act 1925, s 45 to do so. Hopefully, the covenants referred to in the 1956 covenant will reconcile with the D(ii) entry revealed by the Land Charges Department search dated 20 June 1967.

(4)  Clause 2 of the 1967 conveyance is an indemnity covenant given by the buyers under that conveyance in respect of the existing restrictive covenants. It is usual

to find a chain of indemnity covenants passing down the chain of transactions, covering both positive and restrictive covenants.

(5) The certificate of value had the effect of reducing the amount of stamp duty payable on the document. Note the stamp duty and PD stamp underneath the date in the left-hand column.

(6) The document is then 'executed by both parties and attested'. The seller must always sign the deed in order to convey the legal estate, the buyer will sign if he covenants to do something. In this case, the buyer has given an indemnity covenant and so his signature is required. Conveyances executed before 1 August 1990 were not required by law to be attested (witnessed), but it was conventional to have a witness to the parties' signatures, as has been done in this case.

(7) Concurrently with her purchase, Miss Smith mortgaged the property to the Countryside Building Society. This mortgage is the next abstracted document. Mortgages granted before August 1971 required stamp duty, which this one correctly bears. A legal mortgage will be signed by the borrower, but not by the lender. This document appears to be in order except that, since the property has subsequently passed to other owners, one would expect the mortgage to have been paid off, at the very latest on the date when the next owner, Peter William Marshfield, took the property. A note of the discharge of the mortgage should appear in the abstract. A requisition must be raised with the seller to ensure that this mortgage was in fact properly discharged and is not still subsisting.

(8) The abstract then notes that SJ Smith died on 28 September 1976. She dies intestate and a grant of representation to her estate is taken out by her administrators on 20 November 1976. They then make an assent of the property to Mr Marshfield on 1 January 1977. The assent has been made by all the proving personal representatives, it names the beneficiary in whose favour it is made, and thus can be assumed to have been made in favour of the correct person, ie the buyer need not check the intestacy rules to ensure that Mr Marshfield was the proper person entitled to inherit this property. Mr Marshfield correctly gives an indemnity covenant in respect of the restrictive covenants contained in the 1956 conveyance (see earlier) but, where an assent contains a covenant, the document must be a deed and at that date should have borne stamp duty. There is no evidence that this assent is a deed and the document does not appear to bear duty. Both of these omissions must be queried with the seller. A note of the assent should have been made on the grant by the personal representatives (see the Administration of Estates Act 1925, s 36) in order to protect Mr Marshfield against a second disposition of the same property to other buyers. This does not appear to have been done and a query should be raised in relation to it. The grant of administration forms part of the title, showing how the land passed from SJ Smith to Mr Marshfield, but the original document would be retained by the personal representatives so that they could complete their administration of the estate. Mr Marshfield therefore needs an acknowledgment in the assent, given by the personal representatives, confirming Mr Marshfield's right (and that of his successors in title) to the production of the original grant. The assent does not appear to contain such a clause. This omission must be queried with the seller.

(9) The Land Charges Department search of 14 September 1988 is clear (n.s.e.) and the subsequent conveyance falls within the priority period given by that search. No problems arise here.

(10) The conveyance dated 20 September 1988 has a certificate of value but no produced stamp. This omission must be rectified at the seller's expense. The conveyance also appears not to have been executed – the words 'executed by all parties and attested' which were present at the foot of the earlier conveyance do not appear here. Possibly a typing error in the preparation of the abstract has occurred and the explanation of the omission of these words is that they were left out by mistake. Their omission should be queried with the seller. In the absence of proper execution by the seller no legal estate will have passed to the buyer. This may be a situation where the buyer's solicitor feels that he should exercise his right to verify his abstract against the original deeds at this stage of the transaction in order to check that the document was indeed correctly executed.

(11) Concurrently with their purchase on 20 September 1988, Mr and Mrs Bowen mortgaged the property to the Mercia Building Society. As Mr and Mrs Bowen are the present sellers, it is to be expected that this mortgage is still subsisting, but the buyer will require it to be discharged on or before completion, and a requisition to this effect should be raised with the seller.

# ABSTRACT OF THE TITLE

of

Mr and Mrs J R Bowen

to

freehold property known as 17 Lakeside Road

Burley Westshire

| | |
|---|---|
| 20th June 1967 | L.C.R. search against ALAN CHARLTON AND SYBIL JANET SMITH showing D (ii) entry against ALAN CHARLTON but otherwise n.s.e. |
| 23rd June 1967<br>Stamp £24-10s<br>P.D. Stamp | CONVEYANCE of this date made between ALAN CHARLTON of 17 Lakeside Road Burley (vendor) (1). and SYBIL JANET SMITH of 5 Dean Close Burley (purchaser) (2). |

RECITING: –

(1)  Seisin of Vendor

(2)  Agreement for sale

WITNESSED:

1.  In consideration of £4,900 paid by purchaser to vendor (receipt acknowledged) vendor as beneficial owner conveyed to purchaser

> ALL THAT piece or parcel of land with the dwellinghouse thereon known as 17 Lakeside Road Burley Westshire more particularly delineated on the plan attached to a conveyance (hereinafter called 'the conveyance') dated 14th March 1956 made between GRAHAM ARTHUR SOUTHFORD (1) and the Vendor (2) and thereon edged red TOGETHER WITH the rights and easements granted by the conveyance.

TO HOLD the same unto the purchaser in fee simple subject to the exceptions reservations covenants and conditions in the conveyance contained

2.  Covenant by purchaser to perform and observe covenants and conditions in the conveyance and to keep vendor and his estate and effects indemnified

3.  Certificate of value £6,000

> Executed by both parties and attested.

BY MORTGAGE of this date made between said S.J. SMITH (borrower) (1) and Countryside Building Society (lender) (2) the borrower charged the before abstracted property to the lender to secure the sum of £4,000 and interest as therein mentioned

> Executed by the borrower and attested.

| | |
|---|---|
| 28th September 1976 | Said S.J. SMITH died on this date |
| 20th November 1976 | Letters of Administration to the estate of said S.J. SMITH granted to GRAHAM DEMPSTER and MARGARET ELIZABETH BONNER out of the Bamford District Probate Registry |
| 1st January 1977 | BY ASSENT of this date said G. DEMPSTER and M.E. BONNER as Personal Representatives of the said S.J. Smith ASSENTED to the vesting of the before abstracted property in PETER WILLIAM MARSHFIELD of 17 Lakeside Road Burley for all the estate and interest of the said S.J. Smith at the date of her death |

INDEMNITY COVENANT by said P.W. Marshfield in respect of covenants in conveyance of 14th March 1956

Executed by all parties attested

| | |
|---|---|
| 14th September 1988 | L.C.R. search against said P.W. MARSHFIELD showing n.s.e. |
| 20th September 1988 | CONVEYANCE of this date between PETER WILLIAM MARSHFIELD (vendor) (1) and JOHN RICHARD BOWEN and ANGELA EMMA BOWEN (purchasers) (2) |

RECITING seisin of vendor and agreement of sale

WITNESSED:

1. In consideration of £28,000 paid by purchasers to vendor (receipt acknowledged) vendor as beneficial owner conveyed to purchasers

   ALL THAT the before abstracted property

   TO HOLD the same unto the purchasers in fee simple subject to the exceptions reservations covenants and conditions contained in the said conveyance of 14th March 1956 as joint tenants upon trust for sale

2. Joint tenancy clauses

3. Indemnity covenant in respect of covenants in said conveyance of 14th March 1956

4. Certificate of value £30,000

| | |
|---|---|
| 20th September 1988 | BY MORTGAGE of this date made between said J.R. BOWEN and A.E. BOWEN (borrowers) (1) and MERCIA BUILDING SOCIETY (lender) (2) the borrowers charged the before abstracted property to the lender to secure £21,000 and interest as therein mentioned |

Executed by the borrowers and attested

# Chapter 18

# SEARCHES AND ENQUIRIES BEFORE CONTRACT

## 18.1 REASONS FOR MAKING SEARCHES

It is the responsibility of the buyer's solicitor to find out as much as possible about the property before allowing his client to enter into a binding contract to buy. At this stage the buyer can freely withdraw from the transaction if he discovers something about the property he does not like; if something was discovered after exchange which might lead the buyer to wish to withdraw, he may well not be able to do so without incurring liability for breach of contract. As we have seen (at **14.7.1**), when drafting the contract the seller has only a very limited duty to disclose certain matters affecting the title to the property. He does not have to disclose physical defects, hence the need for a structural survey (see Chapter 12), nor matters such as the authorised use of the property for planning purposes, or whether a new motorway is to be built just over the back hedge. The buyer's solicitor must, therefore, as far as possible take steps to ensure that the property is suitable for the buyer's purpose.

Failure by the buyer's solicitor to make these searches may give rise to liability in negligence to the buyer client if, as a result, the buyer suffers loss (see *Cooper v Stephenson* (1825) Cox M and H 627, 21 LJQB 292).

It is, of course, not sufficient just to make the searches; the buyer's solicitor must ensure that the buyer is fully advised of the information discovered and its implications for his proposed purchase.

## 18.2 WHO SHOULD MAKE THE SEARCHES AND ENQUIRIES?

Since the risk of buying the property subject to undiscovered defects rests with the buyer, it is up to the buyer to ensure that all necessary pre-contract searches have been made and that the results are satisfactory.

However, under the Protocol, the seller of unregistered land should supply an index map search and land charges searches as part of the pre-contract package. This requirement of the Protocol is, however, sometimes departed from, in which case the buyer will need to do these searches himself.

The Government's Homes Bill was lost when the May 2001 election was called. However, the Government still intends, when Parliamentary time permits, to reintroduce the Bill. This will make it compulsory for sellers of residential property to prepare a 'Seller's Pack' before marketing the property. This will have to contain prescribed information, which is likely to include replies to standard searches and a form of structural survey.

## 18.3 NATIONAL LAND INFORMATION SERVICE

The buyer's solicitor should make search applications as soon as firm instructions to proceed are received from his client. Search applications should always be submitted without delay, since some authorities take a long time to reply to them. In order to reduce delays in obtaining results of searches (and as part of the transition to e-conveyancing) the National Land Information Service (NLIS) has now been expanded nationwide. This enables subscribers to one of the 'channels' ie commercial providers, to order all necessary searches from the provider through the means of a computer link. As well as avoiding the need (and time and cost) of sending search applications to numerous separate bodies, the ultimate aim is that all such information will be available electronically. The results of searches will then be sent electronically to the solicitor's computer within a matter of minutes of the search request being made. At the moment, however, not all authorities where searches need to be made have their data available electronically.

## 18.4 WHICH SEARCHES SHOULD BE MADE?

### 18.4.1 All transactions

The following searches are regarded as 'usual' and should be undertaken in every transaction:

(1)  search of the local land charges register;
(2)  enquiries of the local authority and, if appropriate, additional enquiries;
(3)  pre-contract enquiries of the seller;
(4)  water and drainage enquiries.

These searches should be made whether the property being purchased is residential or commercial.

### 18.4.2 Additional searches

Depending on the circumstances of the transaction, the following searches may need to be made:

(1)  commons registration search;
(2)  mining search;
(3)  Index Map search, if dealing with unregistered land;
(4)  a Land Charges Department search against the seller's name (for insolvency) and in unregistered land also against other previous owners of the land (to discover incumbrances);
(5)  environmental matters;
(6)  any of the less usual searches which may be applicable in the circumstances (see **18.12**).

### 18.4.3 Less usual searches

This chapter summarises only the main searches which are relevant to a normal conveyancing transaction. For a detailed explanation of the contents of the various search forms and of the less usual searches, reference should be made to a specialist work such as Silverman *Searches and Enquiries – A Conveyancer's Guide* (Butterworths, 1992).

## 18.5 LOCAL LAND CHARGES SEARCH

A local authority is bound by statute to keep a register of certain matters. This register, which is open to public inspection, is called the Local Land Charges Register. It is divided into the 12 parts which are listed on the reverse of the search application form (Form LLC1).

### 18.5.1 Making the search

A local land charges search should be made in every transaction by submitting Form LLC1 to the unitary, district or London borough council in which the property is situated. Where the application is made by post, the form should be completed in duplicate. A plan of the land (also in duplicate) must be submitted if the land cannot clearly be identified from its postal address. A fee is payable for the search. A search should be made in all parts of the register.

### 18.5.2 The search result

The search result is given by way of certificate, signed by an officer of the council, which shows whether and, if so, how many entries are revealed by the search. This certificate is accompanied by a schedule which contains a summary of the relevant entries. Further details of the entries can be obtained either by attending at the council offices to inspect documents or by obtaining office copies of documents from the council. A fee is payable for copies of documents.

### 18.5.3 What the search reveals

The search result will reveal any entries kept by the council under the statutory obligations mentioned above. Such matters might include the following:

- financial charges (eg for roadworks; see **41.2.4**);
- tree preservation orders. These prevent the protected tree(s) being felled without permission;
- smoke control orders. These restrict the use of non-smokeless fuels in domestic fireplaces;
- some compulsory purchase orders;
- planning permissions granted;
- any restrictions on permitted development (eg Article 4 Direction; see **5.5**);
- orders revoking or modifying planning permissions.

The buyer should be advised of the entries affecting the property and their significance, for example in the case of a tree preservation order that the tree in question cannot be felled or lopped without permission. Consideration should also be given as to how the entries will affect the buyer's proposed use for the property. If financial charges are revealed, the seller should be requested to discharge these prior to completion or to reduce the purchase price accordingly.

### 18.5.4 Liability

Where a person suffers as a result of an error in an official certificate of search, compensation may be payable under the Local Land Charges Act 1975, s 10.

## 18.6 ENQUIRIES OF LOCAL AUTHORITY

### 18.6.1 Making the search

The enquiries of the local authority search should be made in every transaction by submitting Form CON29 to the appropriate unitary, district or London borough council in which the property is situated. Where the search is made by post, two copies of the form are required. Some local authorities now accept electronic requests for search applications via computer link. The local authority may insist on submission of a plan with the search application, even in cases where the land can clearly be identified from its postal address. The fee for this search varies from authority to authority.

The form is divided into two parts. The Part I enquiries are relevant to every transaction and are covered by the authority's quoted fee. The Part II enquiries are more specialised in nature and not all the questions will be relevant in every transaction. It should always be considered which, if any, of the Part II enquiries should be raised in each transaction, and those enquiries which are raised should then be indicated by placing a tick in the box against the relevant question number at the foot of the front page of the search form. A separate fee is chargeable for each Part II enquiry raised.

If it is necessary to raise additional enquiries covering matters which are not dealt with by the printed questions, such additional questions should be typed on a separate sheet of paper and submitted in duplicate with the search application. An additional fee is chargeable for each supplementary question raised. Some local authorities refuse to answer questions other than those on the printed form.

### 18.6.2 What the search reveals

A local authority keeps records of a great quantity of information relating to a large number of different matters, extending beyond the limited confines of the local land charges register. It is this enormous quantity of non-statutory information which the search application is designed to reveal. The information revealed by this search will assist the buyer to build up a complete picture of the property he is proposing to buy and is essential to his decision as to whether or not to proceed with the purchase. Examples of the type of entry which might be revealed are as follows:

- whether the roads serving the property are maintained at the public expense;
- roads and railways proposed within 200 metres of the property;
- planning applications made (ie including those refused);
- enforcement and stop notices served and whether they have been complied with (see **5.9**);
- proposed enforcement and stop notices;
- proposed tree preservation orders;
- proposed restrictions on permitted development;
- proposed compulsory purchase orders;

- whether any notices have been served in relation to remediation of contaminated land.

The Part II (optional enquiries) include the following:

- whether the property is crossed by a public path or bridleway;
- whether there are any proposals for permanently stopping up roads or footpaths or putting any other traffic schemes into operation, for example one-way streets, parking restrictions etc;
- whether radon gas precautions are required for new dwellings.

As with the local search, the replies should be considered carefully and the client advised accordingly. If the roads and sewers are not maintained at the public expense, the client should be warned of the potential expense should the local authority subsequently decide to 'adopt' the road. However, as long as the enquiries reveal that there is a Highways Act 1980, s 38 agreement and bond (for the roads) and a Water Industry Act 1991, s 104 agreement and bond (for the sewers), there will be no such problem. See **41.2.4** and **41.2.5** for details of these.

The client should also be advised that, generally, both the local search and enquiries merely reveal matters directly affecting the land being bought; they will not reveal matters relating to adjoining land which may indirectly affect the property. So if a new supermarket is planned for the field at the rear of the house, this will not be revealed. The main exceptions to this are new roads and railways. Those planned within 200 metres of the property will be revealed. However, a new motorway 300 metres away would not be revealed and might still cause disturbance to the occupiers of the property.

However, 'Plansearch' available from Jordans Ltd can provide information on:

- applications for planning consent made within the previous 5 years in respect of land within 250 metres of the property;
- Local Authority Development Plans (see **5.1**) in respect of land within 500 metres;
- whether the property is within a natural river or coastal floodplain.

### 18.6.3  Liability

Subject to the validity of the exclusion clause printed on the front sheet of the search application form, a local authority could be sued in negligence for an erroneous reply to the printed enquiries.

### 18.6.4  Differences between Forms LLC1 and CON29

In practice, the two search applications are submitted simultaneously to the same authority with one cheque covering both fees. It is unusual to do one search without the other and, for that reason, the two searches are often treated as being indistinguishable and are together referred to as 'the local search'. In fact they are two totally separate and distinct searches having different functions. Their differences are summarised below.

(1) Form LLC1 will only reveal matters which fall within the statutory definition of a local land charge (eg planning permissions granted); Form CON29 covers a wider range of subject matter and is not restricted to land charges (eg planning applications made, including refusals).

(2) The liability of the local authority for errors is different (see **18.5.4** and **18.6.3**). For the enquires, negligence has to be established; this is not necessary for the local search.

(3) Form LLC1 is restricted to information which is on the register at the moment the search is made; Form CON29 may reveal information which has affected the property in the past (eg history of planning applications made on the property) or will do so in the future (eg a compulsory purchase order which is pending but which has not yet been registered as a local land charge).

## 18.7 PRE-CONTRACT ENQUIRIES OF THE SELLER: THE SELLER'S PROPERTY INFORMATION FORM

### 18.7.1 Purpose of the search

Pre-contract enquiries of the seller are the third of the 'usual' searches and are made in every transaction. The purpose of this search is to elicit from the seller information, mainly relating to the physical aspects of the property, which he is not bound by law to disclose (see **14.7.1**). The information obtained should enable the buyer to gain a complete picture of the property which he is proposing to buy, and can thus be influential in his making the decision whether or not to proceed with the purchase.

Since the object of the exercise is to obtain information which the seller is not by law bound to disclose, it follows that the seller could refuse to answer the buyer's enquiries altogether. Such a refusal would, however, be unusual and would serve no useful purpose, since it would make the buyer suspicious and would, at best, hinder the speedy progress of the transaction or, at worst, cause the buyer to abort his purchase.

### 18.7.2 Protocol cases

In cases where the Protocol is used, the seller's solicitor should ask his client to complete the Seller's Property Information Form (SPIF). This contains various questions about the property, phrased in layman's language so that the average client should be able to complete this form with minimal help from his solicitor. An erroneous or misleading reply to these questions could give rise to liability in misrepresentation and the seller should be advised to fill in this form very carefully in order not to incur such liability. The form is then submitted to the buyer's solicitor as part of the pre-contract package.

The Seller's Leasehold Information Form contains additional questions which are relevant in leasehold transactions.

### 18.7.3 Non-Protocol cases

The buyer should ask similar questions to those included on the SPIF. Law stationers produce a standard form of pre-contract enquiries and many solicitors have their own version on word processor. In such a case, two copies of the form should be sent to the seller's solicitor (with any enquiries which are not relevant to the transaction in hand deleted from the forms). The form should be submitted to the seller's solicitor as soon as possible after firm instructions are received from the buyer, although, in practice, many solicitors will not send the form until they have received the draft contract from the seller's solicitor, so that any queries arising out of that document can be raised as additional enquiries.

### 18.7.4 Supplementary enquiries

Where there are genuine areas of enquiry which are not covered by the questions on the standard forms, but which are relevant to the buyer's situation, these should be raised as supplementary enquiries either on space at the bottom of the printed form or on a separate sheet (in duplicate). Additional enquiries may extend to queries arising out of the provisions of the draft contract or from the evidence of title supplied by the seller.

Additional enquiries should, in any event, be confined to those matters to which an answer cannot be obtained from reading the documentation supplied by the seller, from the estate agent's particulars, or from a survey or physical inspection of the property. The submission of a large number of irrelevant supplementary enquiries may irritate the seller's solicitor who may decline to answer them.

### 18.7.5 Summary of information to be obtained from search

The following enquiries should be made as a minimum in every case:

- whether there are any disputes with neighbouring owners/occupiers;
- who is in occupation of the property;
- whether there have been any alterations or other building work carried out on the property and if so whether planning permission/building regulation consent was obtained;
- whether there has been any change in the use of the property;
- whether services (eg water) to the property pass through adjoining land;
- whether services to other properties pass through the land to be sold.

The replies should be studied carefully and the client advised of any which will affect his proposed use of the property. For the kind of problems which can be revealed, see **18.14**.

### 18.7.6 Liability

An incorrect reply to pre-contract enquiries may lead to liability in misrepresentation. Any exclusion clause purporting to avoid or minimise liability for misrepresentation will be subject to the reasonableness test in the Unfair Contract Terms Act 1977, s 11 and cannot therefore be guaranteed to afford protection to the seller (see Standard Condition 7.3 and *Walker v Boyle* [1982] 1 All ER 634). Some forms of pre-contract enquiries also contain an exclusion clause.

Where the erroneous reply stems from the seller's solicitor's negligence, he will be liable to his own client (*CEMP Properties (UK) Ltd v Dentsply Research and Development Corporation (No 1)* (1989) 2 EGLR 192) but in this respect does not owe a duty directly to the buyer (see *Gran Gelato v Richcliffe (Group)* [1992] 1 All ER 865).

## 18.8 WATER AND DRAINAGE ENQUIRIES

Information about water and sewerage matters is no longer available from local authorities so drainage and water enquiries should now be made using form CON 29DW. This should be submitted, with the appropriate fee, to the water service company serving the property. These enquiries should be made in every transaction. The enquiry will reveal (inter alia) the following:

• whether the property has foul drainage to the public sewer;
• whether the property has surface water drainage to the public sewer;
• whether there is a water main within the boundaries of the property;
• whether the property is connected to the public water supply.

## 18.9  LAND CHARGES DEPARTMENT SEARCH

A Land Charges Department search should be made in all cases when dealing with unregistered land. Although this search is often undertaken at a later stage of the transaction, it is sensible to make the search prior to exchange so that any problems which do emerge can be dealt with in good time before completion is due. Although strictly not relevant to land registered with an absolute title, it is sensible for the seller's solicitor to make a search against his own client's name to ensure that there are no bankruptcy proceedings pending. The search is made by submitting either Form K15 (full search) or Form K16 (bankruptcy only) to the Land Charges Department at Plymouth, or it can be made by telephone. In Protocol cases, the seller should provide searches against the seller and all previous estate owners within the title.

The register comprises a list of names of proprietors of land, and a fee is payable for each name searched against. A search should be made against the names of all previous estate owners revealed by the epitome. The search is therefore made not against the land itself but against the names of the previous owners. Although the seller has a duty of disclosure, under Standard Condition 3 (see **14.7.1**), and should therefore reveal to the buyer any matters which are the subject of registered entries at HM Land Charges Department, it is nevertheless sensible for the buyer to undertake this search before contracts are exchanged if only to obtain an early warning of potential problems (eg the seller's bankruptcy, Family Law Act 1996 rights, estate contracts). If the seller supplies correctly made searches with the epitome (see **17.6.9**), the buyer need not repeat searches against these names. Unless completion takes place within 15 working days of the issue of the search certificate (the protection period afforded by an official search) the search, at least against the seller's name, will need to be repeated before completion (see Chapter 28).

The register is maintained by computer which will, basically, search only against the version of the name as shown on the application form. It is essential to ensure, therefore, that the search is made against the full name of the owner as revealed by the deeds and that the spelling of that name is correct. It is necessary to indicate on the search application the period of years for which the search should be made. This should be the period for which that person was the owner of the land.

## 18.10 COMPANY SEARCH

When the seller is a company, a company search should be made to check that the company:

(1) exists;
(2) has power to buy and sell land (although these powers are normally implied by law);
(3) has no undisclosed fixed or floating charge which affects the land being purchased; and
(4) is not in administration, receivership or liquidation.

Although the company search is conventionally undertaken at a later stage in the transaction, it is sensible to make the search before exchange so that any problems which do emerge from the search result can be dealt with in good time before completion is due. If required, a search made before exchange can be updated just before completion. There is no official search procedure for this search.

The solicitor or his agent (there are specialist firms who offer company search services) should apply to Companies House in London or Cardiff for a search to be made. A form of application is supplied by Companies House and a charge is made for the search. The search result, which confers no protection or priority on the applicant, is in the form of microfiche sheets showing copies of all the documents which the company has lodged at Companies House. These will include its memorandum and articles of association (constitutional documents), details of its officers (directors and secretary), filed accounts and details of mortgages. The microfiche sheets can be read by placing them in a microfiche reader which will magnify the sheets to a legible size. Microfiche readers are provided at Companies House for personal callers and some agents and larger firms will possess a machine on their own premises.

## 18.11 INDEX MAP SEARCH

An Index Map search at HM Land Registry should be made in all cases when buying an interest in unregistered land. Application is made to the district registry for the area in which the land is situated on Form 96, accompanied by a large-scale plan of the property and the fee. The search result will reveal whether the land is already registered or is subject to a pending application or caution against first registration. If the search result turns out to be inaccurate, compensation from the Land Registry indemnity fund is available. In Protocol cases the seller should provide the result of this search as part of the Protocol package.

## 18.12 ENVIRONMENTAL MATTERS

The public have become much more aware of environmental issues in recent years and these are matters which ought to be considered on a purchase of land. One obvious problem is the possibility of the land being contaminated – see **5.14**. Apart from the potential expense of clean-up liabilities, the dangers posed by the contamination to the owners and occupiers must also be considered. The Law Society has issued a Warning Card to solicitors reminding them of the need to consider the potential problems posed by contaminated land in every property transaction. The advice to be given to clients is considered at **5.14**.

But other environmental matters might also affect the potential buyer's decision whether or not to proceed. Is the property near a landfill site, or are there factories in the area discharging hazardous substances? Because of issues such as these, it is now regarded as best practice to obtain an environmental report in all property transactions. A useful and inexpensive method of doing this in residential purchases is to make use of Envirosearch Residential. This is available from Jordans Ltd and makes use of environmental information gathered by the Landmark Information Group. More detailed information in relation to commercial properties can be obtained using 'Sitecheck', also available through Jordans Ltd.

Note also that the cover given by the NHBC in relation to new houses has now been extended to cover contaminated land. See **41.2.3**. However, this extended cover applies only to houses registered with the NHBC after 1 April 1999; there is no cover in relation to other properties.

## 18.13  LESS USUAL SEARCHES

The buyer's solicitor should be aware of any features of the property or its location which indicate that one of the less usual searches may be appropriate to the situation. The buyer will usually be bound by any incumbrances which exist over the property, whether or not a search was made. A solicitor who fails to carry out a less usual search in circumstances where he should have done so may be liable in negligence to his client (see *G & K Ladenbau (UK) Ltd v Crawley and De Reya* [1978] 1 All ER 682).

Examples of some of the less usual searches appear below.

### 18.13.1  Coal mining search

This search should be made whenever the property is situated in an area where there are or have in the past been coal mining operations. The Law Society's Coal Mining Directory (published by Oyez) will indicate whether or not the parish in which the property is situated is in an area where a coal mining search is recommended. This information is also available on the Coal Authority's website at www.coal.gov.uk.

An application for a search should be made on Form CON29M, accompanied by the fee and a large-scale plan of the property, to the Coal Authority. The result of the search will reveal whether the property is in an area where mining has taken place in the past or is likely to take place in the future, the existence of underground workings which may cause problems with subsidence and whether compensation for subsidence damage has been paid in the past or any claim is pending. No protection is given to the buyer by the search result. Although this search only covers coal mining activities, similar search schemes are available in areas potentially affected by other types of mining, eg tin and china clay in Cornwall and salt in Cheshire.

### 18.13.2  Commons Registration search

A Commons Registration search should be made in any case where the property to be purchased abuts a village green or common land, where property is to be built on previously undeveloped land, or where a verge strip, not owned by the property, separates the property from the public highway. Form CR1 should be completed in duplicate and submitted to the appropriate county or unitary council. A large-scale plan is needed in every case. A fee is charged for this search.

The search result will show whether any land is registered under the Commons Registration Act 1965. Where land has been registered under the 1965 Act it is difficult to remove that land from the register and not possible to obtain planning permission for development over the land. Third parties may have rights over the land which is registered (eg rights to graze cattle). No protection is given by the official search result and no personal search facilities exist.

### 18.13.3 Flooding

The Environment Agency state that 2 million homes and businesses are at risk of flooding in England and Wales. This can easily be checked on the Agency's website at www.environment-agency.gov.uk. This information can also be obtained using 'Plansearch' from Jordans Ltd.

### 18.13.4 Land adjoining rivers, streams or canals

Enquiries should be made of the water authority to check on responsibility for maintenance of riverbanks. In the case of a canal, enquiry should be made of British Waterways.

### 18.13.5 Railways

In the case of land adjoining a railway line, enquiry should be made of Railtrack as to maintenance of fences and access rights.

## 18.14 RESULTS OF SEARCHES

On receiving the results of searches, the buyer's solicitor must check the answers given to ensure that the information supplied complies with his client's instructions. Any reply which is unclear must be pursued with the appropriate authority (or seller in the case of pre-contract enquiries) until a satisfactory explanation is received. Failure to pursue an unsatisfactory reply which results in loss being suffered by the client may result in the buyer's solicitor being liable to his own client in negligence (*Computastaff Ltd v Ingledew Brown Bennison & Garrett* (1983) 7 ILR 156).

Any reply which is for any reason not satisfactory must be referred to the client for further instructions. Contracts should not be exchanged until satisfactory results of all searches have been received. A summary of the information received from the searches should be communicated to the buyer by his solicitor. The individual searches should not be looked at in isolation; rather the information from each should be correlated and considered in the light of the particular circumstances of the case. The following scenarios are commonly encountered and need special care.

***Property built within last 10 years***
- Check that you have copies of NHBC (or similar) documentation. (This provides insurance cover against many structural defects; see **41.2.3**.) Revealed by SPIF.

- Check that there is planning permission and you have copies (see **5.9** for enforcement of planning matters). Revealed by SPIF and local search.
- Check that the conditions attached to the planning permission have been complied with (see **5.9**). Enforcement revealed by enquiries of local authority.
- Check that building regulation consent was obtained and a copy provided (see **41.2.2**). Revealed by SPIF; proceedings for breach revealed by enquires of local authority.
- Check that the roads and drains are adopted, or that agreements and bonds exist (see **18.6.2**). Copies should be provided. Revealed by enquiries of local authority.
- If the roads etc are not adopted, check that adequate easements exist for access. Check title documents.

If no agreements and bonds exist, consider whether a retention should be made from the purchase price until they are adopted.

### *Access to property or service to property cross neighbouring land*

- Revealed by pre-contract enquiries. Check title to ensure that there are easements for access, etc. If no express easements exist, will they be implied or presumed by long user? Can seller get a deed of grant now from neighbouring owners?
- What are the arrangements for maintenance and repair? Are there express arrangements in title documents or any informal arrangements?

Unless the property has been recently built, adoption by the local authority will be unlikely.

### *Occupiers*

- Revealed by pre-contract enquiries.
- Do the occupiers claim an equitable interest?
- If so, ensure that they will sign agreement to give up rights and leave on completion (see **19.4.3**).
- In the case of a non-owning spouse, have rights of occupation under Family Law Act 1996 been registered? Whether or not such rights have already been registered, the spouse should be required to agree to leave and remove any registration prior to completion (see **19.4.3**).

### *Extension or alterations carried out by previous owner*

- Are there any guarantees for work? (See pre-contract enquiries.)
- Was planning permission required/obtained for works? (See **5.13**.)
- Are works within GPDO or were permissions withdrawn? (See **5.5**.)
- Copies of planning permission required?
- Have any covenants on title been complied with, for example consents for work?
- If consent required but not obtained, can it be obtained now, or insurance cover obtained? (See **19.4.1**.)
- Was building regulation consent obtained? (See **5.13**.)
- Is a survey even more desirable in such cases to ensure work carried out to a proper standard?

## 18.15  IMPUTED KNOWLEDGE

Knowledge acquired by the solicitor while acting on his client's behalf is imputed to the client (regardless of whether the client had actual knowledge of the matter in question). Thus, a seller may be liable in misrepresentation to the buyer for a statement made by his solicitor without his knowledge. In such a case, indemnity against the seller's liability could be sought from the seller's solicitors (see *Strover v Harrington* [1988] Ch 390).

## 18.16  RELYING ON SEARCHES MADE BY A THIRD PARTY

The results of searches are not personal to the searcher, thus their benefit may be transferred to a third party. Where the seller makes pre-contract searches and passes their results to the buyer, the buyer and his lender may take the benefit of the results. The buyer must check that the seller has undertaken all the searches and enquiries which the buyer deems necessary for the transaction in hand and, if not, he must carry out the additional searches himself. If the buyer is not satisfied with the results of the searches made by the seller because, for example, he considers that insufficient questions have been raised, he should repeat the search himself. Similarly, a lender may rely on searches made by a buyer's solicitor.

## 18.17  INSPECTION OF THE PROPERTY

Inspection of the property should be undertaken by the client in all cases. There is no obligation on the solicitor, either in law or conduct, to carry out an inspection in every transaction, but he should do so if his client so requests or if matters reported by the client's inspection give rise to suspicion on the part of the buyer's solicitor. The client should be advised to look for (and to report their existence to his solicitor) any of the following matters:

(1) a discrepancy or uncertainty over the identity of or boundaries to the property;
(2) evidence of easements which adversely affect the property (eg evidence suggesting that a right of way over the property exists);
(3) the existence and status of non-owning occupiers;
(4) a discrepancy between the fixtures and fittings which the client understood to belong to the property and those actually existing.

## 18.18  CONCLUSION

The results of these searches and enquiries provide valuable information about the property being bought and thus the viability of the transaction and the buyer's proposals for it. The search results should be studied carefully and the buyer kept fully informed about them and their implications. The buyer should not be allowed to exchange contracts until all outstanding queries have been resolved to his satisfaction. The solicitor should also remember that if he is acting for the buyer's lender as well as the buyer, he should keep the lender client informed about any matters affecting the value or saleability of the property or which otherwise might affect the lender's decision to lend on the security of the property.

**Chapter 19**

# LOOKING AT THE CONTRACT FROM THE BUYER'S POINT OF VIEW

## 19.1 THE PRE-CONTRACT PACKAGE

The buyer's solicitor will be supplied with two copies of the draft contract by the seller's solicitor. He should also receive copies of any documents referred to in the contract (eg a conveyance imposing restrictive covenants) and the remainder of the pre-contract package which should include such items as pre-contract search results, copies of planning consents, copies of an insurance policy against structural defects, and the seller's evidence of title.

Except where the buyer is purchasing a plot on a building estate (a new house in the course of construction), the terms of the contract will usually be open to negotiation between the parties, and the buyer's solicitor should therefore consider the terms of the draft contract in the light of his instructions and of the information revealed by the other documents in the pre-contract package.

Style of drafting is to an extent a matter of individual taste, and the buyer's solicitor should not seek to amend the contract simply because it is drafted in a style which he does not like.

## 19.2 AMENDING THE CONTRACT

Amendments should only be made where they are both necessary and relevant to the particular transaction. The primary questions in looking at the contract from the buyer's point of view are as follows.

(1)   Does the clause accord with the client's instructions?
(2)   Does the clause do what it is intended to do?

If the answers to these questions are 'yes', leave the wording alone. If not, alter the clause until it does meet the above criteria.

### 19.2.1  How to amend the contract

Amendments should be inserted clearly on both copies of the draft contract in a distinctive colour. One copy of the amended contract can then be returned to the seller's solicitor for his consideration of the alterations made by the buyer's solicitor. The copy returned to the seller's solicitor should be marked 'amended in (red) on (date)'. Further amendments (by either party) should follow the same procedure and should be made in distinctive colours not previously used, so that it is possible to identify each layer of changes. Traditionally, first amendments are made in red ink and second amendments in green, but it is not obligatory to follow this sequence of colours.

When final agreement is reached over the contents of the contract, one copy should be returned by the buyer's solicitor to the seller's solicitor marked 'Approved as drawn' (where no amendments have been made) or 'Approved as amended in (green)' (where amendments have been made). In many cases, few amendments, other than inadvertent typographical errors, are needed, and minor amendments can be agreed by the parties' solicitors over the phone cutting out the need for the contract formally to be sent to and from the respective solicitors. A document which does pass back and forth between the parties for amendment is often referred to as a 'travelling draft'.

## 19.3 WHAT TO LOOK FOR WHEN CONSIDERING THE DRAFT CONTRACT

The following are particular matters which the buyer's solicitor should bear in mind when considering the draft contract.

- Are the full names and addresses of the parties correctly included?
- Does the description of the property tie in with that on the register or in the deeds?
- Does the property have the benefit of all the easements necessary for the use to which the buyer intends to put the property or any other reasonable use?
- Is the estate being sold (freehold or leasehold) correctly stated?
- Is the class of title stated (registered land)?
- Is the root of title a 'good root' (unregistered land)? (See **14.7.3**.)
- Is the title number correctly stated (registered land)?
- Are the incumbrances stated in the contract the only ones which the deeds/office copies/searches reveal the land is subject to?
- Will the incumbrances restrict the buyer's proposed use of the property in any way?
- Is full title guarantee being offered? If not, why not?
- Is the contract rate more than the Law Society's Rate (ie more than 4% above base rate)?
- Is the purchase price as agreed?
- Is the amount of the deposit as agreed?
- Is the amount payable for chattels and the identity of the chattels as agreed?
- Is the balance correct?
- Is vacant possession to be given on completion? If not, was this agreed?
- Have requisitions been barred out? If so title must be investigated prior to exchange.
- Have any of the Standard Conditions been amended/made inapplicable by a special condition? If so, will this adversely affect the buyer?
- In particular, has Standard Condition 5 been amended so that the buyer will need to insure on exchange?

## 19.4 RESTRICTIVE COVENANTS

Many properties are subject to restrictive covenants imposed on a previous sale of the land. In most cases, the nature of the covenants is consistent with the type of property being sold. It is common, for example, to find covenants imposed on residential property which restrict the use of the property to a private dwelling house in the occupation of a single family, which prevent alterations from being made to the property without the consent of a named third party, and which prohibit the keeping of animals other than ordinary domestic pets. In such cases, provided that they will not seriously impede the buyer's intended use of the property, no further action need be taken other than informing the buyer of the extent of the covenants and telling him that he has a liability for breach of the covenants.

### 19.4.1　Problematical covenants

Instructions may reveal that the buyer's intended use of the property after completion will cause a breach of existing covenants. For example, if there is a restrictive covenant which prevents use of the property except as a single private dwelling-house and the client wants to convert the property into flats, a breach of covenant will occur.

The first step to be taken in such cases is to check to see whether the covenants are registered. Post-1925 covenants which are not registered either on the charges register of a registered title or as Class D(ii) entries in unregistered land are unenforceable. Usually the covenants are registered. Next, look at the wording of the covenants to see whether they have been annexed effectively to the land and are prima facie binding. Unless it is very clear on the face of the covenants that they are invalid, it is safest to assume that they are enforceable and to consider whether it is possible to obtain an insurance policy which will cover liability for the future breach of covenant. An insurance company will need the following information or documents when considering whether or not to issue a policy.

(1)　A copy of the document imposing the covenant or, if this is not available, a copy of the exact wording of the covenant.
(2)　The exact nature of the breach which has occurred or details of the action which is contemplated which will cause the breach.
(3)　The date when the covenant was imposed.
(4)　Whether or not the covenant is registered.
(5)　The nature of other properties in the immediate neighbourhood. This is to enable the insurance company to assess the risk of enforcement of the covenant. Taking the example given above of a potential breach being caused by a conversion of a dwelling into flats, if many of the neighbouring properties have already been converted into flats, the likelihood of this particular covenant being enforced if breached is more remote than if the surrounding properties remain in single ownership. A plan which shows the property in the context of the surrounding locality is often useful.
(6)　A copy of any planning permission which permits the development to be undertaken by the client.
(7)　What steps have been taken (if any) to trace the person(s) with the benefit of the covenant and the results of those enquiries.

If a policy is issued, it is normally a single premium policy (a single sum is paid on the issue of the policy). The benefit of the policy can be passed on to successors in title. The buyer's lender should be consulted about the proposed breach of covenant and his approval obtained to the terms of the insurance policy.

### 19.4.2  Other methods of dealing with covenants

If no policy can be obtained (the risk of enforcement might cause the insurance company to charge a prohibitive premium), consideration might be given to one of the solutions suggested below. If, however, it appears that valid and enforceable covenants will impede the client's proposed use of the land and that no viable solution to this problem can be achieved, the client should be advised not to proceed with his proposed purchase.

#### *Obtaining the consent of the person with the benefit of the covenant*

Obtaining the consent of the person with the benefit of the covenant is rarely a viable option. If the covenant was imposed many years ago, it will be difficult to trace the person with the benefit (unless the covenant was imposed by the owner of a large estate such as the Duke of Westminster). If the covenant has been imposed during the last 20 or so years, it may be possible to trace the person with the benefit, but the price for granting a release or modification of the covenant may be prohibitive.

The person with the benefit will be the present owner of the land for the benefit of which the covenant was taken. Remember also that, if the covenant was taken for the benefit of a piece of land which has now been divided between several owners, you will need to obtain the consent of all the present owners of that land.

#### *Application to the Lands Tribunal*

The Lands Tribunal has power in certain circumstances under the Law of Property Act 1925, s 84 to grant a modification or discharge of a restrictive covenant, but this solution may not be quick or cheap to pursue. The county court enjoys a similar, but more limited, jurisdiction.

### 19.4.3  Occupiers

If the SPIF, or the buyer's inspection, reveals that someone other than the seller is occupying the property, it will be necessary to ensure that they will vacate the property on or before completion. See **3.8.3** for the law on this issue. Even if the sale is to be made by two trustees (which would thus overreach the equitable interest of the occupier) it is still necessary to get a written agreement by the occupier to leave. Although the occupier's rights may be overreached and so not binding on a buyer, there is a risk of the buyer turning up on completion and finding the occupier still in possession. He may have no defence to a court action by the buyer for possession, but the buyer would have much preferred not to have had to go to court in order to obtain possession. By asking the occupier to confirm in writing that he will leave, this should ensure that any potential problems will be revealed at an early stage of the transaction by the occupier refusing to sign such an agreement.

#### *Suggested form of wording for release of rights*

> In consideration of the Buyer entering into this Agreement, I ...........
> [name of occupier] ...... agree:
>
> (1) to the sale of the Property on the terms of this Agreement; and
>
> (2) not to register any rights I may have in relation to the Property (whether under the Family Law Act 1996 or otherwise); and

**(3) to remove any registrations made by me in relation to these rights before completion; and**

**(4)  to give vacant possession of the Property on completion.**

This form of wording is appropriate for inclusion in the contract; alternatively, it could be amended slightly and set out as a separate document. If the occupier is not the seller's spouse, the reference to the Family Law Act 1996 should be deleted.

An alternative solution, if the occupier is claiming an equitable interest in the property, is to appoint the occupier as a second trustee of the property. The appointment should be made prior to exchange so that the occupier is a party to the contract and is thus bound by the contractual terms as to selling free from incumbrances and giving vacant possession on completion.

**Chapter 20**

# MORTGAGE OFFERS

## 20.1 ACCEPTANCE OF OFFER

Where the buyer is purchasing a property with the assistance of mortgage finance, his solicitor must ensure that the client has received and accepted a satisfactory offer before advising the client to exchange contracts. Advice given to the client about the terms of a mortgage offer may be 'investment business' within the terms of the Financial Services Act 1986. The types of mortgage available to the client are discussed in Chapter 9.

## 20.2 TERMS OF OFFER

A mortgage offer made by an institutional lender in respect of a loan to be made for the purchase of residential property will normally deal with some or all of the matters listed below.

(1) A description of the property which is to be mortgaged, its purchase price and tenure (ie freehold or leasehold).

(2) The amount of the advance (loan) and period of the mortgage (eg 25 years).

(3) The interest rate applicable to the loan. Unless the mortgage is a 'fixed rate' mortgage, this rate may from time to time be altered in line with changes in bank base rates.

(4) The amount of the borrower's initial monthly repayments to the lender. This sum is subject to fluctuation if the interest rate charged under the mortgage is altered, and will be quoted gross and net of tax.

(5) Whether the mortgage is to be repayment or endowment. In the case of the latter, the offer will usually stipulate the details of the life policy which is to be taken out over the borrower's life and the time by which this must be done (eg by completion date).

(6) Where the lender is to insure the property, the amount of cover and when that cover will start. The solicitor must ensure that the time when the lender's policy is to come into force coincides with the contractual provisions relating to insurance; see Chapter 22. The amount of cover taken out by the lender is usually index-linked and may appear to be for an amount in excess of the current purchase price. This is because the insurance is to cover the cost of rebuilding the property in the event of its total destruction and, where the property is not detached, must also cover the cost of repairs to any adjoining or neighbouring property which is damaged by the accident.

(7) Details of any repair works which the lender requires to be carried out to the property, including the time-limit by which these works must be done. Where repairs are required, the lender may also decide to hold back a part of the loan until he is satisfied that the repairs have been completed. This 'retention' from the mortgage advance will cause a shortfall in the money available on completion and a recalculation of the client's finances will be necessary to

ensure that sufficient funds will be available both to complete the transaction and to carry out the necessary repairs.

(8) The amount of any 'guarantee premium' which is payable by the borrower. Where the lender is agreeing to lend a larger sum than he feels is advisable in the circumstances of the case, some lenders insist that an insurance policy is taken out to insure against the risk of the borrower defaulting on the mortgage and the lender not being able to recover the full amount owing on resale of the property. A single premium is payable for this insurance. The cost is borne by the borrower (see **9.2.2**).

(9) It is usually a term of a mortgage offer for a first mortgage over property that any existing mortgage which the client has (eg over his present house) should be discharged on or before completion of the new loan. The buyer's solicitor must ensure that his client is aware of and can comply with this condition.

## 20.3 CONDITIONS ATTACHED TO OFFER

Before accepting the offer or committing his client to the purchase, the buyer's solicitor should ensure that his client understands the conditions and terms attached to the mortgage offer and will be able to comply with them. Conditions may be general (eg a condition that the property must not be let to a tenant without the lender's consent) or special, having application to this offer only (eg a condition that the buyer carries out certain repairs to the property). The solicitor should check the offer to see whether or not the lender requires a formal acceptance of the offer. If a formal acceptance is required, the client must be advised to do this within the time-limit stipulated by the lender. Failure to accept a formal offer (where required) will result in the mortgage funds not being available to complete the transaction.

## 20.4 INSTRUCTIONS TO ACT

At the same time as a mortgage offer is sent to the client, the lender will instruct solicitors to act for him in connection with the grant of the new mortgage. These solicitors will receive a number of documents from the lender, including instructions to act (which contain similar information to the mortgage offer sent to the borrower), blank mortgage deeds and any other documents relevant to the transaction. In many cases, the solicitor who is instructed to act for the lender will be the same solicitor who is acting for the borrower. The objectives of these two clients coincide in that both seek a property which is structurally sound and has a good safe legal title; the risk of conflict of interests nevertheless exists and the solicitor must always bear in mind that he owes a duty to both clients (see *Mortgage Express v Bowerman & Partners (A Firm)* [1996] 2 All ER 836). Acting for both clients in this way has advantages in terms of time and costs since the same solicitor can do the work required for both clients at the same time.

### 20.4.1 The *Lenders' Handbook*

If a solicitor is to act for both lender and borrower, then the conditions laid down by Solicitors' Practice Rules 1990, Rule 6(3) must be complied with – see **6.3**. Most lenders have adopted the *Lenders' Handbook* promulgated by the Council of Mortgage Lenders. This is a set of standardised mortgage instructions, written in plain English, and use of it guarantees compliance with the Rule 6(3) requirements. The instructions in the *Handbook* are in two parts. Part 1 applies to all lenders using the *Handbook*; Part 2 sets out the requirements of each individual lender in cases where they differ from Part 1. Part 1 of the *Lenders' Handbook* is set out in Appendix 8. The solicitor must ensure that he carries out his lender client's instructions as set out in the two parts of the *Lenders' Handbook*.

## 20.5 CONFLICT OF INTERESTS

Where some of the conditions attached to the mortgage offer are unacceptable or prejudicial to the buyer client and where the buyer's solicitor has also been instructed to act for the lender, a conflict arises between the interests of the buyer client and the lender client. Unless the conflict can be resolved to the satisfaction of both clients, the solicitor cannot continue to act for either. If it comes to the notice of the solicitor that the buyer client will be in breach of the terms of the mortgage offer (eg where the purchase price for the property has been misrepresented to the lender), the lender must be informed of the breach.

### 20.5.1 Duty of confidentiality

Where a conflict of interests exists between the buyer client and the lender client, the solicitor, acting in his capacity of adviser to the buyer, may only disclose the nature of the conflict to the lender with the consent of the buyer client (see *Halifax Mortgage Services v Stepsky* [1996] 1 FLR 620). Disclosure of information without the buyer client's consent will be a breach of the solicitor's duty of confidentiality.

# Chapter 21

# THE DEPOSIT

## 21.1 NEED FOR DEPOSIT

It is customary for a buyer, on exchange of contracts, to pay to the seller a deposit of 10% of the purchase price. Standard contractual conditions (such as Standard Condition 2.2) reflect this practice. In law, a deposit is unnecessary, and neither common law nor statute provides for any deposit to be payable.

### 21.1.1 Purpose of deposit

The payment of a deposit acts as part payment of the purchase price, demonstrates the buyer's good intentions of completing the contract and gives the seller leverage to ensure the fulfilment of the contract, since he is usually able to forfeit the deposit if the buyer defaults.

## 21.2 PRELIMINARY DEPOSITS

Neither party needs to pay a preliminary deposit since neither is committed to the sale and purchase until contracts have been exchanged. An estate agent will frequently ask a prospective buyer to pay a preliminary deposit as an indication of the buyer's good intentions to proceed with negotiations. If a preliminary deposit is paid, the buyer should ensure that the agent has the seller's authority to receive the deposit. In the absence of the seller's authority, the buyer has no recourse against the seller if the agent misappropriates the money (see *Sorrell v Finch* [1977] AC 728). A preliminary deposit is normally fully refundable to the buyer if the transaction does not proceed.

### 21.2.1 Buying a newly built property

A seller who is a builder or developer will invariably require a prospective buyer to pay a preliminary deposit. Since this type of preliminary deposit often buys an option to purchase a numbered plot at a stated price, it is not unusual to find that the deposit is not returnable to the buyer in any circumstances, although it will be credited as part of the purchase price if the matter proceeds.

## 21.3 AMOUNT OF DEPOSIT

No deposit at all is payable unless the contract expressly makes provision for one. A deposit of 10% of the purchase price has until recently been standard practice and is the figure provided by Condition 2.2 in both sets of Standard Conditions unless specifically amended. Deposits of less than 10% are not uncommon in residential transactions.

### 21.3.1  Reduced deposit

It is clearly to the seller's advantage to demand a 10% deposit. If, however, he is asked by the buyer to accept a reduced amount, the following matters should be considered by the seller's solicitor.

(1)  The risk of the sale going off, with the consequent need to forfeit the deposit to compensate for loss.
(2)  The amount of the buyer's mortgage offer. (It may be reasonable to accept a less than 10% deposit from a buyer who has a firm offer of advance for the whole of the balance of the purchase price, taking into account the amount of the reduced deposit.)
(3)  The likely amount of loss which the seller would suffer if the buyer were to default (eg the cost of bridging finance or interest needed to complete a related purchase, the length of time which will be taken to effect a resale and the costs of such a resale).

### 21.3.2  Seller's solicitor's duty

The seller's solicitor must explain the consequences of taking a reduced deposit to his client and obtain his client's express authority before agreeing to accept a reduced deposit. *Morris v Duke-Cohan & Co* (1975) 119 Sol J 826 suggests that it may be professional negligence for a solicitor to accept a reduced deposit without the client's express authority.

### 21.3.3  No deposit payable

Only in exceptional circumstances should the transaction proceed without any deposit being taken. Examples might include family transactions or sales to sitting tenants. However, in commercial transactions, some major institutions will refuse to pay a deposit on the basis that they are of such standing that there is no risk of loss to the buyer.

### 21.3.4  Calculating the deposit

The amount of the deposit actually payable on exchange will take into account any preliminary deposit already paid but, unless the contract provides otherwise, is calculated exclusive of the value of chattels which are to be paid for in addition to the purchase price of the land.

## 21.4  FUNDING THE DEPOSIT

Instructions should be obtained from the buyer client as to how he proposes to fund the deposit. When initial instructions are taken from the client, it is best to assume that the seller will require payment of a full 10% deposit. If the buyer wishes to pay a reduced deposit, the matter will have to be raised during negotiations with the seller's solicitor.

### 21.4.1  From an investment account

Where the buyer intends to fund the deposit from money in an investment account held by him, the length of notice which the buyer needs to give to withdraw his funds without losing a significant amount of interest should be borne in mind.

### 21.4.2  Bridging finance

Bridging finance from a bank or other lender may be needed in a situation where the purchase is dependent on a related sale. Bridging finance will be required in the situation where the buyer will have sufficient funds for all of the purchase price on completion (eg because of a related sale), but does not have sufficient funds at exchange of contracts to fund the deposit. A loan will then be required to 'bridge the gap' between when the money is needed (exchange) and when it will be available (completion of the sale). It should be apparent at an early stage in the transaction that bridging finance will be required and arrangements should be made as soon as possible, so that the money is immediately available when required on exchange. An undertaking to repay the bridging loan out of the proceeds of sale of the client's existing property will often be required from the solicitor.

The client should be advised about the costs and risks of bridging finance, such as the high interest rate which will be payable over an uncertain period if the sale goes off, and the arrangement fees charged by the lender for negotiating the loan. If the client has a high cash flow passing through his current account, it may be more cost effective for him to take advantage of the lower interest rates payable on the overdraft on current account.

### 21.4.3  Deposit guarantees

A deposit guarantee, obtainable from some insurance companies, is an insurance policy which is bought by the buyer and tendered to the seller on exchange in place of payment of a money deposit. If the buyer wishes to fund the deposit in this way, the seller's consent must be obtained and the contract amended to provide for payment by way of the guarantee. The guarantee should be taken out in the sum required as deposit (ie normally 10% of the purchase price). The seller will be able to enforce the guarantee against the insurance company, and so recover the deposit in cash in the event of the buyer defaulting on completion. Although guarantees which can be moved up through a chain of transactions can be obtained (ie their benefit can be assigned), they are not popular with sellers and are not commonly used.

### 21.4.4  Use of deposit from related sale

If the buyer is also selling his existing house, he will be receiving a deposit on that sale. Can that money be used to fund (or partly fund) the deposit on the purchase? Standard Condition 2.2.2 permits this in certain circumstances (see **21.6.1**). If, as is likely, the deposit received on the sale is less than the deposit required on the purchase, the balance can be funded in one of the ways previously mentioned. Alternatively, it may be possible to persuade the seller to accept a reduced deposit, ie to try and get the deposit reduced to the amount being received by the buyer on the sale of his present house.

Such a provision is obviously inapplicable in a commercial transaction and so the Standard Commercial Property Conditions of Sale do not include a similar provision.

## 21.5  CLEARING FUNDS

The buyer's solicitor must ensure that he receives the amount of the deposit from his own client in sufficient time to allow the client's cheque to be cleared through the solicitor's client account before drawing the cheque in favour of the seller.

## 21.6  CAPACITY IN WHICH DEPOSIT IS HELD

The deposit is held in one of the three capacities listed below:

(1)   agent for the seller;
(2)   agent for the buyer;
(3)   stakeholder.

Most deposits are paid to the seller's solicitor in the capacity either of agent for the seller or stakeholder.

### 21.6.1  Capacity implied by law

In the absence of contrary agreement, solicitors and estate agents hold in the capacity of agent for the seller, but an auctioneer holds as stakeholder (see *Edgell v Day* (1865) LR 1 CP 80; *Ryan v Pilkington* [1959] 1 All ER 689). This general rule may be varied by express contractual condition. Both sets of Standard Conditions of Sale (Condition 2.2) generally provide for the deposit to be held as stakeholder. However, Residential Standard Condition 2.2 allows the seller to use the deposit as deposit on his related purchase of a house for his own occupation, provided that in such related purchase it will be held on the same terms as the Standard Condition. This is a very important provision as it allows the seller to use the deposit to fund his own deposit on a related purchase without the need for the express permission of the buyer. It is widely taken advantage of in practice. Such a provision is inapplicable in a commercial transaction and so the Standard Commercial Property Conditions do not include a similar provision.

### 21.6.2  Agent for the buyer

The capacity of agent for the buyer is rarely used, since in most situations the seller will be reluctant to agree to the deposit being held in this way. It may, however, be necessary to use this capacity where the seller is represented by an unqualified person.

### 21.6.3  Agent for the seller

If the deposit is held as agent for the seller, the agent may hand the money over to the seller before completion. This capacity is advantageous to the seller who can, if he wishes, use the money immediately for any purpose he wishes. Where this occurs, the buyer may have difficulty in recovering the money if the seller defaults on completion, because the money will have passed into the hands of a third party who may be unknown to the buyer and with whom the buyer has no contractual relationship. In commercial sales, it is usually the case that the deposit is to be held as agent. If either set of the Standard Conditions are being used, a special condition will be required to state that this capacity is to apply.

### 21.6.4 Stakeholder

A stakeholder is a middle-man standing between both parties and, where this capacity is used, the money cannot generally be handed to either party without the consent of the other. Where the seller's solicitor holds the deposit in this capacity, his client will be unable to use the money towards the deposit on his related purchase. This capacity is disadvantageous to the seller (because he cannot use the money), but advantageous to the buyer who knows that the money is safe in the solicitor's bank account and will therefore be recoverable in the event of the sale going off due to the seller's default.

## 21.7 METHODS OF PAYMENT OF DEPOSIT

Residential Standard Condition 2.2 requires payment to be made either by bankers' draft or solicitors' cheque, except where the contract is made at auction.

Except in the case of a sale by auction, the Standard Commercial Property Conditions require the deposit to be paid by direct credit into the seller's solicitors' bank account.

### 21.7.1 Bankers' draft

A bankers' draft is a cheque drawn by a bank on its own funds. It is therefore unlikely to bounce and represents one of the safest methods of payment as far as the seller is concerned because he is guaranteed to get his money. A draft is regarded as being the equivalent of cash.

## 21.8 THE DEPOSIT CHEQUE BOUNCES

If a cheque taken in payment of the deposit bounces, this constitutes a fundamental breach of contract which gives the seller the option either of keeping the contract alive or of treating the contract as discharged by the breach, and in either event of suing for damages (*Millichamp v Jones* [1983] 1 All ER 267). A separate cause of action arises out of the cheque itself. The contract should be drafted to indicate precisely what the rights of the parties are in the event of the dishonour of the deposit cheque. Standard Condition 2.2.4 allows the seller to give notice to the buyer that the contract has been discharged by his breach, provided that he does so within seven working days of his being informed of the cheque being dishonoured. There is no similar provision in the Standard Commercial Property Conditions, so the common law position would apply.

The option of treating the contract as discharged is of little consolation to a seller who, on the strength of his sale contract, has exchanged contracts for the purchase of another property. Provision is therefore made in the contract to ensure that the deposit is payable by a method which will be honoured on presentation (see Standard

Condition 2.2 which requires payment by bankers' draft or solicitors' cheque and Standard Commercial Property Condition 2.2.2, which requires payment to be made by a direct credit to the seller's solicitors' bank account). The seller should insist on compliance with these conditions.

## 21.9  INTEREST ON THE DEPOSIT

Where the deposit is held by a solicitor, irrespective of the capacity in which the money is held, interest may be payable under the Solicitors' Accounts Rules 1998, Rule 24. Standard Condition 2.2.3 (Condition 2.2.2 of the Standard Commercial Property Conditions) provides that, where the deposit, or part of it, is held in the capacity of stakeholder, interest on the deposit will be payable to the seller on completion. If the buyer negotiates an agreement that he is to be credited with interest on the deposit, a special condition must be inserted in the contract to that effect.

### 21.9.1  The Solicitors' Accounts Rules 1998

The Solicitors' Accounts Rules 1998 apply to all money held by a solicitor on behalf of a client, including a deposit held by a solicitor as agent or stakeholder in a conveyancing transaction. Where the rules apply, interest must be paid to the client irrespective of whether the money was held on deposit or current account.

Where clients' money is held in a separate designated account, the solicitor must account to the client for the interest actually earned on that account. A separate designated account must be a deposit account. If the money is held in a general client account, the duty to pay interest depends on the amount of money held and the period for which it is held. Interest must be paid when the money is held for as long or longer than the number of weeks set out in the table below and the minimum balance held during that period equals or exceeds the amounts set out in the table.

| No of weeks | Minimum balance (£) |
|:-----------:|:-------------------:|
| 8 | 1,000 |
| 4 | 2,000 |
| 2 | 10,000 |
| 1 | 20,000 |

If a sum exceeding £20,000 is held for less than one week and it is fair and reasonable to do so, the solicitor must pay interest on that sum to the client.

### 21.9.2  Rate of interest

The rate of interest for money not held in a separate designated account is the rate currently payable on small deposits by the bank or building society where the money is held. Where money is held in a separate designated account (which should be a deposit account with a building society or major clearing bank), the amount of interest payable is the sum actually earned on that money while on deposit.

## 21.10 BUYER'S LIEN

From the moment when he pays the deposit to the seller in the capacity of agent (but not stakeholder), the buyer has a lien over the property for the amount of the deposit. The lien is enforceable only by a court order for sale of the property and may be protected as a notice or caution (registered land) or Class C(iii) land charge (unregistered land). If the buyer is in occupation, his lien may be an overriding interest in registered land under the Land Registration Act 1925, s 70(1)(g). It is not usual to register the lien unless problems arise in the transaction.

# Chapter 22

# INSURANCE

## 22.1 RISK IN THE PROPERTY

At common law, and unless the contract provides otherwise, the risk of accidental damage to the property passes to the buyer from the moment of exchange of contracts. The buyer bears the risk of loss or damage, except where it can be shown that the loss or damage is attributable to the seller's lack of proper care (*Clarke v Ramuz* [1891] 2 QB 456; *Phillips v Lamdin* [1949] 2 KB 33). The buyer should therefore normally insure the property from exchange of contracts onwards. A solicitor who fails to advise his client of the consequences of failure to insure, or who fails to carry out his client's instructions to insure the property, will be liable in negligence if the client suffers loss as a result of the lack of insurance.

## 22.2 INSURING THE PROPERTY

It is essential that the buyer's insurance arrangements have been made in advance of actual exchange so that the policy will be effective immediately upon exchange. Insurance is generally effected by one of the following methods.

(1) By noting the property on a block policy held by the buyer's solicitor which covers all properties currently being handled by the firm.

(2) Where the buyer is financing his purchase with the assistance of a mortgage, the lender will normally insure the property on being requested to do so by the buyer's solicitor. The lender's standing instructions to solicitors should be checked to ensure that:

   (a) the amount of cover will be adequate both in terms of the value of the property and the type of risks covered;

   (b) the property will be put on cover from the time of exchange;

   (c) the lender's insurance requirements do not conflict with the terms of the contract or of any lease to which the property is subject.

(3) By the buyer taking out a policy which will cover the property from exchange.

## 22.3 PROPERTY AT SELLER'S RISK

In some cases, and commonly with new property which is in the course of construction, the contract will provide that the property is to remain at the seller's risk until completion.

### 22.3.1 Standard Condition 5.1

Standard Condition 5.1 provides for the seller to bear the risk in the property until completion, and permits rescission if the property is substantially damaged between exchange and completion. Except in certain cases applicable to the sale of leaseholds, the seller is not obliged by the condition to maintain his own insurance policy after exchange. Where the risk in the property remains with the seller, the buyer need not take out his own policy until completion.

Condition 5.1 is sometimes expressly excluded by special condition, in which case the insurance position under the contract reverts to the common law principles, ie the buyer takes the risk from exchange and therefore must insure from that time. Irrespective of the terms of the contract, the buyer's lender will frequently insist that the property is insured in the buyer's name from the date of exchange. The lender's instructions must therefore be checked to ensure that they do not conflict with the provisions of the contract.

### 22.3.2  The Law of Property Act 1925, s 47

Condition 5.1 of the Standard Conditions of Sale excludes the Law of Property Act 1925, s 47 which would otherwise give the buyer the right, in certain circumstances, to claim off the seller's policy in the event of damage to the property.

### 22.3.3  The Standard Commercial Property Conditions

Condition 5 of the Commercial Conditions takes a completely different approach to the Residential Standard Conditions. It does not change the common law position that the risk passes to the buyer on exchange. Condition 5.1.1(a) provides that the seller is under no obligation to insure the property, except where required by the terms of any lease or the contract of sale. It is, therefore, essential for a buyer to take out his own policy of insurance as from exchange.

However, in practice, it is likely that the seller will keep up his policy until completion, and Condition 5.1.1(b) deals with such a case of dual insurance. Where there are two policies on the same property, there is a danger that, on a claim being made, an insurance company would reduce the amount they were prepared to pay out because of the existence of the other policy. Condition 5.1.1(b) thus provides that where there is a reduction in any payment made to the buyer because of the existence of the seller's policy, the purchase price is to be reduced accordingly. The seller could then claim that reduction from his insurers.

The Commercial Conditions also envisage the possibility of a condition being included in the sale contract requiring the seller to maintain his insurance until completion. If such a special condition is included, Condition 5.1.2 requires the seller (inter alia) to maintain the policy until completion. If, before completion, the property suffers damage, the seller must pay to the buyer all policy monies received or assign to the buyer all rights under the policy.

### 22.4  MAINTENANCE OF SELLER'S POLICY

Except where the seller is required by a condition of the contract of sale or his mortgage or lease to maintain his policy, he could cancel his insurance policy on exchange of contracts but, in practice, he would be unwise to do so (eg in case the buyer failed to complete). The seller should also be advised not to cancel his contents or other policies until completion.

## 22.5 OTHER TYPES OF INSURANCE

In appropriate cases, the buyer should be advised to take out insurance to cover other risks (eg life insurance). These policies should be taken out immediately after exchange of contracts, so that their proceeds would be available to the buyer's personal representatives in the unlikely event of the buyer dying before completion takes place. If the buyer did die at this stage of the transaction the personal representatives could be forced to complete the sale and without the proceeds of a life policy would not have the funds to do so since the buyer's mortgage offer would have been revoked by his death. Advice given by the solicitor to his client about the terms of a life insurance policy will in most cases be subject to the provisions of the Financial Services Act 1986. A house contents policy does not need to be taken out until the buyer moves his furniture into the property (ie normally on completion day).

# Chapter 23

# PREPARING TO EXCHANGE

## 23.1 INTRODUCTION

A binding contract will come into existence on exchange of contracts, after which time neither party will normally be able to withdraw from the contract without incurring liability for breach. It is therefore essential to check that all outstanding queries have been dealt with and that all financial arrangements are in order before the client is advised to commit himself to the contract.

## 23.2 MATTERS TO BE CHECKED

Consideration should be given to the following matters before exchange takes place. The matters marked with an asterisk in the lists concern both seller and buyer; the unmarked items are mainly of concern to a buyer client.

### 23.2.1 Searches

(1)  Have all necessary searches and enquiries been made?
(2)  Have all the replies to searches and enquiries been received?
(3)  Have all search and enquiry replies been checked carefully to ensure that the replies to individual questions are satisfactory and accord with the client's instructions?
(4)* Have all outstanding queries been resolved ?
(5)  Has a survey of the property been undertaken and if so is the result satisfactory?

### 23.2.2 Financial arrangements

(1)  Has a satisfactory offer been made and (where necessary) accepted by the client?
(2)  Are arrangements in hand to comply with any conditions attached to the advance (eg obtaining estimates for repairs to the property)?
(3)  Taking into account the deposit, the mortgage advance (less any retention) and the costs of the transaction (including disbursements), is there sufficient money for the client to proceed with the purchase?
(4)* Have arrangements been made to discharge the seller's existing mortgage(s) or on a sale of part to release the part being sold from the mortgage?

### 23.2.3 Deposit

(1)* How much (if any) preliminary deposit has been paid?
(2)* How much money is needed to fund the deposit required on exchange?
(3)  Has a suitable undertaking been given in relation to bridging finance?
(4)* To whom is the deposit to be paid?
(5)  Have the deposit funds been obtained from the client and cleared through clients' account?

### 23.2.4  The contract

(1)* Have all outstanding queries been satisfactorily resolved?
(2)* Have all agreed amendments been incorporated clearly in both parts of the contract?
(3)* Has the approved draft been returned to the seller?
(4)* Is a clean copy of the contract available for signature by the client?
(5)* Have the terms of the contract been explained to the client?
(6)* Has the list of fixtures and fittings been agreed between the parties?

### 23.2.5  Insurance

(1)  Have steps been taken to insure the property?
(2)  Have steps been taken to obtain any life policy required under the terms of the buyer's mortgage offer?

### 23.2.6  Completion date

(1)* Has a completion date been agreed?

### 23.2.7  Method of exchange

(1)* Which method of exchange is most suitable to be used in this transaction?
(2)* Where the client requires a simultaneous exchange on both sale and purchase contracts, are both transactions and all related transactions in the chain also ready to proceed?

### 23.2.8  Signature of contract

(1)* Has the client signed the contract?

### 23.2.9  Occupiers

(1)* Has the consent of all non-owning occupiers been obtained?

## 23.3  REPORTING TO CLIENT

When the buyer's solicitor has completed his searches and enquiries and the form of the draft contract has been agreed, he should report to his client either orally or (preferably) in writing explaining the results of his investigations and the terms of the contract and mortgage offer to the client. Some firms prepare a 'Buyer's Report' for this purpose.

## 23.4  SIGNATURE OF CONTRACT

Both parties must sign the contract (or each must sign one of two identical copies) in order to satisfy the Law of Property (Miscellaneous Provisions) Act 1989, s 2. The signature need not be witnessed. Where two or more individuals are named in the contract as comprising one of the parties, all such individuals must sign.

### 23.4.1 Signature by the client

Signature by the client in the presence of his solicitor, the solicitor first having ensured that the client understands and agrees with the terms of the contract, is desirable but is not always practicable. Where the contract is to be sent to the client for signature, the accompanying letter should clearly explain where and how the client is required to sign the document. If not already done, the letter should also explain the terms of the contract in language appropriate to the client's level of understanding, and request a cheque for the deposit indicating by which date the solicitor needs to be in receipt of cleared funds.

### 23.4.2 Signature by solicitor on behalf of client

A solicitor needs his client's express authority to sign the contract on behalf of the client (*Suleman v Shahsavari* [1989] 2 All ER 460). Unless the solicitor holds a valid power of attorney, it is recommended that such authority should be obtained from the client in writing, after the client has been informed of the legal consequences of giving such authority (ie signature implies authority to proceed to exchange, and exchange creates a binding contract). Failure to obtain authority may render the solicitor liable in damages for breach of warranty of authority (*Suleman v Shahsavari* (above)).

### 23.4.3 Companies

Provided that the transaction has been authorised by the company, an officer of the company (usually a director or the secretary) may be authorised to sign on behalf of the company.

### 23.4.4 Occupiers

A non-owning occupier may be joined as a party to the contract in order to give a release of his or her purported interest in the property. Where this occurs the non-owning occupier must sign a release of his rights (see **19.4.3**).

# Chapter 24

# EXCHANGE OF CONTRACTS

## 24.1 THE PRACTICE OF EXCHANGE

The physical exchange of contracts between the parties is not a legal requirement for a contract for the sale of land, but where a contract is drawn up by solicitors acting for the parties it is usual for the contract to be prepared in two identical parts, one being signed by the seller, the other by the buyer. When the two parts are physically exchanged, so that the buyer receives the part of the contract signed by the seller and vice versa, a binding contract comes into existence. The actual time when the contract comes into being depends on the method which has been used to effect the exchange.

Since exchange is not a legal necessity, it is possible for the contract to comprise a single document which is signed by both parties. In such a case, the contract becomes binding and enforceable as soon as the second signature has been put on the document (*Smith v Mansi* [1962] 3 All ER 857). This situation is uncommon because the same solicitor is usually forbidden to act for both parties by Rule 6 of the Solicitors' Practice Rules 1990.

## 24.2 AUTHORITY TO EXCHANGE

A solicitor who exchanges contracts without his client's express or implied authority to do so will be liable to the client in negligence. In *Domb v Isoz* [1980] 1 All ER 942, it was held that once the solicitor has his client's authority to exchange he has the authority to effect the exchange by whichever method the solicitor thinks most appropriate to the situation.

## 24.3 METHODS OF EXCHANGE

Whichever method is chosen, the exchange is usually initiated by the buyer indicating to the seller that he is now ready to commit himself to a binding contract. Once contracts have been exchanged, neither party will be able to withdraw from the contract. It is therefore essential that the parties' solicitors have checked that all necessary arrangements are in order before proceeding to exchange. Also, in residential transactions, where the purchase of one property is dependent on the sale of another, the solicitor must ensure that the exchange of contracts and completion dates on both properties are synchronised to avoid leaving his client either owning two houses or being homeless. Failure to synchronise the exchange where the client has instructed that his sale and purchase transactions are interdependent constitutes professional negligence. The solicitor must ensure, therefore, that he either exchanges on both the sale and the purchase or exchanges on neither; he does not want to be in the position of exchanging on one transaction, only to find that the other party to the dependent transaction has decided to withdraw. Ideally, the exchange on the two transactions should take place simultaneously in order to avoid this danger, but this is not practical. The best that the solicitor can do is to ensure that there is as little time delay as is practically possible between exchanging on one transaction and on the other.

### 24.3.1  Telephone

Exchange by telephone is now the most common method of effecting an exchange of contracts. Legal recognition of the practice was given by the Court of Appeal in *Domb v Isoz* [1980] 1 All ER 942. With the exception of personal exchange, this method represents the quickest way of securing an exchange of contracts and is particularly useful in a chain of transactions.

The method is not free of risk. Where exchange is effected by telephone, the contract between the parties becomes effective as soon as the parties' solicitors agree in the course of a telephone conversation that exchange has taken place. The telephone conversation is followed by a physical exchange of documents through the post, but the existence of the contract is not dependent on this physical exchange, the contract already exists by virtue of the telephone conversation. If one party were subsequently to change his mind about the contract, it would be easy to dispute or deny the contents of the telephone conversation and thus the existence of the contract itself. The problems arising out of a telephonic exchange are as follows:

- neither party is able to check that the other's contract has been signed;
- neither party is able to check that the other's contract is in the agreed form and incorporates all agreed amendments.

If one part of the contract has not been signed, or if the two parts are not identical, then there can be no contract, even if the parties purport to exchange. The seller may also be exchanging without having received a deposit. This would be professional negligence on the part of his solicitors.

To avoid the uncertainties arising out of this method of exchange, the parties' solicitors must agree prior to exchange that the telephonic exchange will be governed by one of The Law Society's formulae which were drawn up by the Society in response to the decision in *Domb v Isoz* (above). An accurate attendance note recording the telephone conversation must also be made as soon as possible. The formulae rely on the use of solicitor's undertakings to overcome these problems.

### 24.3.2  Use of the formulae for exchange

There are three Law Society formulae:

(1)  Formula A: this is used where one solicitor (usually the seller's solicitor) already holds both parts of the contract before the exchange is initiated;

(2)  Formula B: this is used where at the time of the telephone exchange each party's solicitor is still in possession of his own client's signed contract;

(3)  Formula C: this is designed to be used in chain transactions.

The wording of the formulae is set out in Appendix 4. Whichever formula is used, the client's express authority to exchange must be obtained before the procedure to exchange is commenced. If any variation to a formula is to be made, that variation must be expressly agreed and noted in writing by all the solicitors involved before exchange takes place. Subject to agreed variations, the conditions attached to the formula in use must be strictly adhered to.

### Formula A

This is little used in practice. The buyer will have sent his part of the contract, together with the deposit cheque, to the seller, with an instruction to hold both of these to his order. When ready to exchange, the buyer will telephone the seller and a completion date will be agreed. The seller will then confirm that he holds his client's part of the contract duly signed by the seller and that this is in the agreed form. It will then be agreed that exchange takes place as at that moment. The seller then undertakes to send his client's part of the contract to the buyer on the same day.

In practice, Formula A is the safest of the three formulae to use because, before actual exchange takes place, the seller's solicitor has the opportunity of seeing the buyer's signed part of the contract and can check that it is identical to his own client's part. He is also usually in possession of the buyer's deposit cheque, which will have been sent to him with the buyer's part of the contract. Although the seller cannot bank the cheque until exchange has taken place, he is secure in the knowledge that the deposit will be paid.

### Formula B

This is the most commonly used of the formulae. Each solicitor still holds their own client's part of the contract. In the telephone conversation, both will confirm that their respective parts of the contract are signed and in the agreed form. After the exchange has taken place, both parties will undertake to send their respective parts of the contract to the other, the buyer also undertaking to send the deposit. Although not specifically designed for use in chain transactions, it is frequently used in such situations.

Imagine a chain of transactions in which A is selling to B, who, in turn, is selling to C. We act for B, who thus has a dependent sale (to C) and purchase (from A). Before exchanging with C, we will check with A that he is ready to exchange and agree a completion date. We will then exchange with C, with completion fixed for the same day. (Agreeing the same completion date for both transactions may in reality need further telephone calls.) Having exchanged with C, we will then immediately telephone A and exchange with him. There is, of course, a risk that since first speaking to A, his client may have decided to withdraw, but this is often thought an acceptable risk as long as contracts can be exchanged on the same day as the initial assurance was received. The other main problem comes if we (B) wish to use the deposit received from C as the deposit on our purchase from A. When we exchange with A we will not have then received the money from C and so will not be able to give the Formula B undertaking that we will send it 'that day'. Prior to exchanging on either transaction, therefore, we will have had to obtain A's approval to an amendment to the formula. We could either undertake to get C to send the money direct to A, or alternatively undertake that we have exchanged with C and will send the money on as soon as it is received by us.

### Formula C

This is specifically designed for use in chain transactions and will avoid any risk of a client exchanging on one transaction without also exchanging on the dependent transaction. It also makes provision for the seller using the buyer's deposit towards the deposit he will need to pay on his dependent purchase. It is, however, somewhat complex and because of this is little used in practice in many areas of the country. Again assuming the same chain, A selling to B who is selling to C and we are acting for B, we will initially obtain an undertaking from A that he will exchange on the sale to us provided that we get back to him by a specified time later today. This then gives us time to exchange on our sale to C, secure in the knowledge that if we do, we will be able to exchange on our purchase also – provided, of course, that we get back to A by the specified time. The undertakings on the exchanges will be similar to those in Formula B, except that if we wish to use the deposit from our sale as the deposit on the purchase we will not send the deposit ourselves. We will obtain an undertaking from our buyer's solicitor that they will send it direct to our own seller rather than to us. The undertaking under Part 2 of Formula C is that we will 'arrange' to send the deposit to the seller. We will comply with this by virtue of the undertaking we have already received from our own buyer. Note, however, that before using Formula C, we will need to have obtained our client's express permission to use that formula. For a worked example of an exchange using Formula C, see **24.5**.

### 24.3.3  Personal exchange

By this method, the solicitors for the parties meet, usually at the seller's solicitor's office, and the two contracts are physically exchanged. A contract exists from the moment of exchange. Although this type of exchange represents the safest and most instantaneous method of exchange, it is frequently not practical to use personal exchange because the physical distance between the offices of the respective solicitors makes it impractical to do so. Personal exchange is infrequently used in residential transactions, but is still used in high-value commercial contracts. This method has two benefits: it is instantaneous, thus leaving no uncertainty over the timing of the creation of the contract, and it enables both parties to see the other party's part of the contract before exchange actually takes place, so that both can check that the parts of the contract are identical in form and have been properly signed. The seller can also ensure that he is in receipt of the deposit before exchanging.

### 24.3.4  Postal exchange

Where exchange is to take place by post, the buyer's solicitor will send his client's signed contract and the deposit cheque to the seller's solicitor who, on receipt of these documents, will post his client's signed contract back to the buyer.

Generally, a contract does not come into being until the buyer has received the seller's contract. Exchange of contracts by post forms an exception to this rule and the contract is made when the seller posts his part of the contract to the buyer (*Adams v Lindsell* (1818) 1 B and Ald 6813). It follows from the above that a contract will be formed even if the seller's part of the contract is lost in the post and never received by the buyer.

Using the post as a method of exchange is reasonably satisfactory when dealing with a single sale or purchase which is not dependent on another related transaction, but even in this situation there will inevitably be a delay between the buyer sending his contract to the seller and the seller posting his part back, during which time the buyer is uncertain of whether he has secured the contract. There is also no guarantee that the seller will complete the exchange by posting his part of the contract back to the buyer. Until he actually does so, he is free to change his mind and withdraw from the transaction. Although these risks are small where a single sale or purchase is being undertaken, they assume a much greater significance where a chain of transactions is involved and the use of postal exchange is not advised in linked transactions.

### 24.3.5 Document exchange

A document exchange, or DX, is a private postal system not under the control of the Post Office. Most solicitors belong to a document exchange. A document exchange can be used to effect an exchange of contracts in a similar way to the normal postal service and is subject to the same risks. The court has approved the use of document exchanges for the service and delivery of documents in non-contentious matters in *John Wilmott Homes v Reed* (1986) 51 P & CR 90. The rules on postal acceptance do not apply to document exchanges and, unless the contract contains a contrary provision, the contract will come into existence when the seller's part of the contract is received by the buyer. Where either set of Standard Conditions is used, Condition 2 provides that the contract is made when the last copy of the contract is deposited at the document exchange. If the Standard Conditions of Sale do not form the basis of the contract, the contract probably comes into existence when the last part of the contract is placed in the recipient's box at the document exchange, but there is no decided case in this area.

### 24.3.6 Fax

The main use of fax in the context of exchange of contracts is to transmit the messages which activate the Law Society formulae. Fax is merely a substitute for using the telephone. Condition 1.3.3 in both sets of Standard Conditions does not permit fax to be used as a valid method of service of a document where delivery of the original document is essential (as it is with the contract), thus effectively ruling out an exchange by faxing copies of the signed contract. Further, an exchange of faxes is not a valid exchange of contracts under s 2 of the Law of Property (Miscellaneous Provisions) Act 1989 (*Commissioner for the New Towns v Cooper (Great Britain) Ltd* [1995] Ch 259).

### 24.3.7 E-mail

At the moment, contracts for the sale of land must be in writing so cannot be entered into electronically via e-mail or the internet. However, e-mail can be used to transmit the messages activating The Law Society formulae.

The Government has, however, published draft legislation, intended to be in force by December 2001, which would allow contracts to be made electronically. There would then be only one copy of the contract which would be stored and 'signed' electronically. Thus there would no longer be exchange of contracts; instead the contract, once 'signed' by both parties would come into existence at a time agreed between the parties. An electronic 'signature' will consist of the transmission of an encrypted message which is certified as coming only from the person transmitting it.

## 24.4 STANDARD CONDITIONS OF SALE

Condition 2.1 in both sets of Standard Conditions governs the making of the contract and allows contracts to be exchanged by document exchange, post, or by telephone using the Law Society formulae.

## 24.5 EXAMPLE OF EXCHANGE USING FORMULA C

Jane has a linked sale and purchase. She is buying from Greg and selling to Zoe. They agree to use Formula C.

Jane wants to use the deposit she will receive from Zoe to fund part of the deposit she pays to Greg (see Standard Condition 2.2.2). Greg and Zoe agree to this.

- Zoe calls to say that she can exchange today. Jane checks when Zoe wants to complete.
- Jane calls Greg to see if he can also exchange today. Jane must agree the same completion date with Greg, so she may have to call Zoe back, if Greg wants a different date. At this stage no one is bound.
- Now Jane calls Zoe. Zoe agrees to Formula C Part 1. She will exchange later today, if Jane calls her before 3.30 pm.
- Jane calls Greg and, because Jane still has her part of the contract, they use Formula B. They amend Formula B because Zoe will send the deposit cheque to Greg. Jane and Greg check the contracts, fill in the completion date and agree to exchange. They date the contracts.
- Jane undertakes to send her part of the contract and the balance of the deposit to Greg, and to arrange for Zoe to send her deposit cheque straight to Greg. Greg undertakes to send his part of the contract to Jane.
- Jane calls Zoe and reminds her that they are using Formula C. They exchange contracts.
- Jane undertakes to send her part of the contract to Zoe. Zoe undertakes to send her part of the contract to Jane and, on Jane's directions, to send the deposit cheque to Greg.

## 24.6 INSURANCE

If the buyer is to insure the property from exchange (see Chapter 22), the buyer's solicitor should immediately after exchange put in hand the previously decided arrangements. So, for example, if the buyer's lender is to effect the insurance, the lender should be telephoned immediately and informed that contracts have been exchanged and that the property should be placed on risk. Written or faxed confirmation of the telephone call should also be given.

Part IV

# AFTER EXCHANGE

**Chapter 25**

# THE CONSEQUENCES OF EXCHANGE

## 25.1 THE EFFECTS OF EXCHANGE

Following exchange a binding contract exists from which normally neither party may withdraw without incurring liability for breach. At common law, the beneficial ownership in the property passes to the buyer, who becomes entitled to any increase in value of the property but also bears the risk of any loss or damage; hence the need to ensure that insurance of the property is effective from the moment of exchange.

The seller retains the legal title to the property until completion, but holds the beneficial interest on behalf of the buyer. During this period, the seller is entitled to remain in possession of the property and to the rents and profits (unless otherwise agreed). He must also pay the outgoings (eg water rates) until completion. He owes a duty of care to the buyer and will be liable to the buyer in damages if loss is caused to the property through neglect or wanton destruction (*Clarke v Ramuz* [1891] 2 QB 456; *Phillips v Lamdin* [1949] 2 KB 33). This duty continues so long as the seller is entitled to possession of the property and does not terminate because the seller vacates the property before completion.

## 25.2 AFTER EXCHANGE

### 25.2.1 The seller

The seller's solicitor should inform the client and estate agent that exchange has taken place and enter the completion date in the his diary or file-prompt system. Where exchange has taken place by telephone, the copy of the contract signed by the seller should immediately be sent to the buyer's solicitor to fulfil any undertaking given in the course of an exchange by telephone, having first checked that the contract is dated and contains the agreed completion date. Any deposit received must immediately be paid into an interest-bearing clients' deposit account.

### 25.2.2 The buyer

The buyer's solicitor should inform the client and his lender that exchange has taken place and enter the completion date in his diary or file-prompt system. Where exchange has taken place by telephone, he should immediately send to the seller (or as directed by him) the signed contract and deposit cheque in accordance with the undertaking given, having first checked that the contract is dated and contains the agreed completion date. Where appropriate, the contract should be protected by registration. Where the buyer is to insure (see Chapter 22), the buyer's solicitor should immediately put in hand the insurance arrangements previously decided upon.

## 25.3  REGISTRATION OF THE CONTRACT

### 25.3.1  Registered land

The contract constitutes a minor interest which, in order to bind future buyers of an interest in the land, needs to be protected by entry of a notice or caution on the register of the title. A buyer who is in possession of the property has an overriding interest within the Land Registration Act 1925, s 70(1)(g), in which case protection of the contract by registration is not necessary.

### 25.3.2  Unregistered land

The contract is an estate contract within the Class C(iv) category of land charge and will be void against a buyer of the legal estate for money or money's worth if not registered. Registration must be made against the name of the legal estate owner for the time being.

## 25.4  WHEN TO REGISTER THE CONTRACT

Since completion of most contracts occurs within a very short period following exchange, in practice registration of the contract is uncommon.

However, the contract should always be registered if any of the circumstances listed below apply:

(1)  there is to be a long interval (eg more than 2 months) between contract and completion;
(2)  there is reason to doubt the seller's good faith;
(3)  a dispute arises between the seller and buyer;
(4)  the seller delays completion beyond the contractual date.

## 25.5  DEATH OF A CONTRACTING PARTY

The death of one of the contracting parties between contract and completion does not affect the validity of the contract; the benefit and burden of the contract passes to the deceased's personal representatives who are bound to complete.

If completion does not take place on the contractual completion date, a breach of contract will occur (irrespective of whether time was of the essence of the completion date) and remedies (eg compensation, damages) will be available to the innocent party.

If time was not originally of the essence of the completion date, it can be made so by service of a notice to complete addressed to the deceased and the executor(s) named in the seller's will. A copy of the notice must be sent to the Public Trustee. If the deceased died intestate, notice can be served on the Public Trustee.

### 25.5.1  Death of one co-seller

Property owned by beneficial co-owners is held on a trust of land, and all the trustees must join in any conveyance of the legal estate. The death of one trustee between contract and completion does not, however, affect the validity of the contract. Where following the death there still remain at least two trustees of the legal estate, the transaction can proceed to completion without delay. In other cases, another trustee may have to be appointed so that the minimum number of two trustees is accomplished. It will be necessary to produce the death certificate of the deceased in order to provide the buyer with evidence of the death, and the purchase deed will need to be redrawn to reflect the change of parties to the transaction.

## 25.6  DEATH OF BUYER

The personal representatives step into the shoes of the deceased and will be bound to complete the contract. Some delay in completion may occur because the purchase deed will have to be redrafted to reflect the change in parties and the personal representatives cannot complete until they obtain the grant of representation. Where the purchase was due to be financed by a mortgage, the death of the buyer will usually mean that the offer of mortgage is revoked and the personal representatives may find themselves with insufficient funds to complete unless an alternative source of finance can be found.

The survivor of joint buyers remains bound by the contract and can be forced to complete. Finance may have to be rearranged and a new mortgage deed prepared. Some delay will be inevitable, and the seller will have a claim against the buyer for loss caused by the delay.

## 25.7  BANKRUPTCY OF SELLER

A buyer will only be affected by the bankruptcy of the seller if there is a bankruptcy entry shown on the result of his official search or on office copy entries. On the bankruptcy of an individual, the legal estate in property owned by him passes to his trustee in bankruptcy and the buyer must from that time deal only with the trustee and not the seller. The trustee may complete the sale subject to his right to disclaim onerous property. Property is defined as 'any unprofitable contract'. However, the trustee is not allowed to disclaim the contract just because he could raise more money by selling to someone else. In any event, if he were to disclaim the contract, he would also have to disclaim the land, and as a disclaimer would not destroy the equitable interest acquired by the buyer on exchange, the buyer would then be entitled to the property. The trustee will thus normally proceed with the sale.

However, a trustee also has powers to apply to court to set aside transactions at an undervalue. There will be such a transaction if the consideration provided by the buyer is 'significantly' less than the value of the property being sold.

Where the matter proceeds to completion, the purchase deed will have to be redrafted to show the trustee as the seller. The bankrupt is not a party to the deed. Some delay may occur pending appointment of the trustee and while the purchase deed is re-drafted and re-executed.

The legal estate in property held by co-owners does not vest in a bankrupt's trustee, but one co-owner's beneficial interest will do so on the latter's bankruptcy. Therefore, on the bankruptcy of one co-owner, the legal estate is unaffected and completion may proceed, the trustee joining in the purchase deed to give his consent to the sale of the beneficial interest.

## 25.8  BANKRUPTCY OF BUYER

If the buyer goes bankrupt, the benefit of the contract passes to the buyer's trustee in bankruptcy who may complete the transaction, subject to his right to disclaim onerous contracts. Where the transaction was to be financed by a mortgage, the buyer's mortgage offer will have been revoked by the bankruptcy, and there will obviously be no other available funds to complete the purchase. Some delay is inevitable pending the appointment of the trustee and while waiting for his decision whether or not to disclaim.

Where one of two or more co-purchasers goes bankrupt, the bankrupt's equitable interest will pass to his trustee. The remaining buyer(s) may have difficulty in completing on the contractual completion date, or at all, since a joint mortgage offer may have been vitiated by the co-purchaser's bankruptcy.

## 25.9  APPOINTMENT OF LIQUIDATOR

Every disposition of a company's property after presentation of a winding-up petition to the court is void unless sanctioned by the court. The presentation of a petition for the compulsory winding-up of a company thus freezes the transaction until a liquidator is appointed. On a voluntary liquidation, the directors' powers cease on appointment of the liquidator. The liquidator can complete a sale transaction on behalf of the company and can (with the consent of the court) bring proceedings to force the buyer to complete. Where a seller company goes into liquidation the liquidator will normally complete the transaction. The company normally remains as 'seller', the liquidator attesting the deed on the company's behalf. The liquidator will be the 'seller' in the purchase deed only if an order vesting the legal estate in him has been made by the court. Such an order is rare in practice.

A copy of the liquidator's deed of appointment should be supplied on completion. Where the liquidator is appointed to a company which is buying land, the liquidator has power to complete or to disclaim onerous contracts, but lack of money may present practical problems in proceeding to completion. Some delay is inevitable in this situation, for which the innocent party may seek compensation by claiming in the liquidation.

## 25.10  THE BUYER IN POSSESSION

In many cases, the seller will be in physical occupation of the property until completion and the question of the buyer taking possession before completion does not arise. The seller is entitled to retain possession until completion unless he agrees to do otherwise. The buyer's request to enter and occupy the premises before completion should be regarded with caution by the seller, because once the buyer takes up occupation he may lose his incentive to complete on the contractual completion date and if, ultimately, he does not complete the transaction at all, it may be difficult for the seller to regain possession of the property. Where the seller has a subsisting mortgage on the property, his lender's consent must be obtained before the buyer is allowed into occupation.

### 25.10.1 Occupation as licensee

In order to avoid problems relating to security of tenure arising from the buyer's occupation, it is essential to ensure that the buyer's occupation is as licensee and not as tenant. Condition 5.2 of both sets of Standard Conditions expressly states that the buyer's occupation is to be construed as a licence and this statement will probably be effective in most circumstances to prevent an inadvertent tenancy from arising. Even where a licence is granted, a court order will always be necessary to remove a residential occupier who does not voluntarily vacate the property (see the Protection from Eviction Act 1977, s 2) and may be necessary in non-residential cases where the tenant will not peaceably surrender his occupation.

### 25.10.2 Conditions of the buyer's occupation

#### *Standard Conditions of Sale*

Where the seller agrees to allow the buyer into possession, some restrictions or conditions should be attached to the buyer's occupancy. Condition 5.2 sets out that the terms of the licence are that the buyer:

- cannot transfer it;
- may permit members of his household to occupy;
- is to pay for or indemnify the seller against all outgoings;
- is to pay the seller a fee calculated at the contract rate on the balance of the purchase price;
- is entitled to the rents and profits from the property;
- is to keep the property in as good a state of repair as it was when he took possession;
- is not to make any alterations;
- is to insure the property for not less than the purchase price;
- is to assume the risk of damage to the property.

Either party can terminate the licence on 5 working days' notice.

The buyer may wish to renegotiate some of these terms. He may wish, for example, to take possession for the purpose of carrying out building works for alterations, improvements, etc, which is not permitted under the Standard Condition. In deciding whether to agree to possession for this purpose, the seller should bear in mind that if the contract fails for some reason he may be left with a property severely damaged because of half-finished works of alteration or improvement. Standard Condition 5.2.4 provides that the buyer is not deemed to be in occupation for the purposes of this condition if he is merely allowed access to carry out work agreed by the seller. Accordingly, if the seller does allow the buyer access for such purposes, express provision will need to be made as to termination of the licence, making good any damage caused, etc.

As an alternative solution, the seller may consider granting the buyer a licence for access only (eg for measuring up for carpets and curtains or to obtain estimates for alterations to be made to the property after completion).

*Standard Commercial Property Conditions*

These are very similar, but do not include any reference to occupation by members of the buyer's household and there is no obligation on the buyer to insure. Remember, that under Condition 5 of the Commercial Conditions the risk passes to the buyer on exchange anyway. Also, the proviso that access for works does not amount to occupation is not included, so allowing access for works could bring the Condition into play.

## 25.11 PRE-COMPLETION STEPS

Traditionally, the major task to be undertaken between exchange and completion was the deduction of title by the seller and its investigation by the buyer. Nowadays it is almost universal practice for proof of title to be dealt with at the pre-contract stage of the transaction. Thus, once contracts have been exchanged, most of the legal work in the conveyancing transaction has already been done by the parties' solicitors and the interval between exchange and completion is used to tidy up outstanding matters and to prepare for completion itself. There are, however, four important matters which must be dealt with at this stage:

(1) preparation of the purchase deed;
(2) dealing with redemption of the seller's mortgage and the creation of the buyer's mortgage;
(3) pre-completion searches made by the buyer; and
(4) ensuring that the financial aspects of the transaction are in order.

## 25.12 THE INTERVAL BETWEEN EXCHANGE AND COMPLETION

The interval between exchange and completion in residential transactions was conventionally a 4-week period giving ample time for the above tasks to be undertaken. In many cases, however, the clients will want completion to follow more quickly after exchange, a completion date which is 14 days or less after exchange being commonly encountered. In such a case, the solicitors will need to plan their timetable of pre-completion steps carefully to ensure that all necessary matters can be accomplished within the available time. Alternatively, in order to save time at this stage of the transaction, some of the pre-completion steps may be brought forward and dealt with at the pre-contract stage of the transaction. Pre-completion searches should be made as close to the date of actual completion as possible (see Chapter 31) because of the protection period given to the buyer with the result of an official search. There is no reason, however, why the preparation of the purchase deed should not be undertaken as soon as the contents of the contract have been agreed between the parties. It is sometimes the case that exchange and completion take place on the same day.

# Chapter 26

# REQUISITIONS ON TITLE

## 26.1 PURPOSE OF REQUISITIONS

The purpose of requisitions on title is to require the seller's solicitor to clarify and, if necessary, to rectify matters on the title supplied which the buyer's solicitor finds unsatisfactory. In practice, they are commonly used also to resolve administrative queries relating to the arrangements for completion.

## 26.2 TIME FOR RAISING REQUISITIONS

By Condition 4.1.1 of both sets of Standard Conditions, written requisitions on the title supplied must be raised within 6 working days after either the date of the contract or the day of delivery of the seller's evidence of title, whichever is the later. The buyer will lose his right to raise requisitions if he does not do so within the time-limits prescribed by this condition.

### 26.2.1 Evidence of title supplied before exchange

In most cases, the seller's evidence of title will be supplied to the buyer before exchange of contracts, and the contract will contain a clause excluding the buyer's right to raise requisitions once contracts have been exchanged. In such cases, the time-limits contained in the Standard Conditions (or other form of contract used) are irrelevant and, unless requisitions are raised before exchange of contracts, the buyer will be unable to query the title. Note, however, that such a special condition prevents the buyer only raising requisitions on the title as presented to him by the seller. If, after exchange, he discovers an undisclosed incumbrance or other defect, he will still be able to require it to be remedied or assert his remedies for non-disclosure (see Chapter 33).

## 26.3 STANDARD FORM REQUISITIONS

Most law stationers produce a standard form of requisitions on title which include many commonly asked questions (eg confirmation that the seller's mortgage on the property will be discharged on or before completion). In addition, the printed questions frequently deal with the administrative arrangements for completion itself (eg method of payment of money, the time and place for completion, whether completion can take place by post, etc). Queries which are specific to the title under consideration may either be added to the end of the standard form or typed on a separate sheet. Where title has been investigated before exchange, the only question relating to title is to ask the seller to confirm that nothing has altered since the date of exchange. The buyer's solicitor should send two copies of the form to the seller's solicitor, who will return one copy with his answers, keeping the other copy on his own file for reference. In Protocol cases, use of the Completion Information and Requisitions on Title form is recommended. This form, as well as asking for the usual information, also contains a request for confirmation that existing mortgages will be discharged on completion. The answer to this question takes effect as an undertaking to discharge the mortgages referred to and avoids the need for such an undertaking to be handed over on completion. Note, however, that if the lender intends to make use of the Electronic Notification of Discharge (END) system, then this undertaking will need modifying: see **30.7.1**.

### 26.3.1 Replies to requisitions

Condition 4.1.1 of both sets of Standard Conditions requires the seller's solicitor to reply to requisitions 4 working days after receiving them from the buyer's solicitor. This time-limit does not apply to requisitions which are raised before exchange of contracts.

### 26.3.2 Further queries

The buyer's solicitor should ensure that the answers given to his requisitions are satisfactory in relation both to the title and to the client's interests. Any replies which are unsatisfactory should be taken up with the seller's solicitor and further written queries raised until the matter is resolved. Condition 4.1.1 governs the time-limits for raising further queries.

# Chapter 27

# THE PURCHASE DEED

## 27.1 WHO PREPARES THE DEED?

It is normally the buyer's duty to prepare the purchase deed, but the seller may, by the Law of Property Act 1925, s 48(1), reserve the right by contractual condition to prepare the deed himself. This right is usually only used in sales of new houses where the seller will supply an engrossment (top copy) of the purchase deed after attaching a draft of this deed to the contract.

## 27.2 TIME FOR PREPARATION OF THE DEED

Traditionally, the purchase deed is prepared after the buyer has completed his investigation of title but, in practice, the deed is usually prepared shortly after exchange of contracts and sent to the seller for his approval with the buyer's requisitions on title. At common law, the buyer is deemed to have accepted the seller's title when he submits the purchase deed for approval, and so the submission of the purchase deed at the same time as requisitions are raised would preclude the buyer's right to raise requisitions on the seller's title. This problem is resolved by Condition 4.5.1 of both sets of Standard Conditions, which preserves the buyer's right to raise requisitions in such circumstances, subject to any express condition in the contract barring out requisitions. By Condition 4.1.2, the buyer is required to submit the draft purchase deed to the seller at least 12 working days before contractual completion date. Under the Protocol, the buyer's solicitor is required to submit the draft purchase deed simultaneously with his requisitions on title, as soon as possible after exchange of contracts and in any case within the time-limits specified in the contract.

## 27.3 FORM OF THE DEED

The purchase deed must be a deed in order to transfer the legal estate in the land to the buyer (Law of Property Act 1925, s 52). However, draft legislation was published in March 2001 which would allow an electronic version of a purchase 'deed' to be used. This is expected to be in force by December 2001. The purchase deed puts into effect the terms of the contract and so must reflect its terms. The form of the deed varies depending on whether the land concerned is registered or unregistered, freehold or leasehold. This chapter concentrates on the form of the purchase deed in freehold transactions. Leaseholds are dealt with in Chapters 35 and 36.

### 27.3.1 Registered land

Where the property being transferred is registered land, the form of the purchase deed is prescribed by rules made under the Land Registration Act 1925 and, subject to permitted variations, the prescribed form of wording must be used. Many of the standard Land Registry forms are reproduced by law stationers and in straightforward transactions these can be used as the basis of the purchase deed. In more complex cases, it will be necessary to produce an individually drafted deed, but in either case the form of wording prescribed by the rules should be followed as closely as circumstances permit. A traditional conveyance cannot be used to transfer registered land. The same form of transfer is used whether the registered estate is freehold or leasehold.

### 27.3.2 Unregistered land

No prescribed form of wording exists for a conveyance of unregistered land. The buyer is thus free to choose his own wording, subject to the seller's approval and provided that it accurately reflects the terms of the contract. As the transaction will lead to an application for first registration of title after completion, instead of using a traditional conveyance the buyer may prepare his purchase deed as a Land Registry transfer.

## 27.4 DRAFTING THE DEED

When drafting the purchase deed the buyer's solicitor needs to have access to:

(1)  the contract, because the purchase deed must reflect the terms of the contract;
(2)  the office copy entries/title deeds, because the contract may refer to matters on the title which need to be repeated or reflected in the purchase deed; and
(3)  except in straightforward cases, a precedent on which to base the deed under preparation.

## 27.5 SELLER'S APPROVAL OF THE DRAFT DEED

When the draft has been prepared, two copies should be sent to the seller's solicitor for his approval. A further copy of the draft should be kept by the buyer's solicitor so that amendments can be agreed over the telephone if required.

On receipt of the draft, the seller's solicitor should check it carefully to ensure that the document accurately reflects the terms of the contract. Amendments should be restricted to those which are necessary for the fulfilment of the document's legal purpose, bearing in mind that the choice of style and wording is the buyer's prerogative. Small amendments may be agreed with the buyer's solicitor by telephone in order to save time. More substantial amendments should be clearly marked in a distinct colour on both copies of the draft, one copy being returned to the buyer's solicitor for his consideration, the other being retained in the seller's solicitor's file for reference. By Condition 4.1.2 of both sets of Standard Conditions, the seller's solicitor is to approve or return the revised draft document 4 working days after delivery of the draft transfer by the buyer's solicitor.

## 27.6 ENGROSSMENT

When amendments (if any) to the draft deed have been finalised, the buyer's solicitor should prepare an engrossment (clean copy) of the deed. The engrossment must be checked carefully to ensure that all agreed amendments have been incorporated. A copy of the engrossment should be kept on the buyer's solicitor's file for reference. The completed engrossment should then be sent to the seller's solicitor for execution (signature) by his client.

Where the buyer is required to execute the deed, it is common practice for him to do so before it is sent to the seller for his signature. By Condition 4.1.2, the buyer must deliver the engrossment of the purchase deed to the seller at least 5 working days before completion.

## 27.7 EXECUTION

To be valid in law a deed must:

(1) indicate clearly that it is a deed (eg by containing the words 'This deed');
(2) be signed by the necessary parties in the presence of a witness; and
(3) be delivered (Law of Property (Miscellaneous Provisions) Act 1989, s 1). (See also Land Registration (Execution of Deeds) Rules 1990.)

Signature by the seller is always required in order to transfer the legal estate (Law of Property Act 1925, s 52). The buyer is required to execute the deed if it contains a covenant or declaration on his behalf. Execution by the buyer will be needed where the document contains an indemnity covenant in respect of existing covenants or a declaration by the buyers relating to the trusts on which they hold the property. Where other parties are joined in the deed (eg a lender to release the property from a mortgage), they should also sign the document. The provisions relating to execution of deeds are further explained in **17.6.8** above.

### 27.7.1 Signature by an individual

Signature by an individual must be made by him in person, preferably in ink. Where an individual is incapable of signing the document himself (eg because he is blind or illiterate), another person may execute it on his behalf. In such a situation the document should be read over to the individual, or its contents clearly explained to him, before signature. Two witnesses are required to the signature in these circumstances (Law of Property (Miscellaneous Provisions) Act 1989, s 1).

### 27.7.2 Attorneys

A person who holds a power of attorney on behalf of another can execute a deed on that person's behalf. The attorney may sign either in his own name or in that of the person on behalf of whom he is acting (eg 'A by his attorney B' or 'B as attorney on behalf of A').

### 27.7.3 Companies

The requirements for execution of a deed by a company are set out at **17.6.8** above.

### 27.7.4  Witnesses

Any responsible adult person may be a witness to the signature of an individual. There is no legal restriction on one party to a document being a witness to the other party's signature, nor on one spouse being a witness to the signature of the other spouse, but an independent witness is preferable because, if the validity of the document was ever challenged in court, the independent witness would provide a stronger testimony. The witness should sign his name and add, underneath the signature, his address and occupation. It is sensible to ask the witness also to write his full name in block capitals after his signature.

### 27.7.5  Delivery

In addition to being signed, a deed must be delivered, ie the parties must intend to be bound by it. A deed takes effect on its delivery. When the buyer delivers the engrossment to the seller for execution by him, he does not normally intend the deed to become effective at that time. It is therefore common practice for the buyer to deliver the deed to the seller 'in escrow', ie conditionally, so that the operation of the deed is postponed until completion. In the case of a company, delivery is presumed at the date of execution unless the contrary is proved (Companies Act 1985, s 36A).

## 27.8  EXPLAINING THE DOCUMENT TO THE CLIENT

A solicitor should always ensure before submitting a document for signature that the client understands the nature and contents of the document. Where the solicitor invites his client to sign the purchase deed in the solicitor's presence, the deed can be explained to the client before signature and may actually be signed in the presence of the solicitor who can then act as a witness to the signature. If this is not possible, the purchase deed may be sent to the client for signature and return. The letter which accompanies the purchase deed should:

(1)  explain the purpose and contents of the document;
(2)  contain clear instructions relating to the execution of the deed;
(3)  tell the client when the signed document must be returned to the solicitor; and
(4)  ask the client not to date the document (it is dated on actual completion).

## 27.9  PLANS

If the contract provides for the use of a plan, the purchase deed will also refer to the plan. In other cases, the buyer is not entitled to demand that a plan is used with the purchase deed unless the description of the property as afforded by the contract and title deeds is inadequate without one. If the buyer wishes to use a plan in circumstances where he is not entitled to demand one, he may do so with the seller's consent, but he will have to pay for its preparation.

Where the sale is of the whole of the seller's property, use of a plan is not normally considered necessary. On a sale of part (including flats and office suites), a plan is highly desirable and, where the land is registered, generally must be used. The plan(s) to be used with the purchase deed should be checked for accuracy, including all necessary colourings and markings, and firmly bound into the engrossment of the deed which should in its wording refer to the use of the plan(s). In registered land cases, all parties who execute the deed must also sign the plan as an acknowledgment of its inclusion as an integral part of the document. In unregistered land cases, signature of the plan is not compulsory but is highly desirable. Signatures on a plan need not be witnessed. Where a company seals the purchase deed, it should also seal the plan.

The preparation and use of plans are discussed at **14.5.1**.

## 27.10 PARTIES

Anyone whose consent is necessary in order to transfer the legal estate or who is to give a valid receipt for capital money arising out of the transaction must be joined as a party to the deed. The seller and buyer will usually be the only parties to the deed, but it may be necessary to join, for example, a receiver or liquidator, where a selling company is insolvent, or a non-owning occupier who will release his or her rights in the property. Where the seller is bankrupt, his trustee in bankruptcy will transfer the property so the seller is not a party to the deed. If the seller is a company which is in liquidation or under receivership, the company itself transfers the property, with the receiver or liquidator joining in the deed to give a receipt for the purchase price. In such a case, the liquidator actually executes the deed.

## 27.11 TRANSFER OF WHOLE

A transfer of the whole of a registered title will usually follow Land Registry Form TR1. A copy of this form is set out below. It is divided into a number of boxes and is designed so that it can be reproduced on a word processor.

**Transfer of whole**
**of registered title(s)**

**HM Land Registry**

*(if you need more room than is provided for in a panel, use continuation sheet CS and staple to this form)*

| |
|---|
| **1. Stamp Duty** |
| *Place "X" in the box that applies and complete the box in the appropriate certificate.* |
| ☐    I/We hereby certify that this instrument falls within category   ☐   in the Schedule to the Stamp Duty (Exempt Instruments) Regulations 1987 |
| ☐    It is certified that the transaction effected does not form part of a larger transaction or of a series of transactions in respect of which the amount or value or the aggregate amount or value of the consideration exceeds the sum of |
|      £ |
| **2. Title Number(s) of the Property** *(leave blank if not yet registered)* |
| |
| **3. Property** |
| |
| *If this transfer is made under section 37 of the Land Registration Act 1925 following a not-yet-registered dealing with part only of the land in a title, or is made under rule 72 of the Land Registration Rules 1925, include a reference to the last preceding document of title containing a description of the property:* |
| **4. Date** |
| **5. Transferor** *(give full names and Company's Registered Number if any)* |
| |
| **6. Transferee for entry on the register** *(Give full names and Company's Registered Number if any; for Scottish Co. Reg. Nos., use an SC prefix. For foreign companies give territory in which incorporated.)* |
| |
| *Unless otherwise arranged with Land Registry headquarters, a certified copy of the transferee's constitution (in English or Welsh) will be required if it is a body corporate but is not a company registered in England and Wales or Scotland under the Companies Acts.* |
| **7. Transferee's intended address(es) for service in the U.K.** *(including postcode)* **for entry on the register** |
| |
| **8. The Transferor transfers the property to the Transferee.** |
| **9. Consideration** *(Place "X" in the box that applies. State clearly the currency unit if other than sterling. If none of the boxes applies, insert an appropriate memorandum in the additional provisions panel.)* |
| ☐    The Transferor has received from the Transferee for the property the sum of *(in words and figures)* |
| ☐    *(insert other receipt as appropriate)* |
| ☐    The Transfer is not for money or anything which has a monetary value |

**10.** The Transferor transfers with *(place "X" in the box which applies and add any modifications)*

☐ full title guarantee     ☐ limited title guarantee

.

---

**11.** Declaration of trust *Where there is more than one transferee, place "X" in the appropriate box.*

☐   The transferees are to hold the property on trust for themselves as joint tenants.

☐   The transferees are to hold the property on trust for themselves as tenants in common in equal shares.

☐   The transferees are to hold the property *(complete as necessary)*

---

**12.** Additional Provision(s) *Insert here any required or permitted statement, certificate or application and any agreed covenants, declarations, etc.*

---

**13.** *The Transferors and all other necessary parties should execute this transfer as a deed using the space below. Forms of execution are given in Schedule 3 to the Land Registration Rules 1925. If the transfer contains transferees' covenants or declarations or contains an application by them (e.g. for a restriction), it must also be executed by the Transferees.*

### 27.11.1  Stamp duty

Box 1 starts with a space where the Inland Revenue will impress the appropriate stamps if stamp duty is payable on the transfer. There is then the certificate, which needs completing appropriately if the transfer is exempt from duty or a reduced rate can be claimed (see **31.7.3** as to which instruments are exempt, eg transfers on divorce or for no consideration). Where a consideration (excluding any amount payable for chattels) of £500,000 or less is payable, a certificate of value must be included in order to claim one of the reduced rates of duty. The certificate is printed on the form and is worded so as to prevent the avoidance of duty by subdividing a larger transaction into a series of smaller ones each below the stamp duty threshold. If the transaction can be certified as not exceeding £60,000, no duty will be payable; if not exceeding £250,000, then duty will be payable at 1% of the price; if not exceeding £500,000, then duty is payable at 3%. If the price exceeds £500,000, no certificate is required and duty will be payable at 4%. The appropriate amount has to be inserted in the box provided, so that if the purchase price is £150,000 it will be certified as not exceeding £250,000. No duty is payable on transactions relating to property within certain specified disadvantaged areas of the country.

### 27.11.2  Title number and property

The next two boxes contain spaces for the title number and a description of the property. All of this information can be obtained from the office copy entries supplied by the seller. The description should include the postcode.

### 27.11.3  Date

The date will be left blank until completion.

### 27.11.4  Transferor

Box 5 contains space for the name of the transferor to be entered. If the transferor is a company, the registered number should be included. There is no need to include the transferor's address. Note that Form TR1 uses the terms 'transferor' and 'transferee'. If preferred, these can be changed to 'seller' and 'buyer'.

### 27.11.5  Transferee

The transferee's name and address (including postcode) should then be inserted in boxes 6 and 7. Again, a company's registration number should be included. The address will be the one which is entered on the register and is intended as an address at which any notices concerning the property can be served. It should, therefore, be the address which will be relevant after the purchase, ie in the case of a house purchase, it will normally be the address of the property being purchased, assuming that the buyers do intend to reside there.

### 27.11.6  Operative words and consideration

The operative words, ie 'the transferor transfers the property to the buyer', are printed in box 8 and need no amendment. The amount of consideration must be expressly stated in box 9 to comply with the Stamp Act 1891 and should be set out in box 8 in both words and figures. Where VAT is payable, the amount stated should include VAT. It is on this amount that the liability to stamp duty will be calculated. There is a pre-printed receipt clause which renders unnecessary the need for any other receipt and is authority for the buyer to pay the money over to the seller's solicitor. Note that if chattels are being purchased for an additional sum, a separate receipt will need to be prepared for this amount.

### 27.11.7 Title guarantee

On the reverse of the form, box 10 requires an X to be inserted to indicate whether the transfer is with full or limited title guarantee. There is also space to include any modifications to the covenants which may have been agreed in the contract.

### 27.11.8 Declaration of trust

Where there is more than one transferee, box 11 requires the buyers to declare whether they will hold the land as joint tenants or tenants in common. If they are to hold as tenants in common, it is necessary for the precise shares to be set out. If the trusts are complicated, they should be continued onto the prescribed continuation sheet (form CS). Whenever trusts are being declared, as the original transfer will be kept by the Land Registry, it is advisable to prepare a duplicate of the transfer and have this executed by the buyers. This can then be kept by the buyers themselves in case of any future dispute as to the terms of the trust.

### 27.11.9 Additional provisions

There is then a box in which any other agreed clauses can be inserted. The most common will be an indemnity covenant. Remember, that additional clauses can be included only if they were agreed in the contract. Where the sale is subject to any obligation on which the seller will remain liable after the sale, Condition 4.5.4 of both sets of Standard Conditions will provide that the buyer should enter into an indemnity covenant. A typical form of wording to comply with the Standard Condition would be as follows:

> **The transferees jointly and severally covenant to observe and perform the covenants referred to in Entry No 1 on the charges register and to indemnify the transferor against any future liability for their breach or non-observance.**

### 27.11.10 Execution

The form then ends with space for the execution by the parties. The seller must always execute; a buyer need only execute if he is entering into covenants or making some form of declaration in the transfer. Due to the inclusion of the declaration of trust for co-owners, co-owners will always need to execute the deed. The form of execution is laid down by the Land Registration Rules 1997 and will vary depending upon the identity of the signatory, but a witness will always be required.

## 27.12 CONVEYANCE

As a conveyance of unregistered land will lead to first registration, it is possible under r 72 of the Land Registration Rules 1997 to use the usual form of Land Registry transfer, ie Form TR1 (see **27.11**). This is very commonly used in practice. The only amendments required to the printed form will be the omission of the title number in box 2 – as the land is not registered there will not be one – and the need to include a fuller description of the property in box 3. This need contain only a reference to another document in the title which contains a full description. This might read, for example:

> **10, Coronation Street, Weatherfield, GM4 8YY, as is more particularly described in a conveyance dated 4 February 1962 and made between.....**

Where a traditional conveyance is to be used, it will contain the same information as in Form TR1, but in a different format.

An example of a conveyance drafted in a modern style is given below.

## Specimen modern form: Conveyance

This Conveyance is made on 2001

between FREDERICK ALBERT BROWN and CLAIRE BROWN both of Brookside, 73A Manor Grove Avenue, Newton, Blankshire ('the Sellers') and LEONARD ARTHUR JOHNSON and JENNIFER JOHNSON both of 27 Albert Road, Newton, Blankshire ('the Buyers').

1. In consideration of twenty-nine thousand eight hundred pounds (£29,800) paid by the Buyers to the Sellers (the receipt of which the Sellers acknowledge) the Sellers convey to the Buyers with full title guarantee the freehold property known as Brookside 73A Manor Grove Avenue, Newton, Blankshire described in a Conveyance dated 18th November 1970 and made between John Edward Smith and the Sellers ('the Property') subject to the matters in that Conveyance so far as they affect the Property and are still effective.

2. The Buyers hold the Property on trust for themselves as joint tenants.

3. The Buyers jointly and severally covenant with the Sellers to observe and perform the restrictions covenants and conditions contained in a conveyance dated 23rd April 1938 and made between Hedley Verity of the one part and Wilfred Rhodes of the other and to indemnify the Seller against any future breach or non-observance.

4. It is certified that the transaction hereby effected does not form part of a larger transaction or of a series of transactions in respect of which the amount or value or aggregate amount or value of the consideration exceeds £60,000.

Signed as a deed and delivered by
Frederick Albert Brown
and Claire Brown
in the presence of:

Signed as a deed and delivered by
Leonard Arthur Johnson
and Jennifer Johnson
in the presence of:

# Chapter 28

# PRE-COMPLETION SEARCHES

## 28.1  WHO MAKES THE SEARCHES?

It is the buyer's solicitor's responsibility to ensure that such pre-completion searches as are relevant to the transaction are carried out, and that their results are satisfactory to his client. The buyer's lender also has an interest in the soundness of the title to the property and the solvency of the borrower, so searches will need making on the lender's behalf also.

## 28.2  REASON FOR MAKING SEARCHES

The main reason for making pre-completion searches is for the buyer's solicitor to confirm that information obtained about the property before exchange remains correct.

## 28.3  WHEN TO MAKE SEARCHES

The searches must be made in sufficient time to guarantee that the results are received by the buyer's solicitor in time for completion to take place on contractual completion date. Pre-completion searches should generally be made about 7 days before contractual completion date, but may be left until closer to completion date if, for example, a telephone, computer or fax search is to be made.

## 28.4  WHICH SEARCHES TO MAKE

The following searches should be made:

(1)  for registered land, search against title number at the district land registry (see **28.5**);
(2)  for unregistered land, including an unregistered reversion to a lease, search at the Land Charges Department against names of estate owners of the land (see **28.6**);
(3)  if acting for a lender, a bankruptcy search against the name of the borrower (see **28.7**);
(4)  such other of the searches listed in **28.8–28.13** as are relevant to the transaction.

## 28.5  LAND REGISTRY SEARCH

When buying registered land, a pre-completion search should be made at the appropriate district land registry. The object of the search is to ascertain whether any further entries have been made on the register of title to the property since the date of the office copies supplied prior to exchange. A fee is payable whether the search is made by post, or requested by telephone or fax by a credit account holder. Fees can be paid by cheque or credit account, provided in the case of the latter that the applicant's solicitor's key number is quoted on the application form. Prescribed forms of wording should be followed when requesting a search by telex or fax. The Land Registry Direct Service now enables solicitors to make searches via computer terminal and modem.

### 28.5.1 Search of whole title

Where the interest being purchased, leased or mortgaged concerns the whole of a registered title, the search application should be made on Form 94A. The application will give details of the title number of the property to be searched, a brief description of its situation, ie postal address, county and district, and the names of the registered proprietors. The applicant's name must also be given, together with his reason for making the search, ie he intends to purchase/lease/take a charge on the land.

Where a solicitor is acting both for a buyer and his lender, the search application should be completed in the name of the lender client. If this is done, the buyer can take the benefit and protection of the search and a separate search in the buyer's name is unnecessary. However, a search made on behalf of the buyer will not protect a lender.

The search application form asks the registrar to supply information relating to any fresh entries which have been made on the register since a stated date, which will usually be the date of the office copy entries given to the buyer and must be a date no earlier than 12 months before the date of the search application. An official certificate of search made on this form confers on the searcher a priority period of 30 working days from the date of the certificate. This provides protection to the buyer (and lender, if the search was made on his behalf) against any subsequent entries which may be placed on the register after the date of the search but before the buyer is registered as proprietor. The buyer will take free from any such entries provided that he submits his application for registration within the priority period.

## 28.6  LAND CHARGES DEPARTMENT SEARCH

This search is only of relevance to unregistered land and is made by submitting Form K15 to the Land Charges Department at Plymouth with the appropriate fee. Fees can be paid by credit account, provided the applicant's solicitor's key number is stated on the application form. An official certificate of result of search confers a priority period of 15 working days on the applicant. This protects the buyer against any entries which may be made on the register after the date of the search but before he completes the purchase. Provided that he completes the transaction within the 15 working days priority period, the buyer will take free from such entries. The search application can be made by post, telephone, telex or fax by a credit account holder. Where title was deduced prior to exchange, and this search was carried out at the pre-contract stage of the transaction, the search need only now be made against the current seller's name. This is to ensure that no further entries have been made against the seller's name since the date of the previous search. No further entries can validly be made against the names of previous estate owners once they have disposed of the land, so these need not be searched against again.

### 28.6.1 Form of the register

The register comprises a list of the names of estate owners of land, with details of charges registered against those names. The search is therefore made not against the land itself but against the names of the estate owners. A fee is payable for each name searched. The search must be made against the names of all the estate owners whose names appear on the abstract or epitome of title supplied by the seller, including those who are merely referred to in the bodies of deeds (as opposed to being parties to the deeds themselves) or in schedules attached to deeds which form part of the title. There is no need to repeat searches where a proper search certificate made against previous estate owners has been supplied with the abstract of title.

The register is maintained on a computer which will search only against the exact version of the name as shown on the application form. It is therefore important to check that the name inserted on the application form is identical to that shown on the title deeds and that, if any variations of that name appear in the deeds, for example if Samuel Smith is variously referred to as 'Sam Smith', 'Samuel James Smith' and 'Samuel Smyth', all the given variations of the name are separately entered on the search form and a separate fee paid in respect of each. Guidance on filling in the application form, together with a list of accepted abbreviations and variations which the computer will search against, is given in Land Charges Department Practice Leaflet No 2.

### 28.6.2 Period to be searched against

It is generally only possible for an effective entry to be made against a name in relation to that person's (or company's) period of estate ownership of the land in question. It is therefore usually only necessary to search against a name for the period during which the estate owner owned the land and for the period between his death and the date of the appointment of personal representatives. For the purposes of the search form, periods of ownership must be stated in whole years and can be ascertained by looking at the abstract or epitome of title supplied by the seller. If the estate owner's period of ownership is not known, as will be the case when searching against the name of the person who was the seller in the document forming the root of title, the search is, in practice, made from 1926 (the year when the register was opened). Where there is a voluntary disposition in the title which is, at the date of the contract, less than 5 years old, it is necessary to search against the donor's name for a period up to and including the current year to ensure that no bankruptcy of the donor occurred during this period. The bankruptcy of the donor during this period could lead to the disposition being set aside by the trustee in bankruptcy (see **17.7.8**).

### 28.6.3 Description of the land

Unless a description of the land is inserted on the search application form, the computer will produce entries relating to every person of the given name in the whole of the county or counties specified. In order to avoid having to read through and then reject multiple search entries revealed by the certificate of search, a brief description of the land, sufficient to clearly identify it, should be included on the application form. Although the intention of describing the land is to curtail the number of irrelevant entries produced by the computer, care should be taken in supplying the description, because an inaccurate description of the land may result in a relevant entry not being revealed by the search.

Particular care is needed when the abstract shows that the land formerly was part of a larger piece of land (eg when buying one plot on a building estate where the estate is being built on land which was previously part of a farm), because the land may previously have been known by a description other than its current postal address. If the search is limited to the present postal address, entries registered against its former description will not be revealed by the search. In such a case, both the present address and former description of the land should be entered on the search application form.

There is a possibility that because of local government reorganisation the land was formerly situated in a different administrative county to that in which it is now.

For the reasons given above, both the present and former county must be included in the description of the land given on the search application form. Where the postal address of the property differs from its actual address (eg the village of Rogate is in the administrative county of West Sussex, but its postal address is Hampshire) the search must be made against the actual address of the property, not its postal address.

### 28.6.4  Pre-root estate owners

The buyer does not need to search against estate owners who held the land prior to the date of the root of title supplied to him, except insofar as the names of such persons have been revealed to him in documents supplied by the seller.

### 28.6.5  Official certificate of search

An official certificate of search is conclusive in favour of the searcher provided that the search has been correctly made, ie it extends over the whole period of the title supplied by the seller and has been made:

(1)  against the correct names of the estate owners for this period;
(2)  against the correct county or former county; and
(3)  for the correct periods of ownership of each estate owner.

In order to ensure that the buyer gains the protection afforded by the search and the accompanying priority period, it is vital to check that the search application form is accurately completed.

### 28.6.6  Search certificates supplied by the seller

Where the seller provides previous search certificates as part of the evidence of title, it is not necessary to repeat a search against a former estate owner provided that the search certificate supplied by the seller reveals no adverse entries and was made:

(1)  against the correct name of the estate owner as shown in the deeds;
(2)  for the correct period of ownership as shown in the title deeds;
(3)  against the correct description of the property as shown in the deeds; and
(4)  the next disposition in the chain of title took place within the priority period afforded by the search certificate.

If any of the conditions outlined above is not met, a further search against the previous estate owner must be made.

## 28.7 BANKRUPTCY SEARCH

Irrespective of whether the transaction relates to registered or unregistered land, a lender will require a clear bankruptcy search against the name of the buyer before releasing the mortgage funds. Unless a full search of the register has been made on Form K15 (which includes a bankruptcy search) (see **28.6**), the lender's solicitor should submit Form K16 to the Land Charges Department, completed with the full and correct names of the borrower(s). A search certificate will be returned by the Department. In the unusual event of there being an adverse entry revealed by the search, the lender's instructions must be obtained immediately. If a solicitor certifies a search entry as not relating to his client, this certification is construed as an undertaking.

## 28.8 COMPANY SEARCH

A company search may be done as one of the pre-contract searches and the information updated at this stage of the transaction. The procedure for making a company search is discussed at **18.9**.

### Registered land

When buying registered land from a company, it is prima facie unnecessary to make a company search in addition to a Land Registry search (see the Land Registration Act 1925, s 60). However, floating charges and impending insolvency will not generally be revealed by a Land Registry search and it is suggested that a company search (which will reveal these things) should still be made, even in the case of registered land. A floating charge is a type of mortgage which can be created by a company but not by an individual. The charge 'floats' over all the assets of the company so that the company is free to deal with its assets without the lender's consent, perhaps selling some, free of the charge, to a third party and buying others, which become subject to the charge as soon as they are acquired by the company. The charge only fixes and attaches to particular assets of the company (which then cannot be dealt with without the lender's consent) when it crystallises. Crystallisation occurs when a specified event happens which makes the sum due under the mortgage payable (eg default in payment of an instalment). A certificate of non-crystallisation given in a letter signed by the lender may be needed where a floating charge subsists.

### Unregistered land

When buying unregistered land from a company or where the title reveals that a company had previously owned the land, a company search ought to be undertaken in order to ensure that there are no adverse entries which would affect the buyer. Adverse entries would include such matters as fixed or floating charges, or the appointment of a receiver or liquidator.

## 28.9 ENDURING POWERS OF ATTORNEY

Where the purchase deed is to be executed by a person who is acting under the authority of an enduring power of attorney, a search should be made at the Court of Protection on Form EP4 to check whether or not registration of the power has been effected or is pending. If no registration has been made or is pending, the transaction may proceed to completion. If the power has been registered, the attorney may deal with the land and thus, provided the donor is still alive, completion may proceed, because the power is no longer capable of revocation without notification to the Court of Protection. While registration is pending, the transaction may only proceed if it is within one of the limited categories permitted by the Enduring Powers of Attorney Act 1985.

## 28.10 LOCAL LAND CHARGES SEARCH AND ENQUIRIES

These searches are invariably made before exchange of contracts and are discussed in Chapter 18. Although the local land charges search shows only the state of the register at the time of issue of the search certificate, and neither search confers a priority period on the buyer, a repeat of these searches before completion is not normally considered to be necessary, provided that completion takes place within a short time after receipt of the search results. Delay in receipt of the replies to these searches sometimes makes it impracticable for them to be repeated at this stage of the transaction. These searches should however be repeated prior to completion if:

(1) there is to be a period of 2 months or more between exchange of contracts and completion and the search has not been covered by insurance or replaced by insurance; or

(2) information received by the buyer's solicitor suggests a further search may be advisable in order to guard against a recently entered adverse entry on the register; or

(3) the contract was conditional on the satisfactory results of later searches.

The discovery of a late entry on such a search is not a matter of title and will not entitle the buyer either to raise requisitions about the entry or to refuse to complete.

## 28.11 INSPECTION OF THE PROPERTY

Inspection or re-inspection of the property may be necessary just before completion. Such a step is advisable in the case of the purchase of a house which is in the course of construction (and may be done by the buyer's lender's surveyor in such cases) or where there has been a problem with non-owning occupiers. Inspection of the property is dealt with in Chapter 18.

## 28.12 RESULTS OF SEARCHES

Completion cannot proceed until the search results have been received and are deemed to be satisfactory to the interests of the client. In the majority of cases, the results of searches will either show no subsisting entries or merely confirm information already known, such as an entry on the register protecting existing restrictive covenants. In such circumstances, no further action on the search results is required from the buyer's solicitor. If an unexpected entry (other than a Class D(ii) protecting restrictive covenants, which cannot generally be removed) is revealed by the search result, the buyer's solicitor should:

(1) find out exactly what the entry relates to;
(2) if the entry appears adversely to affect the property, contact the seller's solicitor as soon as possible to seek his confirmation that the entry will be removed on or before completion;
(3) in the case of a Land Charges Department search, apply for an office copy of the entry using Form K19 (the office copy consists of a copy of the application form which was submitted when the charge was registered and will reveal the name and address of the person with the benefit of the charge who may have to be contacted to seek his consent to its removal);
(4) keep the client, his lender and, subject to the duty of confidentiality, other solicitors involved in the chain of transactions informed of the situation, since negotiations for the removal of the charge may cause a delay in completion. Any such delay will give rise to contractual remedies for breach of contract. Further, if the seller is unable or unwilling to remove an entry which the contract did not make the sale subject to, this will also be a breach of contract. For remedies for breach of contract, see Chapter 33.

### 28.12.1 Removing an entry from the register

An application form for the removal of an entry from the register in either registered or unregistered land will only be accepted by the Chief Land Registrar if it is signed by the person with the benefit of the charge or a person acting on his behalf. An application form signed by the seller's solicitors or an undertaking given by them on completion to secure the removal of the charge may not, therefore, suffice, unless the seller is the person with the benefit of the charge (see *Holmes v Kennard (H) and Son (A Firm)* (1985) 49 P & CR 202). The court has a discretion to remove entries which are redundant but which cannot be removed from the register because the person with their benefit either will not consent to their removal or cannot be contacted. Entries protecting a spouse's rights under the Family Law Act 1996 can be removed on production of the death certificate of the spouse or a decree absolute of divorce. In the absence of these items, the charge can only be removed with the consent of the spouse who has the benefit of the charge.

### 28.12.2 Irrelevant land charges entries

Charges which are registered at the Land Charges Department can only validly be entered against the name of an estate owner in relation to the period during which he was the owner of the land in question. Thus, an entry which was made before or after this time cannot prejudice the buyer. The computerised system which is used to process these searches will sometimes throw up entries which are clearly irrelevant to the transaction in hand, particularly where the name searched against is a very common one such as John Jones. Having checked that the entry is irrelevant, it may either be disregarded or, at completion, the seller's solicitor may be asked to certify the entry as being inapplicable to the transaction. A solicitor's certificate is construed as an undertaking and should therefore only be given where the solicitor is sure that the entry is irrelevant. Particular care is needed in relation to bankruptcy entries.

### 28.12.3 Official certificates of search

*Registered land*

An official certificate of search issued by HM Land Registry is not conclusive in favour of the searcher, who will thus take his interest in the land subject to whatever entries are on the register, irrespective of whether or not they were revealed by the search certificate (see *Parkash v Irani Finance Ltd* [1970] Ch 101). However, where a person suffers loss as a result of an error in an official certificate of search he may be able to claim compensation under the Land Registration Act 1925, s 83(3).

*Unregistered land*

An official certificate of search issued by the Land Charges Department is conclusive in favour of the searcher, who will thus take his interest in the land free of any entries which are on the register but which were not revealed by the search certificate. Where a person suffers loss as a result of an error in an official certificate of search, he may be able to claim compensation from the Chief Land Registrar, but there is no statutory right to compensation in these circumstances. No liability will attach to the solicitor who made the search, provided that a correctly submitted official search was made (Land Charges Act 1972, s 12).

## 28.13 PRIORITY PERIODS

*Registered land*

An official certificate of search issued by HM Land Registry following a search made on Form 94A gives a priority period to the searcher of 30 working days from the date of the search. A buyer will also take advantage of this protection where a search was made on his behalf in the name of his lender. The searcher will take priority over any entry made during the priority period, provided that completion takes place and a correct application for registration of the transaction is received by the appropriate district land registry by 9.30 am on the day when the priority period given by the search expires.

*Unregistered land*

An official certificate of search issued by the Land Charges Department gives a priority period of up to 15 working days from the date of the certificate, during which time the searcher will take free of any entries made on the register between the date of the search and the date of completion, provided that completion takes place during the priority period given by the search.

*Date of expiry of priority period*

The date of expiry of the priority period is shown on the search certificate. It should be marked on the outside of the client's file and entered in the solicitor's diary or file-prompt system to ensure that it is not overlooked. The priority period given by these searches cannot be extended, so if completion is delayed and cannot take place within the priority period given by the search, a new search application will have to be made. The new search certificate will give another priority period, but does not extend the original priority period from the first search. This means that entries made in the intervening period may be binding.

## 28.14 COMPARISON OF LOCAL AND CENTRAL LAND CHARGES SEARCHES

|  | *Local* | *Central* |
|---|---|---|
| Form: | LLC1 | K15 |
| When to make: | in every transaction | unregistered land only |
| Time to make: | before exchange | part of investigation of title |
| Send to: | district council | Plymouth |
| Search against: | description of land | owners' names |
| Information revealed: | mainly public incumbrances | mainly private incumbrances |
| Protection of search: | none | priority for 15 working days |

## 28.15 COMPARISON OF LAND REGISTRY AND LAND CHARGES DEPARTMENT SEARCHES

|  | *Land Registry* | *Land Charges Department* |
|---|---|---|
| Form: | 94A or 94B | K15 |
| When to use: | registered land | unregistered land |
| Search against: | title number | owners' names |
| Protection given: | search not conclusive | conclusive in favour of searcher |
| Fee: | standard fee for each search | fee for each name searched |
| Priority period: | 30 working days | 15 working days |

# Chapter 29

# PREPARING FOR COMPLETION

## 29.1 INTRODUCTION

Both parties need to carry out a number of preparatory steps to ensure that completion proceeds smoothly. Most of these steps have been explained in other chapters of this book. This chapter contains a summary of the matters to be dealt with at this stage of the transaction by way of checklists, with some additional commentary.

## 29.2 SELLER'S CHECKLIST

(1) Check that purchase deed has been approved and requisitions answered.
(2) Receive engrossed purchase deed from buyer? Has buyer executed the deed (where appropriate) and plan (if used)?
(3) Obtain seller's signature (and witness) to purchase deed in time for completion.
(4) Obtain redemption figure(s) for seller's mortgage(s).
(5) Obtain last receipts etc (eg rent receipts for leasehold property) where apportionments are to be made on completion.
(6) Prepare completion statement (where necessary) and send two copies to buyer in good time before completion.
(7) Remind client to organise final readings of meters at the property.
(8) Prepare forms for discharge of land charges where necessary (unregistered land).
(9) Approve any memorandum which the buyer has requested to be placed on retained deeds (unregistered land).
(10) Place land certificate on deposit at HM Land Registry and obtain deposit number (sale of part or grant of registrable lease of registered land).
(11) Prepare any undertaking which needs to be given on completion (eg for discharge of seller's mortgage if also acting for the lender).
(12) Contact lender to confirm final arrangements for discharge of seller's mortgage, method of payment, etc.
(13) Check through file to ensure all outstanding queries have been dealt with.
(14) Prepare list of matters to be dealt with on actual completion.
(15) Locate deeds and documents which will need to be inspected or handed over on completion and prepare certified copies for the buyer of those documents which are not being handed to the buyer on completion.
(16) Prepare two copies of schedule of deeds to be handed to buyer on completion.
(17) Prepare inventory of and receipt for money payable for chattels.
(18) Check arrangements for vacant possession and handing over keys.
(19) Receive instructions from buyer's solicitor to act as his agent on completion and clarify instructions with him if necessary.
(20) Make final arrangements with buyer's solicitor for time and place of completion.
(21) Inform estate agents of completion arrangements.

(22) Prepare bill for submission to client.


## 29.3  BUYER'S CHECKLIST

(1) Ensure purchase deed has been approved and requisitions satisfactorily answered.
(2) Engross purchase and mortgage deeds.
(3) Get buyer to execute mortgage deed, purchase deed and plan (if necessary) and return it to solicitor.
(4) Send (executed) purchase deed to seller's solicitor for his client's execution in time for completion.
(5) Make pre-completion searches and ensure their results are satisfactory.
(6) Make report on title to lender and request advance cheque in time for completion.
(7) Receive completion statement (where necessary) and copies of last receipts in support of apportionments and check it is correct.
(8) Remind client of arrangements for completion.
(9) Obtain seller's approval of the wording of any memorandum which is to be endorsed on retained deeds (unregistered land).
(10) Prepare and agree the form of wording of any undertaking which needs to be given or received on completion (eg in relation to the discharge of the seller's mortgage).
(11) Contact lender to confirm final arrangements for completion.
(12) Ensure that any life policy required by the lender has been obtained and check with client that any other insurances required for the property (eg house contents insurance) have been taken out.
(13) Check through file to ensure all outstanding queries have been dealt with.
(14) Prepare statement of account and bill for client and submit, together with a copy of the completion statement, requesting balance due from client be paid in sufficient time for the funds to be cleared before completion.
(15) Receive advance cheque from lender and balance of funds from buyer. Pay into client account and clear funds before completion.
(16) Arrange for final inspection of property if necessary.
(17) Prepare list of matters to be dealt with on actual completion.
(18) Check arrangements for vacant possession and handing over keys.
(19) Instruct seller's solicitor to act as agent on completion if completion not to be by personal attendance.
(20) Make final arrangements with seller's solicitor for time and place of completion.
(21) Ensure estate agents are aware of completion arrangements.
(22) Make arrangements to send completion money to seller's solicitor (or as he has directed).


## 29.4  THE CLIENT'S MORTGAGE

### 29.4.1  The seller

The seller's solicitor must ensure that he has obtained from the seller's lender or lenders a statement, known as 'a redemption statement', which shows the exact amount required to discharge the seller's mortgage, or mortgages, on the day of completion. The lender will usually also indicate the daily rate which applies to the seller's mortgage so that the redemption figure can be adjusted if completion takes place earlier or later than anticipated.

The form of discharge of the mortgage must be prepared for signature by the lender. Form DS1 is used for this purpose when dealing with registered land. Some lenders are now making use of an Electronic Notification of Discharge (END) system. Where this is in use, the Land Registry will accept an electronic message from the lender notifying the discharge of the loan in place of Form DS1. In such a case, the seller's solicitor will need to draft Form END 1 requesting the lender to send the discharge message to the Registry. This is then sent to the lender instead of Form DS1. A receipt endorsed on the reverse of the mortgage deed is commonly used in unregistered land.

## 29.4.2 The buyer

Once he has completed his investigation of title and is satisfied as to it, the solicitor acting for the buyer's lender will report to the lender that the title to the property is safe, marketable and acceptable as security for the loan. This is usually done on a standard form of report on title supplied by the lender. Any problems or queries relating to the title should have been clarified with the lender before this stage of the transaction is reached.

It will also be necessary for the solicitor acting for the buyer's lender to make a formal request for the advance cheque from the lender. Depending on the practice of the particular lender, this request may form part of the report on title form or may be made on a separate form.

The mortgage deed should be prepared for signature by the borrowers. Many lenders insist that the mortgage deed is executed by the borrowers in the presence of their solicitor.

## 29.5 APPORTIONMENTS

Where completion does not take place on a date when outgoings (eg rent or water rates) on the property fall due, outgoings which attach to the land can be split between the parties on completion. The calculations of the apportioned sums are shown on the completion statement.

Council tax and water rates can be apportioned, but it is normally considered better practice to inform the relevant authority after completion of the change of ownership and request them to send apportioned accounts to seller and buyer.

Standard Condition 6.3 deals with apportionments, and allows a provisional apportionment to be made where exact figures are not available at completion (eg in respect of service charges). The seller must be asked to produce the last demands or receipts for all sums which are to be apportioned so that the calculations of the amounts due or to be allowed on completion may be made. Copies of these receipts should be sent to the buyer with the completion statement to allow him to check the accuracy of the calculation.

Standard Commercial Property Condition 6.3 is similar, but includes more comprehensive provisions dealing with apportionments when the property is being sold subject to a lease. Note also that under the residential Standard Conditions, the seller is deemed to own the property for the whole of the day of completion, whereas under the Commercial Conditions the buyer is deemed to own the property for the whole of that day.

## 29.6  COMPLETION STATEMENT

A completion statement is prepared by the seller's solicitor which shows the amount of money required to complete the transaction and how that figure is calculated. The statement will be requested by the buyer when he sends his requisitions on title to the seller. It is only necessary to provide the buyer with a completion statement where the sum due on completion includes apportionments or other sums in excess of the balance of the purchase price (*Carne v De Bono* [1988] 3 All ER 485). Two copies of the completion statement should be sent to the buyer, together with copies of any receipts or demands relating to apportionments so that the buyer's solicitor can check the accuracy of the calculations.

The statement should show clearly the total amount due on completion, and how that total sum is made up. Depending on the circumstances, it may be necessary to deal with some or all of the following items:

(1)  the purchase price, giving credit for any deposit paid;
(2)  apportionments of outgoings;
(3)  money payable for chattels;
(4)  compensation if completion is delayed;
(5)  a licence fee if the buyer has been in occupation of the property.

## 29.7  STATEMENT TO CLIENT

The buyer's solicitor should prepare and send to his client a financial statement which shows clearly the total sum due from him on completion and how that sum is calculated. In addition to the matters dealt with on the completion statement, the financial statement should also take account of such of the following matters as are relevant to the transaction:

(1)  the mortgage advance and any costs and/or retentions made in respect of it;
(2)  disbursements (eg stamp duty and Land Registry fees);
(3)  the solicitor's costs.

The financial statement, together with a copy of the completion statement and the solicitor's properly drawn bill, should be sent to the client in sufficient time before completion to allow the client to forward the required balance of funds to the solicitor so that those funds can be cleared by completion.

## 29.8  MONEY

As soon as the buyer's solicitor is informed of the amount required to complete, he should check the figures for accuracy. Any discrepancies must be clarified with the seller's solicitor. If at this stage it appears that there is any shortfall in the buyer's funds, the client must immediately be informed and steps must be taken to remedy the shortfall. If bridging finance or a further loan are necessary in order to complete the transaction, arrangements to secure these funds must be made, otherwise a delay in completion may occur. The buyer's mortgage advance and balance of funds received from the client should be obtained in sufficient time to allow the funds to be cleared through client account before completion. A breach of the Solicitors' Accounts Rules 1998 will occur if uncleared funds are taken from client account.

A solicitor may be guilty of a criminal offence if he assists someone who is known or suspected to be laundering money generated by serious crime. The solicitor must therefore exercise caution in circumstances where the buyer client settles a large property transaction in cash or where payment for the property is made through a third party who is unknown to the solicitor. Reference should be made to The Law Society's guidance on money laundering.

On the day of completion, arrangements must be made to send the amount due to the seller's solicitor in accordance with his instructions.

## 29.9 COMPLETION CHECKLIST

When preparing for completion, the solicitor should make a checklist of the matters which need to be dealt with on actual completion to ensure that nothing is overlooked. Where the buyer instructs a person to act as his agent on completion, he should, when instructing the agent, send him a copy of the checklist so that the agent is aware of the matters which need to be dealt with.

Some or all of the items in the following checklist will need to be attended to on actual completion.

The list should contain an itemised list of the documents which need to be inspected, marked, handed over or received at completion.

(1)  Documents to be available at completion:

    (a)  contract;
    (b)  evidence of title;
    (c)  copy purchase deed;
    (d)  answers to requisitions;
    (e)  completion statement.

(2)  Documents to be inspected by buyer:

    (a)  title deeds, where in unregistered land these are not to be handed over on completion (eg on a sale of part);
    (b)  general or enduring power of attorney;
    (c)  grant of administration;
    (d)  receipts/demands for apportionments if not previously supplied.

(3)  Documents, etc, to be handed to buyer on completion:

    (a)  land or charge certificate(s)/title deeds;
    (b)  original lease (on purchase of a lease);
    (c)  executed purchase deed;
    (d)  undertaking to deposit land certificate or actual deposit number if known (sale of part of registered land);

    (e)  schedule of deeds;

    (f)  Form DS1/discharged mortgage or undertaking in respect of discharge of mortgage(s);

    (g)  receipt for money paid for chattels;

    (h)  keys of the property (if these are not available the seller's solicitor should be asked to telephone the key holder to request the release of the keys);

    (i)  certified copy of any memorandum endorsed on retained deeds.

(4)  Documents, etc, to be handed to seller on completion:

    (a)  banker's draft for amount due on completion;

    (b)  executed duplicate purchase deed/counterpart lease (where appropriate);

    (c)  receipted schedule of deeds received from seller;

    (d)  release of deposit if held by third party in capacity of stakeholder.

(5)  Endorsements on documents (if required by buyer):

    (a)  endorsement of sale on most recently dated retained document of title (sale of part of unregistered land);

    (b)  mark up abstract or epitome as compared against the original deeds (unregistered land in respect of any document the original of which is not handed over on completion).

### Part V

# COMPLETION AND POST-COMPLETION

# Chapter 30

# COMPLETION

## 30.1 PURPOSE AND EFFECT OF COMPLETION

For the client, completion is the culmination and climax of the transaction. It is the day on which he moves into his new home or takes possession of his new factory unit. It is also the day on which the balance of the purchase price has to be paid to the seller in return for the title deeds to the property.

For the modern solicitor, completion is a paperwork transaction frequently conducted via the telephone and postal service from the solicitor's own office. It represents the climax of the past few weeks' work, but not the end of the transaction, since several matters will still need to be attended to by the solicitor even after the client has physically moved house (see Chapter 31).

The drama and excitement attached by the client to his house move is not always shared by the solicitor for whom this client's completion is just one of many which will be carried out by the solicitor on every working day. The drama of completion affects only the solicitor when things go wrong, for example if the money is not received by the seller and he will not allow the buyer into possession, or if the seller's mother-in-law refuses to move out of the property and the buyer's removal van is standing outside the property waiting to unload its contents. An understanding of what happens at completion and why it happens, and careful planning of what appears to be a mundane event (until it goes wrong), will avoid most of the foreseeable problems attached to completion.

### 30.1.1 Effect of completion

The effect of completion differs according to whether the land concerned is registered or unregistered. In unregistered land, legal title to the property passes to the buyer at completion. In registered land, title does not pass to the buyer until the buyer becomes registered at HM Land Registry as proprietor of the land.

On completion, the contract merges with the purchase deed insofar as the contract and purchase deed cover the same ground, so that after completion it is not generally possible to bring an action which arises out of one of the terms of the contract, unless that provision has been expressly left extant by a term of the contract itself. For this reason the contract usually contains a non-merger clause (see Condition 7.4 of both sets of Standard Conditions), which will preserve the right to sue on the contract even though completion has taken place. Actions not based on the contract (eg in tort or for misrepresentation) are not affected by this rule (see Chapter 33).

## 30.2 DATE OF COMPLETION

The date of completion will be agreed between the parties' solicitors (after discussion with their respective clients) shortly before exchange of contracts. Where the buyer's purchase is dependent on his sale of another property, the completion dates in both contracts must be synchronised. It follows that the completion dates in all transactions in a chain of transactions must also be synchronised if the chain is not to break. In residential transactions, a completion date 14 days or less from the date of exchange is common. Sufficient time must be allowed between exchange and completion for the pre-completion steps in the transaction to be carried out. If the parties want to complete very quickly after exchange, arrangements can usually be made for some of the pre-completion steps, such as preparation of the purchase deed, to be done before exchange.

### 30.2.1  Condition 6.1

In the absence of express agreement, Condition 6.1 of both sets of Standard Conditions provides that completion shall take place on the twentieth working day after exchange. Time is not 'of the essence' of the completion date. This means that the stipulation as to time merely has the status of a contractual warranty and not a condition, so that although a delay in completion beyond the date fixed in the contract would give the innocent party the right to bring an action in damages and would activate the compensation provisions of Condition 7.3 (see Chapter 32), the delay would not of itself entitle the innocent party to withdraw from the contract at that stage.

Since delay in completion can occur for reasons beyond the control of the contracting parties (eg postal delays), it is not generally a good idea to make time of the essence of the completion date. If the parties do want to make time of the essence (this would be very unusual in a residential transaction), an express provision to this effect can be inserted in the contract (eg by adding the words 'as to which time shall be of the essence' alongside the insertion of the contractual completion date in the contract).

### 30.3  TIME OF COMPLETION

Where a buyer's purchase is dependent on the receipt of money from a related sale transaction, the solicitor must ensure that arrangements for completion day are made so that the sale transaction will be completed before the purchase transaction (otherwise there will be insufficient funds available to complete the purchase), and with a sufficient interval between the two transactions (eg a minimum of an hour) to allow the money received from the sale to be transferred to and used in the purchase transaction. These arrangements will be made when final completion arrangements are made shortly before the day fixed for completion. Where the transaction is part of a long chain, the arrangements may be complex since, inevitably, the transaction at the bottom of the chain (which will usually involve a buyer who is not selling in a related transaction) must complete first, the money then progressing upwards through the chain. Note that many banks will not accept instructions for same day transmission of funds later than 3 pm. Such a transaction will frequently have to be completed early in the morning of completion day to allow all the subsequent transactions to take place within the same working day. A completion time earlier than 10 am is often difficult to comply with unless the money is sent to the seller on the previous day, because of restrictions on banking hours.

Even where a seller has no related purchase, he should ensure that the completion time agreed allows sufficient time for the proceeds of sale to be banked on the day of completion. If the money is not banked or sent to the lender (to discharge the seller's existing mortgage) until the following working day, the seller will suffer loss of interest on his money. For these reasons, a completion time later than 2.30 pm is inadvisable.

### 30.3.1 Condition 6.1.2

In the absence of contrary provision, Condition 6.1.2 of both sets of Standard Conditions provides that, if completion does not take place by 2 pm on the day of completion, interest for late completion becomes payable, ie completion is 'deemed' to have taken place on the next working day. Non-compliance with this condition is a deemed late completion which invokes the compensation provisions of Condition 7.3, requiring payment of compensation at the contractual interest rate for the delay. Condition 6.1.2 does not apply where the sale is with vacant possession and the seller has not vacated the property by 2 pm on the date of actual completion. Condition 6.1.2 affects only the payment of compensation for late completion. It does not make it a term of the contract that completion shall take place by a specified time. If it is desired to make it a term of the contract that completion takes place by a specified time on contractual completion day, a special condition to this effect must be added to the contract.

## 30.4 PLACE OF COMPLETION

By Condition 6.2 of both sets of Standard Conditions, completion is to take place in England and Wales, either at the seller's solicitor's office or at some other place which the seller reasonably specifies. If completion is not to take place at the seller's solicitor's office, he should give the buyer's solicitor sufficient notice of the chosen venue to allow the buyer's solicitor to make his arrangements for attendance at completion and/or transmission of funds. If possible, the buyer's solicitor should be informed of the venue for completion in the answers given to his requisitions on title.

Where the seller has an undischarged mortgage over the property and the seller's solicitor is not also acting for the lender, completion may have to take place at the offices of the seller's lender's solicitors.

### 30.4.1 Chain transactions

Where there is a long chain of transactions, it may sometimes be convenient for some or all of the solicitors for the parties involved in the chain to meet at a mutually convenient location in order to complete several of the transactions in the chain within a very short interval.

### 30.4.2 Completion by post

Although traditionally the buyer's solicitor attends the seller's solicitor's office in person to effect completion, it is common today (especially in residential transactions) for completion to be effected by using The Law Society's Code for Completion by Post. In such cases, the actual place of completion is of little significance to the transaction so long as both parties' solicitors are able to contact each other by telephone or fax to confirm the transmission and receipt of funds on the day of completion itself (see **30.8** for completion by post).

## 30.5  THE MONEY

### 30.5.1  Method of payment

Standard Condition 6.7 provides that the buyer is to pay the money due on completion in one or more of the following ways:

(1)  legal tender;
(2)  a banker's draft drawn by and on a clearing bank (defined as meaning a bank which is a member of the Clearing House Automated Payment System (CHAPS));
(3)  a direct credit to a bank account nominated by the seller's solicitor;
(4)  an unconditional release of a deposit held by a stakeholder.

In the absence of agreement to the contrary, the seller's solicitor is entitled to refuse payment tendered by any method other than those mentioned in the contract.

CHAPS Clearing Ltd is a company set up by the major banks to operate same day high value transmission and clearing of funds amongst themselves.

The Standard Commercial Property Conditions provide for payment to be made only by a direct credit to a bank account and an unconditional release of a deposit held by a stakeholder.

### 30.5.2  Legal tender

Notes and gold coins are legal tender up to any amount, but other coins are subject to the limits imposed in the Coinage Act 1971, s 2. Payment of money in cash on completion is unusual and would involve the personal attendance of both parties' representatives at actual completion so that the money could be counted.

### 30.5.3  Banker's draft

Where completion is to take place in person, payment by banker's draft is the most common method of payment. A draft can be obtained by taking a cheque drawn on the solicitor's bank account to the bank and exchanging it for a draft. A banker's draft is a cheque drawn by the bank on its own funds and can be regarded as being analogous to cash. It is therefore sensible to take precautions against forgery and theft of a draft. For this reason, it may be unwise to send a banker's draft through the post and, where completion is to take place other than by personal attendance of the parties' solicitors, some other method of transmission of funds should be used.

### 30.5.4  Telegraphic transfer of funds

Frequently, completion will take place using The Law Society's Code for Completion by Post. In such a case, the parties will normally agree to transfer the amount of money needed to complete the transaction through the banks' computerised money transfer system which allows funds to be transmitted direct from one bank account to another, even if with a different bank. This is frequently referred to in practice as a 'telegraphic transfer' (or 'TT'), reflecting methods of money transfer in the pre-computer age. The seller's solicitor should inform the buyer's solicitor of the amount needed to complete the transaction and of the details of the account to which the funds are to be sent. This information is normally given in answer to the buyer's requisitions on title.

The buyer's solicitor will then instruct his bank to remit a specific sum from the buyer's solicitor's client account to the account nominated by the seller's solicitor. The bank will charge a fee for this service. Instructions to the bank must be given sufficiently early on the day of completion to ensure that the funds arrive at their destination before the time-limit for receipt of funds, as specified in the contract, expires. Some delay in the transmission of funds may be experienced where the funds are to be transmitted from one bank to another as opposed to transfers between different branches of the same bank. The seller's bank should be asked to telephone the seller's solicitor to inform him of the receipt of the funds immediately they arrive. Completion can proceed as soon as the seller's solicitor is satisfied about the arrival of the funds in his client account. The transmission of funds can be facilitated by the solicitor having a direct computer link with his bank. This will enable him to effect the transmission of funds himself, rather than having to rely on a telephone call or personal visit to the bank and then waiting for a clerk to effect the transfer.

### 30.5.5  Cleared funds

In order to avoid breach of the Solicitors' Accounts Rules 1998, payment of completion money must only be made from cleared funds in client account. This means that the buyer's solicitor must be put in funds by his client in sufficient time for the money to clear through client account before it becomes necessary to draw against them.

### 30.5.6  Discharge of seller's mortgage

The seller's existing mortgage over the property being sold will often be discharged immediately after completion of the sale using part of the proceeds of sale to make payment to the lender. The seller's solicitor may ask the buyer to draw separate banker's drafts for completion, one in favour of the lender for the amount needed to discharge the mortgage, the other, for the balance of the money due, in the seller's solicitor's favour. Where payment is to be made by telegraphic transfer and the lender is represented by a different solicitor from the solicitor acting for the seller, the seller's solicitor may request that a direct transfer is made to the lender's solicitor, and a second transfer for the balance of funds due is made to the seller's solicitor.

### 30.5.7  Release of deposit

A deposit which is held in the capacity of agent for the seller belongs to the seller and does not need to be released expressly to his use on completion. Where a deposit is held by some person in the capacity of stakeholder, the buyer's solicitor should, on completion, provide the seller's solicitor with a written release addressed to the stakeholder, authorising payment of the deposit to the seller or as he directs.

Where the deposit is being held by the seller's solicitor as stakeholder, a written release is often neither asked for nor provided, the release being given verbally once completion has taken place. If the deposit is being held by a third party (eg an estate agent in the capacity of stakeholder) a written release will be required. This can be done by letter addressed by the buyer's solicitor to the stakeholder, informing the stakeholder that completion has taken place and that the funds are now released to the seller's hands.

## 30.6  METHOD OF COMPLETION

Completion may take place by personal attendance by the buyer's solicitor or his agent or through the post using The Law Society's Code for Completion by Post. The method of completion will usually have been agreed by the parties' solicitors at the requisitions on title stage of the transaction.

## 30.7  COMPLETION BY PERSONAL ATTENDANCE

Personal attendance by the buyer's solicitor on the seller's solicitor or seller's lender's solicitor is the traditional method by which completion takes place, but it is not commonly used in uncomplicated transactions where, particularly in residential conveyancing, it is now more common for completion to take place through the post.

### 30.7.1  What happens at completion

*Appointment for completion*

A few days before the date arranged for completion, the buyer's solicitor should telephone the seller's solicitor to arrange a mutually convenient appointment for completion.

*Banker's draft*

On the morning of completion, a banker's draft for the amount required to complete the transaction should be drawn by the buyer's solicitor and kept in a safe place until it is needed. The amount required will have been notified to the buyer's solicitor on the replies to requisitions on title.

*Documents to be taken to completion*

The representative from the buyer's solicitors who is to attend completion (often a trainee) should take with him to the seller's solicitor's office the following items:

(1)  the contract (queries which arise at completion can sometimes be resolved by checking the terms of the contract);
(2)  evidence of title (in order to verify the title);
(3)  a copy of the approved draft purchase deed and of any other document which is to be executed by the seller and handed over on completion (in case there is any query over the engrossments);
(4)  answers to requisitions on title (some queries which arise (eg over who has the keys) can be resolved by the answers supplied to requisitions on title);
(5)  the completion checklist and completion statement (see Chapter 29);

(6)  banker's draft;

(7)  any documents which are required to be handed over to the seller's solicitor on completion (eg release of deposit).

### *Verifying title*

Verification is the process of comparing the original deeds with the abstract or epitome provided to ensure that the abstract is a true copy of the original. It is usually left until completion and, if photocopies of the original documents have been provided with the epitome, is very much a formality. If discrepancies are discovered, the buyer would not be precluded from objecting to these by the usual clause barring out requisitions as this prevents only requisitions on matters discoverable from the abstract as presented by the seller. There would inevitably be a delay in the transaction however. In the case of registered land, verification is strictly unnecessary since the office copies supplied by the seller's solicitor will show the true up-to-date position of the register and so may be more accurate as to the state of the register than the land or charge certificate in the seller's possession. It is, however, still worthwhile checking the land or charge certificate which the seller is to hand over, if only to ensure that it is the one relating to the correct title to be purchased. All land and charge certificates look very similar on the outside and it is easy for the wrong certificate to be handed over by mistake.

### *Charge certificates*

Where there is more than one mortgage registered against the title, the buyer's solicitor must ensure that he obtains charge certificates relating to all the mortgages. The outside cover of the charge certificate specifies the number of the entry to which the particular certificate relates. Note, however, that many lenders are now taking advantage of Land Registration Act 1925, s 63 which allows them to request that the Registry retains the charge certificate in its own possession. In such a case, there is no need for the charge certificate to be handed over on completion. Where the Registry retains the certificate, there will be an entry on the charges register of the title stating that the charge certificate is being retained by the Registry. On a sale by a lender under his power of sale, it is not essential to obtain either the charge certificates or discharges relating to subsequent mortgages which will be overreached on the completion of the sale by the selling lender.

### *Title documents*

When the buyer's solicitor is satisfied as to the title, he should ask the seller's solicitor to hand over the documents necessary to complete the transaction. These documents, including the land or charge certificate, or title deeds (in unregistered land), will have been agreed previously in a list drawn up between the parties and itemised on the completion checklist. Except where these documents have recently been checked by verification, the buyer's solicitor should check each document to ensure it is as he expects to find it, and tick each off on his list as he receives it.

### *Purchase deed*

The purchase deed will be among the documents to be received by the buyer's solicitor and should be dated at completion, after being checked by the buyer's solicitor to ensure that it has been validly executed and has not been altered since the buyer last saw the document.

### Schedule of deeds

The seller's solicitor will have prepared a schedule of deeds in duplicate. One copy should be handed to the buyer's solicitor to keep, the other should be signed by the buyer's solicitor when he is satisfied that he has received all the documents listed on it and returned to the seller's solicitor as evidence for his file of the handing over of the deeds.

### Inspection of receipts

It may be necessary for the buyer's solicitor to inspect receipts where, for example, the last payments of outgoings have been apportioned on the completion statement. Copies of these receipts should have been supplied to the buyer's solicitor with the completion statement in order to allow him to check the amount of the apportionments.

### Chattels

Where the sale includes fittings or chattels, a separate receipt for the money paid for those items should be signed by the seller's solicitor and handed to the buyer's solicitor. A copy of the receipt should be retained by the seller's solicitor. The receipt clause on the purchase deed only operates as a receipt for the money paid for the land, therefore a separate receipt for the money paid for chattels is necessary.

### Discharge of seller's mortgage

Arrangements for the discharge of the seller's mortgage(s) over the property will have been agreed between the parties at the requisitions on title stage of the transaction. Where the mortgage is a first mortgage of the property in favour of a building society lender, the parties will frequently have agreed to permit the seller to discharge his mortgage after actual completion by using part of the proceeds of sale to make payment to the lender. In such a case, it will often have been agreed that the seller's lender's solicitor should hand to the buyer's solicitor, on completion, an undertaking, in the form of wording recommended by The Law Society, to discharge the mortgage and to forward the receipted deed or Form DS1 to the buyer's solicitor as soon as this is received from the lender. An undertaking to discharge the seller's mortgage should only be accepted from a solicitor or licensed conveyancer because of the difficulties of enforcement of undertakings against unqualified persons. The undertaking should also be in the form of wording approved by The Law Society as follows:

> **In consideration of you today completing the purchase of [insert description of property] we hereby undertake to pay over to [insert name of lender] the money required to discharge the mortgage/legal charge dated [insert date of charge] and to forward the receipted mortgage/Form DS1 to you as soon as it is received by us from [insert name of lender].**

In Protocol cases, this undertaking is given on the Completion Information and Requisitions on Title form.

Increasingly, lenders are making use of the Electronic Notification of Discharge (END) system as a means of discharging registered charges. This consists of the lender sending an electronic message to the Registry as evidence of the discharge of the mortgage instead of Form DS1. The solicitor acting for the borrower will pay off the loan in the normal way but instead of sending Form DS1 to the lender, will send Form END 1 requesting the lender to discharge the charge by sending the END to the Land Registry. Lenders using ENDs have agreed that they will send the END within 21 working days of receiving Form END 1, or tell the solicitor sending Form END 1 why the END cannot be transmitted, for example because the money sent was insufficient to discharge the loan.

Where the END system is in use, the form of undertaking given above will be inappropriate. The Land Registry have suggested use of the following:

> **In consideration of your today completing the purchase of [insert description of property] we hereby undertake forthwith to pay over to the lender the money required to discharge the legal charge dated [insert date of charge] and to forward to it a completed Form END 1, to deal promptly with any queries raised by the lender within the 21 day period, and, at the end of that period, if asked to do so by the buyer's conveyancer, to take such steps as may reasonably be required to ensure that the lender transmits the END to the Land Registry.**

### *Documents to be handed to seller's solicitor*

When the buyer's solicitor is satisfied with the documents received from the seller's solicitor and those which he has inspected, he should hand to the seller's solicitor any documents which the seller's solicitor requires in accordance with the list agreed prior to completion (eg release of deposit held by an estate agent), and a banker's draft for the amount specified on the completion statement or otherwise notified to the buyer's solicitor by the seller's solicitor.

### *Copy documents*

In some cases the buyer will only be entitled to have copies of documents relating to the seller's title and not the originals. This will mainly happen on a sale of part of unregistered land where the seller is entitled to keep the title deeds which relate to the land retained by him. Other examples include purchases from personal representatives where they are entitled to retain the original grant, and purchases from attorneys who hold a general or enduring power. Where a power is a special power, relating only to the sale of this property, the buyer is entitled to the original power.

In any case where an original document relevant to the title is not being handed over, the buyer's solicitor should call for the original document and examine his copy against the original. The copy should then be marked to show that it has been examined against the original and is a true copy of the original document. On a sale of part of unregistered land, all the documents contained in the abstract or epitome of title will have to be so marked, and each examined document should bear the wording:

> **examined against the original at the offices of [insert name of seller's solicitors or as appropriate] signed [by buyer's solicitor's representative either in his own name or in the name of the firm] and dated [insert date of examination].**

Where a certified copy of a document will be required (eg by HM Land Registry of a grant of representation), the certification should be carried out by a qualified solicitor by writing on the document clearly and in a conspicuous position the words:

> **I certify this to be a true copy of the [insert type of document] dated [insert date of document being certified] signed [signature of solicitor] and dated [insert date of certification].**

## 30.8  COMPLETION THROUGH THE POST

In many cases, particularly with simple residential transactions, the buyer's solicitor will not want to attend completion personally. In such a case, arrangements can be made with the seller's solicitor to complete the transaction through the post. These arrangements should be made, at the latest, at the requisitions on title stage of the transaction.

### 30.8.1  The Law Society's Code for Completion by Post

The Law Society's Code for Completion by Post should be used. The text of the code is set out in Appendix 5. The buyer's solicitor should agree any variations to the code in writing with the seller's solicitor well before completion is due to take place. He should also send written instructions to the seller's solicitor, specifying precisely what the buyer's solicitor requires the seller's solicitor to do on the buyer's solicitor's behalf at completion, and agreeing a time on the day of completion itself when completion will take place.

### 30.8.2  The money

The buyer's solicitor must either send the banker's draft to the seller's solicitor to arrive in time for completion and to be held by the seller's solicitor to the buyer's solicitor's order until completion takes place or, more commonly, remit the necessary funds by telegraphic transfer to the seller's solicitor's nominated bank account to arrive there in time for completion to take place at the agreed time.

### 30.8.3  The seller's solicitor's role

The seller's solicitor will effectively act as the buyer's solicitor's agent for the purpose of carrying out the completion procedure. The instructions given by the buyer's solicitor should cover such of the matters detailed in **30.7** as the buyer's solicitor would have carried out had he attended personally at completion. On being satisfied as to the proper payment of the completion money, either by draft or telegraphic transfer (see **30.5.4**), the seller's solicitor must carry out the buyer's instructions and effect completion on his behalf. He should then immediately telephone (or fax) the buyer's solicitor to inform him that completion has taken place and post to the buyer's solicitor, by first-class post or document exchange, the documents which the buyer is entitled to receive on completion. Where documents are required to be marked, certified or endorsed, the seller's solicitor will carry out these operations on behalf of the absent buyer's solicitor. Under The Law Society's Code, the seller's solicitor is not entitled to make a charge to the buyer's solicitor for acting as his agent in carrying out completion.

## 30.9  USING AN AGENT

If the buyer's solicitor is unable to attend personally at completion and does not wish to complete through the post, he can appoint another solicitor to act as his agent. The agent will attend completion in person and will carry out the same procedures that the buyer's solicitor would have done had he been present. This is not common in residential transactions.

## 30.10 LENDER'S REQUIREMENTS

The buyer's solicitor will often also be acting for the buyer's lender. In such a case, the buyer's solicitor should check the lender's requirements for completion when he is preparing his own checklist and making arrangements for completion. In most cases the lender's requirements will be identical to the buyer's solicitor's own requirements, but a check on the lender's instructions should always be made to ensure that nothing is overlooked.

**Chapter 31**

# AFTER COMPLETION

## 31.1 INTRODUCTION

The solicitor's role in the transaction does not end when completion has taken place, a number of matters still need to be attended to by both parties, some of which have stringent time-limits attached to them. The steps outlined below should therefore be taken as soon as possible after completion has taken place.

## 31.2 REPORTING TO THE CLIENT

Whichever party the solicitor is acting for, the client is entitled to be informed that completion of his sale or purchase has taken place. The solicitor should therefore contact his client as soon as possible after completion (eg by phone) to inform him of the successful outcome of the transaction. Where the solicitor is also acting for the client's lender, the lender should be informed of completion. A letter sent by first-class post on the day of completion will suffice in this case.

## 31.3 ACTING FOR THE SELLER

Not all of the steps listed below will be relevant in every transaction. Those which are relevant to the circumstances of the case should be carried out promptly.

### 31.3.1 Contact the buyer's solicitor

Where completion has taken place by post, telephone the buyer's solicitor to inform him that completion has taken place.

### 31.3.2 Contact the estate agent

Telephone the estate agent to inform him of completion and to ask him to release the keys of the property to the buyer.

### 31.3.3 Send documents to buyer's solicitor

Where completion has taken place by post, send the purchase deed, land or charge certificate or title deeds and other relevant documents to the buyer's solicitor by first-class post or document exchange.

### 31.3.4 Deal with the proceeds of sale

If part of the proceeds of sale is to be used towards the purchase of another property on the same day, arrangements should be made for the transmission of these funds in accordance with instructions received. Where the client is undertaking simultaneous sale and purchase transactions, the interval between the time of completion of the sale and the proposed time of completion of the purchase may be as short as an hour. The funds for the purchase must, therefore, be dealt with as a matter of urgency. If instructed to do so, pay the estate agent's commission and obtain a receipt for the payment. Account to the seller's bank for the proceeds of sale in accordance with any undertaking given to them. Account to the client for the balance (if any) of the proceeds of sale in accordance with his instructions.

### 31.3.5  Discharge the seller's mortgage(s)

Deal with the discharge of the seller's existing mortgage(s) by sending a client account cheque for the amount required (as per redemption statement previously obtained) to the lender, together with the engrossment of the Form DS1 requesting him to discharge the mortgage and return the receipted Form DS1 as quickly as possible. If the mortgage is over unregistered land, the lender will complete the receipt clause on the reverse of the mortgage deed and forward the receipted deed to the seller's solicitor instead of using a Form DS1. Where necessary, the benefit of a life policy which was assigned to the lender as collateral security in an endowment mortgage should be reassigned to the seller. A lender who has insured the property will also need to be told to cancel the property insurance cover. On receipt of the completed Form DS1 or receipted mortgage from the lender, check it to ensure that it is correct, then send it to the buyer's solicitor and ask to be discharged from the undertaking given on completion.

If the END system is being used (see **30.7.1**), Form DS1 will not be used. Instead, Form END 1 will be sent to the lender requesting the lender to transmit the END to the Land Registry to discharge the charge. There will thus be a saving of work and time in that the notification of the discharge is sent directly by the lender to the Land Registry instead of the lender completing Form DS1, sending it to the seller's solicitors who have to check it and then send it to the buyer who then has to send it to the Land Registry.

### 31.3.6  Send bill to the client

If not already done, a bill of costs should be drafted and sent to the client. Money which is being held by the solicitor on account of costs may be transferred to office account, provided that the client has expressly or impliedly agreed to this being done.

### 31.3.7  Letter to client

The client should be reminded to notify the local authority and water undertaker of the change of ownership of the property and to cancel insurance cover over the property and its contents. In appropriate cases, the client may also be reminded about his liability to capital gains tax.

### 31.3.8  Custody of deeds

Deal with the custody of deeds in accordance with the client's instructions. Most, if not all, original deeds will have passed to the buyer's solicitor on actual completion, but the seller will have retained custody of the deeds on a sale of part, or may have such documents as an original grant of representation or power of attorney.

### 31.3.9  Check file for outstanding matters

Check through the file to ensure that all outstanding matters have been dealt with before sending the file for storage.

## 31.4  ACTING FOR THE BUYER

Where relevant to the transaction, the following steps should be taken by the buyer's solicitor as soon as possible after completion has taken place.

### 31.4.1  Complete mortgage deed

Complete the mortgage deed by insertion of the date and any other information which still has to be completed (eg date when first repayment is due).

### 31.4.2  Complete file copies of documents

Complete file copies of the mortgage, purchase deed and other relevant documents. These are spare copies of the documents which will remain in the file for future reference or, in some cases, will be used as duplicate copies to send to HM Land Registry.

### 31.4.3  Stamp documents

Attend to payment of stamp duty on the purchase deed and other appropriate documents and submit the purchase deed for production to the Inland Revenue (PD stamp) (see **31.7**).

### 31.4.4  Account for bridging finance

Account to the buyer's bank for any bridging finance in accordance with any undertaking given to them, and ask to be released from that undertaking.

### 31.4.5  Send bill to client

If not already done, draft and send a bill of costs to the client. Where money is being held by the solicitor on account of costs, it can be transferred to office account provided that the client has expressly or impliedly agreed to this being done.

### 31.4.6  Discharged mortgage

On receipt of the completed Form DS1 (if END is not being used) or receipted mortgage from the seller's lender's solicitor, check it to make sure it is correct, acknowledge its receipt and release the sender from the undertaking given on completion.

### 31.4.7  Make copies of documents

Make copies of all documents which are to be sent to HM Land Registry to ensure that file copies exist, in case requisitions are raised by the Registry or the documents are lost or damaged before registration is complete. Make copies of any documents of which HM Land Registry require copies (eg the buyer's mortgage, a transfer or conveyance of part which imposes new restrictive covenants). Certify copy documents which are to be sent to HM Land Registry. Certification is effected by writing or typing on the document (in the margin, or at the foot of the document):

> **I/We certify this to be a true copy of the [type of document] dated [insert date] [signed XYZ and Co].**

The certification, which can be signed in the name of an individual or of a firm, can be carried out only by a solicitor who holds a current practising certificate. Except in the case of powers of attorney, which need to be separately certified on each page, one certificate on the reverse of a document will cover the whole document.

### 31.4.8  Register the title

Make application for registration of title within the relevant priority period (land already registered) or within 2 months of completion (application for first registration) (see **31.8**).

### 31.4.9  Register company charges

Register any charge created by a company at Companies House within 21 days of its creation, in accordance with Companies Act requirements. This time-limit is absolute and cannot be extended without an order of the court. Failure to register within the time-limit may prejudice the lender's security. The requirement to register under the Companies Acts is separate and additional to the requirement to register the charge at HM Land Registry.

### 31.4.10  Diary entry for return of land certificate

Make a diary or file prompt entry recording the approximate date when the new land or charge certificate is expected to be received from HM Land Registry (as notified by HM Land Registry) and send a reminder to the registry if the certificate is not received by that time.

### 31.4.11  Notice of assignment of life policy

Where the client has taken out an endowment mortgage, the lender may have required the client to execute a formal deed of assignment of that policy in the lender's favour, although this is unusual nowadays. In such a case and in order to preserve the priority of the lender (in case of subsequent mortgages of the same policy), it is necessary to send notice to the insurance company who issued the policy of the fact that the policy has been assigned. This may be done either on forms supplied for this purpose by the lender or by letter. The notice should identify the policy holder and policy number, give the name and address of the assignee (the lender) and the date when the policy was assigned. Notice should be sent to the insurance company in duplicate, with a request that it signs and return one copy of the notice as an acknowledgment of the fact that notice has been received. The duplicate receipted notice should be kept with the client's title deeds.

### 31.4.12  Discharge entries protecting the contract

Where an entry was lodged to protect the contract (caution or Class C(iv)), an application should now be made for the discharge of that entry which, completion having taken place, is now redundant.

### 31.4.13  Check land certificate

On receipt of the land or charge certificate from HM Land Registry, check its contents carefully. If its contents appear not to be correct, send the certificate back to the Land Registry and ask them to correct the errors.

Under s 63 of the Land Registration Act 1925, a lender may request the Registry to retain the charge certificate in the Registry. Requests by lenders that all their charge certificates be dealt with in this way are becoming common. This practice is often referred to as 'dematerialisation'. Where this has happened, the solicitor will receive a copy of the register and this should be checked in the usual way. An entry will be placed in the charges register stating that the charge certificate has been retained in the Registry.

### 31.4.14  Custody of deeds

Deal with the custody of deeds in accordance with the client's instructions. This will normally involve sending the deeds to the client's lender for safe-keeping. If there is no mortgage on the property, the client may have given instructions for the deeds to be kept in the solicitor's own strong room or sent to the client's bank. A schedule of deeds should be prepared and, where the deeds are sent to a third party for safe custody, the third party should be asked to sign and return a copy of the schedule as an acknowledgment of receipt of the deeds. Deeds should be sent by recorded delivery or insured post.

### 31.4.15  Check file for outstanding matters

Check through the file to ensure that all outstanding matters have been dealt with before sending the file for storage.

## 31.5  THE LENDER'S SOLICITOR

Where a separate solicitor has been instructed to act for the buyer's lender, the lender's solicitor will normally have taken custody of the purchase deed and other title deeds on completion and he will deal with the stamping and registration of the documents instead of the buyer's solicitor.

## 31.6  UNDERTAKINGS

Any undertaking given must be honoured and any obligations accepted must be fulfilled without delay. A solicitor who has performed his undertaking (eg to discharge the seller's mortgage) should formally ask the recipient to release the giver from his undertaking, so that the giver has written evidence of the fulfilment of the undertaking. The recipient may either acknowledge the giver's release by letter or return the original undertaking to the giver. In either case, the evidence of release is to be kept on the giver's file.

## 31.7 STAMPING DOCUMENTS

Certain documents attract stamp duty payable to the Inland Revenue within 30 days of completion. Duty is payable on the value of land, but not on chattels. Non-payment or evasion of duty gives rise to fines and penalties under the Stamp Act 1891 and other statutes, for which the client and his solicitor may face prosecution. A document which is not properly stamped will not be accepted by HM Land Registry and cannot be used in evidence in civil proceedings. The documents which need to be stamped must be taken or sent to an Inland Revenue stamp office. A cheque for the duty payable should accompany the document. Further details of stamp duty are contained in **17.6.5** above.

### 31.7.1 Purchase of freehold property for value

The transfer of freehold property for full value will attract stamp duty at the following rates, depending upon the purchase price:

(1)   purchase price not exceeding £60,000, no duty payable;
(2)   purchase price exceeding £60,000 but not exceeding £250,000, duty payable at 1% of the purchase price;
(3)   purchase price exceeding £250,000 but not exceeding £500,000, duty payable at 3% of the purchase price;
(4)   purchase price exceeding £500,000, duty payable at 4% of the purchase price.

Note that in each case the duty is payable at the stated rate on the full amount of the purchase price and that in the case of the circumstances mentioned in (1), (2) and (3), the nil rate and lower rates of duty can only be claimed if the purchase deed contains the appropriate certificate of value (see **27.11.1**).

Note also that no duty is payable on transactions involving property in specified disadvantaged areas of the country.

### 31.7.2 Transactions at an undervalue

Unless the transfer falls within the Stamp Duty (Exempt Instruments) Regulations 1987, SI 1987/516, duty will be payable on a transfer at an undervalue; the amount will be assessed on adjudication of the transfer after completion.

### 31.7.3 Stamp Duty (Exempt Instruments) Regulations 1987

Where the document falls within one of the categories listed in the Stamp Duty (Exempt Instruments) Regulations 1987 and contains an appropriate certificate, no duty is payable. The most commonly encountered documents which will fall within these regulations are:

(1)   conveyance or transfer to a beneficiary named in the will or under the intestacy rules;
(2)   deed of appointment of a new trustee;

(3) transfers in connection with divorce settlements;

(4) voluntary disposition inter vivos for no consideration in money or money's worth.

### 31.7.4 Time for stamping

Documents should be submitted for stamping as soon as possible after completion has taken place to ensure that they will be returned to the buyer's solicitor in sufficient time for an application for registration of title to be made within the appropriate time-limits. In any event, it must be stamped within 30 days of completion, otherwise penalties will be payable for late stamping.

### 31.7.5 Produced stamp

Certain documents, including a conveyance or transfer of freehold land, must be produced to the Inland Revenue within 30 days of completion under the provisions of the Finance Act 1931. Failure to do this bears the same consequences as non-payment of stamp duty. No fee is payable for this.

Production is normally effected at the same time as stamp duty is paid. Where a document has to be produced to the Inland Revenue under the Finance Act 1931 but is otherwise exempt from stamp duty, the completed LA451 (PD) form may be sent to HM Land Registry with the application for registration of title and the Registry will act as agents for the Inland Revenue in attaching the PD stamp to the document. This procedure avoids any delay which might occur if the document was sent separately to the Inland Revenue for production.

## 31.8 REGISTRATION OF TITLE

It is essential that the relevant time-limits for submission of an application for registration of a client's title are complied with. The time-limits, and the effect of non-compliance with them, differ according to whether it is a first registration of land previously unregistered or whether it is a registration of a dealing with land already registered. Failure to make an application for first registration within 2 months of completion results in the transfer of the legal estate becoming void. Failure to make an application for registration of a dealing within the priority period of 30 working days given by a pre-completion Land Registry search may have the consequence of the client's interest losing priority to another application.

If it is thought that there will be delay in the return of the documents from the Inland Revenue, an application for registration of title can be made before the documents are stamped, so ensuring that the relevant time-limits for registration are complied with. A letter sent with the application for registration should explain that the documents have not yet been stamped and will ask the Registry to return those documents immediately to the buyer's solicitor so that stamping can be effected. The Registry will expect the solicitor to give an undertaking to return the duly stamped documents to them on completion of the stamping requirements. This procedure is necessary because HM Land Registry will not accept unstamped documents for registration, but nevertheless ensures that relevant time-limits for the application for registration are met. A certified copy of the document to be stamped should be submitted with the application for registration, pending return of the properly stamped document to the Registry.

### 31.8.1  Registration of dealings

Where registered land is transferred, an application for registration of the dealing must be made on the appropriate application form, accompanied by the correct documentation and fee, and must be received by the district land registry for the area within the priority period of 30 working days given by the land registry search made before completion. The application must be received by the district land registry by 9.30 am on the day on which protection under the applicant's search expires, in order to preserve the applicant's priority over the registration of other interests. The period of protection under the search cannot be extended (although a second search conferring a separate priority period can be made) and failure to lodge the client's application within the priority period may result in his interest ceding priority to another application.

### 31.8.2  Transfer of whole

The following points apply to any transfer of the whole of the seller's registered title, regardless of whether the interest transferred is freehold or leasehold. Application for registration of the dealing on Form AP1, accompanied by the following documents, should be lodged within 30 working days of the date of issue of the applicant's pre-completion official search certificate:

(1)   the land or charge certificate relating to the title (note that the charge certificate will not be required if it has been retained in the Registry under LRA 1925, s 63);

(2)   the transfer (generally no copy of this document is required);

(3)   the appropriate fee unless to be paid by credit account.

In addition, such of the documents listed below as are appropriate to the circumstances of the transaction should be submitted with the application:

(4)   completed Form DS1 (to show the discharge of the seller's mortgage) (if the lender is using the END system (see **30.7.1**) there is no need for this form);

(5)   mortgage deed relating to the buyer's new mortgage and certified copy;

(6)   office copy or certified copy grant of representation where the seller was personal representative of the deceased proprietor;

(7)   original power of attorney if transfer has been executed under a special power which is limited to the disposal of this property;

(8)   certified copy power of attorney if the transfer has been executed under a power of attorney other than as in (7) above;

(9)   completed PD form where the purchase deed has to be produced to the Inland Revenue under the Finance Act 1931, but only if the deed is not liable to stamp duty;

(10)  if the applicant's solicitor wishes to have the receipt of his application acknowledged by the Registry, a self-addressed postcard in Form C4B should be enclosed with the application.

### 31.8.3 First registration of title

An application for first registration of title (freehold or leasehold) must be made within 2 months of completion of the transaction which induces the registration on Form FR1.

The application form and fee (unless being paid by credit account), accompanied by the documents listed below, should be sent to the district land registry for the area. Documents accompanying the application must be listed in triplicate on Form DL. One copy of this form will be returned to the applicant's solicitor in acknowledgment of receipt of the application. The acknowledgment copy will also give an estimate of the likely time which the registry expects to take to deal with the application. This anticipated time should be noted in the solicitor's diary or file-prompt system, and a reminder should be sent to the registry if the land or charge certificate has not been received within that period.

### 31.8.4 Documents to be submitted on application for first registration of title

The registrar needs to investigate title on an application for first registration in order to decide which class of title can be allocated to the title. He therefore needs to have access to all the documents which formed the evidence of title supplied to the applicant by the seller's solicitor. These documents should be individually numbered in chronological sequence and listed in the same sequence on Form DL. Such of the following documents as are relevant to the transaction should be submitted to the registry:

(1) all the documents which formed the evidence of title supplied by the seller's solicitor;
(2) all the buyer's pre-contract searches and enquiries with their replies (including any variations or further information contained in relevant correspondence);
(3) the contract;
(4) requisitions on title with their replies;
(5) all pre-completion search certificates;
(6) the purchase deed with a certified copy;
(7) the seller's mortgage, duly receipted;
(8) the buyer's mortgage with a certified copy;
(9) where the property is leasehold, the original lease and a certified copy;
(10) PD form, where no stamp duty is payable;
(11) cheque for fee (unless paid by credit account).

## 31.9 FURTHER READING

Quinlan and Sims *Sergeant and Sims on Stamp Duty* (Butterworths, 1996)

Nock and Doye *Stamp Duties for Conveyancers* 6th edn (Sweet & Maxwell, 1995)

**Part VI**

# DELAY AND REMEDIES

# Chapter 32

# LATE COMPLETION

## 32.1 INTRODUCTION

There are many reasons why completion may be delayed and does not take place on the contractual date. Common examples of causes of delay in completion are the buyer not being in receipt of funds from his lender or the seller's solicitor not managing to get the purchase deed signed by his client. Where the transaction forms part of a chain of transactions, all the transactions in the chain may be delayed if there is a problem with one of the links in the chain. In the majority of cases, the delay in completion is merely a temporary hitch in the transaction, causing practical difficulties both to the solicitor and, particularly, to his client, who may not be able to move house on the date when he wished to do so and may now have to alter his removal arrangements. Where the delay is caused by, for example, the buyer not having received his mortgage advance from his lender, there is generally no doubt that completion will occur, even if it takes place a few days later than the anticipated date stipulated in the contract. The provisions for payment of compensation for late completion contained in most contracts (see Standard Condition 7.3) are designed to compensate the innocent party for the losses suffered as a result of minor delays in completion. The provisions relating to delays in completion in the Standard Commercial Property Conditions are somewhat different from those in the residential Standard Conditions. These are, therefore, dealt with separately at **32.6**.

## 32.2 BREACH OF CONTRACT

Any delay in completion beyond the contractual date will be a breach of contract entitling the innocent party to damages for his loss, but will not entitle him immediately to terminate the contract unless time was of the essence of the completion date (*Raineri v Miles* [1981] AC 1050).

### 32.2.1 Time of the essence

Standard Condition 6.1 provides that time is not of the essence of the contract (but it can be made so by express contractual condition), unless a notice to complete has been served.

## 32.3 RELATED TRANSACTIONS

Delay in completing one transaction may affect the client's ability to complete a related sale or purchase. If, for example, completion of the client's sale is delayed, he will not have the money (from the proceeds of sale) with which to complete his synchronised purchase transaction, and failure to complete that purchase on the contractual date for completion will be a breach of contract.

Although the solicitor should try to ensure that no breach of contract occurs (eg by arranging bridging finance in order to complete the purchase transaction on time), he is also under a duty to act in his own client's best interests and, in these circumstances, completion of the purchase with the assistance of bridging finance may not necessarily be the best course of action for the client to take. For example, in the situation outlined above where the client's sale transaction is delayed, if the client does go ahead with completion of his purchase, not only will he incur a heavy charge in interest on the bridging finance used to complete the purchase, he will also be in the position of owning two houses until the sale is completed and, if the sale transaction is not completed within a short space of time, this too will represent an onerous commitment for the client. The reason for the delay on the sale transaction and its likely duration must be taken into account when advising the client whether to complete the purchase on time or to delay completion of the purchase and commit a breach of that contract.

In the converse situation, where the sale can proceed but the purchase is delayed, completion of the sale transaction on the contract date will result in the client becoming homeless for a potentially indefinite length of time with resultant problems relating to alternative accommodation for the period of the delay and storage of furniture.

## 32.4  COMPENSATION FOR DELAY

Damages are payable under normal contractual principles (see **33.2.6**) for delayed completion. In addition, at common law, there are rules dealing with the payment of interest as compensation for late completion. However, these are generally considered inadequate and are replaced in the Standard Conditions of sale by Standard Condition 7.3. This requires the payment of compensation for delayed completion irrespective of whether the innocent party has suffered any loss. Where loss has been suffered in excess of the amount payable under Standard Condition 7.3 (eg the cost of alternative accommodation), this can still be recovered in an action for breach of contract. However, any compensation paid under Standard Condition 7.3 must be taken into account in a claim for breach of contract.

### 32.4.1  Standard Condition 7.3

Standard Condition 7.3 provides for the payment of compensation at the 'contract rate' which is defined by Condition 1.1.1(g) as being 'The Law Society's interest rate from time to time in force' (as published weekly in *The Law Society's Gazette*), although the parties may substitute a different rate by special condition if they wish. Interest is payable on the purchase price, or, where the buyer is the paying party, on the purchase price less the deposit paid. Under Condition 7.3, compensation is assessed using the 'concept of relative fault', so that whoever is most at fault for the delay pays the compensation, it is not simply a matter of the party who delayed in actual completion being liable to pay compensation.

### 32.4.2  Calculating compensation

To calculate the liability for compensation, it is necessary to refer back to the timetable of events contained in Standard Conditions 4.1.1 and 4.1.2 in order to establish whether the delay in completion has been caused by a delay in carrying out a procedural step earlier in the transaction. Delay occurring before completion is assessed by reference to the definition of a 'working day' contained in Condition 1.1.1(n), but this definition ceases to apply once the completion date has passed, after which every day's delay counts towards the liability for compensation. Having apportioned the delay between the parties, the party who is most at fault for the delay pays compensation to the other for the period by which his delay exceeds the delay of the other party, or for the actual period of delay in completion, if this is shorter. Compensation under this provision is neither additional to nor in substitution for common law damages, but merely on account.

*Example*

The seller was 3 days late in delivering his evidence of title under Standard Condition 4.1.1; the buyer was then 5 days late in delivering his requisitions on title and a further 4 days late in delivering his draft purchase deed, but completion itself was delayed 2 days because of the seller's fault.

To assess who is liable for compensation, it is necessary to add up the total periods of default of each party. Here the seller's total default amounts to 5 days, but the buyer's to 9 days. The buyer's default therefore exceeds that of the seller by 4 days and, in this example, the buyer would be liable to pay up to 4 days' compensation to the seller for the delay, even though the delay in actual completion was not his fault; however, since the actual delay was only 2 days, his liability is limited to 2 days' compensation.

The calculation of the delay under Standard Condition 7.3 is thus rather complicated, but does have the merit of recognising that the delay might not be the fault of the party who is actually unable to complete on time. His delay might be the knock-on effect of the other party's delay earlier in the transaction. The complications of Standard Condition 7.3 are further exacerbated by the fact that the timetable laid down in Condition 4.1.1 is based on the traditional practice of title being deduced after exchange, which rarely happens in modern practice, and by the fact that the timetable is based on a minimum period of 15 working days (ie 3 weeks) between exchange and completion. Where, as is usual, completion is to take place earlier than 15 working days after exchange, the time-limits laid down have to be reduced accordingly.

## 32.4.3 Deemed late completion

By Standard Conditions 6.1.2 and 6.1.3, where the sale is with vacant possession and the money due on completion is not paid by 2 pm on the day of actual completion (or such other time as may have been agreed by the parties), for the purposes of the compensation provisions only, completion is deemed to have taken place on the next following working day, unless the seller had not vacated the property by 2 pm (or other agreed time). If this time-limit is not complied with, the buyer may find himself liable to pay compensation to the seller under Standard Condition 7.3. If, for example, completion was due on a Friday, and the buyer's money did not arrive until 2.15 pm, the seller would be able to treat completion as not having taken place until the following Monday and, subject to the application of Condition 7.3, recover compensation for the delay (irrespective of his actual loss). Since the 'working day' definition contained in Standard Condition 1.1.1(n) ceases to apply once completion has taken place, the seller in this example would be able to charge interest for 3 days, ie Saturday and Sunday are included in the calculation.

## 32.5 SERVICE OF A NOTICE TO COMPLETE

Where it appears that the delay in completion is not likely to be resolved quickly (or at all), consideration may be given to the service of a notice to complete which will have the effect of making time of the essence of the contract so that, if completion does not take place on the new completion date specified in the notice, the aggrieved party may then terminate the contract immediately, forfeit or recover his deposit (as the case may be) with accrued interest and commence an action for damages to recover his loss. This then gives the aggrieved party the certainty of knowing that on a stated date he can make a definite decision, either to look for a new property to purchase (if a buyer) or resell the property elsewhere (as a seller).

Making time of the essence imposes a condition which binds both parties. If, therefore, unforeseen events occur between the date of service of the notice and the new date for completion as specified by the notice, which result in the previously aggrieved party being unable to complete on the new date, the previously defaulting party could turn round and terminate the contract, leaving the aggrieved party in breach of contract himself. For this reason a notice to complete should never be served as an idle threat. The server must be sure that he will be able to comply with the new completion date himself before serving the notice.

### 32.5.1  Standard Condition 6.8

Although permitted at common law, the contract normally contains a provision relating to the service of a notice to complete. Standard Condition 6.8 provides that, on service of a notice to complete, completion must take place within 10 working days (exclusive of the date of service) and makes time of the essence of the contract. Standard Condition 6.8.4 requires a buyer who has paid less than a 10% deposit to pay the balance of the full 10% immediately on receipt of a notice to complete.

The parties' rights and obligations where a valid notice has been served but not complied with are governed by Standard Conditions 7.5 and 7.6. Once served, a notice to complete cannot be withdrawn.

### 32.5.2  Non-compliance with a notice to complete

Non-compliance with a notice to complete gives the aggrieved party the right to terminate the contract, but is not in itself an automatic termination of the contract.

#### *Buyer's failure to comply with a notice to complete*
Standard Condition 7.5 provides that, in addition to rescinding the contract, the seller may:

(i)   forfeit and keep the deposit and any accrued interest;
(ii)  resell the property; and
(iii) claim damages.

The seller is expressly stated to retain his other rights and remedies and so would be able to bring an action for specific performance should he so wish.

### Seller's failure to comply with a notice to complete

Standard Condition 7.6 provides that, in addition to rescinding the contract, the buyer is entitled to the return of the deposit and accrued interest. He also keeps his other rights and remedies so he would be able to bring an action for specific performance or damages if he wished.

## 32.6 STANDARD COMMERCIAL PROPERTY CONDITIONS

The provisions of the Standard Commercial Property Conditions relating to time not being of the essence (Condition 6.1.1), deemed late completion (Condition 6.1.2) and service of a notice to complete (Conditon 6.8) are the same as under the residential Standard Conditions. However, Condition 7.3, which deals with compensation for delays in completion, is much changed from the equivalent residential Standard Condition. The concept of relative fault in the residential Standard Conditions (see **32.4**) is not adopted. Instead, a contractual entitlement to compensation is given to the seller where the buyer has defaulted in some way and completion is delayed. If the seller defaults and completion is delayed, there is no contractual right to compensation given to the buyer who would have to bring a claim for damages for breach of contract.

# Chapter 33

# REMEDIES

## 33.1 INTRODUCTION

A contract for the sale of land is subject to the general principles of the law of contract, and remedies for breach of that contract follow normal contractual principles. This chapter contains only a summary of the application of those principles to sale of land transactions, together with a brief reminder of some other remedies which might be available in a sale of land transaction. Contractual remedies need only be considered, however, in the case of a failure to comply with a notice to complete and/or where compensation payable under Standard Condition 7.3 is inadequate (see Chapter 32).

## 33.2 BREACH OF CONTRACT

Remedies for breach of contract depend on whether the breach is of a condition in the contract, entitling the aggrieved party to terminate the contract and/or claim damages, or of a warranty, entitling the aggrieved party to claim damages only.

### 33.2.1 Conditions and warranties

A term of the contract will be a 'condition' if it is a major or fundamental term. Minor terms are classified as 'warranties'.

In some cases, it is not possible to classify a term as specifically falling into one or other of these categories until the consequences of the breach can be seen. Where the consequences are serious or far-reaching, the unclassified term will be treated as a condition; otherwise, it will be treated as a warranty. In conveyancing contracts, all terms are usually called 'conditions', but in law some of those terms will only have the status of warranties. The classification attached to a term by the parties is not necessarily conclusive as to its status.

A defect in title, for example an undisclosed incumbrance, will normally amount to a breach of condition entitling the buyer to treat the contract as discharged by breach. The buyer will also be able to reclaim his deposit and claim damages for any further loss he suffers. Where either set of Standard Conditions apply, Standard Condition 7.1 amends the common law position; see **33.2.4**.

### 33.2.2 Limitation periods

An action on a contract not made by deed has a limitation period under the Limitation Act 1980 of 6 years, running from the date of the breach. A limitation period of 12 years applies where the contract was made by deed.

### 33.2.3 Merger

On completion, the terms of the contract merge with the purchase deed insofar as the two documents cover the same ground, and an action on the contract is no longer sustainable after completion except where it is based on a contract term which remains extant despite completion taking place. For this to happen the contract would generally have to contain a non-merger clause (such as Standard Condition 7.4) which expressly allows a particular clause or clauses to remain alive after completion.

### 33.2.4 Exclusion clauses

Standard Condition 7.1 (in both sets of Standard Conditions) restricts the remedies available for a breach of contract. The buyer is entitled only to damages if there is a material difference in the tenure or value of the property. In addition, he is entitled to treat the contract as at an end only if the error or omission results from fraud or recklessness, or where he would otherwise be obliged to accept property differing substantially in quality, quantity or tenure from what he had been lead to expect. Thus, in the case of an undisclosed incumbrance, the buyer would be entitled to damages only if this caused a material difference in the value of the land. Similarly, he would be able to treat the contract as at an end only if there was fraud or recklessness on the seller's part or if the value of the property was substantially reduced because of the incumbrance. Obviously, a covenant preventing building on land otherwise suitable for development, would have a much greater affect on its value than a covenant restricting a dwellinghouse to use as a house. Note, however, that if there is fraud or recklessness on the seller's part, the buyer will always be entitled to rescind no matter what the effect on the value of the property.

Exclusion clauses contained in contracts for the sale of land (except those relating to the exclusion of liability for misrepresentation) are not subject to the reasonableness test in the Unfair Contract Terms Act 1977.

### 33.2.5 Delayed completion

Unless time was of the essence of the completion date, or had been made so by service of a notice to complete, a delay in completion will be a breach of warranty entitling the aggrieved party to recover damages for any loss suffered as a result of the delay (*Raineri v Miles* [1981] AC 1050). For details of compensation payable for delayed completion under Standard Condition 7.3, see **32.4**, and under Standard Commercial Property Condition 7.3, see **32.6**.

### 33.2.6 Damages for breach

Damages for breach of a contract for the sale of land are assessed under the normal contractual principles established in *Hadley v Baxendale* (1854) 9 Exch 341. Subject to establishing causation, damages for losses naturally flowing from the breach may be claimed and, in addition, damages may be claimed for reasonably foreseeable consequential loss.

#### *Quantum*

The quantum of damages under the consequential loss head is limited to loss which was reasonably foreseeable by the defaulting party in the light of the facts known by him (or by his agent) at the date when the contract was made (not at the date of the breach of contract). The starting-point for damages for breach of a contract for the sale of land is the difference between the contract price and the market price of the property at the date of the breach. To this may be added actual financial loss suffered as a result of the breach, such as wasted conveyancing costs, legal costs involved in the purchase of another property, interest payable on a mortgage or bridging loan, costs of removal or storage of furniture, and/or costs of alternative accommodation pending purchase of another property (see *Beard v Porter* [1948] 1 KB 321).

### Loss of development profit

Loss of development profit, or loss of profit on a sub-sale, can be claimed only if the defendant was aware of the plaintiff's proposals for the property at the time the contract was made (see *Diamond v Campbell Jones* [1961] Ch 22; cf *Cottrill v Steyning and Littlehampton Building Society* [1966] 2 All ER 295).

### Resale by seller

Where the buyer defaults and the seller makes a loss on the resale, that loss can be claimed as damages, but if the seller makes a profit on the resale he would have to give credit for the amount of the profit in his action, because he is entitled only to recover his financial loss and is not entitled to benefit from the buyer's breach. The purpose of contractual damages is to place the parties in the position in which they would have been had the contract been duly performed, not to punish the guilty party.

### Mental distress

As a general principle of contractual damages, it is only possible to recover for financial loss, and no claim can be made in respect of mental distress suffered as a result of the defendant's breach. The practice of awarding a nominal sum in respect of damages for mental distress established by *Jarvis v Swans Tours* [1973] 1 QB 233 seems to be confined to holiday contracts and contracts for leisure activities. (See also *Bliss v South East Thames Regional Health Authority* [1987] ICR 700.)

### Pre-contract losses

Damages can normally be claimed only in respect of losses which have occurred since the contract was made, thus there is generally no possibility of recovering expenses incurred at the pre-contract stage of the transaction (eg for a wasted survey), but, in *Lloyd v Stanbury* [1971] 1 WLR 535, pre-contract expenditure including money spent on repairs to the property was recovered.

### Mitigation

The plaintiff must have attempted to mitigate his loss, for example by trying to purchase another similar property (as disappointed buyer) or by attempting to resell the property (as disappointed seller). If no attempt to mitigate is made, the award of damages may be reduced because of the failure to mitigate. If the plaintiff attempts to mitigate and, in so doing, increases his loss, the defendant will be liable for the increased loss.

### *Giving credit for money received*

Credit must be given in the claim for damages for any compensation received under Standard Condition 7.3 or for any deposit forfeited by the seller.

## 33.3 RESCISSION

In this chapter the word 'rescission' is used in the context of contracts which involve a vitiating element such as misrepresentation, fraud or mistake, and refers to the remedy which is available in those circumstances.

Rescission entails the restoration of the parties to their pre-contract position by 'undoing' the contract and balancing the position of the parties with the payment of compensation by one party to the other. Damages in the conventional sense of that word are not payable, because there will have been no breach of contract. Since rescission is an equitable remedy, its operation is subject to the general equitable bars (eg lapse of time).

### 33.3.1 Contractual right to rescind

A right to rescind may be given by a specific contractual condition which sets out the circumstances in which the right is to operate and the parties' rights and obligations in the event of rescission taking place. Such a clause might be included where, for example, the contract is conditional on the fulfilment of a condition. Under both sets of Standard Conditions of Sale, the right to rescind is available in four situations:

(1) where risk in the property remains with the seller and the property is rendered unusable between contract and completion (Condition 5.1);

(2) for misrepresentation (Condition 7.1);

(3) where a licence to assign is not forthcoming in leasehold transactions (Condition 8.3).

(4) where either the buyer or the seller has failed to comply with a notice to complete (Conditions 7.5 and 7.6).

Where the right to rescind is exercised under one of the above Conditions, the parties' rights on rescission are governed by Condition 7.2 which provides for the repayment of the deposit to the buyer with accrued interest, the return of documents to the seller and the cancellation of any registration of the contract at the buyer's expense.

### 33.3.2 Limitation periods

Where the right to rescind arises out of a contractual provision, it must be exercised within the time-limits given within the condition or, if no time is specified, within a reasonable time. An action based on a contractual rescission clause is subject to the normal 6-year limitation period under the Limitation Act 1980 (unless the contract was by deed when a 12-year limitation period would be available). Actions for rescission arising out of the general law principles (eg for misrepresentation) are subject to the equitable doctrine of laches (lapse of time).

## 33.4 MISREPRESENTATION

### 33.4.1 Definition

A misrepresentation is an untrue statement of fact made by one contracting party which is relied on by the aggrieved party, which induces him to enter the contract, and as a result of which he suffers loss. The statement must be of fact, not law (see *Solle v Butcher* [1950] 1 KB 671). A statement of opinion is not actionable unless it can be proved that the opinion was never genuinely held (*Edgington v Fitzmaurice* (1885) 29 Ch D 459). A misrepresentation may be fraudulent (ie deliberately dishonest) within the definition of fraud laid down in *Derry v Peek* (1889) 14 App Cas 337, negligent (ie made carelessly without having checked the facts, but not necessarily negligent within the tortious meaning of that word), or innocent (ie a genuine and innocently made mistake).

### 33.4.2 Fraudulent misrepresentation

Where the misrepresentation has been made fraudulently, the aggrieved party may bring an action in tort for deceit, which may result in rescission of the contract and damages. The party who alleges fraud must prove fraud. This places a very onerous burden of proof on the plaintiff in the action and, except where there is clear evidence of fraud, it is more usual to treat the misrepresentation as having been made negligently and to pursue a remedy under the Misrepresentation Act 1967.

### 33.4.3 Actions under the Misrepresentation Act 1967

The plaintiff must show that he has an actionable misrepresentation, after which the burden of proof shifts to the defendant who has to disprove negligence. A misrepresentation is negligent if the defendant cannot prove that he had reasonable grounds for believing and did believe the statement he made was true up to the time the contract was made. There is therefore a duty to correct a statement which, although being true at the time when it was made, subsequently becomes untrue.

The remedies for a negligent misrepresentation are rescission of the contract and damages. If the defendant successfully establishes the defence of grounds and belief, thus showing that the misrepresentation was truly innocent, rescission is available, but not damages.

### 33.4.4 Rescission

The award of rescission lies within the equitable jurisdiction of the court and is thus discretionary and subject to the equitable bars. If none of the equitable bars apply but, nevertheless, the court decides not to grant rescission, it may instead award damages in lieu of rescission to the plaintiff under the Misrepresentation Act 1967, s 2(1). Rescission is only likely to be awarded where the result of the misrepresentation is substantially to deprive the plaintiff of his bargain (see *Gosling v Anderson* (1972) *The Times*, February 6, cf *Museprime Properties Ltd v Adhill Properties Ltd* (1990) 36 EG 114). Rescission is available even after completion, although this is subject to the usual equitable rules and so may not be possible where a third party (eg a lender) has acquired an interest in the land.

### 33.4.5  Damages

Damages under the Misrepresentation Act 1967 are awarded on a tortious basis (*Chesneau v Interhome Ltd* (1983) *The Times*, June 9). An award of damages can be made both as an award in lieu of rescission and an award to compensate the plaintiff for his loss, subject to the overriding principle that the plaintiff cannot recover more than his actual loss, thus the awards under the two sub-sections are not cumulative.

### 33.4.6  Limitation period

An action in misrepresentation does not arise out of the contract nor out of tort. The limitation periods prescribed by the Limitation Act 1980 do not therefore apply in this situation, and it seems that the limitation period for an action based on misrepresentation relies on the equitable doctrine of laches.

### 33.4.7  Incorporation as a term of the contract

Where a misrepresentation has become incorporated as a term of the contract it is possible, by the Misrepresentation Act 1967, s 1, to treat the statement as a representation and to pursue a remedy under the Misrepresentation Act 1967. This option gives the plaintiff the right to ask for rescission of the contract as well as damages. If the action was confined to breach of a minor contractual term, the only available remedy would be damages.

### 33.4.8  Imputed knowledge

Knowledge gained by a solicitor in the course of a transaction is deemed to be known by the solicitor's client whether or not this is in fact the case. Thus where a solicitor gives an incorrect reply to pre-contract enquiries, the solicitor's knowledge, and also his misstatement is attributable to the client who will be liable to the buyer in misrepresentation (*CEMP Properties (UK) Ltd v Dentsply Research and Development Corporation (No 1)* (1989) 2 EGLR 192). In such a situation, the solicitor would be liable to his own client in negligence. Similarly, if the seller makes a misrepresentation to the buyer personally but the misrepresentation is later corrected in correspondence between the seller's solicitors and the buyer's solicitors, the buyer is deemed to know of the correction (even if not actually told by his solicitor) and would not in such circumstances be able to bring an action for misrepresentation against the seller (*Strover v Harrington* [1988] Ch 390).

### 33.4.9  Exclusion clauses

By the Misrepresentation Act 1967, s 3, as substituted by the Unfair Contract Terms Act 1977, s 8, any clause which purports to limit or exclude liability for misrepresentation is valid only insofar as it satisfies the reasonableness test laid down in the Unfair Contract Terms Act 1977, s 11 and Sch 2. The reasonableness test is applied subjectively, in the light of the circumstances which were known to the parties at the time when the contract was made. It therefore depends on the circumstances of each particular case as to whether the exclusion clause is valid in that situation.

There is no guarantee that any given form of wording will satisfy the test. Standard Condition 7.1 purports to limit the seller's liability for (inter alia) misrepresentation.

Under the condition, damages are payable only for a misrepresentation if there is a material difference between the property as represented and as it really is. Similarly, rescission is available only where there is fraud or recklessness or where the innocent party would be obliged to accept something differing substantially (in quality, quantity or tenure) from what he had been led to expect. The validity of this clause is subject to its satisfying the reasonableness test on the facts of each particular case.

Some standard forms of pre-contract enquiries (but not the Seller's Property Information Form used in Protocol transactions) have an exclusion clause printed on them. This exclusion clause is also subject to the reasonableness test (see *Walker v Boyle* [1982] 1 All ER 634, where an exclusion clause contained in a then current edition of a standard form of pre-contract enquiries failed the test).

## 33.5 MISDESCRIPTION

Misdescription occurs when an error is made in the particulars of sale of the contract, for example, misdescribing the tenure of the property as freehold when it is in fact leasehold, or wrongly describing the physical extent of the land to be sold. Standard Condition 7.1 (in both sets of Standard Conditions) (see **33.4.9**) also controls the remedies available for misdescription as well as for misrepresentation, in cases where the Standard Conditions are in use.

## 33.6 NON-DISCLOSURE

Non-disclosure arises out of the seller's failure to comply with his duty of disclosure (see Chapter 14). Where either set of Standard Conditions of Sale is in use, the remedies for non-disclosure are again governed by Condition 7.1.

## 33.7 SPECIFIC PERFORMANCE

Although specific performance is an equitable remedy which is granted at the discretion of the court, an order for specific performance is not uncommon in sale of land cases where, since no two pieces of land are identical, an award of damages would be inadequate compensation for the injured party's loss. The claim can be made either on its own or in conjunction with a claim for damages or rescission, depending on the circumstances.

### 33.7.1 General bars to the award

The award of a decree of specific performance is subject to the usual principles of equity. It will not therefore be awarded where (inter alia):

(1) an award of damages would adequately compensate for the loss sustained by the breach;
(2) the contract contains a vitiating element such as mistake, fraud or illegality;
(3) a third party has acquired an interest for value in the property;
(4) the seller cannot make good title.

### 33.7.2 Delay

The doctrine of laches (lapse of time) applies to equitable remedies. The remedy may therefore be barred if the innocent party delays in seeking an award.

### 33.7.3 Damages in lieu

If, in a situation where specific performance would otherwise be available to the injured party, the court decides not to make such an order, it can award damages in lieu of specific performance under the Supreme Court Act 1981, s 50. These damages are assessed using normal contractual principles as outlined in **33.2**. Where an award of specific performance has been made but has not been complied with, the injured party may return to the court asking the court to withdraw the order and to substitute the decree of specific performance with an award of damages (*Johnson v Agnew* [1980] AC 367).

## 33.8  RETURN OF DEPOSIT

Where the buyer defaults on completion, the seller will want to forfeit the deposit, but the Law of Property Act 1925, s 49(2) gives the court an absolute discretion to order the return of the deposit to the buyer. Where the seller retains the deposit, this must be taken into account in any assessment of damages for breach of contract.

Where the seller defaults on completion, the buyer will have a right to the return of the deposit under Condition 7.6 of both sets of Standard Conditions.

## 33.9  RECTIFICATION

### 33.9.1  Rectification of the contract

Where the parties have reached agreement over a particular matter but that matter is either omitted from the written contract in error or is wrongly recorded in the written agreement, an application for rectification of the contract to correct the error can be made. Under the Law of Property (Miscellaneous Provisions) Act 1989, s 2(4), where rectification is ordered, the court has a discretion to determine the date on which the contract comes into operation.

### 33.9.2  Rectification of the purchase deed

Where a term of the contract is either omitted from or inaccurately represented in the purchase deed, an application for rectification of the deed may be made to the court.

## 33.10  COVENANTS FOR TITLE

Certain covenants for title will be implied into the purchase deed, the nature of those covenants depending on whether the seller has sold with full or limited title guarantee (or none at all) (see Chapter 14). Because of the principle of merger of the contract with the conveyance on completion, an action arising out of the contract is not generally possible after completion has taken place and the primary post-completion remedy available to the buyer is an action for breach of the implied covenants for title. However, Standard Condition 7.4 in both sets of Conditions preserves the right to sue on the contract even after completion, subject to the normal 6-year limitation period.

### 33.10.1 Enforcement of the covenants

In the case of unregistered land, liability on the covenants is strict. The limitation period of 12 years runs from the date of completion in the case of the 'right to dispose of the property' covenant, and usually from the date of actual breach in other cases. The covenants for title have equal application to registered land (except that liability is not strict) but the state guarantee of a registered title means that, in practice, actions on the covenants are less likely to occur with the transfer of registered land.

**Part VII**

# LEASEHOLDS

# Chapter 34

# INTRODUCTION TO LEASEHOLD PROPERTY

## 34.1 INTRODUCTION

In some parts of England and Wales, for reasons which are largely historic in origin, it is more common to find residential property being sold leasehold rather than freehold. Commercial property, such as shops, office suites and factories, is frequently rented and not sold freehold, and flats, because they constitute a part of a larger building, are almost invariably sold on leases. Freehold flats are rare and are difficult to mortgage.

### 34.1.1 Advantages of leaseholds

There are distinct advantages to the property owner in granting a lease rather than selling off the freehold, in that he retains an interest in the property (ie the freehold estate) which is a saleable capital asset which can be disposed of separately from the leasehold interest. He can also retain control over who lives in the property, what it is used for and how it is maintained and repaired by means of imposing conditions on the tenant through the terms of the lease. The owner may be able to charge a capital sum for the grant of a long lease almost equivalent to the price for which he could have sold the freehold and, at the same time, be able to charge the tenant rent for the property, so providing income from the property. Another advantage is that the owner (landlord) is more easily able to enforce covenants which are imposed on leasehold land than is the case with freehold land. In freehold land, positive covenants (eg a covenant to repair) are not enforceable against future owners of the land. In the case of leasehold land, almost all covenants, both positive and negative, are enforceable against the successors in title of the original tenant (see **34.4**).

### 34.1.2 Disadvantages of leaseholds

The disadvantages of leasehold property are mainly on the tenant's side. He does not own the property outright and so is not free to alter it at will (the lease may impose restrictions on what the tenant does to the property and how he uses it), nor to dispose of it as and when he wishes, since the lease may require him to obtain his landlord's consent before selling the property or sub-letting it.

A lease is a capital asset in the tenant's hands, and as such has a market value and is saleable, but it is also a wasting asset, in that its value will gradually erode as time passes, and the fewer years there are left to run on the lease, the less it will be worth. In addition to paying a capital sum (premium) for the lease, the tenant will also have to pay rent to the landlord. This is an outgoing for which the tenant sees no visible return on his investment, it is purely income for the landlord. The lease may also impose on the tenant strict repairing obligations with which it will be expensive to comply.

For these reasons, many lay persons consider leases to be a 'second class' type of tenure, inferior to a freehold. This prejudice exists mainly in relation to residential property, where a leasehold house will tend to command a slightly lower price than a similar freehold house. No such prejudice exists in the commercial sector where a large proportion of property is leasehold.

From the landlord's point of view, the main disadvantage of granting a lease rather than selling the property outright is that, together with the rights which he retains in the property, he may also retain various obligations in relation to matters such as repairs and insurance. The burden of these obligations must, however, be set against the benefit of the income received from the rent of the property.

### 34.1.3 Commonhold

The Government has signalled its intention of introducing a new form of land ownership called 'commonhold' which is designed to overcome some of the disadvantages of leases in dispositions of units in interdependent premises, for example flats, office blocks and shopping centres. Each 'unit' (eg each flat) will be held freehold, and the common parts held by a Commonhold Association, which will be responsible for repairs etc to the common parts. This will be a private limited company of which the unit owners will be members. There will also be a Commonhold Community Statement which will set out the obligations of each unit holder, including the obligation to pay a service charge.

As each flat or other unit will be held freehold, the problem of leases being a wasting asset will disappear. Also the fact that a company owned by the tenants will own the common parts will avoid problems that can sometimes arise in blocks of flats of landlords charging excessive service charges. Commonhold will be available both for new developments and for existing developments. The conversion of existing blocks will only be possible, however, at the request of the landlord and with the consent of all the tenants. It is unlikely that the Commonhold and Leasehold Reform Act 2002 will come into force before the middle of 2003.

## 34.2  COMMON ILLUSTRATIONS OF LEASEHOLD PROPERTY

### 34.2.1  Houses

Although some housing estates were sold on long leases (eg 200 years) in the past, this is not common nowadays. The conveyancing aspects of long leasehold houses will be looked at in Chapter 36.

More common today are short-term leases of houses. To some extent, the growth in the private letting market came as a result of the slump of the late 1980s when people could not sell their houses and so chose to let them instead. The procedure on the grant of a short-term lease is normally very informal. The buyer will probably not be legally represented and will make no searches or enquiries at all about the property. The landlord will be most concerned about the status of the tenant rather than legal matters, ie whether the tenant will be a 'good' tenant or not: whether he will pay the rent regularly and will not damage the property. Often such lettings are handled by letting agents, the property lawyer only being called in when things go wrong. Such short-term lettings sometimes give rise to security of tenure and other rights for the tenant, ie a right to continue in possession even after the ending of the contractual tenancy. It is largely in this context that they are of concern to a property lawyer. The rights of tenants are looked at in outline in Chapter 39.

### 34.2.2  Flats

It is in the context of the sale of flats that the property lawyer will most often come across leases of residential property. The drafting of leases of flats is looked at in detail in Chapter 37.

### 34.2.3  Commercial property

Many commercial properties can be regarded in a similar light to flats in that they will be one part of a larger unit owned by the landlord, sharing access ways and other facilities with the tenants of other parts of the building or industrial estate. Like the tenants of flats, the tenants of commercial units will pay both rent and service charge and may, depending on the length of the lease, have to pay a premium for the grant of the lease and sometimes additional sums for fixtures and fittings. Leases for terms of 5 to 25 years are common. The short length of these leases is not a matter for concern, since the tenant will usually have the right to renew his lease under the Landlord and Tenant Act 1954, Part II. Depending on the circumstances, conditions will be imposed on the tenant by the lease restricting the tenant's use of the property and his right to sell it to a third party. The rent payable for a commercial unit is a market rent, much higher relatively than the rent which is payable for residential property, and the rent is usually subject to review every few years under a term to this effect in the lease. The drafting of leases of commercial premises is looked at in Chapter 37.

### 34.2.4  Basic terminology

The owner of the freehold (the landlord) grants a lease to the tenant. This is the head-lease, because the only superior title above it is the freehold (the reversionary interest). The tenant under the head-lease grants a lease of part of the property to another person. This is called a sub-lease (or underlease) and the person with the benefit of the sub-lease is the sub-tenant. The sub-lease cannot be for a period longer than the lease since the tenant has no power to grant a lease which is longer than his own interest in the property. A further lease granted by the sub-tenant would be a sub-underlease; further derivations are not common in the context of residential property.

If the tenant wants to sell his lease then, subject to obtaining his landlord's consent, in appropriate cases he may do so. The sale is called an assignment. The tenant who is selling can be called either the seller (as in freehold conveyancing) or the assignor, and the person who is buying is referred to as the buyer or assignee. All that the tenant can sell is what remains of his lease – the unexpired residue of the term. He cannot sell more than he himself owns.

### 34.2.5  Leasehold conveyancing procedures

Where a long lease is being granted and/or a premium is being paid for its grant the conveyancing procedure undertaken by the parties' solicitors will follow that used on the sale and purchase of freehold land. Pre-contract searches and enquiries and investigation of title will be done in exactly the same way as for freehold land. In some cases, particularly where a commercial lease is concerned, a contract as such will not be entered into and the transaction will continue at the negotiations stage until completion, when the purchase deed (the lease itself) is handed over. The lease, unlike a freehold purchase deed, is usually prepared by the landlord's (seller's) solicitor, and is usually prepared in duplicate, the landlord signing the lease itself, which is given to the tenant, and the tenant signing a counterpart lease which is handed to the landlord. This procedure is similar to an exchange of contracts, but happens at completion and not half way through the transaction. A capital sum or premium payable for the grant of a lease may be raised by way of mortgage by the tenant, and a mortgage deed will be executed in the normal way.

An assignment (sale) of an existing lease follows a similar procedure to a normal sale of freehold property. It must, however, be borne in mind by the assignee (buyer) that he is buying a lease which is already in existence, he is not therefore in a position to negotiate or change the terms of the lease, he either accepts them as they are or chooses not to buy the property.

Where a tenancy agreement or short lease without a premium is being granted, a contract is often dispensed with and the parties simply negotiate the terms of the lease and complete the transaction when agreement over terms has been achieved. Except in the case of very short tenancy agreements, some searches and enquiries should normally be made, but they may not be as extensive as those undertaken in the case of a longer term. Similarly, in the case of a short lease or tenancy agreement, the landlord's title may not be deduced or investigated.

The grant of a sub-lease will follow the same procedure as is used on the grant of a lease, the formalities varying depending largely on the length of the term being granted.

### 34.2.6 How leaseholds are dealt with in this book

The main differences between freehold and leasehold conveyancing lie in the manner in which title is deduced to the prospective tenant. These differences are explained in context in the leasehold chapters of this book, which deal first with the grant of a long lease, then with the sale of an existing lease. Some special provisions which need to be considered when dealing with leases of flats are dealt with in a separate chapter.

Since the conveyancing procedures relating to leaseholds are broadly similar to those applicable to freeholds, these chapters concentrate on highlighting the differences between the two estates and do not contain a full description of leasehold conveyancing. Where a matter is not mentioned in the following chapters on leaseholds, it may be assumed that the procedure is identical to that used in freehold conveyancing and is dealt with in full in the preceding chapters of this book.

### 34.3 ACTING FOR BOTH PARTIES

The Solicitors' Practice Rules 1990, Rule 6, which is explained in Chapter 6, applies equally to leases as to freehold transactions. A solicitor should not act for both landlord and tenant except in the limited circumstances permitted by that rule.

### 34.3.1 Acting for lender and borrower

A solicitor will often act for both the buyer and his lender or, conversely, for the seller and his lender on the discharge of the seller's existing mortgage. Provided there is no conflict or potential conflict of interests and the provisions of the Solicitors' Practice Rules 1990, Rule 6 are complied with, there is no objection to a solicitor acting for both the tenant and his lender or, in the converse situation, the landlord and his lender. This matter is explained further in Chapter 6.

## 34.4 LIABILITY ON COVENANTS IN LEASES

### 34.4.1 Leases granted on or after 1 January 1996

The Landlord and Tenant (Covenants) Act 1995 applies to leases granted on or after 1 January 1996. The original landlord (who granted the lease) and original tenant will be bound by all covenants in the lease while the tenant remains as tenant, but when the tenant lawfully assigns the lease he is automatically released from future liability under the lease covenants unless he has agreed to enter an 'authorised guarantee agreement' with his landlord. The authorised guarantee agreement has the effect of making the outgoing tenant guarantee the performance of the lease covenants by his immediate successor in title but no further. The outgoing tenant remains liable for any breaches of covenant which were committed before the date of the assignment. Similar provisions apply to subsequent assignees, ie they are automatically released from future liability on assignment, subject to the terms of any authorised guarantee agreement which they have agreed to enter. The automatic release provisions do not apply if the assignment is in breach of a covenant in the lease nor if it occurs by operation of law (eg on death of the tenant the lease passes to his personal representatives).

The original landlord (and any subsequent assignee of the landlord's interest) is not automatically released from his covenants when he sells the reversion but can apply to the tenant for the time being to be released from future liability before or within 4 weeks of the date of the assignment of the reversion.

An indemnity covenant given by the assignee to the assignor in the transfer is only necessary in situations where the assignor will continue to be liable on the covenants after completion. The indemnity covenant must be given expressly as the law does not imply such a covenant in this situation.

### 34.4.2 Leases granted before 1 January 1996

The Landlord and Tenant (Covenants) Act 1995 generally does not apply to these leases and the basic principle is that the original tenant remains bound by the covenants in the lease for the whole of the contractual term of the lease unless the landlord expressly agrees to release him. This is regardless of the fact that the tenant, with the landlord's consent, assigns the lease to a third party during the term.

#### (a) Liability of original landlord and tenant

Unless released by the landlord, the original tenant is liable on all the express covenants in the lease for breaches committed at any time during the term of the lease, ie he is liable not only for breaches which he commits himself but also for those committed by his successors in title (assignees and/or sub-tenants). His liability is to the landlord for the time being, because on a transfer of the reversion all rights of action attached to the reversion pass to the transferee, including the right to sue for an existing breach of covenant (Law of Property Act 1925, s 141 and see *In re King (deceased); Robinson v Gray* [1963] Ch 459).

### (b) Continuing liability

Although in most cases the landlord will choose to seek his remedy against the tenant for the time being, the principle of continuing liability means that he has the choice of suing either the original tenant, with whom he shares privity of contract, or the assignee in possession, with whom he shares privity of estate. This choice becomes important to the landlord when, for example, the assignee has become insolvent and is therefore not worth suing. For the original tenant, his continuing liability can lead to serious consequences if an assignee of the lease cannot meet his obligations to the landlord. For example, the original tenant will be liable for the rent due under the lease if the assignee does not pay it.

### (c) The original landlord

The original landlord remains contractually bound to the original tenant throughout the term of the lease because of the principles of privity of contract (*Stuart and Others v Joy and Another* [1904] 1 KB 362). If an original landlord is unable through his own act or default (eg by transferring the reversion to a third party) to carry out an obligation imposed on him by the lease, the landlord may be liable in damages to the tenant. See, for example, *Eagon v Dent* [1965] 2 All ER 334, where a landlord sold the reversion to a third party and the original tenant, who failed in his attempt to exercise an unregistered option against the buyer of the reversion, recovered damages from the original landlord for breach of covenant.

### (d) Landlord and tenant for the time being

The relationship between a transferee of the reversion and the tenant for the time being, and between an assignee of the lease and the landlord for the time being, rests on the doctrine of privity of estate. Liability under this doctrine extends to breaches of covenant which touch and concern the land which are committed by a transferee of the reversion while he holds the reversion or by an assignee of the lease while the lease is vested in him.

### (e) The assignee

An assignee of the lease will not be liable to the landlord for breaches of covenant committed after the date of an assignment of the lease by him to a third party unless, as is commonly required, he has entered into direct covenants with the landlord, in which case his liability will continue throughout the remainder of the term. In this respect the liability of an assignee is no different from that of an original tenant.

### (f) Indemnity

An assignee of the lease will usually be required to indemnify his assignor in respect of any breach of covenant committed after the date of the assignment to him, regardless of whether he has parted with the lease. On the transfer of a registered lease, such an indemnity covenant is implied by the Land Registration Act 1925, s 24, whether or not value was given for the assignment. A similar indemnity provision is implied by the Law of Property Act 1925, s 77 on the assignment of an unregistered lease, but only where value has been given for the assignment.

Where in unregistered land there is to be no valuable consideration for the assignment, an express indemnity covenant will be required by the assignor. Condition 4.5.4 of both sets of Standard Conditions of Sale requires the purchase deed to contain an express indemnity covenant, except where one is implied by law.

### 34.4.3 Liability between head-landlord and sub-tenant

No privity of estate exists between a head-landlord and a sub-tenant, although a contractual relationship will exist between them if the sub-tenant has entered into direct covenants with the head-landlord (eg in a licence to sub-let). The sub-tenant will in any event be directly liable to the head-landlord on restrictive covenants in the head-lease of which the former had notice when he took his sub-lease. Irrespective of direct contractual liability, if the sub-tenant breaches a covenant in the head-lease, the head-landlord will have the right to forfeit the head lease, and this will mean that the sub-lease which is derived out of the head-lease will also terminate.

# Chapter 35

# THE GRANT OF A LEASE

## 35.1 INTRODUCTION

This chapter considers the grant of a long lease, mainly in the context of a lease of residential property, for example a flat. The procedure on the grant of a commercial lease, for example an office, will be very similar, except that there will often not be a contract drawn up between the parties. The same steps will be taken as in a residential transaction but it is likely that most of the negotiations between the parties will concern the terms of the lease itself, and, once these have been agreed, the parties will proceed directly to completion. The conveyancing procedure employed in this type of transaction is similar to that used on a freehold sale and purchase. This chapter deals only with those matters where the procedure for the grant of a lease differs from that used in a freehold transaction.

The landlord grants the lease to the tenant on terms stipulated by the landlord (whose duty it is to draft the lease). The draft lease will be annexed to the draft contract and is then open to negotiation with the tenant. The Protocol is expressed to apply to both freehold and leasehold transactions, but makes no express reference to the procedure on the grant of a lease.

## 35.2 TAKING INSTRUCTIONS FROM THE LANDLORD

Much of the information required by the landlord's solicitor from his client will be similar to that required from the seller in the case of a freehold transaction, which is discussed in Chapter 8. In addition, instructions need to be obtained from the client (and advice given to him) relating to such matters as the length of the term to be granted, the rent to be charged to the tenant, the responsibility for repairs to and insurance of the property, and various other matters which will need to be dealt with in the lease itself. These matters are considered in Chapter 37.

Before drafting the lease, the landlord's solicitor should investigate his own client's title to the property to ensure that the client is entitled to grant the lease. This is done in exactly the same way as if the solicitor was acting for a seller in a freehold transaction (see Chapter 17). Where the property is subject to an existing mortgage, the mortgage will frequently contain a provision which prohibits or restricts the borrower's (landlord's) ability to grant a lease of the property. In such a case, the lender must be contacted and his permission to grant the lease obtained before the matter proceeds.

## 35.3 DRAFTING THE LEASE

The landlord's solicitor will draft the lease. The document will then be sent to the prospective tenant's solicitor for negotiation and approval. Some of the most usual terms to be included in a lease are examined in Chapter 37.

A lease for a term of over 3 years must be granted by deed to vest the legal estate in the tenant. A lease for 3 years or less, taking effect in possession at the best rent without a fine may be granted orally or in writing (Law of Property Act 1925, ss 52–54, as amended).

## 35.4 DRAFTING THE CONTRACT

A contract for the grant of the lease is normally entered into in the case of a purchase for a premium of a long-term residential lease, but is not generally entered into on short-term lettings of residential premises nor on commercial leases where in both cases the parties directly enter negotiations on the draft lease. The lease is drafted by the landlord's solicitor and annexed to the draft contract submitted to the tenant's solicitor. Except where the lease is to be for a term not exceeding 3 years, taking effect in possession and with no premium payable for its grant, the contract for the lease must satisfy s 2 of the Law of Property (Miscellaneous Provisions) Act 1989. Standard Condition 8.2 (both sets of Conditions) provides for the lease to be in the form annexed to the draft contract and for the landlord to engross the lease and supply the tenant with the engrossment at least 5 working days before completion date.

The particulars of sale must state that the property is leasehold and give details of the term to be vested in the tenant. Incumbrances affecting the freehold title must be disclosed and indemnity taken from the tenant in respect of future breaches. In other respects, the contract will be similar to that prepared on a freehold transaction.

## 35.5 TITLE

Under an open contract, the tenant is not entitled to call for deduction of the freehold reversionary title on the grant of a lease (Law of Property Act 1925, s 44(2)). Section 110 of the Land Registration Act 1925 (registered land) does not apply to the grant of a lease. This rule is unsatisfactory, particularly where the lease is to be granted for a term in excess of 21 years, where a premium is to be paid for the grant of the lease, or where a tenant is paying a significant rent for commercial premises.

A lender will not accept a lease of residential property as security for a loan unless the freehold title has been satisfactorily deduced. The absence of the freehold title will usually prevent the tenant and his successors from obtaining an absolute leasehold title on the subsequent registration of the lease unless the freehold is already registered. The landlord should therefore be prepared to deduce his freehold title to the tenant in exactly the same way as if he were selling the freehold (see Chapter 16).

Where the lease will exceed 21 years, Standard Condition 8.2.4 (both sets of Conditions) requires the landlord to deduce such title as would enable the tenant to obtain registration with an absolute title at HM Land Registry. This, in effect, means that the landlord must deduce the freehold and all other superior titles to the lease being granted, for example title to any head lease. In circumstances where the condition does not apply, you should remember that the Land Registry is open to public inspection so that if the title to the reversion is registered, details can simply be obtained by obtaining office copy entries in the usual way, whether or not the landlord is prepared to co-operate.

### 35.5.1 Sub-leases

In the case of the grant of a sub-lease, the sub-tenant is entitled to call for the head-lease out of which his sub-lease is to be derived and all subsequent assignments under which the lease has been held for the last 15 years. In the absence of a contractual condition to the contrary, he is not entitled to call for production of the freehold title (Law of Property Act 1925, s 44).

The sub-tenant's inability at common law to call for the deduction of the freehold title may cause problems if a premium is being demanded for the grant of the sub-lease, the sub-lease is to be mortgaged or it requires registration with its own title. Standard Condition 8.2.4 applies to the grant of a sub-lease, but a head-tenant who did not call for deduction of the freehold title when he took his own lease may not be able to comply with this condition and will have to exclude it by special condition in the contract; but remember again that the Land Registry is open to public inspection.

If the head-lease out of which the sub-lease is to be derived is registered with a separate title, the sub-tenant is entitled to call for production of the head-lease, but not of copies of the registered title itself, since the grant of a sub-lease is not covered by the Land Registration Act 1925, s 110. The sub-tenant will normally require the head-tenant to supply office copies of his registered title, and the contract should contain a special condition to this effect. Standard Condition 8.2.4 reflects this requirement, and where this condition is used, no special condition will be necessary. Again, the open registry rules will solve any problems in this regard. Production of the title to the freehold is unnecessary if the head-lease is registered with an absolute title.

## 35.6 PREPARING THE PRE-CONTRACT PACKAGE

The landlord's solicitor should send to the tenant's solicitor the following documents:

(1) draft contract with draft lease annexed;
(2) evidence of the freehold title;
(3) any relevant planning consents;
(4) answers to pre-contract searches and enquiries (including in Protocol cases the Seller's Property Information Form);
(5) where relevant, evidence of the lender's consent to the grant of the lease.

In the case of the grant of a flat lease where there is going to be a management company providing the services, the company will need incorporating and share certificates (if relevant) and company documents will need to be prepared before the completion of the sale of the first flat. Details of the company will be included in the pre-contract package.

## 35.7  ACTING FOR THE TENANT

The information required by the tenant's solicitor from his client will be similar to that required in a freehold purchase transaction (see Chapter 8).

### 35.7.1  The contract and draft lease

The contract will normally require the tenant to accept the draft in the form annexed to the contract (see, eg, Standard Condition 8.2.3), therefore any queries which need to be raised in connection with the lease must be finalised before contracts are exchanged. Even where the lease appears to contain 'usual' clauses appropriate to the particular transaction in hand, the document must be carefully examined by the tenant's solicitor to ensure that it contains provisions which are adequate to protect his client's interests and no onerous clauses.

The particular points to look out for when checking the draft lease are considered in Chapter 37.

### 35.7.2  Searches

The tenant's solicitor should usually undertake the same searches and enquiries (both before and after exchange) as if he were buying the freehold (see Chapters 18 and 28). As with a freehold transaction, some of these searches may be undertaken by the landlord's solicitor and their results supplied to the tenant's solicitor as part of the pre-contract package.

Where a lease is for a very short term, it is not usual for searches and enquiries to be made, since the low risk attached to these lettings does not justify the expense of making the searches.

### 35.7.3  Lender's requirements

The tenant's lender's requirements, contained in the instructions given to the solicitors acting for the lender, must be observed. The *Lenders' Handbook* requires compliance with the following conditions:

(1)  the consent of the landlord's lender has been obtained to the transaction (where relevant);
(2)  the length of the term to be granted provides adequate security for the loan (terms of less than 60 years are often unacceptable for mortgage purposes in the case of residential leases);
(3)  the lease contains adequate insurance provisions relating both to the premises themselves and (where relevant) to common parts of the building and the insurance provisions coincide with the lender's own requirements for insurance;
(4)  title to the freehold reversion is deduced, enabling the lease itself to be registered with an absolute title at HM Land Registry;
(5)  the lease contains proper repairing covenants in respect both of the property itself and (where relevant) the common parts of the building;
(6)  in the case of residential leases, that there is no provision for forfeiture on the insolvency of the tenant.

### 35.7.4  Advising the client

The tenant's obligations under the lease, which are often complex and extensive, should be explained clearly to him. In particular, the tenant should be warned of the likelihood that, when he assigns the lease, he will have to guarantee the performance of the covenants by the assignee under an authorised guarantee agreement (see Chapter 34) and of the danger of losing the lease through forfeiture for breach of covenant.

## 35.8  ENGROSSMENT AND EXECUTION OF THE LEASE

The lease is normally prepared in two parts (lease and counterpart), both engrossed by the landlord's solicitor (see Condition 8.2.6 in both sets of Standard Conditions). If the landlord requires the tenant to pay a fee for the preparation of the engrossment, this must be dealt with by special condition in the contract. The landlord will sign the lease itself in readiness for completion, and the counterpart should be sent to the tenant's solicitor at least 5 working days before contractual completion date (Condition 8.2.6) for execution by the tenant. The requirements for execution of a deed are dealt with in Chapter 27.

## 35.9  APPORTIONMENT OF RENT

Unless completion takes place on a day when rent under the lease falls due, a proportionate amount of rent calculated from the date of completion until the next rent payment day will be payable by the tenant on completion. This applies where the rent reserved by the lease is payable in advance, not in arrears. The apportionment should be shown on the completion statement supplied by the landlord. The Standard Conditions of Sale do not provide for the apportionment of rent on completion of the grant of a lease, therefore an express special condition is required to deal with this matter, unless it is dealt with in the lease itself.

## 35.10  COMPLETION

On completion, in addition to or in substitution for the matters relevant to a freehold transaction the landlord will receive:

(1)  the counterpart lease executed by the tenant;
(2)  any premium payable for the grant (less any deposit paid on exchange of contracts);
(3)  an apportioned sum representing rent payable in advance under the lease (see **35.9**).

The landlord should give to the tenant:

(1)  the lease executed by him;
(2)  if not already done, properly marked or certified copies of the freehold title deeds (unregistered land);
(3)  where the landlord's title is registered and the lease will itself become registered after completion, the deposit number relating to the landlord's land or charge

certificate (this needs to be placed on deposit at HM Land Registry to await the tenant's incoming application for registration of the lease);

(4) where relevant and if not already done, a certified copy of the consent of the landlord's lender to the transaction.

In the case of a flat lease where a management company is to provide the services, the tenant's share certificate in the company (or an undertaking for it) will be handed over on completion. Frequently, however, the company will be limited by guarantee, not shares, so the flat buyer will have been required to become a member of the company, but there will be no share certificate to hand over.

## 35.11 AFTER COMPLETION

### 35.11.1 Registration

*Short leases*

A lease for 21 years or less is not capable of being registered with its own title at HM Land Registry but will take effect as an overriding interest under the Land Registration Act 1925, s 70(1)(k), whether or not the tenant is in actual occupation of the land. In unregistered land, a legal lease is binding on all subsequent owners of the land, irrespective of notice.

*Registrable leases*

The grant of a lease for a term which exceeds 21 years is registrable in its own right after completion, irrespective of whether the freehold title is itself registered. It will be registered with its own separate title and title number and, provided that the landlord's land certificate is placed on deposit (see **35.10**), will also be noted against the landlord's title (see **35.11.2**).

### 35.11.2 The tenant

*Stamp duty*

The lease must be lodged for stamping with duty at the appropriate rate within 30 days of completion. Stamp duty on leases is assessed by reference to the amount of the premium, the length of the term and the rent payable.

If the lease is granted for a term of 7 years or more, it falls within the Finance Act 1931, s 28 and must be produced to the Inland Revenue in accordance with the requirements of that section (see Chapter 31).

*Registration of the lease*

Where applicable, the lease must be registered at HM Land Registry within the relevant priority period or, on first registration, within 2 months of completion. If the freehold is unregistered, the tenant's application is for first registration. If the freehold is itself registered, the tenant's application is for registration of a dealing. Where the landlord's title is registered, the lease will be noted against the reversionary title. When a lease is registered, it is not attached to the land or charge certificate, but is stamped by the Registry to show that they have seen it and returned to the applicant on completion of the registration.

The lease should be kept with the land or charge certificate since it will be needed on any disposal of the land or if any problem arises over its terms or renewal.

### *Notice to landlord*

Where the tenant is, as usual, obliged by the lease to give notice of dealings to the landlord, this covenant may (depending on its wording) include the obligation to give notice of a mortgage created by the tenant. Notice should be given by sending two copies of the notice, together with a cheque for the appropriate fee, to the landlord's solicitor or other person named in the covenant. The landlord should be asked to sign one copy of the notice and to return it to the tenant, so that the receipted notice may be kept with the tenant's title deeds as evidence of compliance with this requirement.

## 35.11.3 The landlord

Where, on completion of the grant, the tenant will make application for registration of the lease with a separate title, a landlord whose own freehold title is registered should place his land certificate on deposit at HM Land Registry and inform the tenant of the deposit number.

After completion, the landlord should stamp the counterpart with the appropriate duty (£5.00). The landlord may receive notice in duplicate from the tenant, in accordance with the tenant's covenant in the lease, of the tenant's mortgage of the property. One copy of the notice should be placed with the landlord's title deeds, the other should be receipted on behalf of the landlord and returned to the tenant's solicitor.

# Chapter 36

# THE ASSIGNMENT OF A LEASE

## 36.1 INTRODUCTION

An assignment is the sale of an existing lease by the tenant (the assignor or seller) to a third party (the assignee or buyer). The seller can sell no more than the unexpired remainder of the term granted by the lease. The terms of the lease are not open to negotiation by the buyer, because the lease is already in existence and the buyer must take it or leave it as it stands. The only way in which the buyer can obtain an alteration to the lease terms is by negotiating a deed of variation of the lease with the owner of the reversion (the landlord).

The procedure on an assignment is similar to that used in a sale and purchase transaction. This chapter deals only with those areas which differ from a freehold transaction.

## 36.2 PRE-CONTRACT MATTERS: THE SELLER'S SOLICITOR

The information required by the seller's solicitor will be similar to that needed in a freehold transaction (see Chapter 8) with the addition of details of the lease to be sold. Of particular importance is the question of whether the landlord's consent to the transaction will be required (see **36.4**). The seller's solicitor should check his own title, in particular, to ensure that no outstanding breaches of covenant exist, before drafting the contract for sale.

The length of the residue of the term should be checked. Where the buyer may be obtaining a mortgage on the property, his lender will usually require that a minimum stated length of the term remains unexpired at the date of acquisition of the buyer's interest in order to provide adequate security for the loan. A lease which only has a short length of its original term left to run may, unless the term is extended, be difficult to sell. For the rights of certain tenants to insist on an extension, see Chapter 39.

### 36.2.1 Documents to be obtained by seller's solicitor

The seller's solicitor should obtain from his client (or, if not available from the client, from his lender or from the landlord) the following documents, all of which will at some stage during the transaction need to be produced or handed to the buyer:

(1) evidence of the freehold title (the buyer will usually require this to be deduced to him);
(2) the original lease;
(3) evidence of the leasehold title including (where relevant) any licence permitting the current assignment and/or use of the property;
(4) the insurance policy relating to the property and receipt for the last premium due;

(5)   receipts for the last payments of rent and outgoings on the property.

In Protocol transactions, in addition to the usual documentation included in the pre-contract package, the seller should also include the Seller's Leasehold Information Form. This requires completion by the client (in the same way as the Seller's Property Information Form, which should also be completed) and contains information about the lease and the landlord.

## 36.3  PRE-CONTRACT MATTERS: THE BUYER'S SOLICITOR

### 36.3.1  Checking the lease

The seller's solicitor will supply the buyer's solicitor with a copy of the lease at the same time as he sends the draft contract. The buyer's solicitor should check the lease carefully and advise his client about his responsibility under the various covenants in the lease.

The terms of the lease should be checked to ensure that it will be acceptable to the buyer's lender (see Chapter 35).

The buyer's solicitor should make the same searches as on a purchase of the freehold (see Chapter 18).

## 36.4  LANDLORD'S CONSENT

### 36.4.1  References

Commercial leases usually provide for the landlord's consent being required for any assignment. The need for the landlord's consent is not usual in long residential leases, except, perhaps, in the last few years of the term, or in the case of high value properties. Where the lease requires the seller to obtain his landlord's consent to the transfer, the landlord will want to take up references on the prospective buyer to ensure that he is a solvent and trustworthy individual. The buyer should be asked to supply his solicitor with the names and addresses of potential referees so that this information may be passed on to the landlord's solicitor via the seller's solicitor as quickly as possible, in order to avoid any delay in obtaining the consent. References are commonly required from all or some of the following sources:

(1)   a current landlord;
(2)   the buyer's bankers;
(3)   the buyer's employer;
(4)   a professional person such as an accountant or solicitor;
(5)   a person or company with whom the buyer regularly trades;
(6)   3 years' audited accounts in the case of a company or self-employed person.

### 36.4.2  Surety

The landlord may also require a surety (guarantor) to the lease as a condition of the grant of his consent.

### 36.4.3 Absolute covenants

If the covenant against alienation in the lease is absolute (eg 'the tenant shall not assign or part with possession of the property'), any assignment (or other dealing depending on the wording of the restriction), although effective, will be a breach of covenant by the tenant and may lead to forfeiture of the lease. An absolute covenant is not subject to any statutory restrictions on its operation, except those imposed by the Sex Discrimination Act 1975 and the Race Relations Act 1976. Where an absolute covenant exists, the tenant may ask the landlord's permission to grant him a variation of the lease to permit assignment, but there is no obligation on the landlord to give consent, nor to give reasons for his refusal. Absolute bars on assignment are never acceptable in long-term residential leases and would not be acceptable to a prospective lender. The landlord may waive the covenant and give consent to this transaction, but there is no guarantee that he would consent to any other disposition and so a buyer runs the risk that the lease would be unsaleable.

### 36.4.4 Qualified covenants

A qualified covenant permits the tenant to assign (or part with possession, as the case may be), provided that the tenant obtains the prior consent of the landlord to the dealing. The Landlord and Tenant Act 1927, s 19 adds to the covenant the non-excludable proviso that consent must not be withheld unreasonably by the landlord. If the landlord does refuse consent, the prospective buyer is unlikely to wish to proceed with the transaction, because he runs the risk of the lease being forfeited against him.

The Landlord and Tenant Act 1988 provides that the landlord must, after having received a written request for consent, give his consent within a reasonable time unless it is reasonable for him to withhold his consent. He must serve written notice of his decision on the tenant within a reasonable time, stating what conditions (if any) are attached to the consent or, if consent is refused, stating his reasons for withholding his consent. Breach of the landlord's duty under the 1988 Act is actionable in tort as a breach of statutory duty, giving a remedy to the tenant in damages. In leases of commercial property granted on or after 1 January 1996 the lease may provide for the circumstances in which the landlord would withhold his consent to an assignment and any conditions subject to which such consent will be granted (Landlord and Tenant (Covenants) Act 1995). A landlord will not be withholding his consent unreasonably if he insists on compliance with these conditions, so both buyer and seller should check them carefully and ensure that they can be complied with. See further Chapter 37 as to the kind of conditions commonly imposed. In an old commercial lease (ie granted prior to 1 January 1996), it is common to find a requirement for the assignee to enter into a direct covenant with the landlord to comply with the covenants in the lease. This should be explained to the client, as it will mean that the assignee will remain liable on the covenants in the lease even after a subsequent disposition by him.

### 36.4.5 Demanding a premium for consent

Unless (unusually) the lease specifically allows the landlord to charge a premium for giving his consent, the landlord may not require a premium to be paid by the tenant as a condition of the grant of consent.

### 36.4.6  Undertaking for landlord's costs

The landlord is entitled to ask the tenant to pay the landlord's solicitor's reasonable charges in connection with the preparation of the deed of consent (licence to assign).

### 36.4.7  Standard Conditions of Sale

Standard Condition 8.3 requires the seller to apply for the landlord's consent at his own expense and to use all reasonable efforts to obtain such consent, the buyer providing all information and references reasonably required. Unless in breach of these obligations, either party may rescind the contract by notice if the consent has not been given 3 working days before completion date or, if by that time, consent has been given subject to a condition to which the buyer reasonably objects. Although the existence of Standard Condition 8.3 allows contracts to be exchanged before the landlord's consent is obtained, it still gives rise to uncertainty as to whether the transaction is to proceed, as this will depend upon the consent being forthcoming. In a residential transaction, and particularly in a dependent sale and purchase, it is safest not to exchange until the landlord's consent has been obtained. Otherwise this transaction may fall through when the landlord refuses his consent, whereas the dependent transaction would still be binding.

### 36.4.8  Standard Commercial Property Conditions

The Commercial Conditions contain much more comprehensive provisions dealing with the situation where consent is needed from a landlord or superior landlord to an assignment or subletting. It requires the seller to enter into an Authorised Guarantee Agreement – but only if the lease so requires. It also provides that if the landlord's consent has not been obtained by the completion date, completion is postponed until 5 working days after the seller notifies the buyer that consent has been given, or until 4 months after the original completion date, whichever is the earlier.

## 36.5  TITLE

### 36.5.1  Lease registered with absolute title

The buyer is entitled to call for copies of the registered title and other documents specified in the Land Registration Act 1925, s 110. By Condition 4.2.1 of both sets of Standard Conditions, copies supplied must be office copies. Since the title to the lease is guaranteed by HM Land Registry there is no need for the buyer to investigate the title to the freehold or superior leases.

### 36.5.2  Lease registered with good leasehold title

The buyer is entitled to call for copies of the registered title and other documents specified in the Land Registration Act 1925, s 110. By Condition 4.2.1 of both sets of Standard Conditions, copies supplied must be office copies. Registration with a good leasehold title provides no guarantee of the soundness of the title to the freehold reversion and thus, although not entitled under the general law to do so, the buyer should insist on deduction of the superior title to him. The provision for deduction of the reversionary title must be dealt with by special condition in the contract, because neither set of Standard Conditions deals with this point.

Without deduction of the reversionary title the lease may be unacceptable to the buyer and/or his lender (see para 5.4.2 of the *Lenders' Handbook* in Appendix 8). The reversionary title will be deduced by the appropriate method applicable to unregistered land (see Chapter 16). The registers of title at HM Land Registry are open to public inspection so that a buyer could make a search and obtain details of the reversionary title (assuming it is registered) if the seller was unable or unwilling to deduce it.

### 36.5.3 Unregistered lease

Under the general law contained in the Law of Property Act 1925, s 44, the buyer is entitled to call for the lease or sub-lease which he is buying and all assignments under which that lease or sub-lease has been held during the last 15 years, but is not entitled to call for evidence of any superior title. Without deduction of the superior title, unless the reversion is already registered with absolute title, the buyer, on registration of the lease at HM Land Registry following completion, would only obtain a good leasehold title, which may be unacceptable to him and/or to his lender. Unless the contract contains a special condition requiring the seller to deduce the reversionary title, the buyer has no right under either the general law or the Standard Conditions of Sale to call for evidence of the reversionary title. Where title is deduced, the buyer will want to see deduction of the freehold title from a good root of title which was at least 15 years old at the date of the grant of the lease (see Chapter 16).

## 36.6 THE PURCHASE DEED

### 36.6.1 Registered land

An assignment of an existing registered lease is the transfer of a registered estate and the purchase deed will be a Land Registry transfer form. The form prescribed under the Land Registration Rules 1997 for the transfer of a leasehold is the same as for the transfer of a freehold (Form TR1).

An indemnity covenant is implied by the Land Registration Act 1925, s 24, irrespective of whether value was given, in transfers of leases dated before 1 January 1996.

### 36.6.2 Unregistered land

In the case of an assignment of a lease exceeding 21 years in length, this will lead to compulsory first registration and so Land Registry Form TR1 will normally be used by virtue of r 72 of the Land Registration Rules 1997. In the case of the assignment of a shorter lease (which will not be registrable), an assignment will be used. This is similar in format to a conveyance of unregistered land.

### 36.6.3 Covenants for title

If a seller is in breach of a repairing covenant in the lease, the lack of repair could involve him in liability to the buyer after completion under the covenants for title which will be implied in the purchase deed (see Chapter 14). It is usual for the contract to contain a provision requiring the buyer to accept the property in its existing state of repair, thus modifying the covenants for title in this respect (see Standard Condition 3.2.2 in both sets of Standard Conditions). This type of contractual condition must be reflected by an express modification of the covenants in the purchase deed itself. A suggested form of wording is as follows:

> **The covenants for title implied by s 4 of the Law of Property (Miscellaneous Provisions) Act 1994 shall not be deemed to imply that any of the covenants contained in the lease on the part of the tenant for repair or decoration have been performed.**

### 36.6.4 Indemnity

In relation to the assignment of leases granted before 1 January 1996, an indemnity covenant is implied except where, in unregistered land, value is not given by the assignee for the transaction (Law of Property Act 1925, s 77). In such a case, an express indemnity covenant will be inserted if required by the contract (see Condition 4.5.4 in both sets of Standard Conditions).

In relation to the assignment of leases granted on or after 1 January 1996, the tenant will normally be released for future liability on the assignment and so will not require indemnity. If, however, the tenant is to remain liable (eg under the terms of an authorised guarantee agreement) an express indemnity covenant must be included in the contract and purchase deed because no implied covenant exists in this situation.

## 36.7 PREPARING FOR COMPLETION

### 36.7.1 The purchase deed

The purchase deed will be prepared by the buyer's solicitor. The form and contents of this document are discussed in **36.6**.

### 36.7.2 Pre-completion searches

Where the lease is registered with an absolute title, the buyer will make a pre-completion search at HM Land Registry in the same way as if he was buying the freehold. Any other searches which would be appropriate to the purchase of a registered freehold should also be undertaken (see Chapter 28). Where the title to the lease is unregistered, a Land Charges Department search against the names of the estate owners of the leasehold title should be made. Where a company is the landlord (or a former tenant in the case of unregistered land) then a company search will also be required. Where the freehold or other reversionary title has been deduced, the names revealed through investigation of that title should also be included in the land charges search application. If the lease is registered with a good leasehold title, a search at HM Land Registry must be made in respect of the registered title and a Land Charges Department search must be made against the estate owners of the unregistered reversion.

### 36.7.3 Landlord's consent

The landlord's solicitor will supply the engrossment of the licence, which must be by deed if it is to contain covenants. Where the buyer is to give direct covenants to the landlord, the licence is usually drawn up in two parts, the landlord executing the original licence which will be given to the seller on completion for onwards transmission to the buyer, the buyer executing the counterpart which will be given to the landlord on completion.

### 36.7.4 Apportionments

Unless completion takes place on a day when rent and other outgoings become due under the lease, it will be necessary for these sums to be apportioned on completion and the seller should supply the buyer with a completion statement which shows the amounts due and explains how they have been calculated. Copies of the receipts or demands on which the apportionments are based should be supplied to the buyer with the completion statement, so that the buyer can check the apportioned sums. In many cases, it will not be possible to make an exact apportionment of outgoings such as service charges, since the figures required in order to make this calculation will not be available. In such a case, a provisional apportionment of the sum should be made on a 'best estimate' basis, in accordance with Condition 6.3.5 in both sets of Standard Conditions.

## 36.8 COMPLETION

The procedure on completion follows closely that in a freehold transaction (see Chapter 30).

### 36.8.1 Documents to be handed over by the seller

The seller will hand to the buyer such of the following documents as are relevant to the transaction in hand:

(1) the lease/sub-lease;
(2) the purchase deed;
(3) the landlord's licence;
(4) the land or charge certificate (registered lease);
(5) marked abstract or other evidence of superior titles in accordance with the contract (lease not registered or not registered with absolute title);
(6) evidence of discharge of the seller's mortgage;
(7) copies of duplicate notices served by the seller and his predecessors on the landlord in accordance with a covenant in the lease requiring the landlord to be notified of any dispositions;
(8) insurance policy (or copy if insurance is effected by the landlord) and receipt (or copy) relating to the last premium due;
(9) receipts for rent and other outgoings;
(10) share certificate/stock transfer form for management company.

### 36.8.2 Documents to be handed over by the buyer

The buyer should hand to the seller such of the following items as are appropriate to the transaction:

(1) money due in accordance with the completion statement;
(2) duly executed counterpart licence to assign;

(3)   a release of deposit.

### 36.8.3  Rent receipts

The Law of Property Act 1925, s 45(2) provides that, on production of the receipt for the last rent due under the lease or sub-lease which he is buying, a buyer must assume, unless the contrary appears, that the rent has been paid and the covenants performed under that and all superior leases. The buyer's solicitor should inspect the receipts on completion and also, where appropriate, receipts for payment of other apportioned outgoings. Condition 6.6 in both sets of Standard Conditions requires a buyer to assume that the correct person gave the receipt.

## 36.9  AFTER COMPLETION

### 36.9.1  Stamp duty

The transfer (assignment) of an existing lease attracts stamp duty at the same rate as that applicable to freehold property. The licence to assign and its counterpart (whether or not made by deed) do not attract stamp duty.

### 36.9.2  Particulars delivered

Irrespective of whether the purchase deed attracts stamp duty, the transfer of a lease or sub-lease which was granted for 7 years or more must be produced to the Inland Revenue in accordance with the Finance Act 1931, s 28.

### 36.9.3  Notice of assignment

Where, following completion, notice has to be given to a landlord of an assignment or mortgage, such notice should be given in duplicate accompanied by the appropriate fee. The CML *Lenders' Handbook* requires notice of a mortgage to be given to the landlord whether or not this is required by the lease. A notice of assignment is set out below. The recipient of the notice should be asked to sign one copy of the notice in acknowledgment of its receipt, and to return the receipted copy to the sender. The receipted copy will then be kept with the title deeds as evidence of compliance with this requirement.

### 36.9.4  Registered lease

Where the lease is already registered at HM Land Registry with separate title, an application for registration of the transfer to the buyer should be made within the priority period given by the buyer's pre-completion search.

### 36.9.5  Unregistered lease

An unregistered lease or sub-lease which, at the date of the transfer to the buyer, still has over 21 years unexpired will need to be registered at HM Land Registry within 2 months of the assignment. An application for registration with absolute title can be made where the buyer can produce to the Registry satisfactory evidence relating to the superior title(s). In other cases, only good leasehold title can be obtained. An application for first registration of title should therefore be made within this time-limit.

If the title to the reversion is already registered, the lease will be noted against the superior title. In other cases, the buyer may consider lodging a caution against first registration against the freehold title, in order to protect his interests against a subsequent buyer of the reversion. If the lease has 21 years or less unexpired, it is incapable of registration with separate title, but will take effect as an overriding interest against a superior title which is itself registered.

## 36.9.6  Outstanding apportioned sums

As soon as the figures are available, the parties' solicitors should make an adjustment of the provisional apportionments which were made on completion. By Condition 6.3.5 of both sets of Standard Conditions, payment must be made within 10 working days of notification by one party to the other of the adjusted figures.

*Example*

Notice of Assignment

To:     Jackson Properties Ltd,
        15 Mount Street,
        Weyford,
        Blankshire

TAKE NOTICE that by an assignment dated the 6th day of July 2001 made between JAMES BLISS (Seller) of the one part and GRAHAM MARTIN WENTWORTH and SARAH JANE WENTWORTH (Buyers) of the other part the property known as 25 Mackintosh Way Marshfield Greatshire comprised in a lease dated 29th July 1964 made between Jackson Properties Ltd of the one part and Mark John Green and Susan Margaret Green of the other part was assigned to the Buyers for all the unexpired residue of the term

    Dated   12 July 2001

Lytham and Co
Bank Chambers
St Bede's Road
Marshfield
Greatshire

Solicitors for the Buyers

WE ACKNOWLEDGE receipt of a duplicate of this notice with a fee of £15 plus VAT this                day of                      2001

Signed

# Chapter 37

# DRAFTING LEASES

## 37.1  WHY USE A LEASE?

### 37.1.1  Problems of repair and maintenance

It is usual to find that, when a block of offices or flats is constructed and the individual units sold off, a lease of each unit is sold, rather than the freehold. This is, partly at least, because of the difficulty of enforcing positive covenants against future owners of freehold land.

Due to the nature of a block of offices or flats, it is necessary to ensure that the whole of the block – including the other units and the communal hallways, stairways, etc – is properly maintained and repaired. It would not be an acceptable state of affairs if your office or flat were well maintained but the only access was through ill-lit, filthy hallways and past other units which were in a semi-derelict state. What you will normally find, in fact, is that one person, either the landlord or a management company, will be responsible for maintenance etc, but will expect to recover the costs incurred by means of a 'service charge' payable by owners of all the units. Again, as the obligation to pay such a service charge is a positive obligation, enforcement against future owners would be difficult in freehold land. There is, of course, no such difficulty in enforcing positive covenants in leasehold land, hence the use of leases of blocks of offices or flats.

The introduction of commonhold (see **34.1.3**) will provide an alternative method of ensuring the maintenance of blocks of flats, offices etc.

### 37.1.2  Commercial considerations

Commercial considerations will also sometimes dictate that you should choose to grant, or take, a lease and not dispose of, or buy, the freehold.

Many people wanting commercial or residential accommodation only want it on a short-term basis. The business might prosper and they might wish to move to larger premises. Alternatively, the business might not be a success and a move to smaller, cheaper premises might be desired. It is much more convenient for many businesses to have short-term leases, which will allow flexibility, should a move be required. Traditionally, many commercial premises used to be let on 25-year terms. However, these days most tenants require something a good deal shorter, so 5-year or 7-year terms are very common.

As well as the flexibility which short leases give, buying the freehold would also involve a business in considerable capital outlay which, in many cases, would not be possible for the business to afford.

Retaining the freehold reversion of office blocks, shopping centres and the like also forms an important investment for insurance companies, pension schemes and the like. The units will be let at the full open market rent without taking a lump-sum premium and so the reversion will be a valuable asset in the hands of the freeholder; an asset with both income and (one hopes) an appreciating capital value.

As far as residential accommodation is concerned, you will also find many people who only want accommodation on a short-term basis and who do not want (or simply cannot afford) to buy the freehold in a property. However, you will find comparatively few blocks of flats which were specifically built for renting out on short-term lettings. Although there is a market of sorts for short-term leases (you may well have had one yourself whilst at college), the security of tenure until recently given to residential tenants and the comparatively low rents chargeable, have meant that the freehold reversion in such a block does not possess the same investment potential as that in a block of offices.

Blocks of flats intended to be sold on long-term leases, are, however, very common throughout the country, but particularly around the larger towns and cities. These flats are aimed not at the short-term market, but at people who are looking for accommodation on a long-term basis: people who can afford to buy but do not want to buy a house.

Flats have attractions to many people. Often flats are smaller than houses, so they are attractive to the young and the old who do not have children. Many of the normal responsibilities of home ownership are taken care of with a flat through the service charge. So there are no worries about the time or expertise needed to maintain the garden or external decorations. Such flats are normally 'sold' in the same way as a freehold house is sold, ie a lump sum is paid on the grant of the lease. This will normally be sufficiently large to cover the developer's costs of construction, etc – and provide him with his profit as well. A comparatively low ground rent is then charged throughout the term. This may be (say) £200 per year. The lease will be granted for a comparatively long term; often 99 years.

## 37.2  DRAFTING LEASES

### 37.2.1  Why are precedent leases so long?

When you first look at a lease of an office or flat you will probably be horrified at its length. Forty pages is common; 100 pages not unknown! But this is again due to the nature of the premises. There will need to be extensive provisions defining precisely what is let, dealing with the responsibility for repairs and services and setting out how these are to be paid for. There will be the need for lengthy provisions granting each tenant various easements over the rest of the block. There will also be numerous covenants designed to ensure that the value of the individual offices and flats (and of the landlord's reversion) is not affected by the conduct of one irresponsible tenant. Leases of self-contained premises, for example a lock-up shop, will not have to deal with as many problem areas and may well be somewhat shorter.

### 37.2.2  How to draft a lease – landlord's solicitor

*Use of precedents*

It is inevitable that when you draft a lease you will start with an established precedent. Many firms will have their own precedents, developed over the years, on word processor. Other firms will rely on a favourite set of published precedents. In the latter case, it is useful if these are also on the word processor as this will facilitate amendment.

However, bringing up on screen a precedent headed 'Flat Lease', for example, is only the start of the drafting, not the end. Just because you have retrieved what claims to be an appropriate precedent does not mean that you can use it as it stands. You will need to check the content carefully to ensure that it does meet the needs of, and instructions you have received from, your landlord client. Quite frequently, you will find that you will need to combine parts of one precedent with clauses from another in order to meet your instructions. You will also need to check the precedents carefully to ensure that the lease will be acceptable to the prospective tenants. It is no good having the most wonderfully drafted lease if the prospective tenants are put off by its harsh terms.

You should also check the drafting of the precedent. Just because a precedent appears in a well-known and respected published series does not necessarily mean that it is free from errors or inconsistencies. Even the best draftsperson has been known to make mistakes!

### Particular problem areas

The following are the matters to which you should pay particular attention:

(1)  the description of the premises to be let;
(2)  the easements to be granted and reserved;
(3)  the arrangements for repair, maintenance and other services;
(4)  the provisions for payment of the service charge (if any);
(5)  the insurance arrangements;
(6)  the restrictions on the use to which the premises may be put;
(7)  any restrictions on assignment and sub-letting;
(8)  any restrictions on the making of alterations and improvements;
(9)  enforcement of covenants;
(10) the provisions for rent and rent review.

Some of these matters will be of more significance to a commercial tenant (eg user), and others of more relevance in the case of a flat (eg the management scheme), but all must be considered in turn. What you should look out for in relation to each particular topic will be considered later in this chapter.

### Style of drafting

You will soon develop your own style of drafting, but initially you might have problems when combining clauses from two (or more) different precedents. You should ensure that the lease is a coherent whole and that it is in a consistent style. You do not want it to look like a hotchpotch of clauses from various sources just cobbled together in a hurry!

Check also that it is in a modern, easy-to-understand style. Remember, that this lease is going to govern the day-to-day relationship of landlord and tenant for many years. If any disputes or problems arise, it will be the lease that is the starting point for finding a solution. It may well need to be referred to at frequent intervals. It should, therefore, be drafted in plain, modern English, using short sentences and proper punctuation. Archaic terms and legal jargon should be avoided. It should be drafted in such a way that both landlord and tenant can understand what it means.

## 37.3  APPROVING THE DRAFT LEASE – TENANT'S SOLICITOR

### 37.3.1  Read, read and read again!

Assuming that you are acting for a prospective tenant and are looking at the lease for the first time, you must accept the fact that you are going to have to read through the lease several times in order to see if it is acceptable from the tenant's point of view.

Just because others have not spotted problems does not necessarily mean that there are none. Further, just because a lease is acceptable for the purposes of one client does not mean that it will be acceptable for the particular client for whom you are now acting. This is particularly the case with regard to office leases, where the requirements of one office tenant may well be very different from those of the tenant in the next door office.

### 37.3.2  Particular problem areas

The matters which you should particularly check are the same as those mentioned from the point of view of the landlord in **37.2.2** and will be considered in turn in **37.4** below. Indeed, in many cases you will see that the landlord's and the tenant's concerns will be the same, for example that the building will be properly maintained. Often, however, they will differ, for example on whether alienation is allowed.

## 37.4  THE CONTENTS OF THE LEASE

### 37.4.1  Commencement

The lease starts with the words 'This lease', followed by the date of its grant (this date will be the date of completion of the transaction and is inserted on actual completion), and the names and addresses of the parties. Where the lease is created out of a registered title, the document will carry the usual Land Registry heading (county and district, landlord's title number, brief description of the property, and date) at the top of its first page.

### 37.4.2  Payment of premium and receipt

Where the landlord is to grant a long lease of residential premises (ie over 21 years) he will usually charge a capital sum, or premium, for its grant. This is broadly equivalent to the price which a buyer pays on purchase of freehold premises, and consideration and receipt clauses, which have the same effect as those included in a freehold purchase deed, are included in the lease. In addition to the premium, the tenant's consideration for the grant also comprises the payment of rent and the promise to perform various obligations under the lease (covenants) and these are mentioned as being part of the consideration (eg 'IN CONSIDERATION of the sum of forty thousand pounds (receipt of which the Landlord acknowledges) and of the rent reserved and of the covenants by the Tenant contained in this lease …').

### 37.4.3  Operative words

The operative words in the lease were traditionally 'hereby demises', but in more modern leases 'grants' or 'lets' or 'leases' are more commonly used.

### 37.4.4 Title guarantee

The landlord may give the tenant the benefit of full or limited title guarantee covenants in the same way as on a transfer of freehold land (see Chapter 14). The appropriate words 'with full title guarantee' or 'with limited title guarantee' together with any express modifications of the covenants will be included in the document after the operative words.

### 37.4.5 Term

The length (term) of the lease, including its starting date, must be set out. Care should be taken with the commencement date of the term as often other matters are tied to it. For example, rent review is usually to occur on specified anniversaries of the commencement date. It is not unusual to find that the date specified is before the actual signature of the lease. So a lease entered into on 1 January 1999 might be stated to commence on 1 October 1998. This is common in lettings of offices and flats where the landlord wants all of the leases in the block to come to an end on the same day. When specifying a commencement date, it should be made clear whether or not the date specified is to be included in the term. So if a lease is stated to run 'from 1 November 1998', it will, in fact, probably commence on 2 November. The use of the word 'from' probably excludes the day stated. It should be made clear by stating 'on and from' or 'from and including'.

### 37.4.6 The parcels clause – the description of the premises to be let

*Certainty*

The precise extent of what is to be transferred must be clearly and exactly stated. This is always the case in any conveyancing document, but is particularly relevant in the case of offices and flats as the letting is likely to be of only part of a larger building. It must be possible to say with absolute precision what is and is not being let.

It is necessary to define precisely where one unit ends and another begins. Think of the wall which separates one office from another: where in that wall is the boundary between the two offices going to be? Similarly with the floor and ceiling which divide the premises to be let from those below and above it: where is the boundary going to be situated in the floor and ceiling? Often the tenants' repairing obligations are co-extensive with ownership, ie if a tenant owns a wall (or floor or ceiling) he has to repair it, so who owns what becomes especially important.

Often it will not be sensible to provide that the whole of a particular wall or floor belongs to one unit; the boundary will have to be somewhere within the wall or floor. Precisely where will depend upon the method of construction of the particular building. It will obviously be meaningless nonsense to talk of floor boards and wooden joists in a modern building constructed with concrete beams.

*Top floor and ground floor units*

Particular care should be taken with top floor and ground floor/basement lettings. In the case of a top floor letting, is it intended to include the roof and the air space above it in the letting? If these are included, this will enable the tenant to extend upwards, which may not be the landlord's intention. The responsibility for repairing the roof may also be affected by such an inclusion. In the case of the ground floor or basement (if there is one), the same problems arise, but allowing a downwards extension rather than upwards.

### Garage/car parking

Sometimes the letting of a unit (and particularly a flat) will also include a garage and/or car parking space.

Car parking may be underground or in the surrounding grounds. If a specific car parking space or garage is allocated, this should be included in the property let to the tenant. If the lease merely gives a right to park a car somewhere in a car park, this will be an easement. You should inform the client precisely which arrangement exists in each particular case. Numerous arguments can arise over car parking.

## 37.4.7 Easements to be granted

### Access and services

As well as the precise definition of what is being let, you should also look closely at the ancillary rights which benefit the property. In a letting of part, the tenant should be granted all necessary easements over the remainder of the block and the surrounding grounds. This not only involves rights of way – on foot over the entrance lobby, hallways, stairways and lifts inside the block, and by car and on foot from the street and over the surrounding grounds – but also easements for the various essential services to reach the office or flat. These may include water, gas, electricity, drains and telephone, depending upon the circumstances. In an office building the need for the tenant to have direct computer links with other premises should be provided for. Do not forget either that the flat tenant will want to watch television. You should check the arrangements for access to a suitable aerial. Is a communal aerial to be provided – and if so a right to run a cable to it? And can the tenant install his own satellite dish, or is there to be a communal one? Or is there an easement allowing each tenant to fix his own aerial? In office lettings, television may be irrelevant, but you will need to think about the erection of microwave/satellite dishes and aerials and the connecting cables.

### Access for repair etc

An easement just to use these pipes and cables is not enough on its own. Rights of access are necessary in order to inspect and to repair and replace them as required. You should check that these are granted as well.

### New rights

In a lease that will run for some years, it is also sensible to make provision for the possible need to install new cables and facilities in addition to those already there on the grant of the lease. Technology makes great advances very quickly and it would be unfortunate if a lease did not allow the installation into the block of some major new development.

### Use of toilets etc

In office blocks (particularly older ones), it is sometimes the case that each office does not have its own separate toilet facilities. There are communal toilets located elsewhere in the block. In this kind of situation, it will be necessary for easements to be granted for the use of these facilities. The cost of maintaining and cleaning them will then be included in the service charge.

### *Rubbish*

The question of disposal of rubbish will also have to be addressed. When acting for the landlord, you will have to find out whether there is to be a communal bin or whether each unit is to have its own, and if so, where. Rights will have to be given for the use of communal facilities or for the placing of individual bins.

## 37.4.8  Easements to be reserved

As well as the benefit of easements over the rest of the block, you must also ensure that corresponding reservations are made in favour of the landlord and the other tenants in the block. Remember that one tenant's grant of an easement will be the next-door tenant's reservation. Each unit let will have to be made subject to similar rights to those granted to it. Each lease should, therefore, expressly reserve such rights. If it does not, it is likely that the rights granted will not have been reserved over the rest of the block and thus could be ineffective. Therefore, something you should check is whether you are acting for a landlord or for a tenant.

## 37.4.9  Rent and rent review – flat leases

In the case of a flat lease, the annual rent will be comparatively low. After all, the tenant will have paid a large premium to 'buy' his flat and therefore cannot be expected to pay a large rent as well. So you will find that the rent will perhaps be in the region of £200 per year. The lease should make it clear what the rent payment date is and whether the rent is to be paid in advance or arrears. Often, the rent is payable half-yearly rather than in one lump sum.

It is usual in a long lease to find some provision dealing with increases in rent. A rent fixed at the start of a 99-year term will very rapidly have its value eroded by inflation. If you are acting for a landlord, you should take instructions on this. The landlord will probably want to be able to increase the rent in order to compensate for this. However, the dictates of the market must be borne in mind. Tenants (and their mortgagees) are not going to find a lease acceptable which gives a landlord an unfettered right to increase the rent. Remember that a substantial premium has already been paid and a tenant (or mortgagee) will wish to recoup this on a subsequent assignment. This will not be possible if the landlord has imposed a large increase in the rent.

So it is usual in a flat lease to find that the rent increases are agreed in advance and set out in the lease. You will usually find that the rent for the first 20 years of the term is (say) £200, and then for the next 20 years £300, and so on. When acting for a tenant you should check the rent provisions and explain these to the client, particularly the provisions for increase.

### *VAT*

The grant of a residential lease is zero rated, so no special provisions are required to deal with the payment of VAT on the rent. However, where the tenant is to be liable for the landlord's legal and other costs, the lease should make clear that the tenant is to pay these plus VAT.

## 37.4.10 Rent and rent review – commercial leases

As with flat leases, the lease should make clear what the rental payment dates are and whether the rent is payable in advance or arrears; advance is usual. In all types of commercial lease, the amount of the rent will be a prime consideration for both landlord and tenant. Often this will be separately negotiated by surveyors acting on behalf of the landlord and the tenant. The provisions for reviewing the rent to take account of inflation, are, however, a legal matter and will be the concern of the landlord's and the tenant's solicitors.

It is not usual to have pre-determined increases, or increases at such long intervals, as in flat leases. The landlord will want to track inflation and market conditions as closely as possible. He will not want his rent to lose its real value because of inflation, or to fall behind increases in rents in the rest of the letting market.

### *Usual method of rent review*

The usual way to review rent, therefore, is to have a comprehensive rent review provision. This will require the rent to be reviewed perhaps every five years. The precise frequency will depend upon negotiation; landlords may prefer to review every three years, tenants every seven! This review will usually seek to determine the rent for a 'hypothetical letting' of the premises at the time of the review. This rent will then become the new rent for the actual letting.

The parties (and their valuers) will have to pretend that the office is to be let afresh at the review date in the market as it then exists. If such a letting was to take place, what rent would this office now command? This method is now generally accepted as being the best way of reviewing rents to take account of changes in market conditions and the value of money. Obviously, the precise terms of any letting can affect the rent dramatically, and so the rent review clause will have to set out carefully the terms on which a hypothetical letting is supposed to be taking place. Whether acting for landlord or tenant, therefore, great care will have to be taken in the negotiation of the rent review clause. These considerations are outside the scope of this book.

### *VAT*

The grant of a commercial lease is an exempt supply, but subject to the landlord's right to elect to waive the exemption and charge VAT. See **7.5.2** as to the purpose of this option to tax. If the landlord decides to elect to tax, it is essential that he should be able to add the VAT onto the agreed amount of rent. However, the effect of VATA 1989, s 89 is that, if the landlord elects before the grant of the lease, he will only be able to add VAT to the rent if the lease contains a provision permitting this; see **7.5.6**. In every lease, therefore, there should be such a provision.

## 37.4.11 Rent suspension

The lease will continue to run and the rent will continue to be payable even if the property is rendered unusable, for example because of a fire. If the block is totally destroyed, it may be that the doctrine of frustration will apply and the lease will be terminated (see *National Carriers Ltd v Panalpina (Northern) Ltd* [1981] AC 675).

However, it is usual to include a provision in the lease suspending the rental payments whilst the premises are unusable. Usually, landlords will wish to limit this to cases where the damage etc has been caused by an insured risk. This means that if you are acting for a tenant, you must look vary carefully at what the insured risks are to make sure that all potential dangers are covered. Otherwise, if damage is caused by a non-insured risk, the rent will continue to be payable – and there will be no insurance money with which to rebuild the block.

## 37.4.12 Alterations and improvements

At common law, the tenant's ability to make alterations or improvements is somewhat unclear. It all depends upon the centuries old doctrine of 'waste'. It is best, therefore, for these matters to be dealt with expressly in the lease.

A landlord will usually want to exercise some form of control over what can and cannot be done on his premises. Whilst some alterations may well increase the value of the office and the reversion, some may not. He will be concerned, particularly in comparatively short office leases, lest any alterations carried out by a particular tenant will decrease the letting value of the premises when he comes to re-let. This will be less of a problem in a 99-year lease of a flat, for example, but alterations may still affect the value of the reversion. There are also safety aspects: tenants cannot be allowed to remove or interfere with structural walls and the like, otherwise the whole block might collapse.

In a short-term lease, the landlord may wish to prohibit all alterations and so will impose an absolute covenant. Prospective tenants should consider this carefully. Are the premises, as they are now, definitely going to be adequate for the tenant's needs throughout the lease and any possible renewal? It is true to say that the landlord could still grant permission for a particular alteration, despite the absolute prohibition, but, of course, he does not have to. The tenant will be at the landlord's mercy. However, in an office or flat lease, bearing in mind the nature of the premises, an absolute prohibition on structural alterations would be acceptable.

A qualified covenant would be preferable with regard to other alterations. This prohibits alterations without the landlord's prior consent. Under s 19(2) of the Landlord and Tenant Act 1927, a term is implied into a qualified covenant against making improvements that the landlord cannot unreasonably withhold his consent. That term cannot be excluded. This provision will thus apply to a covenant against making alterations to the extent that the alteration in question amounts to an improvement. According to *Lambert v FW Woolworth & Co Ltd* [1938] Ch 883, whether an alteration amounts to an improvement for these purposes, must be looked at purely from the point of view of the tenant. If the works in question will increase the value or usefulness of the premises to the tenant, then it will be an improvement even if it will result in the reduction in the value of the landlord's reversionary interest. In relation to improvements, therefore, the landlord will not be able to withhold his consent unreasonably; in relation to other alterations, he can be as awkward as he likes.

Although the *Woolworth* case is beneficial to tenants, they would often prefer a fully qualified covenant, one that makes it clear on the face of it that the landlord cannot withhold his consent unreasonably to an alteration, whether or not it amounts to an improvement. Landlords must think very carefully before agreeing to concede any kind of qualified covenant.

### 37.4.13 Insurance

As a distinguished judge once said, 'Of all points connected with the sale of flats, insurance seems to give the most trouble and the trouble yields the least benefit to any of the parties concerned'. The same sentiment applies equally to commercial leases. So, whether you are acting for a landlord or a tenant, you should therefore take particular care in considering the insurance provisions in a lease.

#### Reason for insurance

When acting for a tenant, you need to make sure that the whole property and, in the case of a letting of part, the building of which it forms part, will not only be repaired but also that it will be replaced if it is damaged by fire, explosion, etc. It may be, of course, in a letting of part, that the landlord/management company would be obliged to repair such damage (depending upon the wording of the repairing covenant) but the individual tenants would then have to fund the possibly substantial costs involved under the service charge. So, just as you would insure your own home, insurance is also necessary in the case of a block of offices or flats.

#### Reason for problems

Insurance involves several parties – landlord, tenant, mortgagee, management company – all of whom have their own interests at heart, which are often in conflict. It also introduces into the equation another document, the insurance policy, additional to the lease, which governs the rights and responsibilities of the parties. Like leases, insurance policies do tend to be somewhat complex. In order to ascertain the rights of the various parties, the lease and the insurance policy must be read together.

#### Lettings of part – who should insure?

There are two basic alternatives:

(1)  the landlord (or management company) insures the whole block. The cost is then passed on to the tenants through the service charge;
(2)  each tenant insures his own premises and the landlord insures the common parts.

#### Administrative problems if tenants insure

The landlord has to check that the tenants comply with the covenants.

Each tenant needs to rely on every other tenant complying with the insurance covenant. Checking this will be practically impossible. And, if a tenant has not insured, it may well mean that the proceeds from the various policies will not be enough to rebuild. There is also the problem of ensuring that those who have insured actually use the proceeds to make good any damage caused and do not just pocket it and walk away.

Although the lease will usually require all the policies to be taken out with the same company, there will still be a multiplicity of claims should one need to be made.

#### Usual provisions

The normal scheme is for the landlord to covenant to insure the whole block. Sometimes the insurance company to be used will be specified. More usually it is left to the landlord to choose. When drafting the lease, you should then ensure that the landlord can recover the premium through the service charge. You should also ensure that the landlord will be able to keep any discounts or commissions he may receive from the insurance company; otherwise the landlord may have to account for these to the tenants.

When considering the lease you should check the following matters are satisfactory:

- risks insured against;
- amount of cover;
- application of policy monies.

### Risks covered

An obligation 'to insure' is not sufficient; to insure against what? The risks insured against should be stated expressly. There is often an inclusive list of the risks which the landlord must insure against, for example 'fire, storm, flood, etc'. The problem with this, though, is that the landlord may continue to insure against unlikely or expensive risks and, if new risks arise (eg terrorist violence), these may not be covered.

You should inspect the policy itself (and not just rely on the covenant) and ascertain what risks are covered. If an important risk is not covered, it would, in theory, be possible for an individual tenant to arrange extra cover for that risk or renegotiate the clause, but this would probably not be possible in practice.

The following suggested clause covers most foreseeable risks:

> **subject to the reasonable availability of cover, fire, explosion, lightning, tempest, storm, flood, burst pipes, landslip, subsidence, riot, civil commotion, industrial unrest, impact by vehicles, aircraft and other aerial devices and articles dropped therefrom, acts of malicious persons and vandals and such other risks as the landlord may reasonably require or the tenant may reasonably request.**

### Amount of cover

You must ensure that the property is insured to its full reinstatement value, otherwise if the property is totally destroyed there will not be enough money to pay for its rebuilding. Full reinstatement value will include:

- costs of demolition and site clearance;
- professional fees (eg architects, surveyors, etc);
- an allowance for inflation.

A professional valuation or index linking is advisable.

### Application of policy monies

There should be at the very least a covenant by the landlord to use the proceeds to reinstate the premises. Ideally, a tenant would like this extended to include an obligation for the landlord to make good any shortfall in the proceeds out of his own pocket.

You should also check whether there is any provision to deal with the possibility of reinstatement being impossible. Should this provide for the monies to be retained by the landlord, whose building it is, or to be passed over to the tenants who have been paying the premiums?

## 37.4.14 Permitted user

At common law, a tenant can use premises for whatever purposes he wishes – subject, of course, to planning laws and any covenants on the superior title. This may well not be acceptable to the landlord who will want to be able to exercise some control as to the use to which 'his' premises are put. He will want this control both for financial and estate management reasons.

When you are acting for a tenant, you should consider the user provisions carefully, to ensure that they are not going to cause your client any problems in his occupation of the unit, or if he should wish to assign the lease.

### *Flats*

In the case of a lease of a flat, the landlord will usually want to ensure that the block is used solely for residential purposes. This is to preserve the value of the reversion. If one or more flats start to be used for commercial purposes, this may well make the other flats in the block less desirable residences and so more difficult to dispose of. This possibility of non-residential use might influence potential tenants into declining to take the leases when the block is being first developed. Illegal and immoral use will also be prohibited.

So, both landlords and tenants will have the same concerns and a covenant limiting the use to residential only will be acceptable to both. (Sometimes you will find that certain professional uses are permitted, eg doctor, solicitor, presumably on the basis that this kind of use would not affect the value of the other flats adversely.)

### *Commercial leases*

Use is much more of a problem in commercial leases. In lettings of shops, for example, the landlord may need to prevent competition with other premises of his or may wish to ensure a good mix of retail units to make the development attractive to the shopping public. This may cause problems for a tenant who cannot change from an unprofitable shop use to one more profitable.

In a letting of an office block both landlord and tenants will again have a common interest in ensuring that it is all just used for office purposes. Use for (say) a manufacturing purpose would not be acceptable to the other tenants. This would almost certainly cause noise and other forms of pollution which would adversely affect the other tenants. Tenants would leave, offices could not be re-let and the landlord would, thus, suffer financially.

The only matter for the parties to agree upon is the way in which the permitted use is to be defined in the lease. Whether you are acting for landlord or tenant, you should bear in mind that a user clause can have an effect on the rent when it comes to rent review. A very restrictive user clause will inevitably have the effect of reducing the rent that would otherwise be payable; a very wide user clause will tend to increase the rent.

The landlord may be prepared to permit use as an office by any kind of business. This is certainly ideal from a tenant's point of view as it allows him to diversify his business interests or assign without needing to worry about the terms of the lease.

One common way of doing this is by reference to the use classes for planning permission. Class B1 of the Use Classes Order 1987 permits use for any kind of office and the user covenant may permit such use as allowed under that class. Note, however, that B1 does not permit use for financial and professional services provided principally to visiting members of the public; these are within A2. Also, B1 permits light industrial use as well as offices, so care will have to be taken whether you are acting for a landlord or a tenant to ensure that B1 is appropriate in the circumstances.

Alternatively, the landlord may decide to restrict the use to offices for a stated business, for example marketing consultants. This may suit the present tenant in his present business, but inhibits any change (or expansion) of business and limits the class of persons who might be interested in taking an assignment. It is for this same reason, however, that such a clause would almost certainly result in a lower rent at review than if reference were made to the use classes.

The user covenant may be an absolute prohibition on other uses, or it may be qualified, ie provide that a change to another use can be made, but with the landlord's prior consent. There is no implication that the landlord's consent cannot be unreasonably withheld, but s 19(3) of the Landlord and Tenant Act 1927 does provide that the landlord cannot charge a fine or an increased rent as a condition of his giving consent, provided no structural alteration is involved.

## 37.4.15  Assignment and sub-letting

At common law, a tenant is free to dispose of his lease, whether by an outright assignment or by a sub-lease. But a landlord may well want to exercise close control over who will be in occupation of his property.

### *Flat leases*

In long-term flat leases you will recall that the tenant will have paid a substantial premium on the grant of the lease. He will not want his freedom to dispose of the lease, and so recoup this premium, to be substantially restricted. Equally, the landlord must accept that the lease must be acceptable to any prospective mortgagee. The mortgagee will want to be able to sell in exercise of its power of sale without any limitations being imposed. It is usual, therefore, in a long flat lease to find that assignment is freely permitted. There may, however, be restrictions on the assignment or sub-letting of part.

Even where dealings are freely permitted, the landlord will obviously want to know the identity of the new tenants and so you will find that there will be a covenant by the tenant to register any dealings with the landlord and pay a fee.

### *Commercial leases*

Much stricter controls are usual in office and other commercial leases. Such leases are usually for a much shorter term at a much higher rent. The identity and status of the occupier is of much greater significance than in a long flat lease with a low ground rent. An unsatisfactory tenant could greatly damage the value of the landlord's reversion, either by not paying rent or by damaging the property which the landlord has then to try and re-let.

The landlord will wish to control sub-letting as well as assignment. In some circumstances, a sub-tenant can become the direct tenant of the head landlord and so again the landlord could be faced with an unsatisfactory tenant causing financial damage to his interests.

### *Absolute prohibition*

An absolute prohibition on assignment, etc would probably not be acceptable to a tenant, except perhaps in a very short-term letting. Although the landlord could waive the covenant in any given case, the tenant would be completely at the landlord's mercy with regard to this.

### *A qualified prohibition*

A qualified covenant on assignment etc prohibits alienation by the tenant without the landlord's consent. Sometimes the covenant will go further and state that the landlord's consent is not to be unreasonably withheld. This is known as a fully qualified covenant. Such a covenant gives a tenant considerable leeway when seeking licence to assign.

Section 19(1)(a) of the Landlord and Tenant Act 1927 provides that, notwithstanding any contrary provision, a covenant not to assign, underlet, charge or part with possession of the demised premises or any part thereof without the landlord's licence or consent, is subject to a proviso that such licence or consent is not to be unreasonably withheld. In other words, a qualified covenant can be converted into a fully qualified covenant by the operation of s 19(1)(a). As a general rule, a landlord will be acting unreasonably unless his reasons for refusal relate to the status of the proposed assignee, or the use to which the assignee proposes to put the premises.

The Landlord and Tenant Act 1988 further strengthened the position of a tenant seeking consent to assign, sublet, or part with possession. The Act applies where the lease contains a qualified covenant against alienation (whether or not the proviso that the landlord's consent is not to be unreasonably withheld is express or implied by statute). When the tenant has made written application for consent, the landlord owes a duty, within a reasonable time, to give consent, unless it is unreasonable not to do so (the giving of consent subject to an unreasonable condition will be a breach of this duty). In addition, the landlord must serve on the tenant written notice of his decision whether or not to give consent, specifying in addition the conditions he is imposing, or the reasons why he is withholding consent. The burden of proving the reasonableness of any refusal or any conditions imposed is on the landlord.

### *Special rules for covenants against assigning commercial leases*

Under s 19(1A) of the Landlord and Tenant Act 1927 (inserted by s 22 of the Landlord and Tenant (Covenants) Act 1995), special rules apply in relation to covenants against assigning contained in commercial leases granted on or after 1 January 1996. These rules enable the landlord and tenant to agree in advance (ie in the covenant against assigning) specified circumstances in which the landlord may withhold his consent to an assignment and specified conditions subject to which consent to assignment may be given.

If the landlord withholds consent because any of those specified circumstances exist, or imposes any of those specified conditions on his consent, he will not be taken to be acting unreasonably. Hence, by careful use of s 19(1A) in the drafting of the lease, the landlord can provide himself with cast-iron reasonable grounds for withholding consent to an assignment.

The provisions permitted under s 19(1A) may be either of a factual nature (eg whether the assignee is a company quoted on the London Stock Exchange), or discretionary (eg whether in the landlord's opinion the assignee is capable of performing the tenant covenants of the lease). Where the provision involves an exercise of discretion, then s 19(1A) requires either:

(1) that the provision states that discretion is to be exercised reasonably (eg 'if in the landlord's reasonable opinion the assignee is capable of performing the tenant covenants of the lease'); or

(2) that the tenant is given an unrestricted right to have the exercise of the discretion reviewed by an independent third party whose identity is ascertainable from the provision (eg 'if in the landlord's opinion the assignee is capable of performing the tenant covenants of the lease, but if the tenant disagrees with the landlord's opinion, the tenant may apply to an expert appointed in accordance with the terms of the Lease for a second opinion').

### *Sub-lettings*

Sub-lettings of the whole of the premises are usually subject to the same kinds of restrictions as assignments. However, in the case of sub-lettings of part, the lease provisions are usually considerably stricter. Sub-letting of part is often subject to an absolute prohibition. A landlord who let premises to one tenant does not want to find sometime in the future that he now has to deal with a multi-tenanted block.

Section 19(1)(a) of the Landlord and Tenant Act 1927, and the Landlord and Tenant Act 1988 apply to covenants against assignment, sub-letting or parting with possession. However, s 19(1A) of the Landlord and Tenant Act 1927 applies only to assignments.

## 37.4.16 The arrangements for repair, maintenance and other services

You will appreciate by now that, due to the nature of a block of offices or flats, it is essential from the point of view of both the landlord and the tenant that every part of the block is covered by a repairing obligation in order to preserve the value of their respective interests. When he was setting up the development, the landlord will have decided whether he wanted to retain responsibility for some or all of the repairs himself or whether he preferred to drop out of the picture – and the hassle of responsibility – and impose the obligation on someone else. For details of the various management schemes available, see **37.5** below.

### *The landlord's concerns*

The landlord is concerned to ensure that the whole block will be properly maintained in order to preserve its value.

Each tenant may have assumed responsibility for the repair of his particular unit, either the whole of the unit, or possibly only non-structural parts. It must be appreciated, however, that specific performance is not available against a tenant and that due to the restrictions placed on forfeiture of leases for breaches of repairing covenants by the Leasehold Property (Repairs) Act 1938, forfeiture will only be possible in the case of serious lack of repair. So the only real remedy against a defaulting tenant may be damages. But these will not get the necessary repairs done. You should, therefore, ensure that there is some form of back-up provision which allows the landlord to enter and effect any repairs which have not been done by a tenant, and then to charge the tenant with the cost.

The landlord must consider the repair of any part of the block not covered by a tenant's covenant. He may decide to accept responsibility himself or use some form of management company. Whichever management scheme is chosen, he will need to ensure that a right of access is reserved in order to do the repairs and to ascertain what repairs need doing.

He will need to ensure that the service charge provisions enable him to recoup the full amount of the expenditure from the tenants. For details of service charge provisions, see **37.6** below.

### *The tenant's concerns*

The tenant (and any prospective mortgagee, in the case of a flat) will also be concerned to ensure that the whole of the block will be properly maintained in order to preserve the value of their respective interests. A business tenant will also think of the effect on his business of having premises in a potentially run-down building. So, not only the premises let to the tenant must be properly maintained, but the other flats and offices and the common parts: lifts, hallways, stairways, etc.

When checking the lease, you must ensure that there are covenants to repair from the landlord or others responsible so that repair can be enforced should the need arise.

You will often find that obligations to repair are placed on someone other than the tenant's immediate landlord. This is particularly common in flat leases when a management company is often used. If enforcement is not possible under normal landlord and tenant or privity of contract grounds, you will need to ensure that there is some other way in which the tenant will be able to enforce those obligations, should the need arise. Where the obligation to repair the structure and common parts is imposed on a management company, you should check that the management scheme used enables such enforcement (see **37.7**). Sometimes, repairing obligations are imposed on other tenants. In this case, you should check to see that there is a covenant from the landlord that the landlord will enforce them against the other tenants on request, or that the provisions of the Contracts (Rights of Third Parties) Act 1999 are complied with. For details of enforcement of covenants between tenants see **37.7**.

If, as is often the case with flats, the repairs are to be undertaken by a management company specially set up for that purpose, consideration should be given as to the worth of such a covenant and if necessary (and possible) obtain a guarantee from the landlord. The danger here is that the management company may become insolvent and thus unable to carry out its repairing obligations. A guarantee from the landlord will not be implied by the courts.

### *Who does what?*

The express obligations must cover every part of the building; repairing obligations will not normally be implied against either landlords or tenants. Often the landlord will covenant to repair the main structure and exterior of the block, with the individual tenants covenanting to carry out the internal repairs and decoration to their own particular units. Whatever scheme is adopted, you must ensure that there is a clear division of responsibility between the various parties. It must be made certain that every part of the building is covered by a repairing obligation and clear also as to whose responsibility it is to repair each and every part. There must be no grey areas where responsibility is unclear; no black holes where no one has responsibility and no overlaps where two persons are apparently responsible and can then start squabbling as to who will actually have to do the work.

## Operative words

As in any other covenant, the party responsible for the repairs can only be obliged to do what he has agreed to do. You should ensure, therefore, that the operative words of the clause are sufficient to cover all foreseeable repair activities (eg 'to repair maintain cleanse paint decorate ...'). A covenant to 'repair' only would *not* oblige the covenantor to decorate, for example. And if a service charge was being paid by the tenants, if the landlord did in fact decorate the tenants could not be obliged to pay for this where they had promised to pay for 'repairs' alone.

Is the repairing covenant intended to include renewal and/or improvement? Many arguments arise in practice over this simple point. Replacement of defective window frames, for example, is within the ambit of a covenant to 'repair', but what if the old frame is to be replaced with improved double glazed units? This is probably not a repair but an improvement and so is not within the obligation imposed by a covenant to 'repair'. As above, if the landlord did install double glazed units, the tenants would not be obliged to pay for them through the service charge where they had only agreed to pay for 'repairs'.

If the covenant does include improvements, is this acceptable to the tenants? Do the tenants not want the property improved, you may ask? But bear in mind that the tenants will be expected to pay for any work done through the service charge. There is a risk that the landlord/management company could decide to carry out large scale improvements, which the tenants do not want or need, all at the tenants' expense.

Consider a clause 'to improve and renew to the extent such renewals or improvements are necessary or desirable to keep the Building in good and substantial repair...' as a fair compromise.

In the case of inherent defects in design or construction of the building you should appreciate that remedying these will normally be within the obligations imposed by a repairing covenant, and so again the ultimate cost will fall on the tenants through the service charge.

## Notice of breaches

When a landlord enters into a repairing covenant, there will be no breach unless and until he has notice (no matter from what source) of the lack of repair. Even though he may reserve a right of entry to view the state of repair, he is under no obligation to do so and you should advise the tenant to inform the landlord of any lack of repair as soon as it is known.

When acting for a landlord, you should include a tenant's covenant to notify the landlord of the need to repair. If the tenant fails to do this, he will also be in breach of covenant and liable to the landlord for damages (ie any extra cost incurred by reason of the delay in reporting it).

However, if the part of the property in question is in the control of the landlord, for example the common parts, then the landlord's liability does not depend upon his having received notice of the disrepair.

## Occupiers' liability

If the landlord is in occupation of the common parts, he will owe the common duty of care to visitors under the Occupiers' Liability Act 1957. You should look out for clauses which require the tenant to indemnify the landlord against any such claim made by the tenant's visitors.

## 37.5 FLAT MANAGEMENT SCHEMES

### 37.5.1 Introduction

In the case of an office block, the landlord will commonly provide the services himself, either directly or through the use of agents who will manage the block on his behalf. Because of the high rental income and investment value of the reversion, the landlord will have a close personal interest in the management of the block.

In the case of a block of flats, however, the landlord will very often want to rid himself of the responsibility for providing the services – and also the hassle of dealing with complaining tenants. So, some form of management company will often be used. There needs to be some scheme in existence which allows the tenants to enforce the provision of services against the company and enables the company to enforce payment of the service charge against the tenants.

### 37.5.2 Objectives

#### *For the landlord*

The objective for the landlord is to relieve himself of all responsibility for the maintenance of the block, yet provide a system of maintenance which will be acceptable to prospective tenants and their mortgagees. The landlord will also often require a system which preserves for him the rental income and investment value of the reversion to the block and will ensure that the service charge contributions are recoverable from successors in title to the original tenant. Remember the problems of enforcing positive covenants.

#### *For the tenant*

The objective for the tenant is to be able to enforce the maintenance and repairing obligations both as against the landlord and against his successors in title. In the larger schemes, it is usual for a management company to take over the landlord's responsibilities and special problems can then arise.

#### *For the mortgagee*

It is usual for an institutional mortgagee to insist that there should be a satisfactory scheme for enforcing landlord's covenants and that a copy of a management company's memorandum and articles of association, together with the tenant's share certificate, should be deposited with the title deeds.

### 37.5.3 Types of scheme

#### *Direct management by landlord*

Here, the landlord has responsibility for providing the services personally because of his covenant to do so. He will recoup the cost through the service charge. The tenants will then covenant to pay the service charge. The obligations will then be enforceable by and against successors in title under normal landlord and tenant principles.

## Management by agent

In this case, as above, the landlord is responsible for the repairs, etc but he discharges that responsibility by employing agents ('managing agents') to take day-to-day charge of matters. As the ultimate responsibility is the landlord's and the service charge is payable to the landlord, enforceability is as above.

## Use of a management company

The use of a management company has great attractions for both landlords and tenants. The landlord fulfils his objectives; he is free from the responsibility of running the block. The scheme is normally that the management company will be owned and controlled by the flat owners themselves and so the tenants have the bonus of being in control of the maintenance of the block. They will thus be able to ensure that the block is properly maintained and that the service charges are not excessive.

However, the company has to be run. Someone will need to look after the accounts, make the necessary returns to Companies House and arrange for the provision of the services and repairs themselves. Is there someone willing to take on this often thankless job? Is the person who is willing actually able to do the job? Many blocks of flats with tenants' management companies work very well; but some of the most badly maintained are run by tenants' companies, where agreement to undertake work, which some tenants do not think necessary, can never be found.

There are various alternative schemes in use which make use of a management company.

### (A) TRANSFER OF FREEHOLD

Here, the landlord transfers the reversion to the management company. The management company then becomes the tenants' landlord and the covenants are enforceable against and by it under normal landlord and tenant principles. This has the disadvantage to a landlord that he loses his investment in the ownership of the freehold reversion.

### (B) CONCURRENT LEASE

Here, having granted leases of the individual flats, the landlord then grants a concurrent lease of the reversion in the whole of the block to the management company. This concurrent lease takes effect at the same time as and subject to the leases of the individual flats. It thus has the effect of making the management company the flat owners' landlord for the duration of the concurrent lease. (This will usually be perhaps one or two days shorter in length that the flat leases themselves.) In this way, the repairing obligations and the obligation to pay the service charge are enforceable under normal landlord and tenant principles.

As between the landlord and the management company, the terms of the concurrent lease are that the management company agrees to take over responsibility for the landlord's covenants in return for the right to collect the rent and the service charge from the tenants. The management company pays rent to the landlord, the amount being the sum total of that payable by all the flat tenants. Should the need arise, the landlord is able to enforce the covenant given by the management company to comply with the landlord's covenants in the original flat leases.

(C) VARIATIONS

### (i) *Management company joins in the flat leases*

The landlord grants the leases of the flats in the usual way, but the management company joins in those leases to covenant to provide the services. The tenants then covenant to pay the service charge to the management company.

However, there is a problem here. The covenants between the management company and tenants are not covenants between landlord and tenant and so are not enforceable by and against successors in title to the tenant and the management company. However, such schemes may become more popular for 'new leases' (ie those granted on or after 1 January 1996) because of s 12 of the Landlord and Tenant (Covenants) Act 1995. This provides that a covenant in a lease with a management company in these circumstances *will* be enforceable in the same way as covenants between landlord and tenant. Use of this provision will avoid the need for the complications (and slight extra expense) of the concurrent lease. However, where the management company has no legal estate in the common parts, then it is necessary to ensure that it is given adequate rights of access to the building in order to enable it to carry out the repair and maintenance obligations.

### (ii) *Service charge directed to be paid to management company*

In this scheme, the landlord grants the leases of the flats and covenants with the tenants to provide the services in the usual way. The management company joins in the leases and the landlord directs payment of the service charge to it, in consideration of it agreeing to provide the services. The covenants are then enforceable between the landlord and the tenants in the normal way. But, if the management company defaults, the landlord has to provide the services. This is not good for the landlord but it is a worthwhile reassurance for the tenants.

The *Lenders' Handbook* (see Appendix 8) sets out in para 5.11 detailed requirements as to what management arrangements are acceptable for mortgage purposes.

## 37.6 SERVICE CHARGE PROVISIONS

### 37.6.1 Introduction

Although the landlord/management company will usually be responsible for the repairs to the major parts of the block, including the structure and the common parts, the cost of all this will be passed on to the tenants by means of a service charge. The total expenditure in a year will be divided up between the various tenants in the block in proportions set out in the lease. In addition to repairs, the service charge payments will also usually cover other matters such as the painting and decoration of the block and the cleaning and maintenance of the hallways, stairs, lifts, gardens, car parks, toilets, etc.

Many of the problems which arise as between landlord and tenant stem from service charge disputes. This is particularly so in residential leases. Tenants frequently complain of work not being done to proper standards or of costs being too high – or both! Particular care should, therefore, be taken in drafting or approving this clause.

## 37.6.2  Contents of the clause

### *General principle*

Tenants are only obliged to pay for matters which have been agreed in the lease. You should, therefore, take care in drafting the lease to ensure that all necessary expenditure on the building can be recovered from the tenants. When acting for a prospective tenant, you should also check precisely what the tenant will be agreeing to pay for if he enters into the lease. You should also check carefully as to what services the landlord/management company is actually *obliged* to provide.

### *Obligatory and discretionary services*

It is usual to provide that the landlord will be obliged to provide the essential services, for example repairs, and then provide that if the landlord provides various ancillary matters, for example provision of an entry phone system in residential flats, or the employment of security guards in a commercial block, then the tenants will be obliged to pay for it if the landlord actually does provide that facility. You should ensure that there is an obligation to provide all essential services, not just repairs, but also cleaning and maintenance of the common parts. Also, you should check to see what optional items are included and warn the client if there is a potential for considerable extra expense in respect of non-essential items which the landlord might decide to provide.

### *Landlord's obligations*

The landlord's obligations should include:

* repairs and decoration;
* insurance;
* any payments under a head lease;
* furnishing, cleaning and lighting the common parts;
* car park/garden and grounds maintenance;
* maintenance of lifts.

### *Discretionary services*

The optional items may include:

* establishing a reserve or sinking fund;
* improvements;
* entry phone system;
* resident caretaker;
* security staff/other enhanced security arrangements.

### *Other expenditure*

The landlord will probably have to incur other items of expenditure in providing the services. You should make sure that these are expressly made recoverable, for example:

* bank interest and bank charges;
* legal expenses and other professional fees;
* management charge;
* costs of enforcing the obligations under the lease, for example to pay the rent and service charge.

Otherwise, the landlord would have to bear the cost of these personally.

### 37.6.3  Methods of apportioning the cost

There are various formulae which you will find used to apportion the cost amongst the various flat and office tenants. Which one is appropriate in any given situation will depend upon the full circumstances of each particular case. When drafting a lease you should discuss the formula to be chosen with the landlord and the landlord's surveyors at an early stage so that the appropriate formula can be included in the draft lease.

The following are a selection of those you are most likely to come across.

#### *Proportionate to rateable value*

This is common in older developments, the principle being that larger offices and flats (with larger rateable values) should pay a larger share than the smaller ones. With the ending of domestic rates, this method is no longer possible for new flat developments.

#### *Proportionate to floor area*

This is another way of ensuring that larger premises pay a higher proportion than smaller.

#### *Equally between the tenants*

This is only sensible in a block where all the premises are the same size and will make the same use of the services.

#### *A 'fair proportion'*

This allows variations to be made to take into account the fact that different offices and flats may make differing amounts of use of the various services provided. It also allows changes to be made during the term of the lease to take into account differing uses or circumstances, for example an extension of the block. Such a vague provision may, however, lead to disputes with tenants as to what is in fact 'fair'.

#### *A stated proportion of each of the various expenses*

This proportion will vary depending upon the situation and size of the office or flat concerned.

This may be the same proportion of *all* the expenses, or it may allow almost infinite flexibility to apportion different elements of the service charge costs in different proportions amongst the various tenants. For example, why should ground floor tenants have to contribute towards the (often large) cost of maintaining the lift? Care should be taken when you are drafting the leases to ensure that all the different proportions to be paid by the various tenants add up to 100%!

#### *Unlet units*

Both landlord's and tenant's advisers should think carefully as to what is to be done about the contributions due in respect of any offices or flats which are unlet.

If no one is making up the contributions from unlet units, this could have serious implications. It is likely to be the case that the cost of providing the services will still be the same, even though one or more units are unlet. Without the contributions due from those premises, the landlord/management company may well not be able to afford to provide all the services. This may well affect the value and enjoyment of the let units. In the case of a new development, tenants will expect to find that the landlord will covenant to make up these payments until all the units have been sold and the landlord will have little choice than to go along with this.

## 37.6.4 Reserve and sinking funds

### *Purpose and effect*

Although normally the idea behind a service charge is that all expenditure incurred in one year will be covered by the payments made in that year, you will sometimes find that the landlord/management company will set up a reserve or sinking fund to deal with unexpected expenditure which might arise during a year or to cover anticipated major expenditure. For example, every few years the outside of the block will need painting, an expensive task. Similarly, eventually the lifts will need replacing – a very expensive item to be paid for out of one year's service charges.

A large increase in the amounts demanded by way of service charge in one year when compared with the previous year could pose serious financial difficulties for the tenants and, if some are unable or refuse to pay, for the landlord/management company itself and the other tenants. It is often thought sensible, therefore, to build up a fund by small contributions every year so that this can be used in years of expected or unexpectedly high expenditure to even out the amount of the service charge contributions.

Apart from evening out the bills in this way, a sinking fund may also be seen to be fairer when changes in the identity of the tenants are considered. For example, someone buying a flat in the year in which the lift was going to be replaced would have to pay a very large service charge that year to pay for it, whereas the previous owners who had used (and worn out) the lift would have had to pay nothing towards its replacement.

### *Express provisions required*

In order to recover contributions to such a fund, express provision is required in the lease. The lease should declare that the fund is to be held on trust. This is to protect the fund against it being seized by the landlord's creditors should the landlord become insolvent.

### *When can the fund be used?*

When drafting or approving a clause dealing with a reserve or sinking fund, careful thought needs to be given as to when recourse to the fund may or must be made by the landlord. You must appreciate that everything depends upon the wording of the lease itself.

The landlord will not wish to be too tied down or restricted by the terms of the lease. On the other hand, the tenant *will* want to limit the landlord's discretion.

Is there a danger that when a major item of expenditure falls due, the landlord simply charges it to that year's service charge in the normal way and does not make use of the sinking fund? Equally, is there a risk that the landlord uses the reserve fund for items of a recurring nature, for example cleaning bills, rather than the unexpected items for which it is really intended? Perhaps a fair compromise is a provision obliging the landlord to charge at least 50% of the cost of stated major items to the fund, for example painting exterior, replacing lifts, etc.

### Unlet units

As with the service charge itself, there is again the problem of unlet units. Is the landlord required to make the contributions in respect of these? Often he will not wish to do so, and the terms of the lease should make it clear whether the landlord's obligation to make the service charge contributions in respect of unlet units includes the contributions to the sinking fund or not.

### Assignments of the lease

A tenant assigning his lease may wish to be reimbursed by the assignee with the amount of his unexpended contributions to the fund. After all, the incoming tenant will reap the benefit of these in reduced service charge contributions in the future. This will only be possible, however, if the landlord is obliged by the lease to provide information about the size, etc, of the fund. The landlord will probably not wish to agree to this because of the work involved in providing the information.

## 37.6.5  Certificate of amount due

### Who is to prepare the certificate?

The lease should state who is to prepare the accounts and certify the amount due from each tenant. It is usual to state that this certificate is conclusive. It would obviously be inconvenient for the landlord if such a certificate were to be open to challenge. Tenants should be warned that apparently, at common law, if you agree to such a clause then it will be conclusive on matters of law, ie as to the construction of the service charge clause, as well as matters of fact, ie the costs incurred.

### Can an employee be used?

When acting for a tenant, you should check carefully who is to prepare this certificate. It should be someone independent of the landlord and not an employee of the landlord or an associated company.

If the landlord wishes an employee to be able to prepare the certificate, this must be clearly stated. However, if it is clearly stated, then this will be binding upon the tenant. Would you be prepared to accept this on behalf of a client?

In any event, under s 21 of the Landlord and Tenant Act 1985, a residential tenant is entitled to request a written summary of the costs incurred. If the service charges are payable by more than four tenants, then those costs must be certified by a qualified accountant, defined to exclude an employee of the landlord or the landlord's managing agents.

## 37.6.6  Methods of recouping costs

### Payments in advance essential

Provision for advance payments will be essential to ensure that the landlord has sufficient funds in hand to finance the necessary works. The method of calculating the amount of the advance payment must also be specified in the lease. You will find several alternatives in use in precedents.

(a) The previous year's expenditure. This is obviously not going to be practical in the first year of a new development; special provision should be made for the first year. In any event, however, it should be borne in mind that expenditure in the previous year might not accurately reflect the expected expenditure in the following year. For example, one year's accounts may include the cost of decoration which would not need to be repeated in the following year.
(b) A fixed sum. There is a danger, however, that this, if it cannot be changed by the terms of the lease, will rapidly become ineffective due to inflation.
(c) An estimate of probable expenditure. This is often the most sensible as expenditure can vary greatly from year to year due to non-recurring items of expenditure.

### Payment/refund of balance

There must then be provision for a final balance to be paid when the actual costs for the year are known. Any underpayment will then be payable as a lump sum.

What is to happen to any overpayment? Is this to be repaid to the tenant or credited towards the next year's account? Usually, the landlord will require it to be credited to the next year's account.

## 37.7 MUTUAL ENFORCEMENT OF COVENANTS

### 37.7.1 Why the need?

When checking the lease on behalf of a prospective tenant of a flat you will need to ensure that there is some effective scheme for the enforcement of covenants between the tenants. When drafting the lease on behalf of a landlord, therefore, you should ensure that such a scheme is set up.

It is unlikely that this will be necessary with regard to payment of the service charge provisions as the landlord/management company will be able – and anxious – to recover this. But due to the close proximity of flat tenants it is usual to find that the tenants are subject to a wide range of covenants controlling their use of the units. So there will be covenants against business use and against causing a nuisance to the neighbours, for example by noise. If these are to be enforced it will be a matter for the flat owners themselves as they are the ones affected by any breach.

### 37.7.2 What to look for

You should check the following.

(a) There should be a covenant in the lease by the landlord in the lease that he will impose the same covenants in all the flat leases.
(b) There should then be a covenant by the landlord to enforce all the covenants in the lease against another flat owner on the request of another tenant. This will, of course, be at the requesting tenant's expense. There is often a proviso that the landlord is obliged to commence proceedings only if counsel's advice is produced recommending such a course of action. The advantage of this kind of

clause is that it will enable the enforcement of both negative and positive covenants.

(c) Another method of enforcement is a scheme of development, often in freehold land referred to as a 'building scheme', which works in the same way in leasehold flats as well. This will enable any flat owner to sue any other directly, ie without the landlord's assistance. This only works, though, in relation to negative (restrictive) covenants, for example those restricting the use of the property. You should check to ensure that the basic requirements of such a scheme are present, ie that the lease contains statements that it is intended to impose the same covenants on all the flats and that it is the intention of the parties that they should be mutually enforceable.

Another possibility is to make use of the provisions of the Contracts (Rights of Third Parties) Act 1999 which came into force on 11 May 2000. This allows someone who is not a party to a contract to sue on it provided that it purports to confer a benefit on him. The third party must be expressly identified, either by name, or as a member of a class, or as answering a particular description, but need not be in existence when the contract is entered into. Thus, if the covenant purports to benefit 'the Tenants for the time being of the other flats in the Building' this would allow both present and future tenants to enforce the covenant.

## 37.8 FORFEITURE CLAUSE

A proviso for a re-entry or forfeiture clause is an essential part of a fixed-term lease. It enables the landlord to terminate the lease because of the tenant's breach of covenant. An express forfeiture provision is essential; without such a clause a landlord would be unable to remove a tenant until the end of the fixed term even though he was not complying with the covenants in the lease. The clause should give the landlord the right to forfeit if the rent is a specified number of days in arrears (eg 21 days) and for breach of any other covenant. However, despite the existence of the clause, a landlord will not be able to forfeit for covenants other than non-payment of rent unless he has previously served a notice on the tenant under the Law of Property Act 1925, s 146. A court order will be required if possession cannot be acquired peaceably and is always necessary in the case of residential property. When brought into force, the Commonhold and Leasehold Reform Act 2002 will further restrict a landlord's right to forfeit in relation to residential leases.

**Chapter 38**

# THE LANDLORD AND TENANT ACT 1954, PART II

## 38.1 INTRODUCTION

The Act gives security of tenure to tenants who occupy premises for business purposes. A business tenancy will not come to an end at the expiry of a fixed term, nor can a periodic tenancy be terminated by an ordinary notice to quit. Instead, the tenancy will continue after the contractual termination date until it is ended in one of the ways specified by the Act. When it is terminated under the Act, the tenant has the right to apply to the court for a new lease to be granted and the landlord can only oppose this new lease on the grounds laid down in the Act. Any such new tenancy will also be protected under the Act. If the tenant has to vacate the premises, he may be entitled to compensation.

## 38.2 WHEN DOES THE ACT APPLY?

Section 23(1) provides that:

> '... this Act applies to any tenancy where the property comprised in the tenancy is or includes premises which are occupied by the tenant and are so occupied for the purpose of a business carried on by him or for those and other purposes.'

The various parts of this provision must be looked at separately.

### 38.2.1 There must be a 'tenancy'

'Tenancy' includes an agreement for a lease and an underlease, but obviously excludes a licence. Any purported licence will be looked at carefully by the courts and the mere fact that it is described as a 'licence' will not prevent the courts declaring it to be a tenancy if that is what it really is. Basically, if the occupier has exclusive possession of the property and is paying a rent, it is likely that the arrangement will be declared to be a tenancy and not a licence.

Certain tenancies are specifically excluded from the protection of the Act (see **38.2.4**).

### 38.2.2 The premises must be occupied by the tenant

Occupation can be by the tenant personally, or through the medium of an agent or manager. If, however, the premises are occupied by a company owned by the tenant, this will not be sufficient to bring the tenancy within the Act, as the company is a separate legal entity, and it is the company, not the tenant, which is in occupation.

Problems can arise in the case of sub-lettings. There can be no dual occupation for the purpose of the Act. If there is a sub-tenant in occupation, the head tenant cannot be so, and it will be the sub-tenant who will gain the protection of the Act. However, in the case of a sub-letting of part only of the premises, the head tenant will be protected in relation to the part he still occupies for business purposes.

### 38.2.3  Occupied for business purposes

The tenant must be occupying for the purposes of a business carried on by him. 'Business' is widely defined and includes 'a trade, profession or employment and any activity carried on by a body of persons'. 'Any activity' means just that; it need not be a business or commercial activity. So, running a tennis club or running a hospital have both amounted to a business use under the final part of this definition, when carried on by a body of persons.

The business user need not be the sole purpose of occupation; the Act will still apply as long as the business user is the main purpose and not merely incidental to a residential or other purpose. So a shop with a flat above will be within the Act, but, if a residential tenant occasionally brought work home with him, this would not result in his tenancy coming within the Act.

### 38.2.4  Excluded tenancies

The following tenancies are, inter alia, excluded from the Act.

*(1)  Tenancies at will*

Both express and implied tenancies at will are excluded. A tenant let into occupation while negotiations continue for the grant of a new tenancy will be an implied tenant at will and thus outside the Act.

*(2)  Fixed-term tenancies not exceeding six months*

These are excluded unless the tenancy contains provision for renewing or extending the term beyond 6 months. Further, as an anti-avoidance measure, the Act will apply once a tenant has been in occupation for a period exceeding 12 months.

*(3)  Contracted-out tenancies*

Although contracting out of the Act is generally forbidden, s 38(4) allows the parties to agree that a fixed-term letting should be outside the security-of-tenure provisions, provided the court's approval is obtained before the grant. Such approval must be obtained on a joint application, but is readily given where the tenant is legally advised or is otherwise aware of the implications of contracting out.

## 38.3  CONTINUATION TENANCIES

A business tenancy within the Act will not come to an end on the expiry of the fixed term, but will continue on the same terms by virtue of s 24. Although it will continue at the same rent, the landlord is able to apply to the court under s 24A for an interim rent to apply until a new tenancy is granted (see **38.9**).

## 38.4  TERMINATION UNDER THE ACT

A business tenancy can be terminated only in one of the ways laid down by the Act:

- by the service of a landlord's notice under s 25;
- by the service of a tenant's request for a new tenancy under s 26;
- forfeiture;
- surrender;
- in the case of a periodic tenancy, by the tenant giving the landlord a notice to quit;
- in the case of a fixed-term lease, by the tenant serving 3 months' written notice on the landlord under s 27. This cannot expire before the contractual expiry date and if this has already passed when it is served, it must expire on one of the usual quarter days;
- in the case of a fixed-term lease, by the tenant ceasing to be in occupation for business purposes at the end of the lease. In such a situation, the tenant need give no notice or warning to the landlord, see *Esselte AB v Pearl Assurance plc* [1997] 1 WLR 891.

Note that a business lease can still be forfeited for breach of covenant in the usual way. Apart from forfeiture, the usual methods of termination are the s 25 notice and the s 26 request.

## 38.5  THE COMPETENT LANDLORD

It is between the tenant and the 'competent landlord', as defined by s 44 of the Act, that the procedures under the Act must be conducted. Where a freeholder grants a lease, the competent landlord will be the freeholder. However, in the case of a sub-lease, the competent landlord may not always be the sub-tenant's immediate landlord. However, the rules for determining the competent landlord are outside the scope of this book.

## 38.6  THE SECTION 25 NOTICE

### 38.6.1  The prescribed form

The notice must be in the prescribed form, which is set out at the end of the chapter, and must be given not less than 6 months, nor more than 12 months, prior to the date of termination specified in it. The date of termination specified cannot be before the contractual termination date of the lease. Apart from this, there is no requirement for the notice to expire on any particular day, as long as it is of the correct length.

It must also require the tenant, within 2 months of service, to serve a counter-notice stating whether or not he is willing to give up possession on the specified date.

The notice must also state whether or not the landlord will oppose an application by the tenant to the court for a new tenancy, and, if so, on which of the statutory grounds he will rely. The tenant has the right to apply for a new lease, but the landlord can oppose that application on one of seven grounds set out in s 30 of the Act (see **38.8**). The landlord is only able to rely on the grounds of opposition stated in his s 25 notice. However, commonly, the landlord will be willing to grant a new lease. He will be ending the current lease so that a new tenancy can be granted on different terms, usually a higher rent.

### 38.6.2  The tenant's counter-notice

If the tenant wishes to apply for a new lease, he must serve a counter-notice on the landlord within 2 months of the service of the s 25 notice. If he does not serve a counter-notice, he will lose his rights to a new lease under the Act, even if the landlord has stated he would not oppose an application. There is no right to apply for an extension of the time-limit, which therefore must be strictly complied with.

### 38.6.3  The tenant's application to the court

If the landlord has indicated in his s 25 notice that he will not oppose the grant of a new tenancy, the parties will now enter into negotiations for the grant of a new lease. But there is still a danger to the tenant. Unless he applies to the court not less than 2 months, nor more than 4 months, after the service of the s 25 notice, he will again lose his rights under the Act. The application is usually made to the county court. There are, again, no provisions for seeking an extension of this time-limit. Equally, an application to court made within 2 months of the s 25 notice will also be bad as being made too early, although a further application can be made within the correct time-limit if the error is realised in time. Where the landlord is not opposing the grant of a new tenancy, it is unusual for applications to proceed to a hearing, the parties usually reaching agreement as to terms.

If the landlord has indicated that he will oppose the grant of a new tenancy, the tenant's only chance of obtaining a new lease is to apply to the court within the time-limits stated above.

## 38.7  THE SECTION 26 REQUEST

Rather than wait for the landlord to serve a s 25 notice, the tenant can often take the initiative and serve a request for a new tenancy under s 26. However, this procedure is not available to periodic tenants or those for a fixed term of one year or less. The s 26 notice must again be in the prescribed form, which is set out below. It must state the proposed terms of the new tenancy and the date on which it is to begin. This must be not less than 6 months, nor more than 12 months, after service and cannot be before the contractual termination date. The procedure then mirrors the s 25 procedure. The landlord must serve a counter-notice within 2 months stating if he will object to a new lease, and if so on what grounds. However, it is still up to the tenant to make the court application for a new tenancy (not less than 2, nor more than 4, months after service of the s 26 request), and he will lose his right to a new lease if he fails to do so.

Although normally a tenant will be best advised not to serve a s 26 request (the sooner he gets a new lease, the sooner the rent will go up), there are circumstances where this can be advisable.

(1)  If the tenant has plans to sell the lease, he might find it more marketable if he has already been granted a new fixed term.

(2) If the rent in the open market is less than presently payable under the lease, he may want a new lease as soon as possible at a new, lower, market rent.

(3) If the rent in the open market is more than that payable under the lease, it is in the tenant's interest to prolong the old tenancy for as long as possible, and in the landlord's to terminate the old lease as soon as possible. Similarly, if the tenant knows or suspects that the landlord is about to serve a s 25 notice objecting to a new tenancy. However, if the tenant can get in first with his s 26 request and give the maximum 12 months' notice, the old lease and rent will continue for that 12 months and the landlord will not be able to get possession or a new lease at a higher rent until the end of that period.

## 38.8    THE LANDLORD'S GROUNDS FOR OPPOSITION UNDER SECTION 30

When the landlord serves his s 25 notice, or his counter-notice to a tenant's s 26 request, if he wishes to oppose the grant of a new lease he must specify his grounds of opposition. Section 30 sets out seven grounds of opposition. The landlord can rely only on the grounds stated in his notice or counter-notice; no later amendment is possible. The grounds are as follows.

*Ground (a)  Tenant's failure to repair*
*Ground (b)  Persistent delay in paying rent*
*Ground (c)  Substantial breaches of other obligations*

All of these first three grounds are discretionary grounds. It is not sufficient for the landlord just to establish the ground, he also has to show that the tenant 'ought not to be granted a new tenancy in view of' the facts giving rise to the ground.

*Ground (d)  Alternative accommodation*

This must be suitable to the tenant's needs and on reasonable terms.

*Ground (e)  Sub-letting of part where higher rent can be obtained by single letting of whole building*

This is little used, as the necessary requirements are seldom fulfilled. It applies only where the tenancy was created by the sub-letting of part of premises comprised in a superior tenancy and the head landlord wishes to obtain possession so that he can let the whole as the combined rents from the sub-lettings are substantially less than can be obtained on a letting of the whole. Like grounds (a) to (c), this ground is also discretionary in that the landlord also has to show that the tenant 'ought not to be granted a new tenancy' in view of the facts giving rise to the ground.

*Ground (f)  The landlord intends to demolish or reconstruct and could not reasonably do so without obtaining possession*

This is the most frequently used ground. The landlord must show that, on the termination of the tenancy:

(1) he has a firm and settled intention to carry out the relevant work. This is a question of fact in each case, but the landlord's position will be strengthened if he can show that he has obtained the necessary planning permission and that his financial arrangements are in position; and

(2) he intends to demolish or reconstruct the premises (or a substantial part of them), or to carry out substantial works of construction on the holding or a part of it; and

(3) that he cannot reasonably carry out the work without obtaining possession. This again is a question of fact, but the landlord will not succeed if the tenant will agree to terms which allow the landlord access to carry out the work which can then be reasonably carried out without obtaining possession and without substantially interfering with the tenant's use.

*Ground (g)  Landlord's intention to occupy the holding for his own business or a residence*

This is also a frequently used ground; again the landlord must have a firm and settled intention. There is, however, an important restriction on the use of this ground. A landlord cannot rely on it if his interest was purchased or created within 5 years before the ending of the current tenancy. The object of this provision is to prevent a landlord buying the reversion cheaply within five years of the end of the lease and then acquiring vacant possession using this ground. It is important to note, however, that the ground will be available to a landlord who buys property with vacant possession, lets it and then seeks possession within 5 years of buying it.

## 38.9  INTERIM RENT

Where a tenant has applied to the court for a new tenancy, his current tenancy will not end on the expiry of the s 25 notice or s 26 request. Instead it will be continued, at the same rent, until 3 months after the conclusion of the proceedings. It is possible, however, for a landlord to apply for an interim rent to apply pending the outcome of the proceedings.

## 38.10  THE TERMS OF THE NEW LEASE

### 38.10.1  The premises

The tenant is only entitled to a tenancy of the 'holding'. This means the property comprised in the current tenancy, but excluding any part not occupied by the tenant, ie those parts which the tenant has sub-let. However, the landlord (but not the tenant) has the right to insist that any new tenancy will be a tenancy of the whole of the originally demised premise, ie including those parts sub-let.

### 38.10.2  Duration

This will be such as is reasonable in the circumstances but cannot exceed 14 years; it will normally be much less, for example 5 or 7 years.

### 38.10.3  The rent

This is the open market rent having regard to the other terms of the tenancy. But in assessing this, the court must disregard:

(1) the fact that the tenant and his predecessors have been in occupation;
(2) any goodwill attached to the holding;

(3) any effect on rent of any improvements voluntarily carried out by the tenant during the tenancy;

(4) in the case of licensed premises, any addition in value due to the tenant's licence.

The court can insert a rent review clause in the lease, even though there was not one in the previous tenancy.

### 38.10.4 Other terms

In the absence of agreement, these will again be fixed by the court, which must have regard to the terms of the current tenancy and all other relevant circumstances. It is likely that the new terms will be much the same as the old. If a party wishes to change the current terms, the case of *City of London Real Property Co Ltd v O'May* [1983] 2 AC 726, establishes that it is for the party wanting a change to justify that change. The change must also be fair and reasonable.

### 38.10.5 Commencement of the new lease

Any new lease ordered by the court will not commence until 3 months after the proceedings are 'finally disposed of'. This is when the time-limit for appeal has elapsed, ie 4 weeks after the order. The new lease will thus commence 3 months and 4 weeks after the order.

If the tenant finds the terms of a new lease ordered by the court unacceptable (eg as to rent), he may apply for the order to be revoked. Note that the landlord has no such right; if he is unhappy with the terms of the new lease, his only remedy is to appeal.

## 38.11 COMPENSATION FOR FAILURE TO OBTAIN A NEW LEASE

### 38.11.1 Availability

If the tenant does not obtain a new lease, he may be entitled to compensation. It is available only in the following circumstances:

(1) where the landlord's s 25 notice or counter-notice to a s 26 request specifies only one or more of grounds (e), (f) and (g); or

(2) where the landlord has specified one or more of grounds (e), (f) or (g) along with other grounds, and the court refuses to grant a new tenancy solely on one or more of grounds (e), (f) or (g), ie the no-fault grounds.

### 38.11.2 Amount

The amount of compensation will be equivalent to the rateable value of the holding, unless the tenant and his predecessors in the same business have been in occupation for at least 14 years, when it will be twice the rateable value.

### 38.11.3 Contracting out

Any agreement restricting or excluding the payment of compensation is void if the tenant or his predecessors in the same business have been in occupation for 5 years or more. This means that contracting out is permissible in circumstances where the tenant has been in occupation for less than 5 years.

## 38.12 PROPOSED CHANGES

The Department of Transport, Local Government and the Regions has published proposals to reform the current system of security of tenure. It is likely that the procedure under the Regulatory Reform Act 2001 will be used so that the proposals could be in force by early 2003. The following is a summary of the main changes proposed.

- Contracting out will be permitted without the need for a court order.
- It is intended that the landlord's s 25 notice will set out key terms (including rent) for any new tenancy. The requirement for tenants to serve a counter-notice will be abolished. The time-limits for applying to the court for a new tenancy will remain, although it will be possible to extend this by agreement.

FORM NUMBER 1

**LT1**

## Landlord's Notice to Terminate Business Tenancy*

(LANDLORD AND TENANT ACT 1954, Section 25)

To                                                            *(name of tenant)*

of                                                        *(address of tenant)*

---

**IMPORTANT** - This notice is intended to bring your tenancy to an end. If you want to continue to occupy your property you must act quickly. Read the notice and all the notes carefully. If you are in any doubt about the action you should take, get advice immediately e.g. from a Solicitor or Surveyor or a Citizens Advice Bureau.

---

1. This notice is given under section 25 of the Landlord and Tenant Act 1954.

2. It relates to *(description of property)*

 

of which you are the tenant.

See notes 1 and 8.

3. I/We give you notice terminating your tenancy on

See notes 2 and 3.

4. Within two months after the giving of this notice, you must notify me/us in writing whether or not you are willing to give up possession of the property comprised in the tenancy on the date stated in paragraph 3.

**The landlord must cross out one version of paragraph 5. If the second version is used the paragraph letter(s) must be filled in.

[5** If you apply to the court under Part II of the Landlord and Tenant Act 1954 for the grant of a new tenancy, I/we will not oppose your application.]

[5** If you apply to the court under Part II of the Landlord and Tenant Act 1954 for the grant of a new tenancy, I/we will oppose it on the grounds mentioned in paragraph(s)           of section 30(1) of the Act.]

See notes 4 and 5.

6. All correspondence about this notice should be sent to †[the landlord] [the landlord's agent] at the address given below.

Date

†Cross out words in square brackets if they do not apply.

Signature of †[landlord] [landlord's agent]

Name of landlord

Address of landlord

†[Address of agent   Your name
                          Your address
                          Postcode

                                                          ]

---

*This form must *not* be used if-
(a) no previous notice terminating the tenancy has been given under section 25 of the Act, and
(b) the tenancy is the tenancy of a house (as defined for the purpose of Part I of the Leasehold Reform Act 1967), and
(c) the tenancy is a long tenancy at a low rent (within the meaning of that Act of 1967), and
(d) the tenant is not a company or other artificial person.
If the above apply, use form number 13 (LT13) instead of this form.

# NOTES

**Termination of tenancy**

1. This notice is intended to bring your tenancy to an end. You can apply to the court for a new tenancy under the Landlord and Tenant Act 1954 by following the procedure outlined in notes 2 and 3 below. If you do your tenancy will continue after the date shown in paragraph 3 of this notice while your claim is being considered. The landlord can ask the court to fix the rent which you will have to pay while the tenancy continues. The terms of any *new* tenancy not agreed between you and the landlord will be settled by the court.

**Claiming a new tenancy**

2. If you want to apply to the court for a new tenancy you must:-

   (1) notify the landlord in writing not later than 2 months after the giving of this notice that you are not willing to give up possession of the property;

   *AND*

   (2) apply to the court, not earlier than 2 months nor later than 4 months after the giving of this notice, for a new tenancy.

3. The time limits in note 2 run from the giving of the notice. The date of the giving of the notice may not be the date written on the notice or the date on which you actually saw it. It may, for instance, be the date on which the notice was delivered through the post to your last address known to the person giving the notice. If there has been any delay in your seeing this notice you may need to act very quickly.
   If you are in any doubt get advice immediately.

---

### WARNING TO TENANT
**If you do not keep to the time limits in Note 2, you will *lose* your right to apply to the court for a new tenancy.**

---

**Landlord's opposition to claim for a new tenancy**

4. If you apply to the court for a new tenancy, the landlord can only oppose your application on one or more of the grounds set out in section 30(1) of the 1954 Act. These grounds are set out below. The paragraph letters are those given in the Act. The landlord can only use a ground if its paragraph letter is shown in paragraph 5 of the notice.

   **Grounds**

   (a) where under the current tenancy the tenant has any obligations as respects the repair and maintenance of the holding, that the tenant ought not to be granted a new tenancy in view of the state of repair of the holding, being a state resulting from the tenant's failure to comply with the said obligations;

   (b) that the tenant ought not to be granted a new tenancy in view of his persistent delay in paying rent which has become due;

   (c) that the tenant ought not to be granted a new tenancy in view of other substantial breaches by him of his obligations under the current tenancy, or for any other reason connected with the tenant's use or management of the holding;

   (d) that the landlord has offered and is willing to provide or secure the provision of alternative accommodation for the tenant, that the terms on which the alternative accommodation is available are reasonable having regard to the terms of the current tenancy and to all other relevant circumstances, and that the accommodation and the time at which it will be available are suitable for the tenant's requirements (including the requirement to preserve goodwill) having regard to the nature and class of his business and to the situation and extent of, and facilities afforded by, the holding;

   (e) where the current tenancy was created by the sub-letting of part only of the property comprised in a superior tenancy and the landlord is the owner of an interest in reversion expectant on the termination of that superior tenancy, that the aggregate of the rents reasonably obtainable on separate lettings of the holding and the remainder of that property would be substantially less than the rent reasonably obtainable on a letting of that property as a whole, that on the termination of the current tenancy the landlord requires possession of the holding for the purposes of letting or otherwise disposing of the said property as a whole, and that in view thereof the tenant ought not to be granted a new tenancy;

   (f) that on the termination of the current tenancy the landlord intends to demolish or reconstruct the premises comprised in the holding or a substantial part of those premises or to carry out substantial work of construction on the holding or part thereof and that he could not reasonably do so without obtaining possession of the holding;

   (If the landlord uses this ground, the court can sometimes still grant a new tenancy if certain conditions set out in section 31A of the Act can be met.)

   (g) that on the termination of the current tenancy the landlord intends to occupy the holding for the purposes, or partly for the purposes, of a business to be carried on by him therein, or as his residence;

   (The landlord must normally have been the landlord for at least five years to use this ground.)

**Compensation**

5. If you cannot get a new tenancy solely because grounds (e), (f) or (g) apply, you are entitled to compensation under the 1954 Act. If your landlord has opposed your application on any of the other grounds as well as (e), (f) or (g) you can only get compensation if the Court's refusal to grant a new tenancy is based solely on grounds (e), (f) or (g). In other words you cannot get compensation under the 1954 Act if the Court has refused your tenancy on *other* grounds even if (e), (f) or (g) also apply.

6. If your landlord is an authority possessing compulsory purchase powers (such as a local authority) you may be entitled to a disturbance payment under Part III of the Land Compensation Act 1973.

**Negotiating a new tenancy**

7. Most leases are renewed by negotiation. If you do try to agree a new tenancy with your landlord, remember -

   (1) that your present tenancy will not be extended after the date in paragraph 3 of this notice unless you *both*

   (a) give written notice that you will not vacate (note 2(1) above); *and*

   (b) apply to the court for a new tenancy (note 2(2) above);

   (2) that you will lose your right to apply to the court if you do not keep to the time limits in note 2.

**Validity of this notice**

8. The landlord who has given this notice may not be the landlord to whom you pay your rent. "Business" is given a wide meaning in the 1954 Act and is used in the same sense in this notice. The 1954 Act also has rules about the date which the landlord can put in paragraph 3. This depends on the terms of your tenancy. If you have any doubts about whether this notice is valid, get immediate advice.

**Explanatory booklet**

9. The Department of the Environment and Welsh Office booklet "Business Leases and Security of Tenure" explains the main provisions of Part II of the 1954 Act. It is available from the Department of the Environment Publications Store, Building No. 3, Victoria Road, South Ruislip, Middlesex.

---

**LT8**

FORM NUMBER 8

## Tenant's Request for New Tenancy of Business Premises

(LANDLORD AND TENANT ACT 1954, Section 26)

To .           *(name of landlord)*

of ,           *(address of landlord)*

> **IMPORTANT - This is a request for a new tenancy of your property or part of it. If you want to oppose this request you must act quickly. Read the request and all the notes carefully. If you are in any doubt about the action you should take, get advice immediately e.g. from a Solicitor or Surveyor or a Citizens Advice Bureau.**

1. This request is made under section 26 of the Landlord and Tenant Act 1954.

2. You are the landlord of *(description of property)*

3. I/We request you to grant a new tenancy beginning on

4. I/We propose that:

  *(a)* the property comprised in the new tenancy should be

  *(b)* the rent payable under the new tenancy should be

  *(c)* the other terms of the new tenancy should be

†Cross out words in square brackets if they do not apply.

5. All correspondence about this request should be sent to †[the tenant] [the tenant's agent] at the address given below.

Date

Signature of †[tenant] [tenant's agent]

Name of tenant

Address of tenant

†[Address of agent

]

# NOTES

**Request for a new tenancy**

1. This request by your tenant for a new tenancy brings his current tenancy to an end on the day before the date mentioned in paragraph 3 above. He can apply to the court under the Landlord and Tenant Act 1954 for a new tenancy. If he does, his current tenancy will continue after the date mentioned in paragraph 3 of this request while his application is being considered by the court. You can ask the court to fix the rent which your tenant will have to pay whilst his tenancy continues. The terms of any *new* tenancy not agreed between you and your tenant will be settled by the court.

**Opposing a request for a new tenancy**

2. If you do not want to grant a new tenancy, you *must* within two months of the making of this request, give your tenant notice saying that you will oppose any application he makes to the court for a new tenancy. You do not need a special form to do this, but you must state on which of the grounds set out in the 1954 Act you will oppose the application - see note 4.

3. The time limit in note 2 runs from the making of this request. The date of the making of the request may not be the date written on the request or the date on which you actually saw it. It may, for instance, be the date on which the request was delivered through the post to your last address known to the person giving the request. If there has been any delay in your seeing this request you may need to act very quickly. If you are in any doubt get advice immediately.

---

**WARNING TO LANDLORD**

**If you do not keep to the time limit in Note 2, you will *lose* your right to oppose your tenant's application to the court for a new tenancy if he makes one.**

---

**Grounds for opposing an application**

4. If your tenant applies to the court for a new tenancy, you can only oppose the application on one or more of the grounds set out in section 30(1) of the 1954 Act. These grounds are set out below. The paragraph letters are those given in the Act.

**Grounds**

(a) where under the current tenancy the tenant has any obligations as respects the repair and maintenance of the holding, that the tenant ought not to be granted a new tenancy in view of the state of repair of the holding, being a state resulting from the tenant's failure to comply with the said obligations;

(b) that the tenant ought not to be granted a new tenancy in view of his persistent delay in paying rent which has become due;

(c) that the tenant ought not to be granted a new tenancy in view of other substantial breaches by him of his obligations under the current tenancy, or for any other reason connected with the tenant's use or management of the holding;

(d) that you have offered and are willing to provide or secure the provision of alternative accommodation for the tenant, that the terms on which the alternative accommodation is available are reasonable having regard to the terms of the current tenancy and to all other relevant circumstances, and that the accommodation and the time at which it will be available are suitable for the tenant's requirements (including the requirement to preserve goodwill) having regard to the nature and class of his business and to the situation and extent of, and facilities afforded by, the holding;

(e) where the current tenancy was created by the sub-letting of part only of the property comprised in a superior tenancy and you are the owner of an interest in reversion expectant on the termination of that superior tenancy, that the aggregate of the rents reasonably obtainable on separate lettings of the holding and the remainder of that property would be substantially less than the rent reasonably obtainable on a letting of that property as a whole, that on the termination of the current tenancy you require possession of the holding for the purposes of letting or otherwise disposing of the said property as a whole, and that in view thereof the tenant ought not to be granted a new tenancy;

(f) that on the termination of the current tenancy you intend to demolish or reconstruct the premises comprised in the holding or a substantial part of those premises or to carry out substantial work of construction on the holding or part thereof and that you could not reasonably do so without obtaining possession of the holding;

(If you use this ground, the court can sometimes still grant a new tenancy if certain conditions set out in section 31A of the Act can be met.)

(g) that on the termination of the current tenancy you intend to occupy the holding for the purposes, or partly for the purposes, of a business to be carried on by you therein, or as your residence.

(You must normally have been the landlord for at least five years to use this ground.)

You can only use one or more of the above grounds if you have stated them in the notice referred to in note 2 above.

**Compensation**

5. If your tenant cannot get a new tenancy solely because grounds (e), (f) or (g) apply, he is entitled to compensation from you under the 1954 Act. If you have opposed his application on any of the other grounds as well as (e), (f) or (g) he can only get compensation if the court's refusal to grant a new tenancy is based solely on grounds (e), (f) or (g). In other words he cannot get compensation under the 1954 Act if the court has refused his tenancy on *other* grounds even if (e), (f) or (g) also apply.

6. If you are an authority possessing compulsory purchase powers (such as a local authority) you will be aware that your tenant may be entitled to a disturbance payment under Part III of the Land Compensation Act 1973.

**Negotiating a new tenancy**

7. Most leases are renewed by negotiation. If you do try to agree a new tenancy with your tenant-

(1) YOU should remember that you will not be able to oppose an application to the court for a new tenancy unless you give the notice mentioned in note 2 above within the time limit in that note;

(2) YOUR TENANT should remember that he will lose his right to apply to the court for a new tenancy unless he makes the application not less than two nor more than four months after the making of this request.

**Validity of this notice**

8. The landlord to whom this request is made may not be the landlord to whom the tenant pays the rent. "Business" is given a wide meaning in the 1954 Act and is used in the same sense in this request. The 1954 Act also has rules about the date which the tenant can put in paragraph 3. This depends on the terms of the tenancy. If you have any doubts about whether this request is valid, get immediate advice.

**Explanatory booklet**

9. The Department of the Environment and Welsh Office booklet "Business Leases and Security of Tenure" explains the main provisions of Part II of the 1954 Act. It is available from the Department of the Environment Publications Store, Building No. 3, Victoria Road, South Ruislip, Middlesex.

# Chapter 39

# THE RIGHTS OF RESIDENTIAL OCCUPIERS

## 39.1 INTRODUCTION

One major problem for a developer (or, indeed, any other buyer) of the reversion to property let for residential purposes is ascertaining what, if any, security of tenure and other rights the residential tenant may have. The developer will be bound by these rights and they may prevent him from putting the property to the use which he intended.

The law in this area is both extensive and complicated, the pitfalls many and deep, and the consequences for a buyer (and his legal adviser) very serious. A property lawyer needs to be alert to the problems so that, in appropriate circumstances, he knows to research further into the applicable law. The object of this chapter, therefore, is to provide an outline of the different rights which the occupier may have; it does not purport to provide a comprehensive statement of those rights.

## 39.2 WHAT KIND OF RIGHTS MAY A RESIDENTIAL TENANT HAVE?

The kind of rights that a buyer might find himself subject to can be summarised as follows:

(1) security of tenure, ie a right to remain in occupation even though the contractual tenancy may have ended;
(2) a right not to be evicted without a court order;
(3) a right compulsorily to acquire the freehold reversion (ie without the landlord's consent);
(4) a right to take an extended lease (again without the landlord's consent);
(5) a right to have the contractually agreed rent reduced;
(6) a right of first refusal, ie if the landlord wishes to make a disposal of the reversion, a right to compel the landlord to dispose of it to the tenants on the same terms;
(7) a right to have certain parts of the property kept in repair by the landlord, notwithstanding the terms of the tenancy agreement.

You should note that not all tenants will have *all* of these rights; most will have some of them, a few may have none at all.

## 39.3 WHY IS THE LAW SO COMPLICATED?

The protections given to tenants have generally tended to be granted piecemeal over the years as different problems have come to light. Often, legislation has been enacted to deal with a particular problem without any real thought as to how that particular piece of legislation fitted in with earlier legislation or the common law.

Further, social and political attitudes have changed over the years. This has resulted in some rights (particularly security of tenure) changing according to the political complexion of the government of the day. Usually, however, when any such changes are made, people with existing tenancies keep their existing protections; the changes only affecting tenancies granted after a specified date. So both old and new laws continue to be relevant.

## 39.4 HOW DO I DECIDE WHICH TENANTS HAVE WHICH RIGHTS?

Although there are some rights which nearly all tenants will have, the existence of most rights depends upon the type of lease which the tenant has. Before you can advise as to these rights, you will need to obtain a copy of the lease. In particular, you will then need to find out the following:

(1)  the date of the grant of the lease;
(2)  the length of the lease;
(3)  the rent payable under the lease, both currently and at its commencement.

All of these factors are relevant in ascertaining the various rights which the tenant may have. Each of the various protections available to tenants has its own list of qualifying conditions, each of which must be tested against the particular lease with which you are dealing.

However, the protections given can be very broadly broken down into three categories:

Category 1: Rights given to most residential tenants, no matter what type of lease they have. These will include protection against harassment and eviction without a court order.

Category 2: Protections given to tenants of long leases who have bought their house or flat (usually by paying a lump sum 'premium' at the start of the lease) and are just paying a 'ground rent', ie a comparatively small amount just for the use of the land on which the property is built. You should note, however, that this ground rent may well be more than a nominal amount; it could amount to several hundred pounds a year. The protections given may include rights to have a new lease and to buy the freehold. These are in addition to the rights in Category 1.

Category 3: Those rights given to tenants with short-term leases who are paying the full open market rent for the use of the accommodation. These may include security of tenure, the right to have the rent reduced, and repairs. Again, these are additional to the Category 1 rights.

Note that these three categories have no legal significance and are designated purely for explanatory purposes. There are, of course, exceptions. Some tenants with long leases may be paying a full occupation rent; equally some short-term tenants may only be paying a ground rent. In such cases as these, the qualifying conditions of the various statutory protections will need to be carefully studied to ascertain the tenant's rights.

## 39.5 IS IT A LONG LEASE?

The length of the lease is a relevant factor in much, but not all, of the legislation.

The basic dividing line between long and short leases is 21 years. If the lease exceeds 21 years in length, it will normally qualify as a long lease within Category 2; if it is for 21 years or less it will normally be within Category 3.

You should note that when assessing the length of a lease, the deciding factor is the length of the lease when it was originally granted, *not* the length of the lease which remains unexpired. So a lease which has only 3 years left to run until its expiry date will still be a long lease if, when it was originally granted, it was granted for a term of more than 21 years.

## 39.6 CATEGORY 1: RIGHTS GIVEN TO NEARLY ALL RESIDENTIAL TENANTS

### 39.6.1 Protection from Eviction Act 1977

#### *Unlawful eviction*

The right not to be evicted without a court order is given to virtually all residential occupiers by s 1 of the Protection from Eviction Act 1977 (PEA 1977). Unlawful eviction is a criminal offence under this Act and anyone so evicted has a right in civil proceedings to seek an injunction to restore them to occupation. Damages would also be payable.

There are various exceptions to this rule. Eviction will not be unlawful if the tenant and the landlord share living accommodation or in the case of a letting for holiday purposes. It is also a defence for a landlord to establish that he reasonably believed that the tenant no longer lived in the premises.

#### *Harassment*

It is also a criminal offence to harass a tenant if the landlord knows (or has reasonable cause to believe) that the conduct is likely to cause the tenant to leave the premises (PEA 1977, s 1(3A)).

Civil damages will also be available. Exemplary and/or aggravated damages may well be relevant in cases of harassment. If the harassment actually causes the tenant to leave, then substantial damages may be awarded under s 27 of the Housing Act 1988. These will represent the difference between the value of the property to the landlord with the tenant in occupation and the value with vacant possession, ie the damages represent the gain to the landlord rather than the loss to the tenant.

### 39.6.2 Criminal Law Act 1977

#### *Use of violence to obtain entry*

In addition to the prohibitions laid down by the PEA 1977, it is a separate offence under s 6(1) of the Criminal Law Act 1977 to use or threaten violence to secure entry to property if there is someone on the premises who is opposed to that entry.

## 39.7 CATEGORY 2: RIGHTS MAINLY GIVEN TO TENANTS WITH LONG LEASES

### 39.7.1 Landlord and Tenant Act 1987, Part I

*The right of first refusal*

Tenants of flats with long leases at low rents have a collective right to 'take over' any proposed disposal of the reversion by the landlord. This right is given by Part I of the Landlord and Tenant Act 1987.

Exceptionally, the right is also given to statutory and protected tenants under the Rent Act 1977 even though they may not have long leases at low rents.

Prior to making a disposal, a landlord must give the tenants 2 months' notice. This takes effect as an offer to dispose to them on the same terms. This offer can then be accepted by at least 50% of the qualifying tenants.

Criminal sanctions are imposed if the landlord makes a disposition in breach of these requirements. Such a disposition would be valid to pass the legal estate, but the buyer has to notify the tenants of their rights to acquire from him on the same terms as he obtained the property. This is again backed up by criminal sanctions.

### 39.7.2 Leasehold Reform, Housing and Urban Development Act 1993

*Enfranchisement, the right to buy the freehold*

Under the Leasehold Reform, Housing and Urban Development Act 1993 (LRHUDA 1993), tenants with long leases of flats at a low rent have a collective right to compel the landlord to sell the freehold to them. This is so whether or not the landlord intends to make a disposal (cf Landlord and Tenant Act 1987, Part I).

The definition of low rent is complicated, depending upon when the lease was granted. However, if the lease was granted for a 'particularly long term', ie exceeding 35 years, the tenant will be a qualifying tenant whatever the amount of the rent.

At least two-thirds of the tenants in the block must be qualifying tenants and at least two-thirds of those must join in the purchase. So, like the right of first refusal, this is not a right which can be exercised by individual tenants. At least half of the tenants joining in the enfranchisement must have resided in the flat as their only or main home for the previous 12 months.

*The right to an extended lease*

The LRHUDA 1993 also gives qualifying tenants a right to seek a 90-year extension to their lease. This is an *individual* right which can be exercised by a tenant on his or her own without the consent or co-operation of the other tenants in the block. The tenant, however, must have occupied the flat as his only or main home for the previous 3 years.

*Commonhold and Leasehold Reform Act 2002*

When brought into force, this Act will bring about major changes to the qualifying conditions for both enfranchisement and for obtaining an extended lease. The residence requirement and the need for a low rent will be abolished. Further, only 50% of the qualifying tenants in a block need join in the enfranchisement.

### 39.7.3 Landlord and Tenant Act 1954, Part I

*Security of tenure*

You will normally think of security as only being relevant to short-term tenants (see below) but thought also has to be given as to what will be the position of the tenant under a long lease when that comes to an end. A lease for 99 years seems to cause no worries about what will happen when it ends – unless it was granted (say) in the year 1910!

Perhaps the main reason for the abundance of legislation relating to long leases in recent years is that they rapidly become unsaleable (and unmortgageable) as they near their termination date. Many such long leases will thus never actually terminate because the tenants will buy the freehold or will take an extended lease to put off the evil hour of termination for another 90 years. But protection is also given to those tenants who do not (or are unable to afford to) take advantage of such rights.

Protection is given by Part I of the Landlord and Tenant Act 1954 (as amended). At the end of the tenancy, the tenant is allowed to remain in occupation as an assured tenant under the Housing Act 1988 (see **39.8.2**). He will thus have security of tenure, but will have to pay the full market rent for the house, rather than just a ground rent.

### 39.7.4 Leasehold Reform Act 1967

This Act gives tenants of long leases of houses (but not flats) the right to acquire the freehold or to take a 50-year extension of their lease, provided they have occupied the house as their only or main residence for the previous 3 years.

Basically, there must be a long lease (over 21 years) at a low rent. The definition of low rent is complex and depends upon when the lease was granted. However, in the case of leases exceeding 35 years, there is no need for a low rent. When the Commonhold and Leasehold Reform Act 2002 is brought into force the low rent and residence requirements will be abolished.

### 39.7.5 Protections in relation to service charges

Tenants with long leases of flats who pay a service charge often experience problems. They frequently complain that the amounts demanded by way of service charge are excessive, or that the services are not provided to an acceptable standard, or both. There are various statutory protections for tenants, amongst which are the following.

*Restriction on forfeiture for non-payment of service charge (Housing Act 1996, ss 81–82)*

A landlord cannot forfeit for failure to pay a service charge unless the amount of the charge has been agreed to by the tenant or determined by the court or by arbitration.

*Summary of costs incurred*

Under the Landlord and Tenant Act 1985, a tenant is entitled to a summary of the costs incurred by the landlord. If there are more than four flats in the block, this summary must be certified by a qualified accountant.

### Management audit

Under LRHUDA 1993, ss 76–84, tenants can appoint an accountant or a surveyor to conduct a management audit in relation to the provision of services. This will enable the tenant to check whether the landlord is discharging his management obligations effectively and efficiently; and whether the service charge is being applied in an efficient and effective manner.

### Right to appoint surveyor as advisor

Under the Housing Act 1996 (HA 1996), s 84, a recognised tenants' association may appoint a surveyor to advise it about any matters relating to the payment of a service charge. The surveyor is given extensive rights to inspect the property and of access to documents in the landlord's control to enable him to advise on service charge matters.

### Restrictions on the landlord's right to recover costs

By the Landlord and Tenant Act 1985, ss 18–30, costs can only be recovered to the extent that they are reasonably incurred, and where they are incurred in the provision of services or the carrying out of works, only if those services or works are of a reasonable standard.

### Determination of reasonableness of service charges

Either landlord or tenant can apply to the Leasehold Valuation Tribunal for a determination as to whether costs incurred were incurred reasonably, whether services were to a reasonable standard and as to whether the insurance provided or premiums payable are reasonable.

### Estimates and consultation

Where costs are to be incurred on works above the limit specified in Landlord and Tenant Act 1985, s 20(3), the landlord must obtain at least two estimates for the work and submit these to the tenants and have regard to their observations on them. The financial limit is found in the Service Charge (Estimates and Consultation) Order 1988, SI 1988/1285. It is currently £50 × the number of flats in the building, or £1,000, whichever is the greater.

### Appointment of a manager or compulsory acquisition of the freehold

In cases of extreme bad management, the tenants can apply to the Leasehold Valuation Tribunal for a manager to be appointed to run the block and even for the freehold to be acquired by them. These rights are given by the Landlord and Tenant Act 1987.

### Commonhold and Leasehold Reform Act 2002

When this is brought into force it will greatly extend the protections given in relation to service charges. Tenants of flats will have to be provided with a summary of the service charge costs without request. Tenants will also have the right to manage the block as of right without proof of fault on the landlord's part and without any payment.

## 39.8  CATEGORY 3: RIGHTS MAINLY GIVEN TO SHORT-TERM TENANTS

### 39.8.1  Rent Act 1977

*Security of tenure*

This Act primarily protects tenants of dwelling-houses let by private landlords, ie not local authorities, whose tenancies were granted before 15 January 1989. (However, a tenancy granted on or after that date to an existing Rent Act tenant by the person who is then the landlord will, exceptionally, still be within the 1977 Act.)

Tenants are only protected if the rent payable is more than two-thirds of the rateable value of the property.

Security is given to tenants no matter what the length of the lease, but only if and so long as the tenant occupies the property as a home. At the end of a contractual tenancy the tenant can remain in possession as a 'statutory tenant'. The landlord will then only be able to obtain possession if he can prove one of the various grounds. Many of these are based on the tenant's default, eg non-payment of rent.

*Rent control*

Both during a contractual tenancy or a statutory tenancy, the agreed rent can be overridden by the tenant making an application for a 'fair rent'. The application is made to the rent officer (employed by the local authority) who must fix a rent according to a formula laid down by the Act. This is basically the open market rent, but reduced to remove the effects of scarcity.

*Right of first refusal*

Exceptionally, this right is also given to statutory and protected tenants under the Rent Act 1977 even though they do not have long leases at low rents. See Category 2 (**39.7**) for more details of this right.

### 39.8.2  Housing Act 1988 (as amended)

*Security of tenure*

This Act applies to lettings of dwelling-houses by private landlords on or after 15 January 1989 (except those to existing Rent Act tenants by their present landlord). It introduces two types of tenancy: the assured tenancy (sometimes referred to as an 'ordinary' assured tenancy), and the assured shorthold tenancy, which is often just referred to as a 'shorthold'.

*Assured tenancies*

These offer wide-ranging security of tenure, much the same as under the Rent Act 1977. So, a landlord cannot obtain possession unless he can prove a ground for possession, even though the contractual tenancy has ended. This Act only applies, however, if and so long as the tenant occupies the property as his only or main home. There are various other conditions which must be fulfilled, for example the rent must be over £250 per year (£1,000 in Greater London), but not exceeding £25,000 per year.

### *Assured shorthold tenancies*

This is a type of assured tenancy, but offering a tenant no security of tenure; the landlord is guaranteed possession. However, the landlord does need to give the tenant 2 months' notice before possession can be obtained.

For lettings entered into before 28 February 1997, a landlord could create a shorthold only if the letting complied with the following conditions:

(i)    the letting was preceded by the landlord giving the tenant a warning notice in the prescribed form;

(ii)   the letting was for a fixed term (ie not periodic);

(iii)  the letting was for a minimum of 6 months; and

(iv)   the letting contained no power for the landlord to bring it to an end during the first 6 months. However, a normal forfeiture clause would not fall foul of this requirement.

For lettings on or after 28 February 1997, all lettings otherwise within the Act are shortholds (ie there is no need to comply with any of the above provisions) unless the landlord serves a notice stating that the letting is not to be a shorthold. Lettings after that date to existing ordinary assured tenants by their then landlord will, however, remain ordinary assured tenancies unless the tenant serves a notice stating that he wants the new letting to be a shorthold.

### *Rent control*

There are no restrictions on the amount of the rent which a landlord can charge for an ordinary assured tenancy. The rent will be governed entirely by the terms of the agreement between the parties. However, if, in the case of a periodic tenancy, the agreement makes no provision for the landlord to increase the rent, the landlord can only increase the rent if he follows the correct statutory procedure.

There is a limited degree of rent control in relation to shortholds. If the tenant considers the rent to be excessive he can refer it to the Rent Assessment Committee.

For tenancies entered into on or after 28 February 1997, the tenant can only refer the rent to the Rent Assessment Committee during the first 6 months of the letting.

## 39.8.3  Landlord and Tenant Act 1985

### *Repairs*

By ss 11–14 of the Landlord and Tenant Act 1985, repairing obligations are imposed on landlords of certain short leases. The provisions apply to any lease of a dwelling house granted on or after 24 October 1961 provided that the term is for less than 7 years. Periodic tenancies will be within the Act, even though they may have subsisted for longer than 7 years.

In such leases there is an implied covenant by the landlord to repair the structure and exterior of the dwelling and to keep in repair and proper working order the installations in the dwelling for the supply of water, gas, electricity, sanitation and for space and water heating.

These obligations can be contracted out of only with the consent of the court.

**Part VIII**

# SALES OF PART AND NEW PROPERTIES

# Chapter 40

# SALES OF PART

## 40.1 INTRODUCTION

A sale of part is a more complex transaction than the sale of the whole of the seller's interest in a particular piece of land, and some matters additional to those relevant to a sale of whole must be considered. This chapter deals only with those matters which are exclusive to sales of part. Reference should also be made to Chapter 14, which deals with drafting the contract.

## 40.2 DESCRIBING THE LAND

The description of the land in the seller's existing land or charge certificate (or title deeds) must be adapted to provide a new, accurate description of the property which is being sold. It will be necessary to describe the land in the particulars of sale of the contract by reference to a plan which shows clearly the extent of the land being sold and, where relevant, the extent of the land being retained in the seller's ownership. If the plan is not drawn to scale, the measurements of the land should be set out in the verbal description contained in the particulars of sale. For more details on the use of plans, see **14.5.1**.

### 40.2.1 Retained land

It will usually be necessary to refer to the land which is to remain in the ownership of the seller after the sale (eg in relation to easements and reservations). Such land must, therefore, be defined verbally in the contract and marked clearly on the plan attached to the contract. The Standard Conditions of Sale contain no adequate definition of retained land.

### 40.2.2 Form 102 certificate

Where the sale comprises a plot on a building estate, the whole of which is registered at HM Land Registry, the seller will frequently have deposited a site plan at HM Land Registry and the office copies which are issued will give a certificate in Form 102 in lieu of a filed plan. This certificate states that the plot lies within the boundaries of the site plan deposited at the Registry but does not specifically identify the plot. It will also indicate whether any of the matters referred to in the charges register (eg easements or covenants) affect that particular plot.

## 40.3 GRANTS AND RESERVATIONS OF EASEMENTS

On a sale of part of land, the Law of Property Act 1925, s 62 and the rule in *Wheeldon v Burrows* (1879) 12 Ch D 31 may give the buyer certain rights over the land retained by the seller for the benefit of the part sold. Section 62 of the Law of Property Act 1925 may operate to create easements over retained land where, at the time of sale, the two tenements are in separate occupation. Further, the rule in *Wheeldon v Burrows* will impliedly grant to the buyer as easements all rights which are continuous and apparent and reasonably necessary to the enjoyment of the property sold, and actually in use by the seller at the time of the sale. So if, at the time of the sale, a drain from the land being sold passes through the retained land, the right to use this drain will be impliedly granted to the buyer as a legal easement. However, rights that do not already exist cannot be implied under *Wheeldon v Burrows*. So if the land being sold did not already have the benefit of the drain at the time of sale, a right to lay one would not be implied.

So, the rule in *Wheeldon v Burrows* will frequently not give the buyer all the easements he needs. On the other hand, it may inadvertently give a buyer more than the seller intends to grant. It is, therefore, considered preferable to exclude the implied grant rules by a special condition in the contract. Such a condition might be worded as follows:

> **The transfer will contain a declaration that it will only operate to grant those easements expressly referred to and will not operate or be construed to imply the grant of any other easement.**

The question of easements is then dealt with by express conditions in the contract granting specific easements tailored to suit the particular circumstances of the case. In such a case, the buyer should check very carefully to ensure that the property being bought will acquire all the easements necessary for its full use and enjoyment. The following may be relevant, depending upon the circumstances:

- a right of way to gain access to the property. Ensure that this is at all times, for all purposes and allows access both on foot and by motor vehicles;
- a right for the usual services to reach the property – drains, water, gas, electricity, telephone, etc;
- a right of access to maintain all these;
- a right of light;
- a right of support. Although there is a natural right for a piece of land to be supported by neighbouring land, there is no such right for the land to be supported where it has the extra weight of a building on it. This must be expressly granted. Although a right of support will normally be implied between terraced and semi-detached houses, if the implied grant rules are excluded, these will also need expressly granting.

If any rights are to be shared by the buyer and seller, for example use of drains or driveway, a covenant to maintain or contribute to the maintenance costs should also be imposed.

Remember that the seller can grant easements only over his own land; if the services, access, etc, is over someone else's land, the seller must either be passing on the benefit of rights already granted to him or will have to negotiate with the owner of the land for a new deed of grant.

On the sale of, for example, a building plot, it is likely that the drains, etc will not be in existence at the time of the sale so that the easements for laying and using them will arise in the future. So you will be granting a future interest in land which will need to comply with the rule against perpetuities. This basically requires the new easement to come into existence within the perpetuity period of 21 years, so it is often not a problem where the building work, etc is going to be carried out within a much shorter time scale. However, it is thought safest to take advantage of the ability to specify expressly a longer perpetuity period and specify a period of 80 years within which the rights can arise.

Where easements are being granted (or reserved in favour of the seller), the exact route of the right of way/drain, etc will need indicating clearly on the plan.

### 40.3.1 Reservations for the seller

Section 62 of the Law of Property Act 1925 and the rule in *Wheeldon v Burrows* operate only in the buyer's favour. There is no reciprocal section or case which entitles the seller to easements over the land being sold off (other than easements of necessity). For this reason it is important to consider what rights the seller will need to exercise over the land being sold (eg passage of pipelines, drainage etc) and to reserve these expressly in the contract.

### 40.3.2 Rights of light and air

Rights of light and air may pass to the buyer under either s 62 of the Law of Property Act 1925 or the rule in *Wheeldon v Burrows*. If the buyer were to acquire rights of light and air, this might enable him at some future time to frustrate the seller's plans to build close to the boundary of the two properties. Thus the gain of rights of light and air by the buyer may be balanced by a consequent loss of amenity value to the seller's land. As the existence and extent of these rights may be difficult to ascertain, since they are not visible to the eye, it is usually considered necessary to exclude the buyer's right to easements of light and air by an express condition in the contract which provides for the insertion of a provision to this effect in the purchase deed. Condition 3.4.2 of both sets of Standard Conditions contains a provision to this effect, although many solicitors prefer to state it expressly as a special condition. The specimen clause given in **40.3** would exclude rights of light and air along with all other impliedly granted easements. If all implied grants are not to be excluded, then a condition in the following terms should be used:

> **There is not included in the sale any easement of light or air which would or might interfere with or restrict the free use of the retained land for building or any other purpose. The transfer to the buyer must expressly exclude those rights.**

### 40.3.3 Fall-back provisions

Standard Condition 3.4.2 provides for the exclusion of rights of light and air and for the mutual grant of easements and reservations on a sale of part, but the rights given by this condition are limited and imprecise and will in most cases be inadequate to deal effectively with the parties' needs on a sale of part of land. This condition should therefore be regarded as a fall-back provision, to be used only in a case where the contract has omitted to deal expressly with these matters.

## 40.4 IMPOSITION OF NEW COVENANTS

On a sale of part, the seller will frequently wish to impose new covenants on the buyer for the protection of the retained land. All such new covenants will need to be stated expressly in the contract; none will be implied. The seller should consider imposing some or all of the following, depending upon the circumstances of the case:

- restrictions on use, for example use as a single private dwelling house in the occupation of one family only;
- restrictions on building, for example no building without seller's consent; or seller to approve plans; or no building within (say) 10 metres of the boundary line;
- not to cause nuisance or annoyance to seller and neighbouring owners;
- to erect and maintain boundary fence/wall; the materials, height, time-limit for building, etc, must be specified;
- to contribute to the maintenance of shared facilities; for example drains, rights of way.

In the case of restrictive covenants (all of the above except the fencing covenant), care should be taken in the drafting to ensure that both the benefit and the burden will run to future owners of the land. The condition in the contract should state that the covenants, when entered into in the transfer, will be 'given for every part of the Retained Land and that it is intended that the burden of the covenants will run with every part of the Property'.

The seller should be reminded that positive covenants will not be enforceable against the buyer's successors in title.

When acting for a buyer, you should ensure that the covenants being imposed are not too onerous.

## 40.5 CONSENT OF SELLER'S LENDER

Where the land to be sold consists of part of the land which is mortgaged to the seller's lender, the seller must obtain his lender's consent to the sale at the earliest possible opportunity. The lender should be asked whether the repayment of the whole or any part of the mortgage is required out of the proceeds of the sale of part, and if part, how much. Arrangements must be made for the lender to release the land being sold from the mortgage at or before completion. In registered land, the release will be effected by Form DS3 (accompanied by a plan to show the extent of the land being released). In unregistered land, the lender will either give a deed of release or he may prefer to be joined as a party to the conveyance in order both to release the land being sold and to give a receipt for the money being paid to him.

## 40.6 THE PURCHASE DEED

This must be in Land Registry Form TP1. This is similar to Form TR1, used for a transfer of whole, but contains space for the new easements and covenants that may be required on a sale of part. All of the clauses referred to in **27.11** will be relevant to a sale of part, but the following will also be required either in addition to or in substitution for the above.

### 40.6.1 Title number

The seller's existing title number is inserted in the document. A new title number for the part being sold will be allocated by HM Land Registry on registration of the transaction.

### 40.6.2 Description of land to be sold

A clear description of the land being sold must be included with reference to the plan annexed to the transfer. The land retained by the seller should be expressly defined and identified on the plan. The land should be described as 'part of title number LM12037' (or as appropriate). The description of the land given in the contract may be adequate for these purposes.

### 40.6.3 Easements and reservations

Where the contract made provision for the grant of easements to the buyer or reservations in favour of the seller, these contractual provisions must be implemented by insertion expressly into the transfer. The contract will usually provide for the exclusion of the implied grant of easements. A declaration to this effect must be inserted in the transfer to activate this requirement.

### 40.6.4 New restrictive covenants

New restrictive covenants are frequently imposed in a contract for the sale of part of land, and these must be expressly set out in the transfer. Except where the land forms part of a building scheme, covenants are enforceable against subsequent owners of the land sold only if they are for the benefit of land retained by the seller and the burden of them is annexed to the land sold. Express words should be included to give effect to these principles. Frequently, a short reference only to easements, covenants, etc is made in the body of the deed, the detail of such matters being set out in numbered schedules at the end of the document.

### 40.6.5 Schedules

Schedules should appear after the main body of the deed, but above the attestation clauses, to ensure that they are incorporated as part of the signed document and that there cannot be any argument about them having been added to it at a later stage.

### 40.6.6 Building estates

Where the land being sold forms a plot on a building estate, the draft purchase deed will often be prepared by the seller and attached to the draft contract so that in this situation the buyer has no discretion over its form or contents (see Chapter 41).

## 40.7 COMPLETION AND POST-COMPLETION

### 40.7.1 Unregistered land

Where the land is presently unregistered, the seller will not be handing over his title deeds to the buyer on completion. The buyer should therefore verify his abstract or epitome against the original deeds and mark his abstract or epitome as examined against the original. Where the Protocol is used, the seller is required to mark the abstract as examined against the original title deeds before sending it to the buyer. Even where the title to the land bought is to be registered, this procedure is necessary so that immediately after completion the buyer can produce proper evidence of the title to HM Land Registry with his application for first registration.

A note of any restrictive covenants imposed by the conveyance to the buyer (or a copy of that conveyance) should be retained by the seller, otherwise he will not have any evidence of those covenants when he comes to sell his own land at a later stage. New restrictive covenants will automatically be entered on the register of the new title on first registration.

## 40.7.2  Registered land

Where the seller's title is already registered, it is not necessary to provide for an acknowledgment for production of the deeds, because the buyer will obtain his own title number on registration of the sale of part. New restrictive covenants imposed by the transfer of part will automatically be entered on the charges register of the new title on registration.

Since no entry (except a caution) can generally be made against the seller's title without his consent (including removing part of his land from the register), it is necessary under the Land Registration Act 1925, s 64(1) for him to lodge his Land Certificate at HM Land Registry to await the buyer's incoming application for registration. The seller should deposit his certificate prior to completion, accompanied by Form DP1, and state the reason for the deposit (ie the sale of part). On receipt of the certificate, the Land Registry will issue the seller with a deposit number. This number should be communicated to the buyer, who will refer to it on his application for registration.

Application for the registration of the dealing on Form AP1 accompanied by such of the documents listed in **31.8.2** as are relevant to the transaction must be made within the 30 working days protection period given by the pre-completion search. Where the transfer imposes fresh restrictive covenants, a certified copy of it must also be supplied.

**Chapter 41**

# NEW PROPERTIES

## 41.1 INTRODUCTION

The sale of a new property is a more complex transaction than the sale of an existing house or building, and some matters additional to those relevant to a sale of an existing house or building must be considered. This chapter contains a summary of the matters which are exclusive to new and recently built properties.

The main characteristics of this type of transaction which make it different from an ordinary sale and purchase are:

(1) it is a sale/purchase of a 'new property', ie a house or flat being constructed by the seller;

(2) it is a 'sale of part'. The developer usually owns the whole site and is disposing of it in the form of housing plots (or, in the case of a flat development, the developer owns the whole of the block and is disposing of the flats individually);

(3) as the developer is disposing of a number of properties, he may adopt a slightly different conveyancing procedure from that normally encountered. All the usual steps will be taken, but not always by the same person as in a normal transaction and sometimes in a different order. The developer adopts this different system for his own convenience (and to save expense) in dealing with a large number of sales simultaneously.

Note that, although this chapter relates to 'new properties', you should bear the points dealt with in mind not just when buying directly from the developer, but also when buying 'second hand', ie buying a recently constructed house or flat.

## 41.2 NEW PROPERTY

### 41.2.1 Planning permission

Check whether planning permission has been granted. In particular, check whether any attached conditions have been or will be complied with. Bear in mind that the enforcement period for building works in breach of planning control is 4 years, so planning matters must be checked in the case of any purchase of a house or flat within 4 years of its construction. For details of planning control, see Chapter 5.

### 41.2.2 Building regulations consent

Check that building regulations consent was granted.

The Building Regulations control the methods and materials to be used in the construction of a property to ensure that proper standards are maintained in all new properties. Thus, although enforcement proceedings for breach can only be brought within 12 months, the lack of building regulations consent in a recently constructed property may suggest that it may not have been constructed to the proper standards and that it may be sensible to advise the client to point this out to his surveyor in order that a proper check on the structure of the property is made.

### 41.2.3 Structural guarantee

Some form of structural guarantee should be offered. Without this a buyer will not be in a position to secure a mortgage. If any structural defects develop after purchase, the buyer may not be able to obtain compensation from the developer as he may no longer be in business; building companies have a very high failure rate. A structural guarantee from an independent third party is thus essential and will inevitably be a condition of any mortgage offer in relation to a new or recently constructed house or flat.

The NHBC 'Buildmark' scheme provides a two-part guarantee. The developer agrees to be responsible to remedy all defects which occur within 2 years of purchase. In the case of default, the NHBC will itself step in. Similarly, if the developer becomes insolvent before completion of the house, the NHBC will make good any loss to a buyer, for example in respect of the deposit.

After the first 2 years, the NHBC provides an insurance-style guarantee that it will rectify specified structural defects arising in the house during the next 8 years. Structural defects are defined to exclude, for example, defective plasterwork or decorations. There is thus a 10-year guarantee offered. When buying a house (or flat) constructed within the previous 10 years, ensure that the property is covered by such a guarantee. Although the balance of the NHBC guarantee is sometimes expressly assigned to a subsequent buyer, the NHBC has publicly stated that it will honour its obligations whether or not the benefit has been assigned. Statistically, most defects occur between 5 and 10 years after construction, emphasising the importance of obtaining a structural guarantee even when not buying directly from the developer.

In the case of houses registered with the NHBC after 1 April 1999, the cover will also include the cost of cleaning up any contamination in the land on which the house is built; there is no such cover for houses registered with the NHBC before that date.

On the purchase of a new property, the contract with the developer should include a term that he is registered with the NHBC (and will continue to be so until completion) and that on exchange he will offer to enter into this 10-year guarantee. On exchange, a separate 'offer of cover' (form BM 1) will be handed over. The acceptance of cover (form BM 2) should be signed by the client and returned to the NHBC. There is also a comprehensive guidance booklet handed over which the solicitor has to certify that he has given to his client, ie the buyer. Once the property is completed, the NHBC will undertake a final inspection and, if all is satisfactory, will issue a '10-year notice'. This is the document which gives the 10-year guarantee previously explained. In theory, this will be handed to the buyer on completion, but it is often not available and an undertaking for it should be obtained. In the case of flats, in addition to the 10-year notice in respect of the individual flat being bought, there will be a separate notice in relation to the common parts of the block.

Although the NHBC Buildmark scheme is by far the most common, other similar insurance-backed schemes do exist, for example the Zurich Mutual Newbuild scheme. Alternatively, if the building work was supervised by, for example, an architect or surveyor, a certificate to that effect will allow an action to be brought against such person in the case of structural defects arising out of his negligent supervision. The effectiveness of such action, however, may well be dependent upon his having professional indemnity insurance.

Where the new property is to be bought with the aid of a mortgage loan, the *Lenders' Handbook* contains a requirement that one or other of the above forms of protection is in existence. See paragraph 6.6 of the *Lenders' Handbook*.

### 41.2.4  Estate roads

The new estate roads (being, at present, unadopted private roads) are likely to be 'adopted' (ie become publicly maintained) at some point in the future (but be aware that sometimes they might not be). As between the developer and the buyer, there should be a clause in the contract that the developer will be responsible for making up the roads to the local authority's standard and keeping them in that condition until they are adopted at no extra cost to the house buyer.

The roads are usually one of the last things a developer will complete when he is building a housing estate and so there is a risk that if he does become insolvent he will not have completed the roads. In that situation, when the roads are adopted, the properties 'fronting' onto the road might incur road charges if the highway authority have to spend money to 'make up' the road to their standard. The local authority will divide the cost of making up the road between 'frontagers', ie the owners of the properties 'fronting' on to it. In this context, a house 'fronts' onto a road even if it is at the back of the property which adjoins the road and even if the property in question has no access on to the road. There is thus a danger that having paid for the roads as part of the price of the house, the buyer will have to pay for them all over again. Obviously, there would be a right of action against the developer, but this will be only an academic right if he is insolvent.

To protect the owners of such properties from these charges, check to see that a Highways Act 1980 Section 38 Agreement has been entered into by the developer with the highway authority. This is an agreement between the developer and the highway authority that the developer will be responsible for the roads. Obviously, on its own it suffers from the same defect as the similar agreement between the developer and buyer, ie if the developer becomes insolvent. This agreement must therefore be supported by a financial bond, issued by a bank or insurance company, in a sufficient amount to cover against the developer defaulting on the Road Agreement. This, in effect, acts as an insurance policy against the developer defaulting and is paid for by the developer. If the developer does default, the bank, etc, will pay out under the bond and so avoid the risk of the 'frontagers' having to meet the cost of making up the road.

It often takes several years for the roads on a new estate to be adopted, particularly if it is a large estate which takes several years for the development to be completed. Therefore, when buying a house or flat 'second hand', always check the results of the enquiries of the local authority carefully to see whether the roads have been adopted yet. If they have not, then the existence of the agreement and bond will still be relevant.

In cases where there is no agreement and bond, a mortgage lender will usually protect itself against the property owner having to pay 'road charges' by making a retention from the advance of the estimated cost of those charges. This retention will be released only when the roads are adopted and may well cause the buyer financial problems on completion.

If an assessment to road charges is made by a local authority against a property, then this will be registered as a local land charge. It is unlikely that any subsequent buyer would complete a purchase without this being discharged.

### 41.2.5 Drains and sewers

Similar problems can arise with regard to the new drains and sewers which will be necessary to serve the property. Check whether the ownership and maintenance of the drains has been or is to be transferred to the water authority. If the water authority were to adopt the drains without them having been constructed to the proper standards, there is a risk that the properties being served might incur charges. To protect the owners, ensure that a Water Industry Act 1991, s 104 Agreement and bond has been entered into. This works in a similar way to the Highways Act agreement.

## 41.3 SALE OF PART

### 41.3.1 Evidence of title

Evidence of title will be supplied in the form of:

(i) *Unregistered title*: abstract/epitome of title in the usual form. However, as the original deeds, etc, will not be handed over on completion because the developer needs them to prove ownership of the remainder of the land, on completion the abstract/epitome, if not already marked, must be marked as a true copy of the original title documents.

(ii) *Registered title*: office copy entries of the whole site, with filed plan. With estate development, however, a Land Registry Form 102 is often used instead of the filed plan. This confirms that the plot being sold is within the developer's registered title, and indicates if any matters (eg existing covenants in the charges register) affect that plot. On completion, the developer will not hand over his land or charge certificate. Instead, the buyer will receive a Deposit Number of the developer's land or charge certificate in order for the new property to be registered.

### 41.3.2 Description of the property

Ensure that the contract contains a detailed description of the new property in the form of a verbal description and a professionally prepared plan.

### 41.3.3 Easements

Check that the contract provides for the grant to the buyer of all necessary easements. These must include:

- a right of way over the estate roads until adopted;
- a right to use the drains and sewers;

- a right to use all the pipes and cables for all the other services, for example gas, electricity, water, telephone, etc;
- rights of access to maintain all of these.

### 41.3.4 Reservations

The contract should also provide for easements to be reserved for the developer's retained land and the other houses/flats in the development, for example the right to run the services of water, gas and electricity across the buyer's property to the developer's adjoining land. The buyer should be told of the easements which will affect the property prior to exchange of contracts, although it is unlikely that the existence of such rights will restrict the client's proposed use of the property, if only because of the covenants that will be entered into restricting development (see below). However, these easements will include a right of access onto the buyer's property for the purpose of inspection and maintenance of the various services and the buyer must be made aware of this.

### 41.3.5 Covenants

New covenants will be created, some of a restrictive nature (eg to use the property for residential purposes only) and some of a positive nature (eg maintenance of boundary fences). Check that these are not too onerous and ensure that they are brought to the attention of the client. There is frequently a covenant restricting the use of the property to that of a single private dwelling-house and other restrictions are common, for example prohibiting the parking of caravans or boats, or making any alterations without the developer's consent. All of these could pose problems for a buyer with special plans for the property and should always be discussed with the client *before* contracts are exchanged.

### 41.3.6 Existing mortgages

Check to see if the developer's title is mortgaged. If so, the lender's release is required for the sale. This release should be in Form DS3 for a registered title, or a Deed of Release if the title is unregistered. You should ensure that the appropriate document is available at completion and that if there is a floating charge in favour of the developer's bank (to finance the development) a certificate of non-crystallisation will be handed over on completion.

## 41.4 CONVEYANCING PROCEDURES

### 41.4.1 Contract

The contract will be in the developer's standard form. Although this will normally incorporate the Standard Conditions of Sale, it may not be in familiar form. The developer is usually unwilling to accept amendments to this standard form contract. For his own administrative convenience he will want to ensure that every property in the development is sold on exactly the same terms.

In addition to dealing with the sale of the property, the contract may contain clauses dealing with the construction of the property, for example, clauses requiring that the property is to be built in accordance with plans and specifications, time-limits for building, clauses allowing for variations to original plans, etc. (Alternatively, this could be included in a separate building contract.)

### 41.4.2 Transfer

The draft transfer (and the engrossment of the transfer) is prepared by the developer (at the buyer's cost) in standard form and is attached to and forms part of the contract. As with the contract, the developer will usually be unwilling to accept any amendments to this. The purchase deed will contain the detailed description of the property, easements and covenants.

### 41.4.3 Pre-contract package

A developer will not normally adopt the National Protocol for Domestic Conveyancing as such but will at the start of the transaction supply a package of information, which is very similar to the Protocol package, but in a different form. This will usually include copies of the relevant planning permission, building regulation consent, Highways Act Agreement and Bond and the Water Industry Act Agreement and Bond. In addition, the draft transfer will be included, as it is usually annexed to and forms part of the draft contract. Title will be deduced as stated above but the standard Seller's Property Information Form will not be used. However, similar information will be given on a printed sheet prepared specifically for that particular development.

### 41.4.4 Completion date

The completion date in the contract will not be a definite fixed date. This is because, when a property is in the course of construction, the developer cannot predict with certainty the precise date when it will be available for occupation. In such cases, the contract will usually provide for completion of the transaction to take place within a specified number of days (eg 20 days) after the developer certifies that the property is completed and ready for habitation.

This contractual provision could cause further problems for a buyer who has a contract for the sale of his present house. It may prove difficult to synchronise completion of both sale and purchase as it is unlikely that the buyer's purchaser would be willing to agree to a similar condition in the sale contract. There are various practical solutions. The ideal is to wait until the house is completed before exchanging contracts and thus agreeing a fixed completion date. This is sometimes possible. In other cases, the developer will be able to give an indication as to when the property will be finished, for example 'about the last week in February'. Having taken the client's instructions and explained the problem to him, it would be possible to exchange on the dependent sale with a completion date of (say) 1 March. Thus if the house were to be completed as estimated or a week later or even a week earlier, it would still be possible to complete both transactions in accordance with the terms of the respective contracts. The risks must be explained to the client, however, and if there is an exceptionally long delay in the completion of the new property, the danger of having to complete the sale and move into alternative accommodation must be fully discussed. You should ask the client to bear in mind also that in such a case there would be no question of claiming any compensation from the developer for the costs of this alternative accommodation. It has to be said that, although this uncertain completion date could potentially lead to all sorts of disasters, it does not normally do so in practice. Developers and their solicitors are fully aware of the problems involved and will usually do their best to assist purchasers.

PART IX

# INTRODUCTION TO COMMERCIAL CONVEYANCING

# Chapter 42

# COMMERCIAL CONVEYANCING

## 42.1 INTRODUCTION

The procedures to be followed, searches and enquiries to be made, etc, in relation to a sale and purchase of commercial property, are much the same as for residential, or any other, land. However, the work may need to be accomplished in a much shorter timescale than in a residential transaction and different forms of documentation than that under the Protocol may be used. Where the procedure or documentation differs from that under the Protocol, this has been noted in the appropriate part of the book. However, it was thought that it might be useful to give a brief overview of a commercial transaction.

## 42.2 THE STANDARD COMMERCIAL PROPERTY CONDITIONS

### 42.2.1 Why two sets of Conditions of Sale?

The Standard Conditions of Sale were introduced by The Law Society in 1990 as part of the National Protocol which introduced measures designed to streamline domestic conveyancing. They were intended to replace the existing Law Society Conditions of Sale and the National Conditions of Sale. Although they were not specifically intended for use only in residential transactions, their introduction as part of the National Protocol did mean that they contained several provisions which were not appropriate for commercial transactions. As a result, amendments were required (by means of special conditions) to make them suitable for commercial sales.

Partly in response to criticisms as to the unsuitability of the Standard Conditions for commercial transactions, Oyez and The Law Society published in May 1999 a new set of Conditions specifically designed for use in commercial transactions. These conditions are in fact based on the old Standard Conditions, so that many of the provisions of both are identical. The fact that they are called the Standard Commercial Property Conditions (ie no reference to 'Sale') emphasises that they are not just designed for use in commercial sales but also on the grant of a new lease.

### 42.2.2 The Conditions

These are based on the residential Standard Conditions and deal with matters in the same order and using the same condition numbers as the Standard Conditions. The following are some of the more important changes made in order to reflect the differing needs of a commercial transaction.

The front and back pages of the contract form are set out below; the Conditions themselves are set out in Appendix 3.

# CONTRACT

## (Incorporating the Standard Commercial Property Conditions (First Edition))

Contract date : 

Seller : 

Buyer : 

Property
(freehold/leasehold) : 

Root of Title/Title Number : 

Incumbrances on the Property : 

Completion date : 

Contract rate : 

Purchase price : 

Deposit : 

Amount payable for chattels : 

The Seller will sell and the Buyer will buy the Property for the Purchase price.

*The Agreement continues on the back page.*

| WARNING | Signed |
|---|---|
| This is a formal document, designed to create legal rights and legal obligations. Take advice before using it. | |

## SPECIAL CONDITIONS

1. This **contract** incorporates the **Standard Commercial Property Conditions (First Edition)**. Where there is a conflict between those Conditions and any other provision of this Contract, that other provision prevails.

2. The Property is sold subject to the Incumbrances on the Property and the Buyer will raise no requisition on them.

3. The Property is sold with vacant possession on completion.

**or** 3. The Property is sold subject to the following leases or tenancies:

4. The chattels set out on the attached list are included in the sale.

**Seller's Solicitors**  :

**Buyer's Solicitors**  :

### Condition 1 – General

Both sets of conditions open with a list of definitions. One difference here is that the Standard Conditions definition of 'bankers' draft' is replaced by a definition of 'direct credit' in the Standard Commercial Property Conditions. This is because under the Standard Commercial Property Conditions the only authorised method of payment (except on a sale at an auction) is by a direct transfer from one bank account to another.

There is also a new Condition 1.5 in the Standard Commercial Property Conditions which prevents the buyer transferring the benefit of the contract; such a right is not appropriate in a commercial sale.

### Condition 2 – Formation

The main difference here is with regard to the deposit. Both sets of Conditions normally require the deposit to be held as stakeholder, but the provisions in the Standard Conditions dealing with the seller using the deposit in his own purchase are omitted in the Standard Commercial Property Conditions. Also, in the case of a sale by auction, the Standard Commercial Property Conditions make it clear that the auctioneer is to hold the deposit as agent for the seller. There are also provisions allowing the seller to rescind the contract if the deposit cheque is dishonoured.

### Condition 3 – Matters affecting the property

The main change here is the replacement of Condition 3.1.2(d). The Standard Commercial Property Conditions provision is much wider than under the Standard Conditions and in effect means that entries at (for example) HM Land Registry need not be specifically mentioned in the contract, whereas under the Standard Conditions they do need to be. Note also the inclusion of the word 'reasonably' in Condition 3.1.2(c).

Also changed is Condition 3.3. This deals with sales subject to existing leases. This is common in a commercial context and the Standard Commercial Property Condition 3.3 deals comprehensively with the estate management issues which can arise in such cases.

### Condition 5 – Pending completion

The Standard Commercial Property Conditions adopt a completely different approach than the Standard Conditions. Basically, under the Standard Conditions, the seller retains the risk until completion; under the Standard Commercial Property Conditions, the risk passes to the buyer. There are also provisions dealing with the situation that the seller may maintain his insurance until completion and the consequences of double insurance. The Standard Commercial Property Conditions also envisage that in some cases there may be a special Condition providing that the seller's insurance is to continue in force until completion and there are complex provisions dealing with this.

### Condition 6 – Completion

Condition 6.3 deals with apportionments of outgoings on completion. Under the Standard Conditions, it is assumed that the *seller* owns the property for the whole of the day of completion; under the Standard Commercial Property Conditions, it is assumed that the *buyer* owns the property for that day.

There are extra provisions in Standard Commercial Property Conditions 6.3.7–6.3.9 dealing with rent and service charges when the property is being sold subject to a lease or leases.

Standard Commercial Property Condition 6.7 provides that the only authorised means of payment is by a direct credit to a bank account (and the release of a deposit held as stakeholder). The Standard Conditions allows payment by banker's draft or legal tender, ie cash.

### Condition 7 – Remedies

Condition 7.3 deals with late completion. The Standard Commercial Property Condition adopts a much simpler method of dealing with this compared to the concept of relative fault used under the Standard Conditions. A contractual entitlement to compensation is given solely to the seller. Where the seller defaults, the buyer is left to the usual remedies for breach of contract.

Under Condition 7.3.4 of the Standard Conditions, the seller is not entitled to both compensation and the income from the property; under the Standard Commercial Property Conditions, the seller can elect to take both.

### Condition 8 – Leasehold property

Standard Commercial Property Condition 8.3 contains a much more comprehensive set of provisions than the Standard Conditions dealing with the situation where the landlord's consent to an assignment or sub-letting is required. Such a situation is usual in a commercial context but not in a residential one.

### Condition 9 – Chattels

Consistent with the provision in Condition 5 that the risk in the property passes to the buyer on exchange, Condition 9.3 provides that the risk in any chattels is also to pass to the buyer on exchange.

## 42.3  VAT

VAT is always going to be an issue in commercial sales, and both buyer and seller will need to consider the VAT implications of the transaction proposed. Like the residential Standard Conditions, the Commercial Conditions provide that all sums payable under the contract are exclusive of VAT, so there is a possibility that the seller will be able to/may have to add VAT onto any agreed purchase price. For an explanation as to how VAT may affect a commercial sale, see Chapter 7.

## 42.4  BRIEF OVERVIEW OF PROCEDURE

As previously stated, the overall structure of a commercial conveyancing transaction is much the same as a residential transaction. The main differences will be in the documentation used – the Protocol Property Information Form will not be used, for example – and the value and timescale of the transaction.

The seller's solicitor will send a pre-contract package to the buyer in the normal way. This will contain as a minimum the draft contract and details of the title (eg office copies). It may also contain copy planning consents, leases to which the property is subject, etc, as appropriate.

The rest of the Protocol documentation will not be used however, so there will be no Seller's Property Information Form or Fixtures, Fittings and Contents form. However, if contents are to be included in the sale, an inventory of those contents will be required and the buyer will still need to find out as much as possible about the kind of matters dealt with on the Property Information Form. The seller may, therefore, provide with the package answers to a standard form of Enquiries before Contract. Alternatively, the buyer's solicitor will submit a list of questions about the property to the seller on receipt of the pre-contract package. Various forms of Enquiries before Contract are available from law stationers and many solicitors will have their own form which they have developed to suit their own needs.

The same basic searches, etc will be made as in a residential transaction, although more emphasis may well be placed on environmental matters, particularly since the implementation of the remediation provisions in relation to contaminated land. In many cases, lengthy enquiries to try and ascertain the likelihood of the land being contaminated will be made in addition to the usual Enquiries before Contract.

The matter will then proceed to exchange in the usual way. As usual, the buyer's finances will be an issue and the availability of finance will need resolving before exchange. The Standard Commercial Property Conditions provide for the buyer to pay the normal 10% deposit, although some major financial institutions do refuse to pay a deposit when buying property.

As with a residential transaction, it will be necessary to ensure that the buyer's finance is in place prior to exchange. In many cases the lender will employ its own solicitors in connection with the loan. However, it is likely that the lender's solicitors will not undertake their own investigation of title; they will require the buyer's solicitors to give them a Certificate of Title before the loan will be released. This is a certificate signed by the buyer's solicitors to the effect that the title to the property is good and marketable.

Exchange of contracts itself and the procedure leading to completion will be the same as under a residential transaction. It is more likely, however, that completion would take place by personal attendance and that the time scale for the transaction might need to be considerably shorter than that in a residential sale and purchase.

# APPENDICES

# Appendix 1

# NATIONAL PROTOCOL FOR DOMESTIC FREEHOLD AND LEASEHOLD PROPERTY

## THE NATIONAL PROTOCOL (FOURTH EDITION)

### Acting for the seller

#### 1. The first step

The seller should inform the solicitor as soon as it is intended to place the property on the market so that delay may be reduced after a prospective purchaser is found.

#### 2. Preparing the package: assembling the information

On receipt of instructions, the solicitor should then immediately take the following steps, at the seller's expense:

2.1    Whenever possible instructions should be obtained from the client in person.

2.2    Check the client's identity if the client is not known to you.

2.3    Give the client information as to costs, information relating to the name and status of the person who will be carrying out the work and, if that person is not a partner, the name of the partner who has overall responsibility for the matter. Give any other information necessary to comply with Rule 15 of the Solicitors' Practice Rules 1990 and Solicitors' Costs Information and Client Care Code 1999. If given orally this information should be confirmed in writing.

2.4    Give the seller details of whom to contact in the event of a complaint about the firm's services (Rule 15).

2.5    Consider with client whether to make local authority and other searches so that these can be supplied to the buyer's solicitor as soon as an offer is made. If thought appropriate request a payment on account in relation to disbursements.

2.6    Ascertain the whereabouts of the deeds and, if not in the solicitor's custody, obtain them.

2.7    Ask the seller to complete the Seller's Property Information Form.

2.8    Obtain such original guarantees with the accompanying specification, planning decisions, building regulation approvals and certificates of completion as are in the seller's possession and copies of any other planning consents that are with the title deeds or details of any highway and sewerage agreements and bonds or any other relevant certificates relating to the property (eg structural engineer's certificate or an indemnity policy).

2.9    Give the seller the Fixtures, Fittings and Contents Form, with a copy to retain, to complete and return prior to the submission of the draft contract.

2.10    If the title is unregistered make an index map search.

2.11    If so instructed requisition a local authority search and enquiries and any other searches (eg mining or commons registration searches).

2.12    Obtain details of all mortgages and other financial charges of which the seller's solicitor has notice including, where applicable, improvement grants and discounts repayable to a local authority. Redemption figures should be obtained at this stage in respect of all mortgages on the property so that cases of negative equity or penalty redemption interest can be identified at an early stage.

2.13    Ascertain the identity of all people aged 17 or over living in the dwelling and ask about any financial contribution they or anyone else may have made towards its purchase or subsequent improvement. All persons identified in this way should be asked to confirm their consent to the sale proceeding.

2.14    In leasehold cases, ask the seller to complete the Seller's Leasehold Information Form and to produce, if possible:

(1)    A receipt or evidence from the landlord of the last payment of rent.
(2)    The maintenance charge accounts for the last three years, where appropriate, and evidence of payment.
(3)    Details of the buildings insurance policy.

If any of these are lacking, and are necessary for the transaction, the solicitor should obtain them from the landlord. At the same time investigate whether a licence to assign is required and, if so, enquire of the landlord what references or deeds of covenant are necessary and, in the case of some retirement schemes, if a charge is payable to the management company on change of ownership.

### 3.  Preparing the package: the draft documents

As soon as the title deeds are available, and the seller has completed the Seller's Property Information Form and, if appropriate, the Seller's Leasehold Information Form, the solicitor shall:

3.1    If the title is unregistered:

(1)    Make a land charges search against the seller and any other appropriate names.
(2)    Make an index map search in the Land Registry (if not already obtained – see 2.10) in order to verify that the seller's title is unregistered and ensure that there are no interests registered at the Land Registry adverse to the seller's title.
(3)    Prepare an epitome of title. Mark copies or abstracts of all deeds which will not be passed to the buyer's solicitor as examined against the original.
(4)    Prepare and mark as examined against the originals copies of all deeds, or their abstracts, prior to the root of title containing covenants, easements, etc, affecting the property.
(5)    Check that all plans on copied documents are correctly coloured.

3.2    If the title is registered, obtain office copy entries of the register and copy documents incorporated or referred to in the certificate.

3.3    Prepare the draft contract and complete the second section of the Seller's Property Information Form and, if appropriate, the Seller's Leasehold Information Form.

3.4    Check contract package is complete and ready to be sent out to the buyer's solicitor.

3.5 Deal promptly with any queries raised by the estate agent.

## 4. Buyer's offer accepted.

When made aware that a buyer has been found the solicitor shall:

4.1 Check with the seller agreement on the price and, if appropriate, that there has been no change in the information already supplied (Seller's Property Information Form, Seller's Leasehold Information Form and Fixtures, Fittings and Contents Form). Also check the seller's position on any related purchase.

4.2 Inform the buyer's solicitor that the Protocol will be used.

4.3 Ascertain the buyer's position on any related sale and in the light of that reply, ask the seller for a proposed completion date.

4.4 Send to the buyer's solicitor as soon as possible the contract package to include:

    (1) Draft contract.

    (2) Office copy entries of the registered title (including office copies of all documents mentioned), or the epitome of title (including details of any prior matters referred to but not disclosed by the documents themselves) and the index map search.

    (3) The Seller's Property Information Form with copies of all relevant planning decisions, guarantees, etc.

    (4) The completed Fixtures, Fittings and Contents Form. Where this is provided it will form part of the contact and should be attached to it.

    (5) In leasehold cases

        (i) the Seller's Leasehold Information Form, with all information about maintenance charges and insurance and, if appropriate, the procedure (including references required) for obtaining the landlord's consent to the sale;

        (ii) a copy of the lease.

    (6) If available, the local authority search and enquiries and any other searches made by the seller's solicitor.

If any of these documents are not available the remaining items should be forwarded to the buyer's solicitor as soon as they are available.

4.5 Inform the estate agent when the draft contract has been submitted to the buyer's solicitor.

4.6 Ask the buyer's solicitor if a 10 per cent deposit will be paid and, if not, what arrangements are proposed.

4.7 If and to the extent that the seller consents to the disclosure, supply information about the position on the seller's own purchase and of any other transactions in the chain above, and thereafter, of any change in circumstances.

4.8 Notify the seller of all information received in response to the above.

4.9 Inform the estate agent of any unexpected delays or difficulties likely to delay exchange of contracts.

## Acting for the buyer

### *5. The first step*

On notification of the buyer's purchase the solicitor should then immediately take the following steps, at the buyer's expense:

5.1     Wherever possible instructions should be obtained from the client in person.

5.2     Check the client's identity if the client is not known to you.

5.3     Give the client information as to costs, information relating to the name and status of the person who will be carrying out the work and, if that person is not a partner, the name of the partner who has overall responsibility for the matter. Give any other information necessary to comply with Rule 15 of the Solicitor's Practice Rules 1990 and Solicitors' Costs Information and Client Care Code 1999. If given orally this information should be confirmed in writing.

5.4     Give the client details of whom to contact in the event of a complaint about the firm's services (Rule 15).

5.5     Request a payment on account in relation to disbursements.

5.6     Confirm to the seller's solicitor that the Protocol will be used.

5.7     Ascertain the buyer's position on any related sale, mortgage arrangements and whether a 10 per cent deposit will be provided.

5.8     If and to the extent that the buyer consents to the disclosure, inform the seller's solicitor about the position on the buyer's own sale, if any, and of any connected transactions, the general nature of the mortgage application, the amount of deposit available and if the seller's target date for completion can be met, and thereafter, of any change in circumstances.

On receipt of the draft contract and other documents:

5.9     Notify the buyer that these documents have been received, check the price and send the client a copy of the Fixtures, Fittings and Contents Form and, if appropriate, a copy of the filed plan for checking.

5.10    Make a local authority search with the usual part one enquiries and any additional enquiries relevant to the property.

5.11    Make a commons registration search, if appropriate.

5.12    Make mining enquiries and drainage enquiries if appropriate and consider any other relevant searches, eg environmental searches.

5.13    Check the buyer's position on any related sale and check that the buyer has a satisfactory mortgage offer and all conditions of the mortgage are or can be satisfied.

5.14    Check the buyer understands the nature and effect of the mortgage offer and duty to disclose any relevant matters to the lender.

5.15    Advise the buyer of the need for a survey on the property.

5.16    Confirm approval of the draft contract and return it approved as soon as possible, having inserted the buyer's full names and address, subject to any outstanding matters.

5.17    At the same time ask only those specific additional enquiries which are required to clarify some point arising out of the documents submitted or which are relevant to the particular nature or location of the property or which the buyer has expressly requested. Any enquiry, including those about the state and condition of the building, which is capable of being ascertained by the buyer's own enquiries or survey or personal inspection should not be raised. Additional duplicated standard forms should not be submitted; if they are, the seller's solicitor is under no obligation to deal with them nor need answer any enquire seeking opinions rather than facts.

5.18 If a local authority search has been supplied by the seller's solicitors with the draft contract, consider the need to make a local authority search with the usual part one enquiries and any additional enquiries relevant to the property. (The local authority search should not be more than three months' old at exchange of contracts nor six months' old at completion).

5.19 Ensure that buildings insurance arrangements are in place.

5.20 Check the position over any life policies referred to in the lender's offer of mortgage.

5.21 Check with the buyer if property is being purchased in sole name or jointly with another person. If a joint purchase check whether as joint tenants or tenants in common and advise on the difference in writing.

## Both parties' solicitor

### *6. Prior to exchange of contracts*

*If acting for the buyer*

When all satisfactory replies received to enquiries and searches:

6.1 Prepare and send to the buyer a contract report and invite the buyer to make an appointment to call to raise any queries on the contract report and to sign the contract ideally in the presence of a solicitor.

6.2 When the buyer signs the contract check:

    (1) Completion date.

    (2) That the buyer understands and can comply with all the conditions on the mortgage offer if appropriate.

    (3) That all the necessary funds will be available to complete the purchase.

*If acting for the seller*

6.3 Advise the seller on the effect of the contract and ask the seller to sign it, ideally in the presence of the solicitor.

6.4 Check the position on any related purchase so that there can be a simultaneous exchange of contracts on both the sale and purchase.

6.5 Check completion date.

### *7. Relationship with the buyer's lender*

On receipt of instructions from the buyer's lender:

7.1 Check the mortgage offer complies with Practice Rule 6(3)(c) and (e) and is certified to that effect.

7.2 Check any special conditions in the mortgage offer to see if there are additional instructions or conditions not normally required by Practice Rule 6(3)(c).

7.3 Go through any special conditions in the mortgage offer with the buyer.

7.4 Notify the lender if Practice Rule 6(3)(b) or 1.13 or 1.14 of the CML Lenders' Handbook ('Lenders' Handbook') are applicable.

7.5 Consider whether there are any conflicts of interest which prevent you accepting instructions to act for the lender.

7.6 If you do not know the borrower and anyone else required to sign the mortgage, charge or other document, check evidence of identity (Practice

Rule 6(3)(c)(*i*)).

7.7    Consider whether there are any circumstances covered by the Law Society's:

    (1)    Green Card on property fraud

    (2)    Blue Card on money laundering

    (3)    Pink Card on undertakings

7.8    If you do not know the seller's solicitor/licensed conveyancer check that they appear in a legal directory or are on the record of their professional body (see Practice Rule 6(3)(c)(*i*) and the Lenders' Handbook).

7.9    Carry out any other checks required by the lender provided they comply with Practice Rule 6(3)(c).

7.10    At all times comply with the requirements of Practice Rule 6(3) and the Lenders' Handbook and ensure if a conflict of interest arises you cease to act for the lender.

## 8.  Exchange of contracts

On exchange, the buyer's solicitor shall send or deliver to the seller's solicitor:

8.1    The signed contract with all names, dates and financial information completed.

8.2    The deposit provided in the manner prescribed in the contract. Under the Law Society's Formula C the deposit may have to be sent to another solicitor nominated by the seller's solicitor.

8.3    If contracts are exchanged by telephone the procedures laid down by the Law Society's Formulae A, B or C must be used and both solicitors must ensure (unless otherwise agreed) that the undertakings to send documents and to pay the deposit on that day are strictly observed.

8.4    The seller's solicitor shall, once the buyer's signed contract and deposit are held unconditionally, having ensured that the details of each contract are fully completed and identical, send the seller's signed contract on the day of exchange to the buyer's solicitor in compliance with the undertaking given on exchange.

8.5    Notify the client that contracts have been exchanged.

8.6    Notify the seller's estate agent or property seller of exchange of contracts and the completion date.

## 9.  Between exchange and the day of completion

As soon as possible after exchange and in any case within the time limits contained in the Standard Conditions of Sale:

9.1    The buyer's solicitor shall send to the seller's solicitor, in duplicate:

    (1)    Completion Information and Requisitions on Title Form.

    (2)    Draft conveyance/transfer or assignment incorporating appropriate provisions for joint purchase.

    (3)    Other documents, eg draft receipt for purchase price of fixtures, fittings and contents.

9.2    As soon as possible after receipt of these documents the seller's solicitor shall send to the buyer's solicitor:

    (1)    Replies to Completion Information and Requisitions on Title Form.

    (2)    Draft conveyance/transfer or assignment approved.

(3) If appropriate, completion statement supported by photocopy receipts or evidence of payment of apportionments claimed.

(4) Copy of licence to assign from the landlord if appropriate.

9.3 The buyer's solicitor shall then:

(1) Engross the approved draft conveyance/transfer or assignment.

(2) Explain the effect of that document to the buyer and obtain the buyer's signature to it (if necessary).

(3) Send it to the seller's solicitor in time to enable the seller to sign it before completion without suffering inconvenience.

(4) If appropriate prepare any separate declaration of trust, advise the buyer on its effect and obtain the buyer's signature to it.

(5) Advise the buyer on the contents and effect of the mortgage deed and obtain the buyer's signature to that deed. If possible, and in all cases where the lender so requires, a solicitor should witness the buyer's signature to the mortgage deed.

(6) Send the certificate of title (complying with Rule 6(3)(d)) to the lender.

(7) Take any steps necessary to ensure that the amount payable on completion will be available in time for completion including sending to the buyer a completion statement to include legal costs, Land Registry fees and other disbursements and, if appropriate, stamp duty.

(8) Make the Land Registry and land charges searches and, if appropriate, a company search.

9.4 The seller's solicitor shall:

(1) Request redemption figures for all financial charges on the property revealed by the deeds/office copy entries/land charges search against the seller.

(2) On receipt of the engrossment of the conveyance/transfer or assignment, after checking the engrossment to ensure accuracy, obtain the seller's signature to it after ascertaining that the seller understands the nature and contents of the document. If the document is not to be signed in the solicitor's presence the letter sending the document for signature should contain an explanation of the nature and effect of the document and clear instructions relating to the execution of it.

(3) On receipt of the estate agent's or property seller's commission account obtain the seller's instructions to pay the account on the seller's behalf out of the sale proceeds.

## 10. *Relationship with the seller's estate agent or property seller*

Where the seller has instructed estate agents or property seller, the seller's solicitor shall take the following steps:

10.1 Inform them when the draft contracts are submitted (see 4.5).

10.2 Deal promptly with any queries raised by them.

10.3 Inform them of any unexpected delays or difficulties likely to delay exchange of contracts (see 4.9).

10.4 Inform them when exchange has taken place and the date of completion (see 8.6).

10.5 On receipt of their commission account send a copy to the seller and obtain instructions as to arrangements for payment (see 9.4(3)).

10.6    Inform them of completion and, if appropriate, authorise release of any keys held by them (see 11.3(1)).

10.7    If so instructed pay the commission (see 9.4(3) and 11.6(2)).

### 11. Completion: the day of payment and removals

11.1    If completion is to be by post, the Law Society's Code for Completion shall be used, unless otherwise agreed.

11.2    As soon as practicable and not later than the morning of completion, the buyer's solicitor shall advise the seller's solicitor of the manner and transmission of the purchase money and of steps taken to despatch it.

11.3    On being satisfied as to the receipt of the balance of the purchase money, the seller's solicitor shall:

(1)    Notify the estate agent or property seller that completion has taken place and authorise release of the keys.

(2)    Notify the buyer's solicitor that completion has taken place and the keys have been released.

(3)    Date and complete the transfer.

(4)    Despatch the deeds including the transfer to the buyer's solicitor with any appropriate undertakings.

11.4    The seller's solicitor shall check that the seller is aware of the need to notify the local and water authorities of the change in ownership.

11.5    After completion, where appropriate, the buyer's solicitor shall give notice of assignment to the lessor.

11.6    Immediately after completion, the seller's solicitor shall:

(1)    Send to the lender the amount required to release the property sold.

(2)    Pay the estate agent's or property seller's commission if so authorised.

(3)    Account to the seller for the balance of the sale proceeds.

11.7    Immediately after completion, the buyer's solicitor shall:

(1)    Date and complete the mortgage document.

(2)    Confirm completion of the purchase and the mortgage to the buyer.

(3)    Pay stamp duty on the purchase deed, if appropriate.

(4)    Deal with the registration of the transfer document and mortgage with the Land Registry within the priority period of the search.

(5)    If appropriate, send a notice of assignment of a life policy to the insurance company.

(6)    On receipt of the land or charge certificate from the Land Registry check its contents carefully and supply a copy of the certificate to the buyer.

(7)    Send the charge certificate to the lender or deal with the land certificate in accordance with the buyer's instructions.

# Appendix 2

# STANDARD CONDITIONS OF SALE (THIRD EDITION)

## (NATIONAL CONDITIONS OF SALE 23RD EDITION, LAW SOCIETY'S CONDITIONS OF SALE 1995)

## 1. General

### 1.1 Definitions

1.1.1    In these conditions:

(a)    'accrued interest' means:

   (i)    if money has been placed on deposit or in a building society share account, the interest actually earned

   (ii)    otherwise, the interest which might reasonably have been earned by depositing the money at interest on seven days' notice of withdrawal with a clearing bank

   less, in either case, any proper charges for handling the money

(b)    'agreement' means the contractual document which incorporates these conditions, with or without amendment

(c)    'banker's draft' means a draft drawn by and on a clearing bank

(d)    'clearing bank' means a bank which is a member of CHAPS Limited

(e)    'completion date', unless defined in the agreement, has the meaning given in condition 6.1.1

(f)    'contract' means the bargain between the seller and the buyer of which these conditions, with or without amendment, form part

(g)    'contract rate', unless defined in the agreement, is the Law Society's interest rate from time to time in force

(h)    'lease' includes sub-lease, tenancy and agreement for a lease or sub-lease

(i)    'notice to complete' means a notice requiring completion of the contract in accordance with Condition 6

(j)    'public requirement' means any notice, order or proposal given or made (whether before or after the date of the contract) by a body acting on statutory authority.

(k)    'requisition' includes objection

(l)    'solicitor' includes barrister, duly certificated notary public, recognised licensed conveyancer and recognised body under sections 9 or 32 of the Administration of Justice Act 1985

(m)    'transfer' includes conveyance and assignment

(n)    'working day' means any day from Monday to Friday (inclusive) which is not Christmas Day, Good Friday or a statutory Bank Holiday.

1.1.2    When used in these conditions the terms 'absolute title' and 'office copies' have the special meaning given to them by the Land Registration Act 1925.

## 1.2 Joint parties

If there is more than one seller or more than one buyer, the obligations which they undertake can be enforced against them all jointly or against each individually.

## 1.3 Notices and documents

1.3.1    A notice required or authorised by the contract must be in writing.

1.3.2    Giving a notice or delivering a document to a party's solicitor has the same effect as giving or delivering it to that party.

1.3.3    Transmission by fax is a valid means of giving a notice or delivering a document where delivery of the original document is not essential.

1.3.4    Subject to conditions 1.3.5 to 1.3.7, a notice is given and a document delivered when it is received.

1.3.5    If a notice or document is received after 4.00pm on a working day, or on a day which is not a working day, it is to be treated as having been received on the next working day.

1.3.6    Unless the actual time of receipt is proved, a notice or document sent by the following means is to be treated as having been received before 4.00pm on the day shown below:

(a)    by first-class post:    two working days after posting
(b)    by second-class post:    three working days after posting
(c)    through a document exchange:    on the first working day after the day on which it would normally be available for collection by the addressee

1.3.7    Where a notice or document is sent through a document exchange, then for the purposes of condition 1.3.6 the actual time of receipt is:

(a)    the time when the addressee collects it from the document exchange or, if earlier
(b)    8.00am on the first working day on which it is available for collection at that time.

## 1.4 VAT

1.4.1    An obligation to pay money includes an obligation to pay any value added tax chargeable in respect of that payment.

1.4.2    All sums made payable by the contract are exclusive of value added tax.

## 2. Formation

### 2.1 Date

2.1.1    If the parties intend to make a contract by exchanging duplicate copies by post or through a document exchange, the contract is made when the last copy is posted or deposited at the document exchange.

2.1.2    If the parties' solicitors agree to treat exchange as taking place before duplicate copies are actually exchanged, the contract is made as so agreed.

### 2.2 Deposit

2.2.1    The buyer is to pay or send a deposit of 10 per cent of the purchase price no later than the date of the contract. Except on a sale by auction, payment is to be made by banker's draft or by a cheque drawn on a solicitors' clearing bank account.

2.2.2    If before completion date the seller agrees to buy another property in England and Wales for his residence, he may use all or any part of the deposit as a deposit in that transaction to be held on terms to the same effect as this condition and condition 2.2.3.

2.2.3    Any deposit or part of a deposit not being used in accordance with condition 2.2.2 is to be held by the seller's solicitor as stakeholder on terms that on completion it is paid to the seller with accrued interest.

2.2.4    If a cheque tendered in payment of all or part of the deposit is dishonoured when first presented, the seller may, within seven working days of being notified that the cheque has been dishonoured, give notice to the buyer that the contract is discharged by the buyer's breach.

### 2.3 Auctions

2.3.1    On a sale by auction the following conditions apply to the property and, if it is sold in lots, to each lot.

2.3.2    The sale is subject to a reserve price.

2.3.3    The seller, or a person on his behalf, may bid up to the reserve price.

2.3.4    The auctioneer may refuse any bid.

2.3.5    If there is a dispute about a bid, the auctioneer may resolve the dispute or restart the auction at the last undisputed bid.

## 3. Matters affecting the property

### 3.1 Freedom from incumbrances

3.1.1    The seller is selling the property free from incumbrances, other than those mentioned in condition 3.1.2.

3.1.2    The incumbrances subject to which the property is sold are:

(a)    those mentioned in the agreement
(b)    those discoverable by inspection of the property before the contract
(c)    those the seller does not and could not know about

(d)       entries made before the date of the contract in any public register except those maintained by HM Land Registry or its Land Charges Department or by Companies House

(e)       public requirements.

3.1.3    After the contract is made, the seller is to give the buyer written details without delay of any new public requirement and of anything in writing which he learns about concerning any incumbrances subject to which the property is sold.

3.1.4    The buyer is to bear the cost of complying with any outstanding public requirement and is to indemnify the seller against any liability resulting from a public requirement.

### 3.2 Physical state

3.2.1    The buyer accepts the property in the physical state it is in at the date of the contract unless the seller is building or converting it.

3.2.2    A leasehold property is sold subject to any subsisting breach of a condition or tenant's obligation relating to the physical state of the property which renders the lease liable to forfeiture.

3.2.3    A sublease is granted subject to any subsisting breach of a condition or tenant's obligation relating to the physical state of the property which renders the seller's own lease liable to forfeiture.

### 3.3 Leases affecting the property

3.3.1    The following provisions apply if the agreement states that any part of the property is sold subject to a lease.

3.3.2    (a)       The seller having provided the buyer with full details of each lease or copies of the documents embodying the lease terms, the buyer is treated as entering into the contract knowing and fully accepting those terms

(b)       The seller is to inform the buyer without delay if the lease ends or if the seller learns of any application by the tenant in connection with the lease; the seller is then to act as the buyer reasonably directs, and the buyer is to indemnify him against all consequent loss and expense

(c)       The seller is not to agree to any proposal to change the lease terms without the consent of the buyer and is to inform the buyer without delay of any change which may be proposed or agreed

(d)       The buyer is to indemnify the seller against all claims arising from the lease after actual completion; this includes claims which are unenforceable against a buyer for want of registration

(e)       The seller takes no responsibility for what rent is lawfully recoverable, nor for whether or how any legislation affects the lease

(f)       If the let land is not wholly within the property, the seller may apportion the rent.

### 3.4 Retained land

3.4.1    The following provisions apply where after the transfer the seller will be retaining land near the property.

3.4.2    The buyer will have no right of light or air over the retained land, but otherwise the seller and the buyer will each have the rights over the land of the other which they would have had if they were two separate buyers to whom the seller had made simultaneous transfers of the property and the retained land.

3.4.3    Either party may require that the transfer contain appropriate express terms.

## 4. Title and transfer

### 4.1 Timetable

4.1.1    The following are the steps for deducing and investigating the title to the property to be taken within the following time limits:

| Step | | Time Limit |
|---|---|---|
| 1. | The seller is to send the buyer evidence of title in accordance with condition 4.2 | Immediately after making the contract |
| 2. | The buyer may raise written requisitions | Six working days after either the date of the contract or the date of delivery of the seller's evidence of title on which the requisitions are raised whichever is the later |
| 3. | The seller is to reply in writing to any requisitions raised | Four working days after receiving the requisitions |
| 4. | The buyer may make written observations on the seller's replies | Three working days after receiving replies |

The time limit on the buyer's right to raise requisitions applies even where the seller supplies incomplete evidence of his title, but the buyer may, within six working days from delivery of any further evidence, raise further requisitions resulting from that evidence. On the expiry of the relevant time limit the buyer loses his right to raise requisitions or make observations.

4.1.2    The parties are to take the following steps to prepare and agree the transfer of the property within the following time limits:

| Step | | Time Limit |
|---|---|---|
| A. | The buyer is to send the seller a draft transfer | At least twelve working days before completion date |
| B. | The seller is to approve or revise that draft and either return it or retain it for use as the actual transfer | Four working days after delivery of the draft transfer |
| C. | If the draft is returned the buyer is to send an engrossment to the seller | At least five working days before completion date |

4.1.3   Periods of time under conditions 4.1.1 and 4.1.2 may run concurrently.

4.1.4   If the period between the date of the contract and completion date is less than 15 working days, the time limits in conditions 4.1.1 and 4.1.2 are to be reduced by the same proportion as that period bears to the period of 15 working days. Fractions of a working day are to be rounded down except that the time limit to perform any step is not to be less than one working day.

### 4.2  Proof of title

4.2.1   The evidence of registered title is office copies of the items required to be furnished by section 110(1) of the Land Registration Act 1925 and the copies, abstracts and evidence referred to in section 110(2).

4.2.2   The evidence of unregistered title is an abstract of the title, or an epitome of title with photocopies of the relevant documents.

4.2.3   Where the title to the property is unregistered, the seller is to produce to the buyer (without cost to the buyer):

(a)     the original of every relevant document, or

(b)     an abstract, epitome or copy with an original marking by a solicitor of examination either against the original or against an examined abstract or against an examined copy.

### 4.3  Defining the property

4.3.1   The seller need not:

(a)     prove the exact boundaries of the property

(b)     prove who owns fences, ditches, hedges or walls

(c)     separately identify parts of the property with different titles further than he may be able to do from information in his possession.

4.3.2   The buyer may, if it is reasonable, require the seller to make or obtain, pay for and hand over a statutory declaration about facts relevant to the matters mentioned in condition 4.3.1. The form of the declaration is to be agreed by the buyer, who must not unreasonably withhold his agreement.

### 4.4  Rents and rent charges

The fact that a rent or rent charge, whether payable or receivable by the owner of the property, has been or will on completion be, informally apportioned is not to be regarded as a defect in title.

### 4.5  Transfer

4.5.1   The buyer does not prejudice his right to raise requisitions, or to require replies to any raised, by taking any steps in relation to the preparation or agreement of the transfer.

4.5.2   If the agreement makes no provision as to title guarantee, then subject to condition 4.5.3 the seller is to transfer the property with full title guarantee.

4.5.3   The transfer is to have effect as if the disposition is expressly made subject to all matters to which the property is sold subject under the terms of the contract.

4.5.4    If after completion the seller will remain bound by any obligation affecting the property, but the law does not imply any covenant by the buyer to indemnify the seller against liability for future breaches of it:

(a)    the buyer is to covenant in the transfer to indemnify the seller against liability for any future breach of the obligation and to perform it from then on, and

(b)    if required by the seller, the buyer is to execute and deliver to the seller on completion a duplicate transfer prepared by the buyer.

4.5.5    The seller is to arrange at his expense that, in relation to every document of title which the buyer does not receive on completion, the buyer is to have the benefit of:

(a)    a written acknowledgement of his right to its production, and

(b)    a written undertaking for its safe custody (except while it is held by a mortgagee or by someone in a fiduciary capacity).

## 5. Pending completion

### 5.1 Responsibility for property

5.1.1    The seller will transfer the property in the same physical state as it was at the date of the contract (except for fair wear and tear), which means that the seller retains the risk until completion.

5.1.2    If at any time before completion the physical state of the property makes it unusable for its purpose at the date of the contract:

(a)    the buyer may rescind the contract

(b)    the seller may rescind the contract where the property has become unusable for that purpose as a result of damage against which the seller could not reasonably have insured, or which it is not legally possible for the seller to make good.

5.1.3    The seller is under no obligation to the buyer to insure the property.

5.1.4    Section 47 of the Law of Property Act 1925 does not apply.

### 5.2 Occupation by buyer

5.2.1    If the buyer is not already lawfully in the property, and the seller agrees to let him into occupation, the buyer occupies on the following terms.

5.2.2    The buyer is a licensee and not a tenant. The terms of the licence are that the buyer:

(a)    cannot transfer it

(b)    may permit members of his household to occupy the property

(c)    is to pay or indemnify the seller against all outgoings and other expenses in respect of the property

(d)    is to pay the seller a fee calculated at the contract rate on the purchase price (less any deposit paid) for the period of the licence

(e)    is entitled to any rents and profits from any part of the property which he does not occupy

(f)     is to keep the property in as good a state of repair as it was in when he went into occupation (except for fair wear and tear) and is not to alter it

(g)     is to insure the property in a sum which is not less than the purchase price against all risks in respect of which comparable premises are normally insured

(h)     is to quit the property when the licence ends.

5.2.3   On the creation of the buyer's licence, condition 5.1 ceases to apply, which means that the buyer then assumes the risk until completion.

5.2.4   The buyer is not in occupation for the purposes of this condition if he merely exercises rights of access given solely to do work agreed by the seller.

5.2.5   The buyer's licence ends on the earliest of completion date, rescission of the contract or when five working days' notice given by one party to the other takes effect.

5.2.6   If the buyer is in occupation of the property after his licence has come to an end and the contract is subsequently completed he is to pay the seller compensation for his continued occupation calculated at the same rate as the fee mentioned in condition 5.2.2(d).

5.2.7   The buyer's right to raise requisitions is unaffected.

# 6. Completion

## *6.1 Date*

6.1.1   Completion date is twenty working days after the date of the contract but time is not of the essence of the contract unless a notice to complete has been served.

6.1.2   If the money due on completion is received after 2.00pm, completion is to be treated, for the purposes only of conditions 6.3 and 7.3, as taking place on the next working day.

6.1.3   Condition 6.1.2 does not apply where the sale is with vacant possession of the property or any part and the seller has not vacated the property or that part by 2.00pm on the date of actual completion.

## *6.2 Place*

Completion is to take place in England and Wales, either at the seller's solicitor's office or at some other place which the seller reasonably specifies.

## *6.3 Apportionments*

6.3.1   Income and outgoings of the property are to be apportioned between the parties so far as the change of ownership on completion will affect entitlement to receive or liability to pay them.

6.3.2   If the whole property is sold with vacant possession or the seller exercises his option in condition 7.3.4, apportionment is to be made with effect from the date of actual completion; otherwise, it is to be made from completion date.

6.3.3    In apportioning any sum, it is to be assumed that the seller owns the property until the end of the day from which apportionment is made and that the sum accrues from day to day at the rate at which it is payable on that day.

6.3.4    For the purpose of apportioning income and outgoings, it is to be assumed that they accrue at an equal daily rate throughout the year.

6.3.5    When a sum to be apportioned is not known or easily ascertainable at completion, a provisional apportionment is to be made according to the best estimate available. As soon as the amount is known, a final apportionment is to be made and notified to the other party. Any resulting balance is to be paid no more than ten working days later, and if not then paid the balance is to bear interest at the contract rate from then until payment.

6.3.6    Compensation payable under condition 5.2.6 is not to be apportioned.

## 6.4  Amount payable

The amount payable by the buyer on completion is the purchase price (less any deposit already paid to the seller or his agent) adjusted to take account of:

(a)   apportionments made under condition 6.3
(b)   any compensation to be paid or allowed under condition 7.3.

## 6.5  Title deeds

6.5.1    The seller is not to retain the documents of title after the buyer has tendered the amount payable under condition 6.4.

6.5.2    Condition 6.5.1 does not apply to any documents of title relating to land being retained by the seller after completion.

## 6.6  Rent receipts

The buyer is to assume that whoever gave any receipt for a payment of rent or service charge which the seller produces was the person or the agent of the person then entitled to that rent or service charge.

## 6.7  Means of payment

The buyer is to pay the money due on completion in one or more of the following ways:

(a)   legal tender
(b)   a banker's draft
(c)   a direct credit to a bank account nominated by the seller's solicitor
(d)   an unconditional release of a deposit held by a stakeholder.

### *6.8 Notice to complete*

6.8.1    At any time on or after completion date, a party who is ready able and willing to complete may give the other a notice to complete.

6.8.2    A party is ready able and willing:

(a)    if he could be, but for the default of the other party, and

(b)    in the case of the seller, even though a mortgage remains secured on the property, if the amount to be paid on completion enables the property to be transferred freed of all mortgages (except those to which the sale is expressly subject).

6.8.3    The parties are to complete the contract within ten working days of giving a notice to complete, excluding the day on which the notice is given. For this purpose, time is of the essence of the contract.

6.8.4    On receipt of a notice to complete:

(a)    if the buyer paid no deposit, he is forthwith to pay a deposit of 10 per cent

(b)    if the buyer paid a deposit of less than 10 per cent, he is forthwith to pay a further deposit equal to the balance of that 10 per cent.

## 7. Remedies

### *7.1 Errors and omissions*

7.1.1    If any plan or statement in the contract, or in the negotiations leading to it, is or was misleading or inaccurate due to an error or omission, the remedies available are as follows.

7.1.2    When there is a material difference between the description or value of the property as represented and as it is, the injured party is entitled to damages.

7.1.3    An error or omission only entitles the injured party to rescind the contract:

(a)    where it results from fraud or recklessness, or

(b)    where he would be obliged, to his prejudice, to transfer or accept property differing substantially (in quantity, quality or tenure) from what the error or omission had led him to expect.

### *7.2 Rescission*

If either party rescinds the contract:

(a)    unless the rescission is a result of the buyer's breach of contract the deposit is to be repaid to the buyer with accrued interest

(b)    the buyer is to return any documents he received from the seller and is to cancel any registration of the contract.

### *7.3 Late completion*

7.3.1    If there is default by either or both of the parties in performing their obligations under the contract and completion is delayed, the party whose total period of default is the greater is to pay compensation to the other party.

7.3.2    Compensation is calculated at the contract rate on the purchase price, or (where the buyer is the paying party) the purchase price less any deposit paid, for the period by which the paying party's default exceeds that of the receiving party, or, if shorter, the period between completion date and actual completion.

7.3.3    Any claim for loss resulting from delayed completion is to be reduced by any compensation paid under this contract.

7.3.4    Where the buyer holds the property as tenant of the seller and completion is delayed, the seller may give notice to the buyer, before the date of actual completion, that he intends to take the net income from the property until completion. If he does so, he cannot claim compensation under condition 7.3.1 as well.

## 7.4  After completion

Completion does not cancel liability to perform any outstanding obligation under this contract.

## 7.5  Buyer's failure to comply with notice to complete

7.5.1    If the buyer fails to complete in accordance with a notice to complete, the following terms apply.

7.5.2    The seller may rescind the contract, and if he does so:

(a)    he may

(i)    forfeit and keep any deposit and accrued interest
(ii)   resell the property
(iii)  claim damages

(b)    the buyer is to return any documents he received from the seller and is to cancel any registration of the contract.

7.5.3    The seller retains his other rights and remedies.

## 7.6  Seller's failure to comply with notice to complete

7.6.1    If the seller fails to complete in accordance with a notice to complete, the following terms apply.

7.6.2    The buyer may rescind the contract, and if he does so:

(a)    the deposit is to be repaid to the buyer with accrued interest
(b)    the buyer is to return any documents he received from the seller and is, at the seller's expense, to cancel any registration of the contract.

7.6.3    The buyer retains his other rights and remedies.

## 8. Leasehold property

### *8.1 Existing leases*

8.1.1    The following provisions apply to a sale of leasehold land.

8.1.2    The seller having provided the buyer with copies of the documents embodying the lease terms, the buyer is treated as entering into the contract knowing and fully accepting those terms.

8.1.3    The seller is to comply with any lease obligations requiring the tenant to insure the property.

### *8.2 New leases*

8.2.1    The following provisions apply to a grant of a new lease.

8.2.2    The conditions apply so that:

'seller' means the proposed landlord
'buyer' means the proposed tenant
'purchase price' means the premium to be paid on the grant of a lease.

8.2.3    The lease is to be in the form of the draft attached to the agreement.

8.2.4    If the term of the new lease will exceed 21 years, the seller is to deduce a title which will enable the buyer to register the lease at HM Land Registry with an absolute title.

8.2.5    The buyer is not entitled to transfer the benefit of the contract.

8.2.6    The seller is to engross the lease and a counterpart of it and is to send the counterpart to the buyer at least five working days before completion date.

8.2.7    The buyer is to execute the counterpart and deliver it to the seller on completion.

### *8.3 Landlord's consent*

8.3.1    The following provisions apply if a consent to assign or sub-let is required to complete the contract.

8.3.2    (a)    The seller is to apply for the consent at his expense, and to use all reasonable efforts to obtain it
         (b)    The buyer is to provide all information and references reasonably required.

8.3.3    The buyer is not entitled to transfer the benefit of the contract.

8.3.4    Unless he is in breach of his obligation under condition 8.3.2, either party may rescind the contract by notice to the other party if three working days before completion date:

         (a)    the consent has not been given or
         (b)    the consent has been given subject to a condition to which the buyer reasonably objects.

In that case, neither party is to be treated as in breach of contract and condition 7.2 applies.

## 9. Chattels

9.1     The following provisions apply to any chattels which are to be sold.

9.2     Whether or not a separate price is to be paid for the chattels, the contract takes effect as a contract for sale of goods.

9.3     Ownership of the chattels passes to the buyer on actual completion.

# Appendix 3

# STANDARD COMMERCIAL PROPERTY CONDITIONS (FIRST EDITION)

## *1. GENERAL*

## *1.1 Definitions:*

*1.1.1*     *In these conditions*

   *(a)*     *'accrued interest' means:*

      *(i)*     *if money has been placed on deposit or in a building society share account, the interest actually earned*

      *(ii)*     *otherwise, the interest which might reasonably have been earned by depositing the money at interest on seven days' notice of withdrawal with a clearing bank less, in either case, any proper charges for handling the money*

   *(b)*     *'clearing bank' means a member of CHAPS Clearing Limited*

   *(c)*     *'completion date', unless otherwise defined, has the meaning given in condition 6.1.1*

   *(d)*     *'contract rate', unless otherwise defined is the Law Society's interest rate from time to time in force*

   *(e)*     *'direct credit' means a direct transfer of cleared funds to an account nominated by the seller's solicitor and held at a clearing bank*

   *(f)*     *'lease' includes sub-lease, tenancy and agreement for a lease or sub-lease*

   *(g)*     *'notice to complete' means a notice requiring completion of the contract in accordance with condition 6*

   *(h)*     *'public requirement' means any notice, order or proposal given or made (whether before or after the date of the contract) by a body acting on statutory authority*

   *(i)*     *'requisition' includes objection*

   *(j)*     *'service charge' has the meaning given to it by section 18 of the Landlord and Tenant Act 1985 (disregarding the words 'of a dwelling')*

   *(k)*     *'solicitor' includes barrister, certificated notary public, licensed conveyancer and recognised body under sections 9 or 32 of the Administration of Justice Act 1985*

   *(l)*     *'transfer' includes conveyance and assignment*

(m)      *'working day' means any day from Monday to Friday (inclusive) which is not Christmas Day, Good Friday or a statutory Bank Holiday.*

1.1.2    *When used in these conditions the terms 'absolute title' and 'office copies' have the special meanings given to them by the Land Registration Act 1925.*

## 1.2  Joint parties

*If there is more than one seller or more than one buyer, the obligations which they undertake can be enforced against them all jointly or against each individually.*

## 1.3  Notices and documents

1.3.1    *A notice required or authorised by the contract must be in writing.*

1.3.2    *Giving a notice or delivering a document to a party's solicitor has the same effect as giving or delivering it to that party.*

1.3.3    *Transmission by fax is a valid means of giving a notice or delivering a document where delivery of the original document is not essential.*

1.3.4    *Subject to conditions 1.3.5 to 1.3.7, a notice is given and a document delivered when it is received.*

1.3.5    *If a notice or document is received after 4.00 pm on a working day, or on a day which is not a working day, it is to be treated as having been received on the next working day.*

1.3.6    *Unless the actual time of receipt is proved, a notice or document sent by the following means is to be treated as having been received before 4.00 pm on the day shown below:*

(a)      *by first class post: two working days after posting*

(b)      *by second class post: three working days after posting*

(c)      *through a document exchange: on the first working day after the day on which it would normally be available for collection by the addressee.*

1.3.7    *Where a notice or document is sent through a document exchange, then for the purpose of condition 1.3.6 the actual time of receipt is:*

(a)      *the time when the addressee collects it from the document exchange or, if earlier*

(b)      *8.00 am on the first working day on which it is available for collection at that time.*

## 1.4  VAT

1.4.1    *An obligation to pay money includes an obligation to pay any value added tax chargeable in respect of that payment.*

1.4.2    *All sums made payable by the contract are exclusive of value added tax.*

## 1.5 Assignment and Sub-Sales

*1.5.1*    *The buyer is not entitled to transfer the benefit of the contract.*

*1.5.2*    *The seller may not be required to transfer the property in parts or to any person other than the buyer.*

## 2. FORMATION

### 2.1 Date

*2.1.1*    *If the parties intend to make a contract by exchanging duplicate copies by post or through a document exchange, the contract is made when the last copy is posted or deposited at the document exchange.*

*2.1.2*    *If the parties' solicitors agree to treat exchange as taking place before duplicate copies are actually exchanged, the contract is made as so agreed.*

### 2.2 Deposit

*2.2.1*    *The buyer is to pay a deposit of 10 per cent of the purchase price no later than the date of the contract.*

*2.2.2*    *Except on a sale by auction the deposit is to be paid by direct credit and is to be held by the seller's solicitor as stakeholder on terms that on completion it is paid to the seller with accrued interest.*

### 2.3 Auctions

*2.3.1*    *On a sale by auction the following conditions apply to the property and, if it is sold in lots, to each lot.*

*2.3.2*    *The sale is subject to a reserve price.*

*2.3.3*    *The seller, or a person on its behalf, may bid up to the reserve price.*

*2.3.4*    *The auctioneer may refuse any bid.*

*2.3.5*    *If there is a dispute about a bid, the auctioneer may resolve the dispute or restart the auction at the last undisputed bid.*

*2.3.6*    *The auctioneer is to hold the deposit as agent for the seller. If any cheque tendered in payment of all or part of the deposit is dishonoured when first presented, the seller may, within seven working days of being notified that the cheque has been dishonoured, give notice to the buyer that the contract is discharged by the buyer's breach.*

## 3. MATTERS AFFECTING THE PROPERTY

### 3.1 Freedom from incumbrances

3.1.1       *The seller is selling the property free from incumbrances, other than those mentioned in condition 3.1.2.*

3.1.2       *The incumbrances subject to which the property is sold are:*

     (a)       *those mentioned in the contract*

     (b)       *those discoverable by inspection of the property before the contract*

     (c)       *those the seller does not and could not reasonably know about*

     (d)       *matters, other than monetary charges or incumbrances, disclosed or which would have been disclosed by the searches and enquiries which a prudent buyer would have made before entering into the contract*

     (e)       *public requirements*

3.1.3       *After the contract is made, the seller is to give the buyer written details without delay of any new public requirement and of anything in writing which it learns about concerning any incumbrance subject to which the property is sold.*

3.1.4       *The buyer is to bear the cost of complying with any outstanding public requirement and is to indemnify the seller against any liability resulting from a public requirement.*

### 3.2 Physical state

3.2.1       *The buyer accepts the property in the physical state it is in at the date of the contract, unless the seller is building or converting it.*

3.2.2       *A leasehold property is sold subject to any subsisting breach of a condition or tenant's obligation relating to the physical state of the property which renders the lease liable to forfeiture.*

3.2.3       *A sub-lease is granted subject to any subsisting breach of a condition or tenant's obligation relating to the physical state of the property which renders the seller's own lease liable to forfeiture.*

### 3.3 Leases affecting the property

3.3.1       *The following provisions apply if any part of the property is sold subject to a lease.*

3.3.2       *The seller having provided the buyer with full details of each lease or copies of the documents embodying the lease terms, the buyer is treated as entering into the contract knowing and fully accepting those terms.*

3.3.3       (a)       *The seller is to inform the buyer without delay if the seller learns of any application by the tenant in connection with the lease.*

(b)     The seller is not to agree to any application by the tenant nor to grant or withhold licences, consents or approvals required under the lease without the consent of the buyer.

(c)     The buyer is not to withhold its consent or attach conditions to the consent where to do so might place the seller in breach of an obligation to the tenant or a statutory duty.

(d)     In all other circumstances the seller is to act as the buyer reasonably directs, and the buyer is to indemnify it against all consequent loss and expense.

3.3.4     The seller is not to agree to any proposal to change the lease terms without the consent of the buyer and is to inform the buyer without delay of any change which may be proposed or agreed.

3.3.5     The seller is to manage the property in accordance with the principles of good estate management until completion.

3.3.6     The seller is to inform the buyer without delay if the lease ends and is not to serve any notice to end the lease.

3.3.7     The buyer is to indemnify the seller against all claims arising from the lease after actual completion; this includes claims which are unenforceable against a buyer for want of registration.

3.3.8     If the property does not include all the land let, the seller may apportion the rent and, if the lease is a new tenancy, the buyer may require the seller to apply under section 10 of the Landlord and Tenant (Covenants) Act 1995 for the apportionment to bind the tenant.

## 3.4 Retained land

3.4.1     The following provisions apply where after the transfer the seller will be retaining land near the property.

3.4.2     The buyer will have no right of light or air over the retained land, but otherwise the seller and the buyer will each have the rights over the land of the other which they would have had if they were two separate buyers to whom the seller had made simultaneous transfers of the property and the retained land.

3.4.3     Either party may require that the transfer is to contain appropriate express terms.

## 4. TITLE AND TRANSFER

### 4.1 Timetable

4.1.1     *The following are the steps for deducing and investigating the title to the property to be taken within the following time limits:*

| Step | | Time Limit |
|------|---|------------|
| 1. | The seller is to send the buyer evidence of title in accordance with condition 4.2 | Immediately after making the contract |
| 2. | The buyer may raise written requisitions | Six working days after either the date of the contract or the date of delivery of the seller's evidence of title on which the requisitions are raised is the later |
| 3. | The seller is to reply in writing to any requisitions raised | Four working days after receiving the requisitions |
| 4. | The buyer may make written observations on the seller's replies | Three working days after receiving the replies |

*The time limit on the buyer's right to raise requisitions applies even where the seller supplies incomplete evidence of its title, but the buyer may, within six working days from delivery of any further evidence, raise further requisitions resulting from that evidence. On the expiry of the relevant time limit the buyer loses its right to raise requisitions or make observations.*

4.1.2     *The parties are to take the following steps to prepare and agree the transfer of the property within the following time limits:*

| Step | | Time Limit |
|------|---|------------|
| A. | The buyer is to send the seller a draft transfer | At least twelve working days before completion date |
| B. | The seller is to approve or revise that draft and either return it or retain it for use as the actual transfer | Four working days after delivery of the draft transfer |
| C. | If the draft is returned the buyer is to send an engrossment to the seller | At least five working days before completion date |

4.1.3     *Periods of time under conditions 4.1.1 and 4.1.2 may run concurrently.*

*4.1.4*　　*If the period between the date of the contract and completion date is less than 15 working days, the time limits in conditions 4.1.1 and 4.1.2 are to be reduced by the same proportion as that period bears to the period of 15 working days. Fractions of a working day are to be rounded down except that the time limit to perform any step is not to be less than one working day.*

## 4.2 Proof of title

*4.2.1*　　*The evidence of registered title is office copies of the items required to be furnished by section 110(1) of the Land Registration Act 1925 and the copies, abstracts and evidence referred to in section 110(2).*

*4.2.2*　　*The evidence of unregistered title is an abstract of the title, or an epitome of title with photocopies of the relevant documents.*

*4.2.3*　　*Where the title to the property is unregistered, the seller is to produce to the buyer (without cost to the buyer):*

　　　　*(a)　　the original of every relevant document, or*

　　　　*(b)　　an abstract, epitome or copy with an original marking by a solicitor of examination against the original or against an examined abstract or against an examined copy.*

## 4.3 Defining the property

*4.3.1*　　*The seller need not:*

　　　　*(a)　　prove the exact boundaries of the property*

　　　　*(b)　　prove who owns fences, ditches, hedges or walls*

　　　　*(c)　　separately identify parts of the property with different titles*

　　　　*further than it may be able to do from information in its possession.*

*4.3.2*　　*The buyer may, if to do so is reasonable, require the seller to make or obtain, pay for and hand over a statutory declaration about facts relevant to the matters mentioned in condition 4.3.1. The form of the declaration is to be agreed by the buyer, who must not unreasonably withhold its agreement.*

## 4.4 Rents and rent charges

　　　　*The fact that a rent or rent charge, whether payable or receivable by the owner of the property, has been or will on completion be, informally apportioned is not to be regarded as a defect in title.*

## 4.5 Transfer

*4.5.1*　　*The buyer does not prejudice its right to raise requisitions, or to require replies to any raised, by taking any steps in relation to the preparation or agreement of the transfer.*

4.5.2    *If the contract makes no provision as to title guarantee, then subject to condition 4.5.3 the seller is to transfer the property with full title guarantee.*

4.5.3    *The transfer is to have effect as if the disposition is expressly made subject to all matters to which the property is sold subject under the terms of the contract.*

4.5.4    *If after completion the seller will remain bound by any obligation affecting the property and disclosed to the buyer before the contract is made, but the law does not imply any covenant by the buyer to indemnify the seller against liability for future breaches of it:*

(a)      *the buyer is to covenant in the transfer to indemnify the seller against liability for any future breach of the obligation and to perform it from then on, and*

(b)      *if required by the seller, the buyer is to execute and deliver to the seller on completion a duplicate transfer prepared by the buyer.*

4.5.5    *The seller is to arrange at its expense that, in relation to every document of title which the buyer does not receive on completion, the buyer is to have the benefit of:*

(a)      *a written acknowledgement of the buyer's right to its production, and*

(b)      *a written undertaking for its safe custody (except while it is held by a mortgagee or by someone in a fiduciary capacity).*

## 5. PENDING COMPLETION

### 5.1 Responsibility for property

5.1.1    *Unless condition 5.1.2 or condition 8.1.3 applies:*

(a)      *the seller is under no obligation to the buyer to insure the property*

(b)      *if payment under a policy effected by or for the buyer is reduced, because the property is covered against loss or damage by an insurance policy effected by or for the seller, the purchase price is to be abated by the amount of that reduction.*

5.1.2    *If the contract provides that the policy insuring the property against loss or damage effected by or for the seller should continue in force after exchange of contracts, the seller is to:*

(a)      *do everything required to continue to maintain the policy, including to pay promptly any premium which falls due*

(b)      *increase the amount or extent of the cover as requested by the buyer, if the insurers agree and the buyer pays the additional premium*

(c)      *permit the buyer to inspect the policy, or evidence of its terms, at any time*

(d) *obtain or consent to an endorsement on the policy of the buyer's interest, at the buyer's expense*

(e) *pay to the buyer immediately on receipt, any part of an additional premium which the buyer paid and which is returned by the insurers*

(f) *if before completion the property suffers loss or damage:*

    (i) *pay to the buyer on completion the amount of policy moneys which the seller has received; and*

    (ii) *if no final payment has then been received, assign to the buyer, at the buyer's expense, all rights to claim under the policy in such form as the buyer reasonably requires; and pending execution of the assignment, hold any policy moneys received in trust for the buyer*

*and the buyer is to pay the seller a proportionate part of the premium which the seller paid in respect of the period from the date when the contract is made to the date of actual completion.*

5.1.3 (a) *The following provisions apply if any part of the property transferred is subject to a lease.*

(b) *On completion the seller is to cancel the insurance policy relating to the property transferred.*

(c) *The seller is to pay the buyer, immediately on receipt the amount of refund of premium received which relates to any part of the premium which was paid or reimbursed by a tenant or third party*

(d) *The buyer is to hold the money paid subject to the rights of that tenant or third party.*

5.1.4 *Section 47 of the Law of Property Act 1925 does not apply.*

## 5.2 *Occupation by buyer*

5.2.1 *If the buyer is not already lawfully in the property, and the seller agrees to let the buyer into occupation, the following terms apply.*

5.2.2 *The buyer is a licensee and not a tenant. The terms of the licence are that the buyer:*

(a) *cannot transfer it*

(b) *is to pay or indemnify the seller against all outgoings and other expenses in respect of the property*

(c) *is to pay the seller a fee calculated at the contract rate on the purchase price (less any deposit paid) for the period of the licence*

(d) *is entitled to any rents and profits from any part of the property which the buyer does not occupy*

(e) *is to keep the property in as good a state of repair as it was in when the buyer went into occupation (except for fair wear and tear) and is not to alter it*

(f)      *is not to infringe a statutory requirement relating to it*

(g)      *is to quit the property when the licence ends.*

5.2.3    *The licence ends on the earliest of: completion date, rescission of the contract or when five working days' notice given by one party to the other takes effect.*

5.2.4    *If the buyer is in occupation of the property after the licence has come to an end and the contract is subsequently completed the buyer is to pay the seller compensation for its continued occupation calculated at the same rate as the fee mentioned in condition 5.2.2(c).*

5.2.5    *The buyer's right to raise requisitions is unaffected.*

## 6. COMPLETION

### 6.1 Date

6.1.1    *Completion date is twenty working days after the date of the contract but time is not of the essence of the contract unless a notice to complete has been served.*

6.1.2    *If the money due on completion is received after 2.00 pm, completion is to be treated, for the purposes only of conditions 6.3 and 7.3, as taking place on the next working day.*

### 6.2 Place

*Completion is to take place in England and Wales, either at the seller's solicitor's office or at some other place which the seller reasonably specifies.*

### 6.3 Apportionments

6.3.1    *Subject to condition 6.3.7 income and outgoings of the property are to be apportioned between the parties so far as the change of ownership on completion will affect entitlement to receive or liability to pay them.*

6.3.2    *If the whole property is sold with vacant possession or the seller exercises its option in condition 7.3.4, apportionment is to be made with effect from the date of actual completion; otherwise, it is to be made from completion date.*

6.3.3    *In apportioning any sum, it is to be assumed that the buyer owns the property from the beginning of the day on which the apportionment is to be made.*

6.3.4    *A sum to be apportioned is to be treated as accruing*

(a)      *from day to day throughout the period for which it is payable or receivable by instalments, and*

(b)      *at the rate from time to time applicable during the period for which the apportionment is made.*

6.3.5    *When a sum to be apportioned is not known or easily ascertainable at completion, a provisional apportionment is to be made according to the best estimate available. As soon as the amount is known, a final apportionment is to be made and notified to the other party. Any resulting balance is to be paid no more than ten working days later, and if not then paid the balance is to bear interest at the contract rate from then until payment.*

6.3.6    *Compensation payable under condition 5.2.4 is not to be apportioned.*

6.3.7    *This provision applies where any lease subject to which the property is sold obliges the tenant to pay a service charge.*

    *(a)    On completion the buyer is to pay the seller the amount of any service charge expenditure already incurred by the seller but not yet due from the tenant.*

    *(b)    On completion the seller is to credit the buyer with service charge payments already recovered from the tenant but not yet incurred by the seller.*

6.3.8.    *Condition 6.3.9 applies if*

    *(a)    any part of the property is sold subject to a lease*

    *(b)    on completion any rent or service charge payable under the lease is due but not paid*

    *(c)    the contract does not provide that the buyer is to assign to the seller the right to collect any arrears due to the seller under the terms of the contract, and*

    *(d)    the seller is not entitled to recover any arrears from the tenant.*

6.3.9    *(a)    The buyer is to seek to collect all the arrears in the ordinary course of management, but need not take legal proceedings or distrain*

    *(b)    A payment made on account of arrears is to be apportioned between the parties in the ratio of the sums owed to each, unless the tenant exercises its right to appropriate the payment in some other manner*

    *(c)    Any part of a payment on account of arrears received by one party but due to the other is to be paid no more than ten working days after the receipt of cash or cleared funds and, if not then paid, the sum is to bear interest at the contract rate until payment.*

## 6.4 Amount payable

*The amount payable by the buyer on completion is the purchase price (less any deposit already paid to the seller or its agent) adjusted to take account of:*

    *(a)    apportionments made under condition 6.3*

    *(b)    any compensation to be paid under condition 7.3*

    *(c)    any sum payable under condition 5.1.2*

### 6.5  Title deeds

6.5.1       *As soon as the buyer has complied with all its obligations on completion the seller must part with the documents of title.*

6.5.2       *Condition 6.5.1 does not apply to any documents of title relating to land being retained by the seller after completion.*

### 6.6  Rent receipts

*The buyer is to assume that whoever gave any receipt for a payment of rent or service charge which the seller produces was the person or the agent of the person then entitled to that rent or service charge.*

### 6.7  Means of payment

*The buyer is to pay the money due on completion by direct credit and by an unconditional release of any deposit held by a stakeholder.*

### 6.8  Notice to complete

6.8.1       *At any time on or after completion date, a party who is ready, able and willing to complete may give the other a notice to complete.*

6.8.2       *A party is ready, able and willing:*

   *(a)       if it could be, but for the default of the other party, and*

   *(b)       in the case of the seller, even though a mortgage remains secured on the property, if the amount to be paid on completion enables the property to be transferred freed of all mortgages (except those to which the sale is expressly subject).*

6.8.3       *The parties are to complete the contract within ten working days of giving a notice to complete, excluding the day on which the notice is given. For this purpose, time is of the essence of the contract.*

6.8.4       *On receipt of a notice to complete:*

   *(a)       if the buyer paid no deposit, it is forthwith to pay a deposit of 10 per cent*

   *(b)       if the buyer paid a deposit of less than 10 per cent, it is forthwith to pay a further deposit equal to the balance of that 10 per cent.*

### 7.  REMEDIES

### 7.1  Errors and omission

7.1.1       *If any plan or statement in the contract, or in the negotiations leading to it, is or was misleading or inaccurate due to an error or omission, the remedies available are as follows.*

7.1.2   *When there is a material difference between the description or value of the property as represented and as it is, the injured party is entitled to damages.*

7.1.3   *An error or omission only entitles the injured party to rescind the contract:*

(a)   *where that error or omission results from fraud or recklessness, or*

(b)   *where that party would be obliged, to its prejudice, to transfer or accept property differing substantially (in quantity, quality or tenure) from that which the error or omission had led it to expect.*

## 7.2  Rescission

*If either party rescinds the contract:*

(a)   *unless the rescission is a result of the buyer's breach of contract the deposit is to be repaid to the buyer with accrued interest*

(b)   *the buyer is to return any documents received from the seller and is to cancel any registration of the contract*

(c)   *the seller's duty to pay any returned premium under condition 5.1.2(e) (whenever received) is not affected.*

## 7.3  Late completion

7.3.1   *If the buyer defaults in performing its obligations under the contract and completion is delayed, the buyer is to pay compensation to the seller.*

7.3.2   *Compensation is calculated at the contract rate on the purchase price (less any deposit paid) for the period between completion date and actual completion, but ignoring any period during which the seller was in default.*

7.3.3   *Any claim by the seller for loss resulting from delayed completion is to be reduced by any compensation paid under this contract.*

7.3.4   *Where the sale is not with vacant possession of the whole property and completion is delayed, the seller may give notice to the buyer, before the date of actual completion, that it will take the net income from the property until completion as well as compensation under condition 7.3.1.*

## 7.4  After completion

*Completion does not cancel liability to perform any outstanding obligation under the contract.*

## 7.5  Buyer's failure to comply with notice to complete

7.5.1   *If the buyer fails to complete in accordance with a notice to complete, the following terms apply.*

7.5.2   *The seller may rescind the contract, and if it does so:*

(a)   *it may*

> > > *(i)          forfeit and keep any deposit and accrued interest*
> > > *(ii)          resell the property*
> > > *(iii)          claim damages*
> >
> > *(b)          the buyer is to return any documents received from the seller and is to cancel any registration of the contract.*

*7.5.3          The seller retains its other rights and remedies.*

## 7.6  Seller's failure to comply with notice to complete

*7.6.1          If the seller fails to complete in accordance with a notice to complete, the following terms apply.*

*7.6.2          The buyer may rescind the contract, and if it does so:*

> *(a)          the deposit is to be repaid to the buyer with accrued interest*

> *(b)          the buyer is to return any documents it received from the seller and is, at the seller's expense, to cancel any registration of the contract.*

*7.6.3          The buyer retains its other rights and remedies.*

## 8.  LEASEHOLD PROPERTY

### 8.1  Existing leases

*8.1.1          The following provisions apply to a sale of leasehold land.*

*8.1.2          The seller having provided the buyer with copies of the documents embodying the lease terms, the buyer is treated as entering into the contract knowing and fully accepting those terms.*

*8.1.3          The seller is to comply with any lease obligations requiring the tenant to insure the property.*

### 8.2  New leases

*8.2.1          The following provisions apply to a grant of a new lease.*

*8.2.2          The conditions apply so that:*

*'seller' means the proposed landlord*
*'buyer' means the proposed tenant*
*'purchase price' means the premium to be paid on the grant of a lease.*

*8.2.3          The lease is to be in the form of the draft attached to the contract.*

*8.2.4          If the term of the new lease will exceed 21 years, the seller is to deduce a title which will enable the buyer to register the lease at HM Land Registry with an absolute title.*

*8.2.5          The seller may not be required to grant a lease to any person other than the buyer.*

8.2.6   *The seller is to engross the lease and a counterpart of it and is to send the counterpart to the buyer at least five working days before completion date.*

8.2.7   *The buyer is to execute the counterpart and deliver it to the seller on completion.*

## 8.3 Landlord's consent

8.3.1   *The following provisions apply if the property is leasehold and the terms of the lease require a reversioner whether or not immediate (a 'landlord') to consent to an assignment or sub-letting.*

8.3.2   *The seller is to:*

   (a)   *apply for the consent at its expense, and to use all reasonable efforts to obtain it*

   (b)   *give the buyer notice forthwith on obtaining the consent*

   (c)   *enter into an authorised guarantee agreement if the lease so requires.*

8.3.3   *Where the landlord lawfully requires, the buyer is to:*

   (a)   *use reasonable endeavours to provide promptly all information and references*

   (b)   *covenant directly with the landlord to observe the tenant's covenants and the conditions in the seller's lease*

   (c)   *use reasonable endeavours to provide guarantees of the performance and observance of the tenant's covenants and conditions in the seller's lease*

   (d)   *execute or procure the execution of the licence.*

8.3.4   *If the landlord's consent has not been obtained by the original completion date:*

   (a)   *the time for completion is to be postponed until five working days after the seller gives written notice to the buyer that the consent has been obtained or four months from the original completion date whichever is the earlier*

   (b)   *the postponed date is to be treated as the completion date.*

8.3.5   *At any time after four months from the original completion date, either party may rescind the contract by notice to the other if:*

   (a)   *consent has still not been given, and*

   (b)   *no declaration has been obtained from the court that consent has been unreasonably withheld.*

8.3.6   *Neither party may object to a consent subject to a condition:*

   (a)   *which under section 19(1A) of the Landlord and Tenant Act 1927 is not regarded as unreasonable,*

   (b)   *which is lawfully imposed under an express term of the lease.*

8.3.7    *If the contract is rescinded under condition 8.3.5 the seller is to remain liable for any breach of condition 8.3.2 and the buyer is to remain liable for any breach of condition 8.3.3 but in all other respects neither party is to be treated as in breach of contract and condition 7.2 applies.*

8.3.8    *A party in breach of its obligations under condition 8.3.2 or 8.3.3 cannot rescind under condition 8.3.5 for so long as its breach is a cause of the consent's being withheld.*

## 9.  CHATTELS

9.1     *The following provisions apply to any chattels which are to be sold.*

9.2     *Whether or not a separate price is to be paid for the chattels, the contract takes effect as a contract for sale of goods.*

9.3     *Ownership of the chattels passes to the buyer on actual completion but they are at the buyer's risk from the contract date.*

**Appendix 4**

# THE LAW SOCIETY'S FORMULAE FOR EXCHANGING CONTRACTS BY TELEPHONE, FAX OR TELEX

## INTRODUCTION

It is essential that an agreed memorandum of the details and of any variations of the formula used should be made at the time and retained in the file. This would be very important if any question on the exchange were raised subsequently. Agreed variations should also be confirmed in writing. The serious risks of exchanging contracts without a deposit, unless the full implications are explained to and accepted by the seller client, are demonstrated in *Morris v Duke-Cohan & Co* (1975) 119 SJ 826.

As those persons involved in the exchange will bind their firms to the undertakings in the formula used, solicitors should carefully consider who is to be authorised to exchange contracts by telephone, fax or telex and should ensure that the use of the procedure is restricted to them. Since professional undertakings form the basis of the formulae, they are only recommended for use between firms of solicitors and licensed conveyancers.

## LAW SOCIETY TELEPHONE/TELEX EXCHANGE – FORMULA A (1986)

(For use where one solicitor holds both signed parts of the contract.)

A completion date of        20  is agreed. The solicitor holding both parts of the contract confirms that he or she holds the part signed by his or her client(s), which is identical to the part he or she is also holding signed by the other solicitor's client(s) and will forthwith insert the agreed completion date in each part.

Solicitors mutually agree that exchange shall take place from that moment and the solicitor holding both parts confirms that, as of that moment, he or she holds the part signed by his or her client(s) to the order of the other. He or she undertakes that day by first-class post, or where the other solicitor is a member of a document exchange (as to which the inclusion of a reference thereto in the solicitor's letterhead shall be conclusive evidence) by delivery to that or any other affiliated exchange, or by hand delivery direct to that solicitor's office, to send his or her signed part of the contract to the other solicitor, together, where he or she is the purchaser's solicitor, with a banker's draft or a solicitor's client account cheque for the deposit amounting to £. . . . . . . .

**Note**

1. A memorandum should be prepared, after use of the formula, recording:

> (a) date and time of exchange;
> (b) the formula used and exact wording of agreed variations;
> (c) the completion date;
> (d) the (balance) deposit to be paid; and
> (e) the identities of those involved in any conversation.

## LAW SOCIETY TELEPHONE/TELEX EXCHANGE – FORMULA B (1986)

(For use where each solicitor holds his or her own client's signed part of the contract.)

A completion date of          20   is agreed. Each solicitor confirms to the other that he or she holds a part contract in the agreed form signed by the client(s) and will forthwith insert the agreed completion date.

Each solicitor undertakes to the other thenceforth to hold the signed part of the contract to the other's order, so that contracts are exchanged at that moment. Each solicitor further undertakes that day by first-class post, or, where the other solicitor is a member of a document exchange (as to which the inclusion of a reference thereto in the solicitor's letterhead shall be conclusive evidence) by delivery to that or any other affiliated exchange, or by hand delivery direct to that solicitor's office, to send his or her signed part of the contract to the other together, in the case of a purchaser's solicitor, with a banker's draft or a solicitor's client account cheque for the deposit amounting to £. . . . . . . .

**Notes**

1. A memorandum should be prepared, after use of the formula, recording:

> (a) date and time of exchange;
> (b) the formula used and exact wording of agreed variations;
> (c) the completion date;
> (d) the (balance) deposit to be paid;
> (e) the identities of those involved in any conversation.

2. Those who are going to effect the exchange must first confirm the details in order to ensure that both parts are identical. This means in particular, that if either part of the contract has been amended since it was originally prepared, the solicitor who holds a part contract with the amendments must disclose them, so that it can be confirmed that the other part is similarly amended.

*9 July 1986, revised January 1996*

## LAW SOCIETY TELEPHONE/FAX/TELEX EXCHANGE – FORMULA C (1989)

### Part I

The following is agreed:
Final time for exchange:    pm
Completion date:    20
Deposit to be paid to:

Each solicitor confirms that he or she holds a part of the contract in the agreed form signed by his or her client, or, if there is more than one client, by all of them. Each solicitor undertakes to the other that:

(a) he or she will continue to hold that part of the contract until the final time for exchange on the date the formula is used, and

(b) if the vendor's solicitor so notifies the purchaser's solicitor by fax, telephone or telex (whichever was previously agreed) by that time, they will both comply with part II of the formula.

The purchaser's solicitor further undertakes that either he or she or some other named person in his or her office will be available up to the final time for exchange to activate part II of the formula on receipt of the telephone call, fax or telex from the vendor's solicitors.

### Part II

Each solicitor undertakes to the other henceforth to hold the part of the contract in his or her possession to the other's order, so that contracts are exchanged at that moment, and to despatch it to the other on that day. The purchaser's solicitor further undertakes to the vendor's solicitor to despatch on that day, or to arrange for the despatch on that day of, a banker's draft or a solicitor's client account cheque for the full deposit specified in the agreed form of contract (divided as the vendor's solicitor may have specified) to the vendor's solicitor and/or to some other solicitor whom the vendor's solicitor nominates, to be held on formula C terms.

'To despatch' means to send by first-class post, or, where the other solicitor is a member of a document exchange (as to which the inclusion of a reference thereto in the solicitor's letterhead is to be conclusive evidence) by delivery to that or any other affiliated exchange, or by hand delivery direct to the recipient solicitor's office. 'Formula C terms' means that the deposit is held as stakeholder, or as agent for the vendor with authority to part with it only for the purpose of passing it to another solicitor as deposit in a related property purchase transaction on these terms.

### Notes

1. Two memoranda will be required when using Formula C. One needs to record the use of Part I, and a second needs to record the request of the vendor's solicitor to the purchaser's solicitor to activate Part II.

2. The first memorandum should record:

    (a) the date and time when it was agreed to use Formula C;

    (b) the exact wording of any agreed variations;

    (c)  the final time, later that day, for exchange;

    (d)  the completion date;

    (e)  the name of the solicitor to whom the deposit was to be paid, or details of amounts and names if it was to be split; and

    (f)  the identities of those involved in any conversation.

3. Formula C assumes the payment of a full contractual deposit (normally 10%).

4. The contract term relating to the deposit must allow it to be passed on, with payment direct from payer to ultimate recipient, in the way in which the formula contemplates. The deposit must ultimately be held by a solicitor as stakeholder. Whilst some variation in the formula can be agreed this is a term of the formula which must not be varied, unless all the solicitors involved in the chain have agreed.

5. If a buyer proposes to use a deposit guarantee policy, Formula C will need substantial adaptation.

6. It is essential prior to agreeing Part I of Formula C that those effecting the exchange ensure that both parts of the contract are identical.

7. Using Formula C involves a solicitor in giving a number of professional undertakings. These must be performed precisely. Any failure will be a serious breach of professional discipline. One of the undertakings may be to arrange that someone over whom the solicitor has no control will do something (ie to arrange for someone else to despatch the cheque or banker's draft in payment of the deposit). An undertaking is still binding even if it is to do something outside the solicitor's control.

8. Solicitors do not as a matter of law have an automatic authority to exchange contracts on a Formula C basis, and should always ensure that they have the client's express authority to use Formula C. A suggested form of authority is set out below. It should be adapted to cover any special circumstances:

I/We . . . . . . . . . . . understand that my/our sale and purchase of . . . . . . . . . . . . . are both part of a chain of linked property transactions, in which all parties want the security of contracts which become binding on the same day.

I/We agree that you should make arrangements with the other solicitors or licensed conveyancers involved to achieve this.

I/We understand that this involves each property-buyer offering, early on one day, to exchange contracts whenever, later that day, the seller so requests, and that the buyer's offer is on the basis that it cannot be withdrawn or varied during that day.

I/We agree that when I/we authorise you to exchange contracts, you may agree to exchange contracts on the above basis and give any necessary undertakings to the other parties involved in the chain and that my/our authority to you cannot be revoked throughout the day on which the offer to exchange contracts is made.

*15 March 1989, revised January 1996*

# Appendix 5

# THE LAW SOCIETY'S CODE FOR COMPLETION BY POST 1998

## PREAMBLE

The Code provides a procedure for postal completion which practising solicitors may adopt by reference. It may also be used by licensed conveyancers.

Before agreeing to adopt this Code, a solicitor must be satisfied that doing so will not be contrary to the interests of the client (including any mortgagee client).

When adopted, the Code applies without variation, unless agreed in writing in advance.

## PROCEDURE

### General

1. To adopt this Code, all the solicitors must expressly agree, preferably in writing, to use it to complete a specific transaction.
2. On completion, the seller's solicitor acts as the buyer's solicitor's agent without any fee or disbursements.

### Before completion

3. The seller's solicitor will specify in writing to the buyer's solicitor before completion the mortgages or charges secured on the property which, on or before completion, will be redeemed or discharged to the extent that they relate to the property.
4. The seller's solicitor undertakes:

    (i) to have the seller's authority to receive the purchase money on completion; and
    (ii) on completion to have the authority of the proprietor of each mortgage or charge specified under paragraph 3 to receive the sum intended to repay it,

BUT
if the seller's solicitor does not have all the necessary authorities then:

    (iii) to advise the buyer's solicitor no later than 4.00pm on the working day before the completion date that they do not have all the authorities or immediately if any is withdrawn later; and
    (iv) not to complete until he has the buyer's solicitor's instructions.

5. Before the completion date, the buyer's solicitor will send the seller's solicitor instructions as to any of the following which apply:

    (i) documents to be examined and marked;
    (ii) memoranda to be endorsed;

(iii) undertakings to be given;

(iv) deeds, documents (including any relevant undertakings) and authorities relating to rents, deposits, keys, etc. to be sent to the buyer's solicitors following completion; and

(v) other relevant matters.

In default of instructions, the seller's solicitor is under no duty to examine, mark or endorse any document.

6.  The buyer's solicitor will remit to the seller's solicitor the sum required to complete, as notified in writing on the seller's solicitor's completion statement or otherwise, or in default of notification as shown by the contract. If the funds are remitted by transfer between banks, the seller's solicitor will instruct the receiving bank to telephone to report immediately the funds have been received. Pending completion, the seller's solicitor will hold the funds to the buyer's solicitor's order.

7.  If by the agreed date and time for completion the seller's solicitor has not received the authorities specified in paragraph 4, instructions under paragraph 5 and the sum specified in paragraph 6, the seller's solicitor will forthwith notify the buyer's solicitor and request further instructions.

## Completion

8.  The seller's solicitor will complete forthwith on receiving the sum specified in paragraph 6, or at a later time agreed with the buyer's solicitor.

9.  When completing, the seller's solicitor undertakes:

(i)  to comply with the instructions given under paragraph 5; and

(ii) to redeem or obtain discharges for every mortgage or charge so far as it relates to the property specified under paragraph 3 which has not already been redeemed or discharged.

## After completion

10. The seller's solicitor undertakes:

(i)  immediately completion has taken place to hold to the buyer's solicitor's order every item referred to in (iv) of paragraph 5 and not to exercise a lien over any such item;

(ii) as soon as possible after completion, and in any event on the same day:

   (a)  to confirm to the buyer's solicitor by telephone or fax that completion has taken place; and

   (b)  to send written confirmation and, at the risk of the buyer's solicitor, the items listed in (iv) of paragraph 5 to the buyer's solicitor by first class post or document exchange.

## Supplementary

11. The rights and obligations of the parties, under the contract or otherwise, are not affected by this Code.

12. (i) References to the seller's solicitor and the buyer's solicitor apply as appropriate to solicitors acting for other parties who adopt the Code.
    (ii) When a licensed conveyancer adopts this Code, references to a solicitor include a licensed conveyancer.

13. A dispute or difference arising between solicitors who adopt this Code (whether or not subject to any variation) relating directly to its application is to be referred to a single arbitrator agreed between the solicitors. If they do not agree on the appointment within one month, the President of The Law Society may appoint the arbitrator at the request of one of the solicitors.

## Notes to the Code:

1. This Code will apply to transactions when the Code is adopted after 1 July 1998.
2. The object of this Code is to provide solicitors with a convenient means for completion on an agency basis when a representative of the buyer's solicitor is not attending at the office of the seller's solicitor.
3. As with The Law Society's formulae for exchange of contracts by telephone and fax, the guide embodies professional undertakings and is only recommended for adoption between solicitors and licensed conveyancers.
4. Paragraph 2 of the Code provides that the seller's solicitors will act as agents for the buyer's solicitors without fee or disbursements. The convenience of not having to make a specific appointment on the day of completion for the buyer's solicitor to attend to complete will offset the agency work that the seller's solicitor has to do and any postage payable in completing under the Code. Most solicitors will from time to time act for both sellers and buyers. If a seller's solicitor does consider that charges and/or disbursements are necessary in a particular case this would represent a variation in the Code and should be agreed in writing before the completion date.
5. In view of the decision in *Edward Wong Finance Company Limited v Johnson, Stokes & Master* [1984] AC 1296, clause 4(ii) of the Code requires the seller's solicitor to undertake on completion to have authority of the proprietor of every mortgage or charge to be redeemed to receive the sum needed to repay such charge.
6. Paragraph 11 of the Code provides that nothing in the Code shall override any rights and obligations of the parties under contract or otherwise.
7. The buyer's solicitor is to inform the seller's solicitor of the mortgages or charges which will be redeemed or discharged (see paragraph 3 above) and is to specify those for which an undertaking will be required on completion (paragraph 5(iii)). The information may be given in reply to requisitions on title. Such a reply may also amount to an undertaking.
8. Care must be taken if there is a sale and sub-sale. The sub-seller's solicitor may not hold the title deeds nor be in a position to receive the funds required to discharge the seller's mortgage on the property. Enquiries should be made to ascertain if the monies or some part of the monies payable on completion should, with either the authority of the sub-seller or the sub-seller's solicitor, be sent direct to the seller's solicitor and not to the sub-seller's solicitor.

9.  Care must also be taken if there is a simultaneous resale and completion and enquiries should be made by the ultimate buyer's solicitor of the intermediate seller's solicitor as to the price being paid on that purchase. Having appointed the intermediate seller's solicitor as agent, the buyer's solicitor is fixed with the knowledge of an agent even without having personal knowledge (see Green Card Warning on Property Fraud).

10. If the seller's solicitor has to withdraw from using the Code, the buyer's solicitor should be notified of this not later than 4.00pm on the working day prior to the completion date. If the seller's solicitor's authority to receive the monies is withdrawn later, the buyer's solicitor must be notified immediately.

These notes refer only to some of the points in the Code that practitioners may wish to consider before agreeing to adopt it. Any variation in the Code must be agreed in writing before the completion date.

**Appendix 6**

# FORM OF UNDERTAKING TO DISCHARGE BUILDING SOCIETY MORTGAGES APPROVED BY THE LAW SOCIETY IN CONVEYANCING MATTERS

In consideration of you today completing the purchase of . . . . . . . . . . . . . . . . . . . .
WE HEREBY UNDERTAKE forthwith to pay over to the . . . . . . . . . . . . . . . . . .
Building Society the money required to redeem the mortgage/legal charge dated

. . . . . . . . . . . . . and to forward the receipted mortgage/legal charge to you as soon

as it is received by us from the . . . . . . . . . . . . . . . . . . . . . . . . . . Building Society.

# Appendix 7

# FORMS OF UNDERTAKING AGREED WITH BANKS

## FORM NO 1

Undertaking by solicitor – Deeds/Land Certificate loaned to the Solicitor for purpose of inspection only and return.

. . . . . . . . . . . . . . . . . . . . . . 20 . . .

To      BANK LIMITED

I/We hereby acknowledge to have received on loan from you the Title Deeds and/or Land Certificate and documents relating to . . . . . . . . . . . . . . . . . . . . . . . . . . . . . . .
. . . . . . . . . . . . . . . . . . . . . in accordance with the schedule hereto.

I/We undertake to hold them on your behalf and to return them to you on demand in the same condition in which they now are and without the property to which they relate or any interest therein being, to our knowledge, in any way charged, conveyed, assigned, leased, encumbered, disposed of or dealt with.

Signature . . . . . . . . . . . . . . . . . . . . . . . . . . .

SCHEDULE

## FORM NO 2

Undertaking by Solicitor – Deed/Land Certificate handed to the Solicitor re Sale or Mortgage of property, or part of it, in consideration of promise to account to Bank for net proceeds.

................................ 20 ...

To      BANK LIMITED

I/We hereby acknowledge to have received from you the Title Deeds and/or Land Certificate and documents *together with a charge to the Bank relating to . . . . . . . . . ........................ in accordance with the schedule hereto for the purpose of the sale/mortgage of this property.

I/We undertake to hold them on your behalf and to return them to you on demand in the same condition in which they now are, pending completion of such transaction. If the transaction is completed I/we undertake

a)   to pay to you the amount of the purchase/mortgage money, not being less than £ . . . . . . . . . . . gross subject only to the deduction therefrom of the deposit (if held by the estate agent(s)), the estate agent's commission and the legal costs and disbursements relating to the transaction, and

b)   if the Title Deeds and/or Land Certificate and documents also relate to other property in addition to that referred to above, to return same to you suitably endorsed or noted.

Signature . . . . . . . . . . . . . . . . . . . . . . . . . . . . .

**Note:** If there are likely to be any deductions from the purchase price other than those shown above, these must be specifically mentioned.

SCHEDULE

* Delete if no charge form has been taken.

# FORM NO 3

Undertaking by Solicitor – to send Deeds/Land Certificate to Bank on completion of a purchase, the Bank and/or its customer having provided the purchase monies.

. . . . . . . . . . . . . . . . . . . . . . 20 . . .

To     BANK LIMITED

If you provide facilities to my/our client . . . . . . . . . . . . . . . . . . . . for the purchase of the Freehold/Leasehold property [Description of Property]

I/We undertake

a)    that any sums received from you or your customer for the purpose of this transaction will be applied solely for acquiring a good marketable title to such property and in paying any necessary deposit legal costs and disbursements in connection with such purchase. The purchase price contemplated is £ . . . . . . . . gross and with apportionments and any necessary disbursements is not expected to exceed £ . . . . . . . . .
     and

b)    after the property has been acquired by . . . . . . . . . . . . . . . . . . . . . . . and all necessary stamping and registration has been completed to send the Title Deeds and/or Land Certificate and documents to you and in the meantime to hold them to your order.

Signature . . . . . . . . . . . . . . . . . . . . . . . . . . .

## FORM NO 4  (BRIDGING FINANCE)

Undertaking by solicitors (with form of authority from client) to account to the bank for net proceeds of sale of the existing property, the bank having provided funds in connection with the purchase of the new property.

### Authority from client(s)

. . . . . . . . . . . . . . . . . . . . . . 20 . . .

To . . . . . . . . . . . . . . . . . . . . . . . . . . . . . . . . . . . . . . . . . . . . . . . . . . . . . . . . . . . . . . . . .

. . . . . . . . . . . . . . . . . . . . . . . . . . . . . . . . . . . . . . . . . . . . . . . . . . . . . . . . . . . . . .

(name and address of solicitors)

I/We hereby irrevocably authorise and request you to give an undertaking in the form set out below and accordingly to pay the net proceeds of sale after deduction of your costs to . . . . . . . . . . . . . . . . . . . . . . . . . . . . . . . . . . . . . . Bank Limited . . . . . . .

. . . . . . . . . . . . Branch.

Signature of client(s) . . . . . . . . . . . . . . . . . . . . . . . . . . . .

Undertaking . . . . . . . . . . . . . . . . . . . . . . . .   20 . . .


To . . . . . . . . . . . . . . . . . . . . . . . . . . . . . . BANK LIMITED


If you provide facilities to our client . . . . . . . . . . . . . . . . . . . . . . . . . . . . . . . . . . . . . . .

. . . . . . . . . . . . . . . . . . . . . . . . . . . . . . . . . . . . . . . . . . . . . . . . . . . . . . . . . . . . . . . .

for the purchase of the Freehold/Leasehold property (the new property) . . . . . . . . . . .

. . .. . . . . . . . . . . . . . . . . . . . . . . . . . . . . . . . . . . . . . . . . . . . . . . . . . . . . . . . . . . . .

(description of property)

pending the sale by our client of the Freehold/Leasehold property (the existing property . . . . . . . . . . . . . . . . . . . . . . . . . . . . . . . . . . . . . . . . . . . . . . . . . . . . . . . . . . . . .

(description of property)


We undertake

1.  That any sums received from you or your customer will be applied solely for the following purposes:

    *a)  in discharging the present mortgage(s) on the existing property
    b)   in acquiring a good marketable title to the new property *subject to the mortgage mentioned below
    c)   in paying any necessary deposit legal fees costs and disbursements in connection with the purchase.

    The purchase price contemplated is £ . . . . . . . gross.

    *We are informed that a sum of £ . . . . . . . . is being advanced on mortgage by . . . . . . . . . . . . . . . . . The amount required from our client for the transaction

including the deposit and together with costs disbursements and apportionments
is not expected to exceed £ . . . . . . . .

2.    To hold to your order when received by us the documents of title of the existing
property pending completion of the sale (unless subject to any prior
mortgage(s)) and of the new property (unless subject to any prior mortgage(s)).

3.    To pay to you the net proceeds of sale of the existing property when received by
us. The sale price contemplated is £ . . . . . . . . and the only deductions which
will have to be made at present known to us are:

(i)    the deposit (if not held by us)
(ii)   the estate agent's commission
(iii)  the amount required to redeem any mortgage and charges which so far as
       known to us at present do not exceed £ . . . . . . . .
(iv)   the legal fees costs and disbursements relating to the transaction.

4.    To advise you immediately of any subsequent claim by a third party upon the
net proceeds of sale of which we have knowledge.

## Note

(1)   If any deductions will have to be made from the net proceeds of sale other than
those shown above, these must be specifically mentioned.
(2)   It would be convenient if this form of undertaking were presented in duplicate
so that a carbon copy could be retained by the solicitor.

*Delete if not applicable.

**Appendix 8**

# THE CML LENDERS' HANDBOOK FOR SOLICITORS AND LICENSED CONVEYANCERS ENGLAND AND WALES (1999)

## CONTENTS

## PART I – INSTRUCTIONS AND GUIDANCE

Those lenders who instruct using the CML Lenders' Handbook certify that these instructions have been prepared to comply with the requirements of Rule 6 (3) of the Solicitors' Practice Rules 1990.

## 1  GENERAL

1.1      The CML Lenders' Handbook is issued by the Council of Mortgage Lenders. Your instructions from an individual lender will indicate if you are being instructed in accordance with the Lenders' Handbook. If you are, the general provisions in part 1 and any specific requirements in part 2 must be followed.

1.2      References to 'we' and 'our' means the lender from whom you receive instructions.

1.3      The Lenders' Handbook does not affect any responsibilities you have to us under the general law or any practice rule or guidance issued by your professional body from time to time.

1.4 The standard of care which we expect of you is that of a reasonably competent solicitor or licensed conveyancer acting on behalf of a mortgagee.

1.5 The limitations contained in rule 6(3)(c) and (e) of the Solicitors' Practice Rules 1990 apply to the instructions contained in the Lenders' Handbook and any separate instructions.

1.6 You must also comply with any separate instructions you receive for an individual loan.

1.7 If the borrower and the mortgagor are not one and the same person, all references to 'borrower' shall include the mortgagor.

1.8 References to 'borrower' (and, if applicable, 'guarantor' or, expressly or impliedly, the mortgagor) are to each borrower (and guarantor or mortgagor) named in the mortgage instructions/offer (if sent to the conveyancer). This applies to references in the Lenders' Handbook and in the certificate of title.

1.9 References to 'mortgage offer' include any loan agreement, offer of mortgage or any other similar document.

1.10 If you are instructed in connection with any additional loan (including a further advance) then you should treat references to 'mortgage' and 'mortgage offer' as applying to such 'additional loan' and 'additional loan offer' respectively.

1.11 In any transaction during the lifetime of the mortgage when we instruct you, you must use our current standard documents in all cases and must not amend them without our written consent. We will send you all the standard documents necessary to enable you to comply with our instructions, but please let us know if you need any other documents and we will send these to you. Check part 2 to see who you should contact. If you consider that any of the documentation is inappropriate to the particular facts of a transaction, you should write to us (see part 2) with full details and any suggested amendments.

1.12 In order to act on our behalf your firm must be a member of our conveyancing panel. You must also comply with any terms and conditions of your panel appointment.

1.13 If you or a member of your immediate family (that is to say, a spouse, co-habitee, parent, sibling, child, step-parent, step-child, grandparent, grandchild, parent-in-law, or child-in-law) is the borrower and you are a sole practitioner, you must not act for us.

1.14 Your firm or company must not act for us if the partner of fee earner dealing with the transaction or a member of his immediate family is the borrower, unless we say your firm may act (see part 2) and a separate fee earner of no less standing or a partner within the firm acts for us.

1.15 If there is any conflict of interest, you must not act for us and must return our instructions.

## 2 COMMUNICATIONS

2.1     All communications between you and us should be in writing quoting the mortgage account or roll number, the surname and initials of the borrower and the property address. You should keep copies of all written communications on your file as evidence of notification and authorisation. If you use PC fax or e-mail, you should keep a paper copy.

2.2     If you require deeds or information from us in respect of a borrower or a property then you must first of all have the borrower's authority for such a request. If there is more than one borrower, you must have the authority of all the borrowers.

2.3     Where you are reporting a matter to us you must do so as soon as you become aware of it so as to avoid any delay. You should provide a concise summary and your recommendations. After reporting a matter you should not complete the mortgage until you have received our further instructions. We recommend that you report such matters before exchange of contracts because we may have to withdraw or change the mortgage offer.

## 3 SAFEGUARDS

3.1     You must follow the guidance in the Law Society's Green Card (mortgage fraud) and Pink Card (undertakings) and, to the extent that they apply, comply with the Money Laundering Regulations 1993 (see the Law Society's Blue Card).

3.2     If you are not familiar with the seller's solicitors or licensed conveyancers, you must verify that they appear in a legal directory or they are currently on record with the Law Society or Council for Licensed Conveyancers as practising at the address shown on their note paper.

3.3     Unless you personally know the signatory of a document, you must ask the signatory to provide evidence of identity, which you must carefully check. You should check the signatory's identity against one of the documents from list A or two of the documents in list B:

**List A**

- a valid full passport; or
- a valid HM Forces identity card with the signatory's photograph; or
- any other document listed in the additional list A in part 2.

**List B**

- a cheque guarantee card, credit card (bearing the Mastercard or Visa Logo) American Express or Diners Club card, debit or multi-function card (bearing the Switch or Delta logo) issued in the United Kingdom with an original account statement less than three months old; or
- a firearm and shotgun certificate; or
- a receipted utility bill less than three months old; or
- a council tax bill less than three months old; or
- a council rent book showing the rent paid for the last three months; or

- a mortgage statement from another lender for the mortgage accounting year just ended; or
- any other document listed in the additional list B in part 2.

You should check that any document you use to verify a signatory's identity appears to be authentic and current, signed in the relevant place. You should take a copy of it and keep the copy on your file. You should also check that the signatory's signature on any document being used to verify identity matches the signatory's signature on the document we require the signatory to sign and that the address shown on any document used to verify identity is that of the signatory.

3.4        All your duties to us under the Lenders' Handbook in relation to identifying signatories of documents will be satisfied by you complying with paragraphs 3.1, 3.2 and 3.3.

## 4 VALUATION OF THE PROPERTY

### 4.1 Valuation

4.1.1      Check part 2 to see whether we send you a copy of the valuation report or if you must get it from the borrower. If you are sent, or are required to obtain, a copy of the valuation report:

4.1.1.1    you must take reasonable steps to verify that there are no discrepancies between the description of the property as valued and the title and other documents which a reasonably competent conveyancer should obtain, and, if there are, you must tell us immediately; and

4.1.1.2    you should take reasonable steps to verify that the assumptions stated by the valuer about the title (for example, its tenure, easements, boundaries and restrictions on its use) in the valuation are correct. If they are not, please let us know as soon as possible (see part 2) as it will be necessary for us to check with the valuer whether the valuation needs to be revised.

We are not expecting you to assume the role of valuer. We are simply trying to ensure that the valuer has valued the property based on correct information.

4.1.2      We recommend that you should advise the borrower that there may be defects in the property which are not revealed by the inspection carried out by our valuer and there may be omissions or inaccuracies in the report which do not matter to us but which would matter to the borrower. We recommend that, if we send a copy of a valuation report that we have obtained, you should also advise the borrower that the borrower should not rely on the report in deciding whether to proceed with the purchase and that he obtains his own more detailed report on the condition and value of the property, based on a fuller inspection, to enable him to decide whether the property is suitable for his purposes.

### 4.2 Re-inspection

Where the mortgage offer states that a final inspection is needed, you must ask for the final inspection at least 10 working days before the advance is required. Failure to do so may cause delay in the issue of the advance. Your certificate of title must be sent to us in the usual way (see part 2).

## 5  TITLE

### *5.1  Surrounding Circumstances*

5.1.1       Please report to us (see part 2) if the owner or registered proprietor has been registered for less than six months or the person selling to the borrower is not the owner or registered proprietor unless the seller is:

5.1.1.1     a personal representative of the registered proprietor; or
5.1.1.2     an institutional mortgagee exercising its power of sale; or
5.1.1.3     a receiver, trustee in bankruptcy or liquidator; or
5.1.1.4     developer or builder selling a property acquired under a part exchange scheme.

5.1.2       If any matter comes to the attention of the fee earner dealing with the transaction which you should reasonably expect us to consider important in deciding whether or not to lend to the borrower (such as whether the borrower has given misleading information to us or the information which you might reasonably expect to have been given to us is no longer true) and you are unable to disclose that information to us because of a conflict of interest, you must cease to act for us and return our instructions stating that you consider a conflict of interest has arisen.

### *5.2  Searches and Reports*

5.2.1       In carrying out your investigation, you must make all usual and necessary searches and enquiries. We must be named as the applicant in the Land Registry search.

5.2.2       In addition, you must carry out any other searches which may be appropriate to the particular property, taking into account its locality and other features.

5.2.3       All searches except where there is a priority period must not be more than three months old at exchange of contracts and six months old at completion.

5.2.4       You must make a mining search (such as a coal, tin, china clay or brine search) where it is reasonable to believe that the property could be affected by underground workings. The search must not be more than six months old at exchange of contracts. In the case of coal mining search, if the result of the search from the Coal Authority are such that the property is not affected by any of the matters mentioned in the report then we do not need to be notified of its contents. Subject to that, you should advise us if any entries are revealed in the same way as you would advise the borrower. You should not simply send us a copy of the mining search.

5.2.5       Check part 2 to see if we accept personal searches or search insurance. If we do, you must take reasonable steps to check that a suitably qualified search agent carries out the personal search or that the search insurance policy adequately protects us. You must be satisfied that you will be able to certify that the title is good and marketable.

### 5.3 *Planning*

5.3.1   You must by making appropriate searches and enquiries take all reasonable steps (including any further enquiries to clarify any issues which may arise) to ensure that there is no evidence of any breach of the conditions of any consent or certificate affecting the property and that no matter is revealed which would preclude the property from being used as a residential property or that the property may be the subject of enforcement action. If there is such evidence and the seller (or the borrower in the case of remortgage) is not providing a sufficient undertaking to satisfy those outstanding conditions by completion, then this must be reported to us (see part 2). Check part 2 to see if copies of planning permissions, building regulations and other consents or certificates should be sent to us.

5.3.2   If the property will be subject to any enforceable restrictions, for example under an agreement (such as an agreement under section 106 of the Town and Country Planning Act 1990) or in a planning permission, which, at the time of completion, might reasonably be expected materially to affect its value or its future marketability, you should report this to us (see part 2).

### 5.4 *Good and Marketable Title*

5.4.1   The title to the property must be good and marketable free of any restrictions, covenants, easements, charges or encumbrances which, at the time of completion, might reasonably be expected to materially adversely affect the value of the property or its future marketability (but excluding any matters covered by indemnity insurance) and which may be accepted by us for mortgage purposes. Our requirements in respect of indemnity insurance are set out in 9. You must also take reasonable steps to ensure that, on completion, the property will be vested in the borrower.

5.4.2   Good leasehold title will be acceptable if:

5.4.2.1   a marked abstract of the freehold and any intermediate leasehold title for the statutory period of 15 years before the grant of the lease is provided; or

5.4.2.2   you are prepared to certify that the title is good and marketable when sending your certificate of title because, for example, the landlord's title is generally accepted in the district where the property is situated; or

5.4.2.3   you arrange indemnity insurance. Our requirements in respect of indemnity insurance are set out in 9.

5.4.3   A title based on adverse possessions or possessory title will be acceptable if:

5.4.3.1   there is satisfactory evidence by statutory declaration of adverse possession for a period of at least 12 years. In the case of lost title deeds, the statutory declaration must explain the loss satisfactorily;

5.4.3.2   we will also require indemnity insurance where there are buildings on the part in question or where the land is essential for access or services;

5.4.3.3      we may not need indemnity insurance in cases where such title affects land on which no buildings are erected or which is not essential for access or services. In such cases, you must send a plan of the whole of the land to be mortgaged to us identifying the area of land having possessory title. We will refer the matter to our valuer so that an assessment can be made of the proposed security. We will then notify you of any additional requirements or if a revised mortgage offer is to be made.

### 5.5 Freehold Flats and Flying Freeholds

5.5.1       If any part of the property comprises or is affected by a flying freehold or the property is freehold flat, check part 2 to see if we will accept it as security.

5.5.2       If we are prepared to accept a title falling within 5.5.1:

5.5.2.1      (unless we tell you not to in part 2) you must report to us that the property is a freehold flat or flying freehold; and

5.5.2.2      the property must have all necessary rights of support, protection, and entry for repair as well as a scheme of enforceable covenants that are also such that subsequent buyers are required to enter into covenants in identical form; and

5.5.2.3      you must be able to certify that the title is good and marketable; and

5.5.2.4      in case of flying freeholds, you must send us a plan of the property clearly showing the part affected by the flying freehold.

If our requirements in 5.5.2.2 are not satisfied, indemnity insurance must be in place at completion (see 9).

5.5.3       We have no objection to a security which comprises a building converted into not more than four flats where the borrower occupies one of those flats and the borrower or another flat owner owns the freehold of the building and the other flats are subject to long leases. Those other leases should contain appropriate covenants by the tenant of each flat to contribute towards the repair, maintenance and insurance of the building. The leases should also grant and reserve all necessary rights and easements. They should not contain any unduly onerous obligations on the landlord.

### 5.6 Restrictions on Use and Occupation

You must check whether there are any material restrictions on the occupation of the property as a private residence or as specified by us (for example, because of the occupier's employment, age or income), or any material restrictions on its use. If there are any restrictions, you must report details to us (see part 2). In some cases, we may accept a restriction, particularly if this relates to sheltered housing or to first time buyers.

## 5.7 Restrictive Covenants

5.7.1    You must enquire whether the property has been built, altered or is currently used in breach of a restrictive covenant. We rely on you to check that the covenant is not enforceable. If you are unable to provide an unqualified certificate of title as a result of the risk of enforceability, you must ensure that indemnity insurance (see 9) is in place at completion of our mortgage.

5.7.2    We will not insist on indemnity insurance:

5.7.2.1    if you are satisfied that there is no risk to our security; and

5.7.2.2    the breach has continued for more than 20 years; and

5.7.2.3    there is nothing to suggest that any action is being taken or is threatened in respect of the breach.

## 5.8 First Legal Charge

On completion, we require a fully enforceable first charge by way of legal mortgage over the property executed by all owners of the legal estate. All existing charges must be redeemed on or before completion, unless we agree that an existing charge may be postponed to rank after our mortgage. Our standard deed or form of postponement must be used.

## 5.9 Other Loans

You must ask the borrower how the balance of the purchase price is being provided. If you become aware that the borrower is not providing the balance of the purchase price from his own funds and/or is proposing to give a second charge over the property, you must report this to us if the borrower agrees (see part 2), failing which you must return our instructions and explain that you are unable to continue to act for us as there is a conflict of interest.

## 5.10 Leasehold Property

5.10.1    Our requirements on the unexpired term of a lease offered as security are set out in part 2.

5.10.2    There must be no provision for forfeiture on the insolvency of the tenant or any superior tenant.

5.10.3    The only situations where we will accept a restriction on the mortgage or assignment (whether by a tenant or a mortgagee) of the lease is where the person whose consent needs to be obtained cannot unreasonably withhold giving consent. The necessary consent for the particular transaction must be obtained before completion. If the lease requires consent to an assignment or mortgage to be obtained, you must obtain these on or before completion (this is particularly important if the lease is a shared ownership lease). You must not complete without them.

5.10.4　You must take all reasonable steps to check that there are satisfactory legal rights, particularly for access, support, shelter and protection. There should also be adequate covenants and arrangements in respect of matters such as insurance and maintenance and repair of the structure, foundations, main walls, roof, common parts, common services and grounds. Where these are the responsibility of one or more of the tenants, we expect the lease to contain adequate provisions for the enforcement of these obligations by the landlord or management company at the request of the tenant. In the absence of a provision in the lease that all the leases of the other flats in the block are in, or will be granted in, similar form, you should take reasonable steps to check that the leases of the other flats are in similar form or, if you are unable to do so, effect indemnity insurance (see 9). This is not essential if the landlord is responsible for the maintenance and repair of the main structure.

5.10.5　We have no objections to a lease which contains provision for a periodic increase of the ground rent provided that the amount of the increased ground rent is fixed or can be readily established and is reasonable. If you consider any increase in the ground rent may materially affect the value of the property, you must report this to us (see part 2).

5.10.6　You should enquire whether the landlord or managing agent foresees any significant increase in the level of the service charge in the reasonably foreseeable future and, if there is, you must report to us (see part 2).

5.10.7　If the terms of the lease are unsatisfactory, you must obtain a suitable deed of variation to remedy the defect or ensure that indemnity insurance (see 9) is put in place.

5.10.8　You must obtain on completion a clear receipt or other appropriate written confirmation for the last payment of ground rent and service charge from the landlord or managing agents on behalf of the landlord. Check part 2 to see if it must be sent to us after completion. If confirmation of the payment from the ground landlord cannot be obtained, we are prepared to proceed provided that you are satisfied that the absence of the ground landlord is common practice in the district where the property is situated, the seller confirms that there are no breaches of the terms of the lease, you are satisfied that our security will not be prejudiced by the absence of such a receipt and you provide us with a clear certificate of title.

5.10.9　Notice of the mortgage must be served on the landlord and any management company immediately following completion, whether or not the lease requires it. Check part 2 to see if a receipted copy of the notice or evidence of service must be sent to us after completion.

5.10.10　We will accept leases which require the property to be sold on the open market if re-building or reinstatement is frustrated provided the insurance proceeds and the proceeds of sale are shared between the landlord and tenant in proportion to their respective interests.

5.10.11　You must report to us (see part 2) if it becomes apparent that the landlord is either absent or insolvent. If we are to lend, we will require indemnity insurance to be arranged (see 9).

5.10.12    If the leasehold title is registered but the lease has been lost, we are
           prepared to proceed provided you have checked an HM Land Registry
           produced copy of the registered lease. Whilst this will not be an office
           copy of the lease you may accept it as sufficient evidence of the lease and
           its terms when approving the title for mortgage purposes provided it is, on
           its face, a complete copy.

## 5.11  Management Company

5.11.1     In paragraph 5.11 the following meanings shall apply:

- 'management company' means the company formed to carry out the
  maintenance and repair of the common parts;
- 'common parts' means the structure, main walls, roof, foundations,
  services, grounds and any other common areas serving the building or
  estate of which the property forms part;
- 'an interest in the land' means such an interest in the common parts as
  enables the management company to fully carry out its obligations in
  respect of the common parts, and such an interest may be by way of
  (a) a lease or (b) the grant of an easement.

           If a management company is required to maintain or repair the common
           parts, the management company should have an interest in the land; if the
           management company's interest in the common parts is not a leasehold
           interest then the tenants of the building should also be the members of the
           management company.

           If this is not the case, there should be a covenant by the landlord to carry
           out the obligations of the management company should it fail to do so.

5.11.1.1   For leases granted before 1 September 2000:

           If the lease does not satisfy the requirements of paragraph 5.11.1 but:

- you are nevertheless satisfied that the existing arrangements affecting
  the management company and the maintenance and repair of the
  common parts are sufficient to ensure the adequate maintenance of the
  common parts; and
- you are able to provide a clear certificate of title,

           then we will rely on your professional judgement.

5.11.2     You should make a company search and obtain and check such
           management company's last three years' published accounts. Any apparent
           problems with the company should be reported to us (see part 2). If the
           borrower is required to be a shareholder in the management company,
           check part 2 to see if you must arrange for the share certificate, a blank
           stock transfer form executed by the borrower and a copy of the
           memorandum and articles of association to be sent to us after completion
           (unless we tell you not to). If the management company is limited by
           guarantee, the borrower (or at least one of them if two or more) must
           become a member on or before completion.

### *5.12 Insolvency Considerations*

5.12.1    You must obtain a clear bankruptcy search against each borrower (and each mortgagor or guarantor, if any) providing us with protection at the date of completion of the mortgage. You must fully investigate any entries revealed by your bankruptcy search against the borrower (or mortgagor or guarantor) to ensure that they do not relate to them.

5.12.2    Where an entry is revealed against the name of the borrower (or the mortgagor or guarantor):

5.12.2.1  you must certify that the entry does not relate to the borrower (or the mortgagor or guarantor) if you are able to do so from your own knowledge or enquiries; or

5.12.2.2  if, after obtaining office copy entries or making other enquiries of the Official Receiver, you are unable to certify that the entry does not relate to the borrower (or the mortgagor or guarantor) you must report this to us (see part 2). We may as a consequence need to withdraw our mortgage offer.

5.12.3    If you are aware that the title to the property is subject to a deed of gift or a transaction at an apparent undervalue completed within five years of the proposed mortgage then you must be satisfied that we will acquire our interest in good faith and will be protected under the provisions of the Insolvency (No 2) Act 1994 against our security being set aside. If you are unable to give an unqualified certificate of title, you must arrange indemnity insurance (see 9).

5.12.4    You must also obtain clear bankruptcy searches against all parties to any deed of gift or transaction at an apparent undervalue.

### *5.13 Powers of Attorney*

5.13.1    If any document is being executed under power of attorney, you must ensure that the power of attorney is, on its face, properly drawn up, that it appears to be properly executed by the donor and that the attorney knows of no reason why such power of attorney will not be subsisting at completion. Where there are joint borrowers the power should comply with section 25 of the Trustee Act 1925, as amended by section 7 of the Trustee Delegation Act 1999 or with section 1 of the Trustee Delegation Act 1999 with the attorney making an appropriate statement under section 2 of the 1999 Act.

5.13.2    A power of attorney must not be used in connection with a regulated loan under the Consumer Credit Act 1974.

5.13.3    Check part 2 to see if:

5.13.3.1  the original or a certified copy of the power of attorney must be sent to us after completion;

5.13.3.2  where the power of attorney is a general power of attorney and was completed more than 12 months before the completion of our mortgage, you must send us a statutory declaration confirming that it has not been revoked.

### *5.14 Title Guarantee*

Whilst we recommend that a borrower should try to obtain a full title guarantee from the seller, we do not insist on this. We, however, require the borrower to give us a full title guarantee in the mortgage deed. The mortgage deed must not be amended.

## 6  THE PROPERTY

### *6.1 Mortgage Offer and Title Documents*

6.1.1    The loan to the borrower will not be made until all relevant conditions of the mortgage offer which need to be satisfied before completion have been complied with and we have received your certificate of title.

6.1.2    You must check your instructions and ensure that there are no discrepancies between them and the title documents and other matters revealed by your investigations.

6.1.3    You should tell us (see part 2) as soon as possible if you have been told that the borrower has decided not to take up the mortgage offer.

### *6.2  Boundaries*

These must be clearly defined by reference to a suitable plan or description. They must also accord with the information given in the valuation report, if this is provided by you. You should check with the borrower that the plan or the description accords with the borrower's understanding of the extent of the property to be mortgaged to us. You must report to us (see part 2), if there are any discrepancies.

### *6.3  Purchase Price*

6.3.1    The purchase price for the property must be the same as set out in our instructions. If it is not, you must tell us (unless we say differently in part 2). You must tell us (unless we say differently in part 2) if the contract provides for:

6.3.1.1   a cashback to the buyer; or
6.3.1.2   part of the price is being satisfied by a non-cash incentive to the buyer.

This may lead to the mortgage offer being withdrawn or amended.

6.3.2    You must report to us (see part 2) if you will not have control over the payment of all of the purchase money (for example, if it is proposed that the borrower pays money to the seller direct) other than a deposit held by an estate agent or a reservation fee of not more that £500 paid to a builder or developer.

### *6.4  Vacant Possession*

Unless otherwise stated in your instructions, it is a term of the loan that vacant possession is obtained. The contract must provide for this. If you doubt that vacant possession will be given, you must not part with the advance and should report the position to us (see part 2).

### 6.5 Properties Let At Completion

6.5.1      Where the property, or part of it, is already let, or is to be let at completion, then the letting must comply with the details set out it the mortgage offer or any consent to let we issue. If no such details are mentioned, you must report the position to us (see part 2).

6.5.2      Check part 2 for whether counterparts or certified copies of all tenancy agreement and leases in respect of existing tenancies must be sent to us after completion.

### 6.6 New Properties – Building Standards Indemnity Schemes

6.6.1      If the property is newly built, or newly converted, or to be occupied for the first time, you must ensure that it was built or converted under whichever of the following is acceptable to us (see part 2):

6.6.1.1      the National House-Building Council (NHBC) Buildmark scheme; or
6.6.1.2      the Zurich Municipal Newbuild scheme; or
6.6.1.3      Zurich Municipal Rebuild scheme; or
6.6.1.4      the Housing Association Property Mutual (HAPM) scheme; or
6.6.1.5      the monitoring of the development by a professional consultant. You should ensure that the professional consultant properly completes the lender's Professional Consultant's Certificate in the form published in the *Law Society's Gazette* of 25 May 2000 and on the Council of Mortgage Lender's website www.cml.org.uk or such other form as the instructing lender may provide. The professional consultant should also confirm to you that he has appropriate experience in the design or monitoring of the construction or conversion of residential or commercial buildings and has one or more of the following qualifications:

6.6.1.5.1      fellow or associate of the Royal Institution of Chartered Surveyors (FRICS or ARICS); or

6.6.1.5.2      fellow or member of the Institute of Structural Engineers (F.I.Struct.E or M.I.Struct.E); or

6.6.1.5.3      fellow or member of the Chartered Institute of Building (FCIOB or MCIOB); or

6.6.1.5.4      fellow or member of the Architects and Surveyors Institute (FASI or MASI); or

6.6.1.5.5      fellow or member of the Association of Building Engineers (FB.Eng or MB.Eng); or

6.6.1.5.6      member of the British Institute of Architectural Technicians (MBIAT); or

6.6.1.5.7      architect registered with the Architects Registration Board (ARB). An architect must be registered with the Architects Registration Board, even if also a member of another institution, for example the Royal Institute of British Architects (RIBA); or

6.6.1.5.8      fellow or member of the Institute of Civil Engineers (FICE or MICE); or

6.6.1.5.9      fellow or associate of the Institution of Valuers and Auctioneers (FSVA or ASVA).

6.6.2      If cover is provided by the NHBC, check part 2 to see if the House Purchaser's Insurance Policy, the Standard Notice of Insurance Cover, the Common Parts Notice of Insurance Cover and where applicable the NHBC agreement itself should be sent to us after completion.

6.6.3       If the property is built under the Buildmark Scheme, check part 2 to see if the Ten Year Notice should be sent to us after completion. If the property is a flat or maisonette and there are common parts, there should also be a Common Parts Ten Year Notice.

6.6.4       We do not insist that notice of assignment of the benefit of the NHBC agreement be given to the builder in the case of a second and subsequent purchase(s) during the period of the insurance cover. Check part 2 to see if any assignments of building standards indemnity schemes which are available should be sent to us after completion.

6.6.5       At the time he issues his certificate of practical completion, the consultant must have professional indemnity insurance in force for each claim for not less than the greater of:

6.6.5.1     the value of the property once completed; and
6.6.5.2     £250,000 if employed directly by the borrower or, in any other case, £500,000.

            Check part 2 to see whether you must verify this. If we require a collateral warranty from any professional adviser, this will be stated specifically in the mortgage instructions.

6.6.6       Check part 2 to see if the consultant's certificate must be sent to us after completion.

## 6.7 Roads and Sewers

6.7.1       If the roads or sewers serving the property are not adopted or maintained at public expense, there must a suitable agreement and bond in existence or you must make an appropriate retention from the purchase price or you must report to us (see part 2).

6.7.2       If there is any such agreement, it should be secured by bond or deposit as required by the appropriate authority to cover the cost of making up the roads and sewers to adoptable standards, maintaining them thereafter and procuring adoption.

## 6.8 Easements

6.8.1       You must take all reasonable steps to check that the property has the benefit of all easements necessary for its full use and enjoyment. This would include, for example, rights of way (both vehicular and pedestrian), the use of services and any necessary rights of entry for repair. All such rights must be enforceable by the borrower and the borrower's successors in title. If they are not, you must report to us (see part 2).

6.8.2       If the borrower owns adjoining land over which the borrower requires access to the property or in respect of which services are provided to the property, this land must also be mortgaged to us.

### 6.9 Release of Retentions

6.9.1        If we make a retention from an advance (for example, for repairs, improvements or road works) we are not obliged to release that retention, or any part of it, if the borrower is in breach of any of his obligations under the mortgage, or if a condition attached to the retention has not been met or if the loan has been repaid in full. You should, therefore not give an unqualified undertaking to pay the retention to a third party.

6.9.2        Check part 2 to see who we will release the retention to.

### 6.10 Neighbourhood Changes

The local search or the enquiries of the seller or the seller's conveyancer should not reveal that the property is in an area scheduled for redevelopment or in any way affected by road proposals. If it is, please report this to us (see part 2).

### 6.11 Rights of Pre-emption and Restrictions on Resale

You must ensure that there are no rights of pre-emption, restrictions on resale, options or similar arrangements in existence at completion which will affect our security. If there are, please report this to us (see part 2).

### 6.12 Improvement and Repair Grants

Where the property is subject to an improvement or repair grant which will not be discharged or waived on completion, check part 2 to see whether you must report the matter to us.

### 6.13 Insurance

Where we do not arrange the insurance, you must:

6.13.1       report to us (see part 2) if the property is not insured in accordance with our requirements (one of our requirements, see part 2, will relate to whether the property is insured in the joint names of us and the borrower or whether our interest may be noted);

6.13.2       arrange that the insurance cover starts from no later than completion;

6.13.3       check that the amount of buildings insurance cover is at least the amount referred to in the mortgage offer (if the property is part of a larger building and there is a common insurance policy, the total sum insured for the building must be not less than the total number of flats multiplied by the amount set out in the mortgage offer for the property);

6.13.4       ensure that the buildings insurance cover is index linked;

6.13.5       ensure that the excess does not exceed the amount set out in part 2;

6.13.6       check that all the following risks are covered:

6.13.6.1     fire;
6.13.6.2     lightning;
6.13.6.3     aircraft;
6.13.6.4     explosion;
6.13.6.5     earthquake;
6.13.6.6     storm;

| 6.13.6.7 | flood; |
|---|---|
| 6.13.6.8 | escape of water or oil; |
| 6.13.6.9 | riot; |
| 6.13.6.10 | malicious damage; |
| 6.13.6.11 | theft or attempted theft; |
| 6.13.6.12 | falling trees and branches and aerials; |
| 6.13.6.13 | subsidence; |
| 6.13.6.14 | heave; |
| 6.13.6.15 | landslip; |
| 6.13.6.16 | collision; |
| 6.13.6.17 | accidental breakage of glass and sanitary ware; and |
| 6.13.6.18 | accidental damage to underground services; |

6.13.7    check that the borrower has insured against public liability to anyone else; and

6.13.8    if we require (see part 2), obtain before completion the insurer's confirmation that the insurer will notify us if the policy is not renewed or is cancelled or if you do not obtain this, report to us (see part 2); and

6.13.9    if we require (see part 2), send a copy of the buildings insurance policy and the last premium receipt to us.

## 7 OTHER OCCUPIERS

7.1    Rights or interests of persons who are not a party to the mortgage and who are or will be in occupation of the property may affect our rights under the mortgage, for example as overriding interests.

7.2    If your instructions state the name of a person who is to live at the property, you should ask the borrower before completing the mortgage that the information given by us in our mortgage instructions or mortgage offer about occupants is correct and nobody else is to live at the property.

7.3    Unless we state otherwise (see part 2), you must obtain a signed deed or form of consent from all occupants aged 17 or over of whom you are aware who are not a party to the mortgage before completion of the mortgage.

7.4    We recognise that in some cases the information given to us or you by a borrower may be incorrect or misleading. If you have any reason to doubt the accuracy of any information disclosed, you should report it to us (see part 2) provided the borrower agrees; if the borrower does not agree, you should return our instructions.

## 8 SEPARATE REPRESENTATION

Unless we otherwise state (see part 2), you must not advise:

8.1    any borrower who does not personally benefit from the loan; or

8.2    any guarantor; or

8.3    anyone intending to occupy the property who is to execute a consent to the mortgage, and you must arrange for them to see an independent conveyancer. If we do allow you to advise any of these people, you must only do so after recommending in the absence of any other person interested in the transaction that such person obtains independent legal advice. Any advice that you give any of these people must also be given in the absence of any other person interested in the transaction. You should be particularly careful if the matrimonial home is being charged to secure a business debt.

## 9 INDEMNITY INSURANCE

You must effect an indemnity insurance policy whenever the Lenders' Handbook identifies that this is an acceptable or required course to us to ensure that the property has a good and marketable title at completion. This paragraph does not relate to mortgage indemnity insurance. The draft policy should not be sent to us unless we ask for it. Check part 2 to see if the policy must be sent to us after completion. Where indemnity insurance if effected:

9.1     you must approve the terms of the policy on our behalf; and

9.2     the limit of indemnity must meet our requirements (see part 2); and

9.3     the policy must be effected without cost to us; and

9.4     you must disclose to the insurer all relevant information which you have obtained; and

9.5     the policy must not contain conditions which you know would make it void or prejudice our interests; and

9.6     you must provide a copy of the policy to the borrower and explain to the borrower why the policy was effected and that a further policy may be required if there is further lending against the security of the property; and

9.7     you must explain to the borrower that the borrower will need to comply with any conditions of the policy and that the borrower should notify us of any notice or potential claim in respect of the policy; and

9.8     the policy should always be for our benefit and, if possible, for the benefit of the borrower and any subsequent owner or mortgagee. If the borrower will not be covered by the policy, you must advise the borrower of this.

## 10 THE LOAN AND CERTIFICATE OF TITLE

10.1    You should not submit your certificate of title unless it is unqualified or we have authorised you in writing to proceed notwithstanding any issues you have raised with us.

10.2    We shall treat the submission by you of the certificate of title as a request for us to release the mortgage advance to you.

10.3    You are only authorised to release the loan when you hold sufficient funds to complete the purchase of the property and pay all stamp duties and registration fees to perfect the security as a first legal mortgage or, if you do not have them, you accept responsibility to pay them yourself. You must hold the loan on trust for us until completion. If completion is delayed, you must return it to us when and how we tell you (see part 2).

10.4    You should note that although your certificate of title will be addressed to us, we may at some time transfer our interest in the mortgage. In those circumstances, our successors in title to the mortgage and persons deriving title under or through the mortgage will also rely on your certificate.

10.5    If, after you have requested the mortgage advance, completion is delayed you must telephone or fax us immediately after you are aware of the delay and you must inform us of the new date for completion (see part 2).

10.6    See part 2 for details of how long you can hold the mortgage advance before returning it to us. If completion is delayed for longer than that period, you must return the mortgage advance to us. If you do not, we reserve the right to require you to pay interest on the amount of the mortgage advance (see part 2).

10.7    If the mortgage advance is not returned within the period set out in part 2, we will assume that the mortgage has been completed, and we will charge the borrower interest under the mortgage. We may make further payments and advances without reference to you.

## 11  THE DOCUMENTATION

### 11.1  The Mortgage

The mortgage incorporates our current mortgage conditions and, where applicable, loan conditions. If the mortgage conditions booklet is supplied to you with your instructions you must give it to the borrower before completion of the mortgage.

### 11.2  Explanation

You should explain to each borrower (and any other person signing or executing a document) his responsibilities and liabilities under the documents referred to in 11.1 and any documents he is required to sign.

### 11.3  Signing and Witnessing of Documents

It is considered good practice that the signature of a document that needs to be witnessed is witnessed by a solicitor, legal executive or licensed conveyancer. All documents required at completion must be dated with the date of completion of the loan.

## 12 INSTALMENT MORTGAGES AND MORTGAGE ADVANCES RELEASED IN INSTALMENTS

### *12.1 Introduction*

12.1.1      If the cost of the building is to be paid by instalments as work progresses (for example, under a building contract) the amount of each instalment which we will be able to release will be based on a valuation made by our valuer at the time. Whilst we will not be bound by the terms of any building contract we will meet the reasonable requirements of the borrower and the builder as far as possible.

12.1.2      The borrower is expected to pay for as much work as possible from his own resources before applying to us for the first instalment. However, we may, if required, consider advancing a nominal sum on receipt of the certificate of title to enable the mortgage to be completed so long as the legal estate in the property is vested in the borrower.

12.1.3      The borrower is responsible for our valuer's fees for interim valuations as well as the first and final valuations.

### *12.2 Applications for Part of the Advance*

As in the case of a normal mortgage account, cheques for instalment mortgages will be made payable and sent to you. However, instalment cheques (apart from the first which will be sent to you to enable you to complete the mortgage) can be made payable to and sent direct to the borrower on request.

### *12.3 Requests for Intermediate Cheques*

To allow time for a valuation to be carried out, your request should be sent to us (see part 2) at least 10 days before the cheque is required.

### *12.4 Building Contract as Security*

We will not lend on the security of a building contract unless our instructions to you specifically state to the contrary. As a result, the mortgage must not be completed and no part of the advance released until the title to the legal estate in the property has been vested in the borrower.

## 13 MORTGAGE INDEMNITY INSURANCE OR HIGH LOAN TO VALUE FEE

You are reminded to tell the borrower that we (and not the borrower) are the insured under any mortgage indemnity or similar form of insurance policy and that the insurer will have a subrogated right to claim against the borrower if it pays us under the policy. Different lenders call the various schemes of this type by different names. They may not involve an insurance policy.

# 14  AFTER COMPLETION

## 14.1  *Application to HM Land Registry*

14.1.1    You must register our mortgage at HM Land Registry. Before making your Land Registry application for registration, you must place a copy of the Land or Charge Certificate relating to the property on your file together with certified copies of the transfer, mortgage deed and any receipt or DS1 from a previous mortgagee.

14.1.2    Our mortgage conditions and mortgage deed have been deposited at HM Land Registry and it is therefore unnecessary to submit a copy of the mortgage conditions on an application for registration.

14.1.3    Where the loan is to be made in instalments or there is any deferred interest retention or stage release, check part 2 to see whether you must apply to the Land Registry on form 113 for entry of a notice on the register that we are under an obligation to make further advances. If the Land Registry code 'CHOBL' appears on the mortgage deed (it is usually in the top right hand corner) there is no need to submit a form 113.

14.1.4    The application for registration must be received by the Land Registry during the priority period afforded by your original Land Registry search made before completion and, in any event, in the case of an application for first registration, within two months of completion.

## 14.2  *Title Deeds*

14.2.1    All title deeds, searches, enquiries, consents, requisitions and documents relating to the property must be held to our order and you must not create or exercise any lien over them. Unless otherwise instructed, they must be sent to us (see part 2) with the schedule in triplicate supplied by us as soon as possible after completion. We expect them to be lodged, in any event, within three months of completion. If it is not possible to return the deeds to us within this period you should advise us in writing with a copy of any correspondence from HM Land Registry explaining the delay.

14.2.2    You must only send us documents we tell you to. You should obtain the borrower's instructions concerning the retention of documents we tell you not to send us.

## 14.3  *Your Mortgage File*

14.3.1    For evidential purposes you must keep your file for at least six years from the date of the mortgage before destroying it. Microfiching or data imaging is suitable compliance with this requirement. It is the practice of some fraudsters to demand the conveyancing file on completion in order to destroy evidence that may later be used against them. It is important to retain these documents to protect our interests. Where you are processing personal data (as defined in the Data Protection Act 1998) on our behalf, you must:

14.3.1.1    take such security measures as are required to enable you to comply with obligations equivalent to those imposed on us by the seventh data protection principle in the 1998 Act; and

14.3.1.2    process such personal data only in accordance with our instructions. In addition, you must allow us to conduct such reasonable audit of your information security measures as we require in order to ensure your compliance with your obligations in this paragraph.

14.3.2    Subject to any right of lien or any overriding duty of confidentiality, you should treat documents comprising your file as if they are jointly owned by the borrower and the lender and you should not part with them without the consent of the both parties. You should on request supply certified copies of documents on the file or a certified copy of the microfiche to either the borrower or the lender, and may make a reasonable charge for copying and certification.

## 15  LEGAL COSTS

Your charges and disbursements are payable by the borrower and should be collected from the borrower on or before completion. You must not allow non-payment of fees or disbursements to delay the stamping and registration of documents. The Law Society recommends that your costs for acting on our behalf in connection with the mortgage should, in the interest of transparency, be separately identified to the borrower.

## 16  TRANSACTIONS DURING THE LIFE OF THE MORTGAGE

### 16.1  Requests for Deeds

All requests for deeds should be made in writing and sent to us (see part 2). In making such a request you must have the consent of all the borrowers to apply for the deeds.

### 16.2  Further Advances

16.2.1    Our mortgage secures further advances. Consequently, when a further advance is required for alterations or improvements to the property we will not normally instruct a member of our conveyancing panel.

16.2.2    If additional land is to be mortgaged or the further advance is required for some other purpose (for example, to purchase a spouse's equitable or other interest in the property), you may receive instructions to act for us in connection with that transaction.

### 16.3  Transfers of Equity

16.3.1    You must approve the transfer (which should be in the Land Registry's standard form) and, if we require, the deed of covenant on our behalf. Check part 2 to see if we have standard forms of transfer and deed of covenant. When drafting or approving a transfer, you should bear in mind:

16.3.1.1    although the transfer should state that it is subject to the mortgage (identified by date and parties), it need give no details of the terms of the mortgage;

16.3.1.2    the transfer need not state the amount of the mortgage debt. If it does, the figure should include both principal and interest at the date of completion, which you must check (see part 2 for where to obtain this);

16.3.1.3    there should be no statement that all interest has been paid to date.

16.3.2    You must ensure that every person who will be a borrower after the transfer covenants with us to pay the money secured by the mortgage, except in the case of:

16.3.2.1    an original party to the mortgage (unless the mortgage conditions are being varied); or

16.3.2.2    a person who has previously covenanted to that effect.

16.3.3    Any such covenant will either be in the transfer or in a separate deed of covenant. In a transfer, the wording of the covenant should be as follows, or as close as circumstances permit:

'The new borrower agrees to pay the lender all the money due under the mortgage and will keep to all the terms of the mortgage.'

If it is in the transfer, you must place a certified copy of the transfer with the deeds (unless we tell you not to in part 2).

16.3.4    If we have agreed to release a borrower or a guarantor and our standard transfer form (if any) includes no appropriate clause, you must add a simple form of release. The release clause should be as follows, or as close as circumstances permit:

'The lender releases .... from [his/her/their] obligations under the mortgage.'

You should check whether a guarantor who is to be released was a party to the mortgage or to a separate guarantee.

16.3.5    You must obtain the consent of every guarantor of which you are aware to the release of a borrower or, as the case may be, any other guarantor.

16.3.6    You must only submit the transfer to us for execution if it releases a party. All other parties must execute the transfer before it is sent to us. See part 2 for where the transfer should be sent for sealing. Part 2 also gives our approved form of attestation clause.

### 16.4 Properties To Be Let After Completion

16.4.1    You should advise the borrower that any letting of the property is prohibited without our prior consent. If the borrower wishes to let the property after completion then an application for consent should be made to us (see part 2). Check part 2 to see whether it is necessary to send to us a copy of the proposed tenancy when making the application.

16.4.2    If the application for our consent is approved and we instruct you to act for us, you must approve the form of tenancy agreement on our behalf.

16.4.3    Please also note that:

16.4.3.1    an administration fee will be payable for our consideration of the application whether or not consent is granted; and

16.4.3.2    the proposed rent should cover the borrower's gross mortgage payments at the time; and

16.4.3.3    we reserve the right to charge a higher rate of interest to the borrower in certain circumstances or change the terms of the mortgage.

### 16.5  Deeds of Variation, Rectification, Easement or Option Agreements

16.5.1    If we consent to any proposal for a deed of variation, rectification, easement or option agreement, we will rely on you to approve the documents on our behalf.

16.5.2    Our consent will usually be forthcoming provided that you first of all confirm in writing to us (see part 2) that our security will not be adversely affected in any way by entering into the deed. If you are able to provide this confirmation then we will not normally need to see a draft of the deed. If you cannot provide confirmation and we need to consider the matter in detail then an additional administration fee is likely to be charged.

16.5.3    Whether we are a party to the deed or give a separate deed or form of consent is a matter for your discretion. It should be sent to us (see part 2) for sealing or signing with a brief explanation of the reason for the document and its effect together with your confirmation that it will not adversely affect our security.

### 16.6  Deeds of Postponement or Substitution

If we agree to enter into an arrangement with other lenders concerning the order of priority of their mortgages, you will be supplied with our standard form of deed or form of postponement or substitution. We will normally not agree to any amendments to the form. In no cases will we postpone our first charge over the property.

## 17  REDEMPTION

### 17.1  Redemption Statement

17.1.1    When requesting a redemption statement you should quote the expected repayment date and whether you are acting for the borrower or have the borrower's authority to request the redemption statement in addition to the information mentioned in paragraph 2.1. You should request this at least five working days before the expected redemption date. You must quote all the borrower's mortgage account or roll numbers of which you are aware when requesting the repayment figure. You must only request a redemption statement if you are acting for the borrower or have the borrower's written authority to request a redemption statement.

17.1.2    To guard against fraud please ensure that if payment is made by cheque then the redemption cheque is made payable to us and you quote the mortgage account or roll number and name of borrower.

### 17.2  Discharge

On the day of completion you should send the discharge and your remittance for the repayment to us.

Part 2 is not reproduced in this book.

# INDEX

**References are to paragraph and Appendix numbers.**